The Word on Fire

VATICAN II
COLLECTION

Constitutions

The Word on Fire

VATICAN II
COLLECTION

Constitutions

Edited by
Matthew Levering

Foreword by
Bishop Robert Barron
with commentary by the postconciliar popes

Published by the Word on Fire Institute, an imprint of
Word on Fire, Park Ridge, IL 60068
© 2021 by Word on Fire Catholic Ministries
Printed in the United States of America
All rights reserved

Commentary excerpts collected by Matthew Levering and Matthew Becklo

Design and layout by Rozann Lee, Cassie Bielak, and Clare Sheaf

Cover and interior art by Cory Mendenhall

Conciliar texts and commentaries used with permission of Libreria Editrice Vaticana.
All rights reserved.

First printing, February 2021
Second printing, June 2023

ISBN: 978-1-943243-93-8

Library of Congress Control Number: 2020924131

"[The Second Vatican Council] has invested its teachings with the authority of the supreme ordinary magisterium, which ordinary magisterium is so obviously authentic that it must be accepted with docility and sincerity by all the faithful, according to the mind of the Council as expressed in the nature and aims of the individual documents."

— *Pope St. Paul VI*

"With the passing of the years, *the Council documents have lost nothing of their value or brilliance.* They need to be read correctly, to be widely known and taken to heart as important and normative texts of the Magisterium, within the Church's Tradition. . . . I feel more than ever in duty bound to point to the Council *as the great grace bestowed on the Church in the twentieth century*: there we find a sure compass by which to take our bearings in the century now beginning."

— *Pope St. John Paul II*

"The Second Vatican Council Documents, to which we must return, freeing them from a mass of publications which instead of making them known have often concealed them, are a compass in our time too that permits the Barque of the Church to put out into the deep in the midst of storms or on calm and peaceful waves, to sail safely and to reach her destination."

— *Pope Benedict XVI*

"Vatican II was a Council on faith, inasmuch as it asked us to restore the primacy of God in Christ to the center of our lives, both as a Church and as individuals. The Church never takes faith for granted, but knows that this gift of God needs to be nourished and reinforced so that it can continue to guide her pilgrim way. The Second Vatican Council enabled the light of faith to illumine our human experience from within, accompanying the men and women of our time on their journey."

— *Pope Francis*

Contents

Foreword
ix

Opening Address
1

1. DEI VERBUM
Dogmatic Constitution on Divine Revelation
13

II. LUMEN GENTIUM
Dogmatic Constitution on the Church
43

III. SACROSANCTUM CONCILIUM
Constitution on the Sacred Liturgy
151

IV. GAUDIUM ET SPES
Pastoral Constitution on the Church in the Modern World
211

Closing Address
339

Afterword
347

Key Terms and Figures
357

Frequently Asked Questions
367

Foreword

Bishop Robert Barron

The Second Vatican Council (1962–1965), a gathering of Catholic bishops from around the world under the headship of Pope St. John XXIII and then Pope St. Paul VI, was one of the most significant cultural and ecclesiastical events of the twentieth century. Though practically everyone acknowledges its importance, Catholics have been debating its precise meaning and application for the past sixty years. As I write these words, a fresh controversy has broken out, this time prompted by "traditionalists" who claim that Vatican II has betrayed authentic Catholicism and produced disastrous consequences in the life of the Church. In the years that I was coming of age, the 1970s and 1980s, the argument was, largely, between advocates of a "hermeneutic of continuity" reading versus a "hermeneutic of rupture" interpretation of the council—which is to say, between those who appreciated Vatican II as a legitimate development of the teaching that preceded it, and those who saw the council as a real break with that tradition and a signal that something altogether new was emerging in the life of the Church.

To understand this rather complex set of positions and counter-positions, it is advisable to look, however briefly, at the council and its immediate aftermath. The great and saintly pope who summoned this gathering of bishops saw the purpose of the council as fundamentally missionary. The Church of the early 1960s did not face major doctrinal questions, but many priests, bishops, scholars, and pastoral practitioners did indeed think that the Church's regnant neo-scholastic theology, a rather dry, superficial version of the thought of St. Thomas Aquinas, was inadequate to the missionary task in the modern world. Thus, what the overwhelming majority of the theological experts and bishops at Vatican II opted for was an updating of the Church, but paradoxically, precisely through a recovery of the more lyrical language of the early Church Fathers and of the Scriptures. This change, they felt, would facilitate the process of bringing the light of Christ to the men and women of our time. It is noteworthy that unlike almost all of the conciliar texts that came before, the documents of Vatican II are not pithy statements of belief or anathemas of heresies, but rather lengthy, meditative theological essays designed to persuade rather than to define or condemn. That this approach won the day at Vatican II is evident in the vote counts for the conciliar documents, almost all of which were passed with only a handful of negative votes out of over two thousand cast.

To be sure, there was a small group of vocal dissenters to the documents, bishops and theologians who preferred to stay within the confines of the standard neo-scholastic approach, but it is fair to say that they were clearly defeated at the council. Now, the victorious party, within five years of the close of Vatican II, split into two camps, one more liberal and the other more conservative. The former, represented by such figures as Karl Rahner, Edward Schillebeeckx, Hans Küng, and Gregory Baum, saw the documents of Vatican II as a first step in the direction of a more radical reform of the Church. They argued that the council was much more than the written texts that it produced; that it had, in fact, unleashed a spirit that should be allowed to blow through the Church, affecting its doctrines, practices, and institutional structures. The latter group, represented by, among others, Joseph Ratzinger, Henri de Lubac, Hans Urs von Balthasar, and Karol Wojtyła, reacted against this liberal reading. In a famous essay from the early seventies, Ratzinger decried the desire to perpetuate an amorphous "spirit of the council." In point of fact, he argued, the Church always turns with a kind of relief from a council, since such gatherings always represent a certain throwing of the Church into suspense. While the theologians and bishops gather to deliberate and discuss, as indeed they must from time to time, the Church is not focused on its basic work of worshiping God, evangelizing, and caring for the poor.

Once the council has completed its task and resolved whatever difficulties needed resolving, the Church returns with renewed enthusiasm and clarity to its mission. Therefore, the perpetuation of the spirit of Vatican II would be tantamount, Ratzinger concluded, to condemning the Church to a permanent state of indecision.

These two camps, corresponding more or less to the hermeneutic of rupture and hermeneutic of continuity approaches referenced above, have battled for the past roughly fifty years, but the latter school came to the fore due to the fact that two of its most distinguished representatives, Wojtyła and Ratzinger, both were elected to the office of Peter. Their papacies, expressed in numerous homilies, talks, encyclicals, and formal statements, stabilized the interpretation of Vatican II. The radical traditionalists of the present moment represent an energetic comeback of the neo-scholastics who lost the day at Vatican II. They reject both the hermeneutic of continuity and the hermeneutic of rupture, preferring to see the entire Vatican II project as misbegotten from the beginning.

With the book you are reading, I am nailing my colors to the mast. I and Word on Fire stand firmly with Vatican II and hence against the radical traditionalists. And we stand firmly with the Wojtyła-Ratzinger interpretation of the council, and hence against the progressives. We are convinced that, even as many voices have argued about the council since the documents appeared in the mid-1960s, vanishingly few Catholics have actually *read* the texts themselves. This book is designed to address that problem. It includes the four "constitutions" of the council—which is to say, the principal essays that most fully articulate its purpose and ethos. But it also features a range of commentaries and explications of these marvelous documents, most drawn from the popes and bishops who provide a magisterial interpretation.

Many years ago, I heard a speaker remark that far too many people in the Church seem to want either Vatican I or Vatican III! That traditionalists and progressives still dominate much of the conversation today proves that his observation still has validity. I believe that the documents of Vatican II are still widely unread, and if they are read, often misunderstood. The needful thing, I am convinced, is a robust and enthusiastic reappropriation of the texts of Vatican II. I hope that this book represents a contribution to that project.

Opening Address to the Council

Pope St. John XXIII

Today, Venerable Brethren, is a day of joy for Mother Church: through God's most kindly providence the longed-for day has dawned for the solemn opening of the Second Vatican Ecumenical Council, here at St. Peter's shrine. And Mary, God's Virgin Mother, on this feast day of her noble motherhood, gives it her gracious protection.

THE CHURCH IN COUNCIL

A positive proof of the Catholic Church's vitality is furnished by every single council held in the long course of the centuries—by the twenty ecumenical councils as well as by the many thousands of memorable regional and provincial ones emblazoned on the scroll of history.

And now the Church must once more reaffirm that teaching authority of hers which never fails, but will endure until the end of time. For that was Our reason for calling this most authoritative assembly, and We address you now as the humble successor, the latest born, of this Prince of Apostles. The present Council is a special, worldwide manifestation by the Church of her teaching office, exercised in taking account of the errors, needs and opportunities of our day.

1

A History of Triumph . . .

We address you, therefore, as Christ's vicar, and We naturally begin this General Council by setting it in its historical context. The voice of the past is both spirited and heartening. We remember with joy those early popes and their more recent successors to whom we owe so much. Their hallowed, momentous words come down to us through the councils held in both the East and the West, from the fourth century to the Middle Ages, and right down to modern times. Their uninterrupted witness, so zealously given, proclaims the triumph of Christ's Church, that divine and human society which derives from its divine Redeemer its title, its gifts of grace, its whole dynamic force.

. . . And of Adversity

Here is cause indeed for spiritual joy. And yet this history has its darker side too, a fact, which cannot be glossed over. These nineteen hundred years have reaped their harvest of sorrow and bitterness. The aged Simeon's prophecy to Mary, the Mother of Jesus, proves true in every age: "Behold, this child is destined for the fall and for the rise of many in Israel, and for a sign that shall be contradicted."[1] Jesus, too, when grown to manhood, made it quite clear that men in times to come would oppose Him. We remember those mysterious words of His: "He who hears you, hears me."[2] St. Luke, who records these words, also quotes Him later as saying: "He who is not with me is against me; and he who does not gather with me scatters."[3]

To Be with Christ or Against Him

Certain it is that the critical issues, the thorny problems that wait upon men's solution, have remained the same for almost twenty centuries. And why? Because the whole of history and of life hinges on the person of Jesus Christ. *Either* men anchor themselves on Him and His Church, and thus enjoy the blessings of light and joy, right order and peace; *or* they live their lives apart from Him; many positively oppose Him, and deliberately exclude themselves from the Church. The result can only be confusion in their lives, bitterness in their relations with one another, and the savage threat of war.

A Pastoral Function

But the function of every ecumenical council has always been to make a solemn proclamation of the union that exists between Christ and His Church; to diffuse the light of truth; to give right guidance to men both as individuals and as members of a family and a society; to evoke and strengthen their spiritual resources; and to set their minds continually on those higher values which are genuine and unfailing.

No study of human history during these twenty centuries of Christendom can fail to take note of the evidence of this extraordinary teaching authority of the Church as voiced in her general councils. The documents are there, whole volumes of them; a sacred heritage housed in the Roman archives and in the most famous libraries of the world.

THE DECISION TO HOLD THE SECOND VATICAN COUNCIL

A Sudden Inspiration

As regards the immediate cause for this great event, which gathers you here together at Our bidding, it is sufficient for Us to put on record once more something which, though trifling in itself, made a deep impression on Us personally. The decision to hold an ecumenical council came to Us in the first instance in a sudden flash of inspiration. We communicated this decision, without elaboration, to the Sacred College of Cardinals on that memorable January 25, 1959, the feast of St. Paul's Conversion, in his patriarchal basilica in the Ostien Way.[4] The response was immediate. It was as though some ray of supernatural light had entered the minds of all present: it was reflected in their faces; it shone from their eyes. At once the world was swept by a wave of enthusiasm, and men everywhere began to wait eagerly for the celebration of this Council.

Arduous Preparation

For three years the arduous work of preparation continued. It consisted in making a detailed and accurate analysis of the prevailing condition of the faith, the religious practice, and the vitality of the Christian, and particularly the Catholic, body.

We are convinced that the time spent in preparing for this Ecumenical Council was in itself an initial token of grace, a gift from heaven.

Hope for Spiritual Enrichment

For We have every confidence that the Church, in the light of this Council, will gain in spiritual riches. New sources of energy will be opened to her, enabling her to face the future without fear. By introducing timely changes and a prudent system of mutual cooperation, We intend that the Church shall really succeed in bringing men, families and nations to the appreciation of supernatural values.

Thus the celebration of this Council becomes a compelling motive for whole-hearted thanksgiving to God, the giver of every good gift, and for exultantly proclaiming the glory of Christ the Lord, the triumphant and immortal King of ages and peoples.

THE TIMING OF THIS COUNCIL

And now, venerable brethren, there is another point that We would have you consider. Quite apart from the spiritual joy we all feel at this solemn moment of history, the very circumstances in which this Council is opening are supremely propitious. May We go on record as expressing this conviction openly before you now in full assembly.

Pessimistic Voices

In the daily exercise of Our pastoral office, it sometimes happens that We hear certain opinions which disturb Us—opinions expressed by people who, though fired with a commendable zeal for religion, are lacking in sufficient prudence and judgment in their evaluation of events. They can see nothing but calamity and disaster in the present state of the world. They say over and over that this modern age of ours, in comparison with past ages, is definitely deteriorating. One would think from their attitude that history, that great teacher of life, had taught them nothing. They seem to imagine that in the days of the earlier councils everything was as it should be so far as doctrine and morality and the Church's rightful liberty were concerned.

We feel that We must disagree with these prophets of doom, who are always forecasting worse disasters, as though the end of the world were at hand.

A Basis for Optimism

Present indications are that the human family is on the threshold of a new era. We must recognize here the hand of God, who, as the years roll by, is ever directing men's efforts, whether they realize it or not, towards the fulfillment of the inscrutable designs of His providence, wisely arranging everything, even adverse human fortune, for the Church's good.

Civil Intervention Eliminated

As a simple example of what We mean, consider the extremely critical problems which exist today in the political and economic spheres. Men are so worried by these things that they give scant thought to those religious concerns, which are the province of the Church's teaching authority. All this is evil, and we are right to condemn it. But this new state of affairs has at least one undeniable advantage: it has eliminated the innumerable obstacles erected by worldly men to impede the Church's freedom of action. We have only to take a cursory glance through the annals of the Church to realize that even those ecumenical councils which are recorded there in letters of gold, were celebrated in the midst of serious difficulties and most distressing circumstances, through the unwarranted intervention of the civil authority. Such intervention was sometimes dictated by a sincere intention on the part of the secular princes to protect the Church's interests, but more often than not their motives were purely political and selfish, and the resultant situation was fraught with spiritual disadvantage and danger.

Earnest Prayer for Absent Bishops

We must indeed confess to you Our deep sorrow over the fact that so many bishops are missing today from your midst. They suffer imprisonment and every kind of disability because of their faith in Christ. The thought of these dear brothers of Ours impels Us to pray for them with great earnestness. Yet We are not without hope; and We have the immense consolation of knowing that the Church, freed at last from the worldly fetters that trammeled her in past ages, can through you raise her majestic and solemn voice from this Vatican Basilica, as from a second Apostolic Cenacle.

THE COUNCIL'S PRINCIPAL DUTY: THE DEFENSE AND ADVANCEMENT OF TRUTH

The major interest of the Ecumenical Council is this: that the sacred heritage of Christian truth be safeguarded and expounded with greater efficacy.

That doctrine embraces the whole man, body and soul. It bids us live as pilgrims here on earth, as we journey onwards towards our heavenly homeland.

Man's Twofold Obligation

It demonstrates how we must conduct this mortal life of ours. If we are to achieve God's purpose in our regard we have a twofold obligation: as citizens of earth, and as citizens of heaven. That is to say, all men without exception, both individually and in society, have a life-long obligation to strive after heavenly values through the right use of the things of this earth. These temporal goods must be used in such a way as not to jeopardize eternal happiness.

Seeking the Kingdom of God

True enough, Christ our Lord said: "Seek first the kingdom of God and His justice,"[5] and this word "first" indicates what the primary direction of all our thoughts and energies must be. Nevertheless, we must not forget the rest of Our Lord's injunction: "and all these things shall be given you besides."[6] Thus the traditional as well as the contemporary Christian approach to life is to strive with all zeal for evangelical perfection, and at the same time to contribute toward the material good of humanity. It is from the living example and the charitable enterprise of such Christians as these that all that is highest and noblest in human society takes its strength and growth.

Contributing to Society

If this doctrine is to make its impact on the various spheres of human activity—in private, family, and social life—then it is absolutely vital that the Church shall never for an instant lose sight of that sacred patrimony of truth inherited from the Fathers. But it is equally necessary for her to keep up to date with the changing conditions of this modern world, and of modern living, for these have opened up entirely new avenues for the Catholic apostolate.

Beyond Science

The Church has never been stinting in her admiration for the results of man's inventive genius and scientific progress, which have so revolutionized modern living. But neither has she been backward in assessing these new developments at their true value. While keeping a watchful eye on these things, she has constantly exhorted men to look beyond such visible phenomena—to God, the source of all wisdom and beauty. Her constant fear has been that man, who was commanded to "subject the earth and rule it,"[7] should in the process forget that other serious command: "The Lord thy God shalt thou worship, and Him only shalt thou serve."[8] Real progress must not be impeded by a passing infatuation for transient things.

BRINGING HOME THE CHURCH'S TEACHING TO THE MODERN WORLD

From what We have said, the doctrinal role of this present Council is sufficiently clear.

Transmitting the Truth Fearlessly

This twenty-first Ecumenical Council can draw upon the most effective and valued assistance of experts in every branch of sacred science, in the practical sphere of the apostolate, and in administration. Its intention is to give to the world the whole of that doctrine which, notwithstanding every difficulty and contradiction, has become the common heritage of mankind—to transmit it in all its purity, undiluted, undistorted.
It is a treasure of incalculable worth, not indeed coveted by all, but available to all men of good will.

And our duty is not just to guard this treasure, as though it were some museum-piece and we the curators, but earnestly and fearlessly to dedicate ourselves to the work that needs to be done in this modern age of ours, pursuing the path which the Church has followed for almost twenty centuries.

Nor are we here primarily to discuss certain fundamentals of Catholic doctrine, or to restate in greater detail the traditional teaching of the Fathers and of early and more recent theologians. We presume that these things are sufficiently well known and familiar to you all.

A Fresh Approach

There was no need to call a council merely to hold discussions of that nature. What is needed at the present time is a new enthusiasm, a new joy and serenity of mind in the unreserved acceptance by all of the entire Christian faith, without forfeiting that accuracy and precision in its presentation which characterized the proceedings of the Council of Trent and the First Vatican Council. What is needed, and what everyone imbued with a truly Christian, Catholic, and apostolic spirit craves today, is that this doctrine shall be more widely known, more deeply understood, and more penetrating in its effects on men's moral lives. What is needed is that this certain and immutable doctrine, to which the faithful owe obedience, be studied afresh and reformulated in contemporary terms. For this deposit of faith, or truths which are contained in our time-honored teaching is one thing; the manner in which these truths are set forth (with their meaning preserved intact) is something else.

This, then, is what will require our careful, and perhaps too our patient, consideration. We must work out ways and means of expounding these truths in a manner more consistent with a predominantly pastoral view of the Church's teaching office.

THE RIGHT WAY TO SUPPRESS ERROR

In these days, which mark the beginning of this Second Vatican Council, it is more obvious than ever before that the Lord's truth is indeed eternal. Human ideologies change. Successive generations give rise to varying errors, and these often vanish as quickly as they came, like mist before the sun.

The Church has always opposed these errors, and often condemned them with the utmost severity. Today, however, Christ's Bride prefers the balm of mercy to the arm of severity. She believes that, present needs are best served by explaining more fully the purport of her doctrines, rather than by publishing condemnations.

Contemporary Repudiation of Godlessness

Not that the need to repudiate and guard against erroneous teaching and dangerous ideologies is less today than formerly. But all such error is so manifestly contrary to rightness and goodness, and produces such fatal results, that our contemporaries show every inclination to condemn it of their own accord—especially that way of life which repudiates God and His law, and which places excessive confidence in technical progress and an exclusively material prosperity. It is more and more widely understood that personal dignity and true self-realization are of vital importance and worth every effort to achieve. More important still, experience has at long last taught men that physical violence, armed might, and political domination are no help at all in providing a happy solution to the serious problems which affect them.

A Loving Mother

The great desire, therefore, of the Catholic Church in raising aloft at this Council the torch of truth, is to show herself to the world as the loving mother of all mankind; gentle, patient, and full of tenderness and sympathy for her separated children. To the human race oppressed by so many difficulties, she says what Peter once said to the poor man who begged an alms: "Silver and gold I have none; but what I have, that I give thee. In the name of Jesus Christ of Nazareth, arise and walk."[9] In other words it is not corruptible wealth, nor the promise of earthly happiness, that the Church offers the world today, but the gifts of divine grace which, since they raise men up to the dignity of being sons of God, are powerful assistance and support for the living of a more fully human life. She unseals the fountains of her life-giving doctrine, so that men, illumined by the light of Christ, will understand their true nature and dignity and purpose. Everywhere, through her children, she extends the frontiers of Christian love, the most powerful means of eradicating the seeds of discord, the most effective means of promoting concord, peace with justice, and universal brotherhood.

PROMOTING UNITY OF THE CHRISTIAN AND HUMAN FAMILY

The Church's anxiety to promote and defend truth springs from her conviction that without the assistance of the whole of revealed doctrine man is quite incapable of attaining to that complete and steadfast unanimity which is associated with genuine peace and eternal salvation. For such is God's plan. He "wishes all men to be saved and to come to the knowledge of the truth."[10]

Unhappily, however, the entire Christian family has not as yet fully and perfectly attained to this visible unity in the truth. But the Catholic Church considers it her duty to work actively for the fulfillment of that great mystery of unity for which Christ prayed so earnestly to His heavenly Father on the eve of His great sacrifice. The knowledge that she is so intimately associated with that prayer is for her an occasion of ineffable peace and joy. And why should she not rejoice sincerely when she sees Christ's prayer extending its salvific and ever increasing efficacy even over those who are not of her fold?

Reflection of That Unity Sought By Christ

Indeed, if we consider well the unity for which Christ prayed on behalf of His Church, it would seem to shine, as it were, with a threefold ray of supernatural, saving light. There is first of all that unity of Catholics among themselves which must always be kept steadfast and exemplary. There is also a unity of prayer and ardent longing prompting Christians separated from this Apostolic See to aspire to union with us. And finally there is a unity, which consists in the esteem and respect shown for the Catholic Church by members of various non-Christian religions.

Universality and Unity

It is therefore an overwhelming source of grief to us to know that, although Christ's blood has redeemed every man that is born into this world, there is still a great part of the human race that does not share in those sources of supernatural grace, which exist in the Catholic Church. And yet the Church sheds her light everywhere. The power that is hers by reason of her supernatural unity redounds to the advantage of the whole family of men. She amply justifies those magnificent words of St. Cyprian: "The Church, radiant with the light of her Lord, sheds her rays over all the world, and that light of hers remains one, though everywhere diffused; her corporate unity is not divided. She spreads her luxuriant branches over all the earth; she sends out her fair-flowing streams ever farther afield. But the head is one; the source is one. She is the one mother of countless generations. And we are her children, born of her, fed with her milk, animated with her breath."[11]

Blazing a Trail

Such, venerable brethren, is the aim of the Second Vatican Council. It musters the Church's best energies and studies with all earnestness how to have the message of salvation more readily welcomed by men. By that very fact it blazes a trail that leads toward that unity of the human race, which is so necessary if this earthly realm of ours is to conform to the realm of heaven, "whose king is truth, whose law is love, whose duration is eternity."[12]

CONCLUSION

Thus, venerable brethren in the episcopate, "our heart is wide open to you."[13] Here we are assembled in this Vatican Basilica at a turning-point in the history of the Church; here at this meeting-place of earth and heaven, by St. Peter's tomb and the tomb of so many of Our predecessors, whose ashes in this solemn hour seem to thrill in mystic exultation.

A Radiant Dawn

For with the opening of this Council a new day is dawning on the Church, bathing her in radiant splendor. It is yet the dawn, but the sun in its rising has already set our hearts aglow. All around is the fragrance of holiness and joy. Yet there are stars to be seen in this temple, enhancing its magnificence with their brightness. You are those stars, as witness the Apostle John;[14] the churches you represent are golden candlesticks shining round the tomb of the Prince of Apostles.[15] With you We see other dignitaries come to Rome from the five continents to represent their various nations. Their attitude is one of respect and warm-hearted expectation.

Saints, Faithful, and Council Fathers

Hence, it is true to say that the citizens of earth and heaven are united in the celebration of this Council. The role of the saints in heaven is to supervise our labors; the role of the faithful on earth, to offer concerted prayer to God; your role, to show prompt obedience to the supernatural guidance of the Holy Spirit and to do your utmost to answer the needs and expectations of every nation on earth. To do this you will need serenity of mind, a spirit of brotherly concord, moderation in your proposals, dignity in discussion, and wisdom in deliberation.

God grant that your zeal and your labors may abundantly fulfill these aspirations. The eyes of the world are upon you; and all its hopes.

Prayer for Divine Assistance

Almighty God, we have no confidence in our own strength; all our trust is in you. Graciously look down on these Pastors of your Church. Aid their counsels and their legislation with the light of your divine grace. Be pleased to hear the prayers we offer you, united in faith, in voice, in mind.

Mary, help of Christians, help of bishops; recently in your church at Loreto, where We venerated the mystery of the Incarnation,[16] you gave us a special token of your love. Prosper now this work of ours, and by your kindly aid bring it to a happy, successful conclusion. And do you, with St. Joseph your spouse, the holy apostles Peter and Paul, St. John the Baptist and St. John the Evangelist, intercede for us before the throne of God.

To Jesus Christ, our most loving Redeemer, the immortal King of all peoples and all ages, be love, power, and glory for ever and ever. Amen.

—October 11, 1962

NOTES

1   Luke 2:34.

2   Ibid. 10:16.

3   Ibid. 11:23.

4   See *The Encyclicals and Other Messages of John XXIII* (Washington, DC: TPS Press, 1964), 20–23.

5   Matt. 6:33.

6   Ibid.

7   Gen. 1:28.

8   Matt. 4:10; Luke 4:8.

9   Acts 3:6.

10   1 Tim. 2:4.

11   *De Catholicae Ecclesiae Unitate,* 5.

12   St. Augustine, Ep. 138, 3.

13   2 Cor. 6:11.

14   Rev. 1:20.

15   Ibid.

16   See *TPS*, VIII. 273–8.

DEI VERBUM

Dogmatic Constitution on
Divine Revelation

SOLEMNLY PROMULGATED *by* HIS HOLINESS
POPE PAUL VI
on NOVEMBER 18, 1965

A Call for Biblical Renewal

Introduction to *Dei Verbum* by Bishop Robert Barron

Vatican II's document on revelation, known by the first two words of the Latin text *Dei Verbum* (the Word of God), is of signal importance in the life of the Church, since it speaks of the process by which God communicates to his people. The entire purpose of this communication is to draw us into friendship with God. What could be more significant for all believers, but especially for teachers, catechists, theologians, and preachers?

It also has great significance for those embarked on the Church's mission of evangelization. The council fathers recognized the need for a renewal when it came to reading and appreciating the Bible. They called for greater study of the Bible among laypeople, placing the Scriptures more fully at the center of the liturgy, and making the sacred writings the "soul of sacred theology" (DV 24). But that dream is still, I believe, largely unrealized.

In point of fact, when we consult the numerous studies of the ever-increasing army of the religiously unaffiliated, we discover that the Bible is often a prime reason why people, especially young people, are alienated from the Christian faith. We hear that it is nonsense written by prescientific people who knew nothing about the way the world works; that it is bronze-age mythology; that it encourages genocide, violence against women, slavery, and militaristic aggression; that its central character is, in the language of one atheist provocateur, like King Lear in Act Five, except more insane.

The insights of *Dei Verbum* can help Catholics recover the depth and power of the Bible in the twenty-first century, and hold off the many charges made against it.

DEI VERBUM
Dogmatic Constitution
on Divine Revelation

INTRODUCTION

1. Hearing the word of God with reverence and proclaiming it with faith, the sacred synod takes its direction from these words of St. John: "We announce to you the eternal life which dwelt with the Father and was made visible to us. What we have seen and heard we announce to you, so that you may have fellowship with us and our common fellowship be with the Father and His Son Jesus Christ" (1 John 1:2–3). Therefore, following in the footsteps of the Council of Trent and of the First Vatican Council, this present council wishes to set forth authentic doctrine on divine revelation and how it is handed on, so that by hearing the message of salvation the whole world may believe, by believing it may hope, and by hoping it may love.[1]

CHAPTER I
Revelation Itself

2. In His goodness and wisdom God chose to reveal Himself and to make known to us the hidden purpose of His will (see Eph. 1:9) by which through Christ, the Word made flesh, man might in the Holy Spirit have access to the Father and come to share in the divine nature (see Eph. 2:18; 2 Pet. 1:4). Through this revelation, therefore, the invisible God (see Col. 1:15, 1 Tim. 1:17) out of the abundance of His love speaks to men as friends (see Exod. 33:11; John 15:14–15) and lives among them (see Bar. 3:38), so

that He may invite and take them into fellowship with Himself. This plan of revelation is realized by deeds and words having an inner unity: the deeds wrought by God in the history of salvation manifest and confirm the teaching and realities signified by the words, while the words proclaim the deeds and clarify the mystery contained in them. By this revelation then, the deepest truth about God and the salvation of man shines out for our sake in Christ, who is both the mediator and the fullness of all revelation.[2]

3. God, who through the Word creates all things (see John 1:3) and keeps them in existence, gives men an enduring witness to Himself in created realities (see Rom. 1:19–20). Planning to make known the way of heavenly salvation, He went further and from the start manifested Himself to our first parents. Then after their fall His promise of redemption aroused in them the hope of being saved (see Gen. 3:15) and from that time on He ceaselessly kept the human race in His care, to give eternal life to those who perseveringly do good in search of salvation (see Rom. 2:6–7). Then, at the time He had appointed He called Abraham in order to make of him a great nation (see Gen. 12:2). Through the patriarchs, and after them through Moses and the prophets, He taught this people to acknowledge Himself the one living and true God, provident father and just judge, and to wait for the Savior promised by Him, and in this manner prepared the way for the Gospel down through the centuries.

4. Then, after speaking in many and varied ways through the prophets, "now at last in these days God has spoken to us in His Son" (Heb. 1:1–2). For He sent His Son, the eternal Word, who enlightens all men, so that He might dwell among men and tell them of the innermost being of God (see John 1:1–18). Jesus Christ, therefore, the Word made flesh, was sent as "a man to men."[3] He "speaks the words of God" (John 3:34), and completes the work of salvation which His Father gave Him to do (see John 5:36; John 17:4). To see Jesus is to see His Father (John 14:9). For this reason Jesus perfected revelation by fulfilling it through his whole work of making Himself present and manifesting Himself: through His words and deeds, His signs and wonders, but especially through His death and glorious resurrection from the dead and final sending of the Spirit of truth. Moreover He confirmed with divine testimony what revelation proclaimed, that God is with us to free us from the darkness of sin and death, and to raise us up to life eternal.

The Christian dispensation, therefore, as the new and definitive covenant, will never pass away and we now await no further new public revelation before the glorious manifestation of our Lord Jesus Christ (see 1 Tim. 6:14 and Titus 2:13).

The Self-Manifestation of God

Dei Verbum 2–4 | Bishop Barron

The first chapter of *Dei Verbum*, which deals directly with the question of revelation, speaks of God's gradual self-manifestation through his Word, culminating in the enfleshment of that Word in Jesus Christ. The document specifies that the purpose of this manifestation is none other than the drawing of human beings into friendship with God and participation in the divine life. Then comes that distinctive word *oeconomia*, which is repeated like a refrain throughout *Dei Verbum*: "This plan of revelation [*revelationis oeconomia*] . . ." One could not speak coherently of an economy unless there were an *economus* (overseer), some great mind and personality responsible for the rational arrangement of nature and history.

Next, *Dei Verbum* specifies that this pattern or economy of salvation unfolds *gestis verbisque*, by both "deeds and words." It thereby implies that revelation is never simply a verbal or intellectual matter but an affair of factual history. In Thomas Aquinas' language, God has authority over both words and "things" and can use both for his communicative purposes. Now, this means that history cannot be construed in a purely linear way but must be interpreted as a coherent and artistically driven narrative, filled with allusions, anticipations, rhymes, echoes, meanings that double back upon themselves, typologies, and prophecies.

On *Dei Verbum*'s reading, this participatory view of history and nature is rooted in the creative power of the Word. God witnesses to himself through the orderliness and beauty of the created world and, in a more pointed way, through salvation history. *Dei Verbum* lays out the contours of sacred history—commencing with the call of Abraham and the other patriarchs, the giving of the Law through Moses, the summoning of the prophets, and finally the arrival of the Messiah—characterizing this *oeconomia* as a succession of covenants made between God and his people.

Not One Word Among Many

Dei Verbum 4

Pope Francis
—
Lumen Fidei 14

The word which God speaks to us in Jesus is not simply one word among many, but his eternal Word (see Heb. 1:1–2). God can give no greater guarantee of his love, as Saint Paul reminds us (see Rom. 8:31–39). Christian faith is thus faith in a perfect love, in its decisive power, in its ability to transform the world and to unfold its history. "We know and believe the love that God has for us" (1 John 4:16). In the love of God revealed in Jesus, faith perceives the foundation on which all reality and its final destiny rest.

5. "The obedience of faith" (Rom. 16:26; see 1:5; 2 Cor. 10:5–6) "is to be given to God who reveals, an obedience by which man commits his whole self freely to God, offering the full submission of intellect and will to God who reveals,"[4] and freely assenting to the truth revealed by Him. To make this act of faith, the grace of God and the interior help of the Holy Spirit must precede and assist, moving the heart and turning it to God, opening the eyes of the mind and giving "joy and ease to everyone in assenting to the truth and believing it."[5] To bring about an ever deeper understanding of revelation the same Holy Spirit constantly brings faith to completion by His gifts.

6. Through divine revelation, God chose to show forth and communicate Himself and the eternal decisions of His will regarding the salvation of men. That is to say, He chose to share with them those divine treasures which totally transcend the understanding of the human mind.[6]

As a sacred synod has affirmed, God, the beginning and end of all things, can be known with certainty from created reality by the light of human reason (see Rom. 1:20); but teaches that it is through His revelation that those religious truths which are by their nature accessible to human reason can be known by all men with ease, with solid certitude and with no trace of error, even in this present state of the human race.[7]

The Knowledge of Faith

Dei Verbum 6

Pope St. John Paul II

———

Fides et Ratio 8

Restating almost to the letter the teaching of the First Vatican Council's Constitution *Dei Filius*, and taking into account the principles set out by the Council of Trent, the Second Vatican Council's Constitution *Dei Verbum* pursued the age-old journey of *understanding faith*, reflecting on Revelation in the light of the teaching of Scripture and of the entire Patristic tradition. At the First Vatican Council, the Fathers had stressed the supernatural character of God's Revelation. On the basis of mistaken and very widespread assertions, the rationalist critique of the time attacked faith and denied the possibility of any knowledge which was not the fruit of reason's natural capacities. This obliged the Council to reaffirm emphatically that there exists a knowledge which is peculiar to faith, surpassing the knowledge proper to human reason, which nevertheless by its nature can discover the Creator. This knowledge expresses a truth based upon the very fact of God who reveals himself, a truth which is most certain, since God neither deceives nor wishes to deceive.

CHAPTER II

Handing on Divine Revelation

7. In His gracious goodness, God has seen to it that what He had revealed for the salvation of all nations would abide perpetually in its full integrity and be handed on to all generations. Therefore Christ the Lord in whom the full revelation of the supreme God is brought to completion (see Cor. 1:20; 3:13; 4:6), commissioned the Apostles to preach to all men that Gospel which is the source of all saving truth and moral teaching,[1] and to impart to them heavenly gifts. This Gospel had been promised in former times through the prophets, and Christ Himself had fulfilled it and promulgated it with His lips. This commission was faithfully fulfilled by

the Apostles who, by their oral preaching, by example, and by observances handed on what they had received from the lips of Christ, from living with Him, and from what He did, or what they had learned through the prompting of the Holy Spirit. The commission was fulfilled, too, by those Apostles and apostolic men who under the inspiration of the same Holy Spirit committed the message of salvation to writing.[2]

But in order to keep the Gospel forever whole and alive within the Church, the Apostles left bishops as their successors, "handing over" to them "the authority to teach in their own place."[3] This sacred tradition, therefore, and Sacred Scripture of both the Old and New Testaments are like a mirror in which the pilgrim Church on earth looks at God, from whom she has received everything, until she is brought finally to see Him as He is, face to face (see 1 John 3:2).

8. And so the apostolic preaching, which is expressed in a special way in the inspired books, was to be preserved by an unending succession of preachers until the end of time. Therefore the Apostles, handing on what they themselves had received, warn the faithful to hold fast to the traditions which they have learned either by word of mouth or by letter (see 2 Thess. 2:15), and to fight in defense of the faith handed on once and for all (see Jude 1:3).[4] Now what was handed on by the Apostles includes everything which contributes toward the holiness of life and increase in faith of the peoples of God; and so the Church, in her teaching, life and worship, perpetuates and hands on to all generations all that she herself is, all that she believes.

This tradition which comes from the Apostles develops in the Church with the help of the Holy Spirit.[5] For there is a growth in the understanding of the realities and the words which have been handed down. This happens through the contemplation and study made by believers, who treasure these things in their hearts (see Luke. 2:19, 51) through a penetrating understanding of the spiritual realities which they experience, and through the preaching of those who have received through Episcopal succession the sure gift of truth. For as the centuries succeed one another, the Church constantly moves forward toward the fullness of divine truth until the words of God reach their complete fulfillment in her.

The words of the holy fathers witness to the presence of this living tradition, whose wealth is poured into the practice and life of the believing and praying Church. Through the same tradition the Church's full canon of the sacred books is known, and the sacred writings themselves are more profoundly understood and unceasingly made active in her; and thus God, who spoke of old, uninterruptedly converses with the bride of His beloved Son; and the Holy Spirit, through whom the living voice of the Gospel resounds in the Church, and through her, in the world, leads unto all truth those who believe and makes the word of Christ dwell abundantly in them (see Col. 3:16).

The Counselor of the Church

Dei Verbum 8

**Pope
St. John Paul II**

---

*Dominum et
Vivificantem 4*

[Jesus tells his disciples:] "But the Counselor, the Holy Spirit, whom the Father will send in my name, he will teach you all things, and bring to your remembrance all that I have said to you" (John 14:26). The Holy Spirit will be the Counselor of the Apostles and the Church, always present in their midst—even though invisible—as the teacher of the same Good News that Christ proclaimed. The words "he will teach" and "bring to remembrance" mean not only that he, in his own particular way, will continue to inspire the spreading of the Gospel of salvation but also that he will help people to understand the correct meaning of the content of Christ's message; they mean that he will ensure continuity and identity of understanding in the midst of changing conditions and circumstances. The Holy Spirit, then, will ensure that in the Church there will always continue the same truth which the Apostles heard from their Master.

9. Hence there exists a close connection and communication between sacred tradition and Sacred Scripture. For both of them, flowing from the same divine wellspring, in a certain way merge into a unity and tend toward the same end. For Sacred Scripture is the word of God inasmuch as it is consigned to writing under the inspiration of the divine Spirit, while sacred tradition takes the word of God entrusted by Christ the Lord and

the Holy Spirit to the Apostles, and hands it on to their successors in its full purity, so that led by the light of the Spirit of truth, they may in proclaiming it preserve this word of God faithfully, explain it, and make it more widely known. Consequently it is not from Sacred Scripture alone that the Church draws her certainty about everything which has been revealed. Therefore both sacred tradition and Sacred Scripture are to be accepted and venerated with the same sense of loyalty and reverence.[6]

Sacred Scripture and Sacred Tradition

Dei Verbum 8–10 | Bishop Barron

Through his providence, God has guaranteed that his revelation is preserved across the centuries, handed down from generation to generation. And Christ himself, the fullness of revelation, commissioned his Apostles to preach, and those Apostles chose successors, the bishops, to maintain this revelation in its integrity. This apostolic preaching, "which is expressed in a special way in the inspired books, was to be preserved by an unending succession of preachers until the end of time."

And this means that there is a very close connection between the Scriptures and what the Church calls "Tradition."

In one of the most celebrated of its passages, *Dei Verbum* affirms that Scripture and Tradition both flow from the Holy Spirit—which is to say, from a power who properly transcends time and hence can effectively unite them. "For both of them, flowing from the same divine wellspring, in a certain way merge into a unity and tend toward the same end." Thus we can say that "Sacred tradition and Sacred Scripture form one sacred deposit of the word of God, committed to the Church."

10. Sacred tradition and Sacred Scripture form one sacred deposit of the word of God, committed to the Church. Holding fast to this deposit the entire holy people united with their shepherds remain always steadfast in the teaching of the Apostles, in the common life, in the breaking of the bread and in prayers (see Acts 2:42, Greek text), so that holding to,

practicing, and professing the heritage of the faith, it becomes on the part of the bishops and faithful a single common effort.[7]

But the task of authentically interpreting the word of God, whether written or handed on,[8] has been entrusted exclusively to the living teaching office of the Church,[9] whose authority is exercised in the name of Jesus Christ. This teaching office is not above the word of God, but serves it, teaching only what has been handed on, listening to it devoutly, guarding it scrupulously and explaining it faithfully in accord with a divine commission and with the help of the Holy Spirit, it draws from this one deposit of faith everything which it presents for belief as divinely revealed.

It is clear, therefore, that sacred tradition, Sacred Scripture, and the teaching authority of the Church, in accord with God's most wise design, are so linked and joined together that one cannot stand without the others, and that all together and each in its own way under the action of the one Holy Spirit contribute effectively to the salvation of souls.

The Religion of the Living Word

Dei Verbum 10

Pope Benedict XVI

———

Verbum Domini 7

Human language operates analogically in speaking of the word of God. In effect, this expression, while referring to God's self-communication, also takes on a number of different meanings which need to be carefully considered and related among themselves, from the standpoint both of theological reflection and pastoral practice. As the Prologue of John clearly shows us, the Logos refers in the first place to the eternal Word, the only Son, begotten of the Father before all ages and consubstantial with him: the word was with God, and the word was God. But this same Word, Saint John tells us, "became flesh" (John 1:14); hence Jesus Christ, born of the Virgin Mary, is truly the Word of God who has become consubstantial with us. Thus the expression "word of God" here refers to the person of Jesus Christ, the eternal Son of the Father, made man.

While the Christ event is at the heart of divine revelation, we also need to realize that creation itself, the *liber naturae*, is an essential part of this symphony of many voices in which the one word is spoken. We also profess our faith that God has spoken his word in salvation history; he has made his voice heard; by the power of his Spirit "he has spoken through the prophets." God's word is thus spoken throughout the history of salvation, and most fully in the mystery of the incarnation, death, and resurrection of the Son of God. Then too, the word of God is that word preached by the Apostles in obedience to the command of the Risen Jesus: "Go into all the world and preach the Gospel to the whole creation" (Mark 16:15). The word of God is thus handed on in the Church's living Tradition. Finally, the word of God, attested and divinely inspired, is sacred Scripture, the Old and New Testaments. All this helps us to see that, while in the Church we greatly venerate the sacred Scriptures, the Christian faith is not a "religion of the book": Christianity is the "religion of the word of God," not of "a written and mute word, but of the incarnate and living Word." Consequently the Scripture is to be proclaimed, heard, read, received, and experienced as the word of God, in the stream of the apostolic Tradition from which it is inseparable.

CHAPTER III
Sacred Scripture's Divine Inspiration and Its Interpretation

11. Those divinely revealed realities which are contained and presented in Sacred Scripture have been committed to writing under the inspiration of the Holy Spirit. For holy mother Church, relying on the belief of the Apostles (see John 20:31; 2 Tim. 3:16; 2 Pet. 1:19–20, 3:15–16), holds that the books of both the Old and New Testaments in their entirety, with all their parts, are sacred and canonical because written under the inspiration of the Holy Spirit, they have God as their author and have been handed on as such to the Church herself.[1] In composing the sacred books, God chose men and while employed by Him[2] they made use of their powers and abilities, so that with Him acting in them and through them,[3] they, as true authors, consigned to writing everything and only those things which He wanted.[4]

The Authorship of God

Dei Verbum 11 I Bishop Barron

We hear that the sacred books were written under the influence of the Holy Spirit and hence "have God as their author" (*Deum habent auctorem*). That this does not amount to a naïve literalism is made clear in the immediately subsequent observation that "God chose men and while employed by Him they made use of their powers and abilities, so that with Him acting in them and through them, they, as true authors, consigned to writing everything and only those things which He wanted." The ground for this paradoxical assertion is in the consistently biblical teaching that God relates to his creation noncompetitively, allowing it to flourish on its own even as he works through it. Perhaps the clearest Old Testament statement of this principle is in the twenty-sixth chapter of Isaiah when the prophet states, "You have accomplished all we have done" (Isa. 26:12).

But the idea comes to richest and most dramatic expression in the New Testament claim that God became human, without ceasing to be God and without compromising the integrity of the creature he became. The Council of Chalcedon honored this biblical logic when it spoke of the two natures in Jesus coming together without mixing, mingling, or confusion. It thereby held off the triple threat of monophysitism (a one-sided stress on divinity), Nestorianism (a one-sided stress on humanity), and Arianism (a compromise of the two). The negation of all three positions was made possible by the distinctively biblical belief in God as Creator.

Extrapolating from this discussion, we can say with *Dei Verbum* that the true God is capable of working decisively through intelligent, created causes but in such a way that the full integrity and purposefulness of those causes is not compromised. On a more Nestorian reading of inspiration—prominent in much of modernity—one might speak of an independent human author speculating according to his lights, with perhaps a vague relationship to a distant God. On a monophysite reading, one might speak—as fundamentalists and literalists do—of a God who uses human agents in a domineering manner, essentially eliminating their own intelligence. Both fall short of the participative view on display in *Dei Verbum*.

Therefore, since everything asserted by the inspired authors or sacred writers must be held to be asserted by the Holy Spirit, it follows that the books of Scripture must be acknowledged as teaching solidly, faithfully, and without error that truth which God wanted put into sacred writings[5] for the sake of salvation. Therefore "all Scripture is divinely inspired and has its use for teaching the truth and refuting error, for reformation of manners and discipline in right living, so that the man who belongs to God may be efficient and equipped for good work of every kind" (2 Tim. 3:16–17, Greek text).

12. However, since God speaks in Sacred Scripture through men in human fashion,[6] the interpreter of Sacred Scripture, in order to see clearly what God wanted to communicate to us, should carefully investigate what meaning the sacred writers really intended, and what God wanted to manifest by means of their words.

To search out the intention of the sacred writers, attention should be given, among other things, to "literary forms." For truth is set forth and expressed differently in texts which are variously historical, prophetic, poetic, or of other forms of discourse. The interpreter must investigate what meaning the sacred writer intended to express and actually expressed in particular circumstances by using contemporary literary forms in accordance with the situation of his own time and culture.[7] For the correct understanding of what the sacred author wanted to assert, due attention must be paid to the customary and characteristic styles of feeling, speaking, and narrating which prevailed at the time of the sacred writer, and to the patterns men normally employed at that period in their everyday dealings with one another.[8]

But, since Holy Scripture must be read and interpreted in the sacred spirit in which it was written,[9] no less serious attention must be given to the content and unity of the whole of Scripture if the meaning of the sacred texts is to be correctly worked out. The living tradition of the whole Church must be taken into account along with the harmony which exists between elements of the faith. It is the task of exegetes to work according to these rules toward a better understanding and explanation of the meaning of Sacred Scripture, so that through preparatory study the judgment of the Church may mature. For all of what has been said about the way of interpreting Scripture is subject finally to the judgment of the Church, which carries out the divine commission and ministry of guarding and interpreting the word of God.[10]

The Diversity and Unity of the Scriptures

Dei Verbum 12 | Bishop Barron

Dei Verbum emphasizes the crucial importance of attending to authorial intention and "literary forms" in biblical interpretation. One should never approach a more straightforwardly historical text such as 1 Samuel with the same hermeneutical assumptions that one might employ to survey a text such as the book of the prophet Jonah.

But then it immediately affirms what would come to be called "canonical criticism," insisting that the Bible as a whole must be used as the interpretive matrix for any part of Scripture. *Dei Verbum* maintains that "since Holy Scripture must be read and interpreted in the sacred spirit in which it was written, no less serious attention must be given to the content and unity of the whole of Scripture if the meaning of the sacred texts is to be correctly worked out." This principle is clearly violated in the measure that the recovery of the mind of the historical authors is the exclusive preoccupation of biblical hermeneutics.

13. In Sacred Scripture, therefore, while the truth and holiness of God always remains intact, the marvelous "condescension" of eternal wisdom is clearly shown, "that we may learn the gentle kindness of God, which words cannot express, and how far He has gone in adapting His language with thoughtful concern for our weak human nature."[11] For the words of God, expressed in human language, have been made like human discourse, just as the word of the eternal Father, when He took to Himself the flesh of human weakness, was in every way made like men.

The Words of God in Human Language

Dei Verbum 13 | Bishop Barron

Dei Verbum declares that the Bible is "the words of God, expressed in human language." That laconic statement packs a punch, for it clarifies why the fundamentalist strategy of scriptural interpretation is always dysfunctional. God did not dictate the Scriptures word for word to people who received the message dumbly and automatically. Rather, God spoke subtly and indirectly, precisely through human agents who employed distinctive literary techniques and who were conditioned by the cultures in which they found themselves and by the audiences they addressed. Thus, one of the most basic moves in scriptural exegesis is the determination of the genre in which a given biblical author was operating. Are we dealing with a song, a psalm, a history, a legend, a letter, a Gospel, a tall tale, an apocalypse? Therefore, to ask, "Do you take the Bible literally?" is about as helpful as asking, "Do you take the library literally?"

A further implication of *Dei Verbum*'s statement is that there is a distinction between, as William Placher put it, what is in the Bible and what the Bible teaches. There are lots of things that are indeed in the pages of the Scriptures but that are not essential to the overarching message of the Scriptures. They were part of the cultural milieu of the human authors, but they are not ingredient in the revelation that God intends to offer. A good example of this would be the references to slavery. The institution of slavery was taken for granted in most ancient cultures, and therefore it is not surprising that biblical authors would refer to it or even praise it. But attention to the great patterns and trajectories of the Bible as a whole reveal that the justification of slavery is not something that "the Bible teaches," which is precisely why the fight against slavery in Western culture was led by people deeply shaped by the Scriptures.

CHAPTER IV
The Old Testament

14. In carefully planning and preparing the salvation of the whole human race the God of infinite love, by a special dispensation, chose for Himself a people to whom He would entrust His promises. First He entered into a covenant with Abraham (see Gen. 15:18) and, through Moses, with the people of Israel (see Exod. 24:8). To this people which He had acquired for Himself, He so manifested Himself through words and deeds as the one true and living God that Israel came to know by experience the ways of God with men. Then too, when God Himself spoke to them through the mouth of the prophets, Israel daily gained a deeper and clearer understanding of His ways and made them more widely known among the nations (see Ps. 21:29; 95:1–3; Isa. 2:1–5; Jer. 3:17). The plan of salvation foretold by the sacred authors, recounted and explained by them, is found as the true word of God in the books of the Old Testament: these books, therefore, written under divine inspiration, remain permanently valuable. "For all that was written for our instruction, so that by steadfastness and the encouragement of the Scriptures we might have hope" (Rom. 15:4).

15. The principal purpose to which the plan of the old covenant was directed was to prepare for the coming of Christ, the redeemer of all and of the messianic kingdom, to announce this coming by prophecy (see Luke 24:44; John 5:39; 1 Pet. 1:10), and to indicate its meaning through various types (see 1 Cor. 10:12). Now the books of the Old Testament, in accordance with the state of mankind before the time of salvation established by Christ, reveal to all men the knowledge of God and of man and the ways in which God, just and merciful, deals with men. These books, though they also contain some things which are incomplete and temporary, nevertheless show us true divine pedagogy.[1] These same books, then, give expression to a lively sense of God, contain a store of sublime teachings about God, sound wisdom about human life, and a wonderful treasury of prayers, and in them the mystery of our salvation is present in a hidden way. Christians should receive them with reverence.

16. God, the inspirer and author of both Testaments, wisely arranged that the New Testament be hidden in the Old and the Old be made manifest in the New.[2] For, though Christ established the new covenant in His blood

(see Luke 22:20; 1 Cor. 11:25), still the books of the Old Testament with all their parts, caught up into the proclamation of the Gospel,[3] acquire and show forth their full meaning in the New Testament (see Matt. 5:17; Luke 24:27; Rom. 16:25–26; 2 Cor. 3:14–16) and in turn shed light on it and explain it.

The Old Testament

Dei Verbum 14–16 | Bishop Barron

"The plan of salvation foretold by the sacred authors, recounted and explained by them, is found as the true word of God in the books of the Old Testament: these books, therefore, written under divine inspiration, remain permanently valuable." With this statement, *Dei Verbum* is eager to hold off all forms of Marcionism, an early heresy of the Church that sought to abstract Jesus from the Old Testament and the history of Israel.

The ultimate purpose of the Old Testament books is to prepare for the coming of Christ—through prophecy, to be sure, but also through what the tradition calls "types." This is a style of reading the Old Testament typical of the Church Fathers, wherein some word, event, or person is construed as a symbolic anticipation of Jesus. So Adam, Noah, Abraham, Moses, Joshua, David, Solomon, etc. are all Old Testament anticipatory signs, as are the Exodus, the conquest of the Promised Land, the Babylonian exile, the bronze serpent in the desert, Mt. Sinai, etc. Salvation history consistently *rhymes*.

Dei Verbum 15 again uses the term *oeconomia* (plan) to describe the structuring logic of both salvation history and the Bible itself, and it states clearly that this *oeconomia* is directed to Christ. To be sure, the Old Testament texts have their own spiritual integrity, but they are particularly reverenced by Christians in the measure that "in them the mystery of our salvation is present in a hidden way," under signs and symbols. Echoing Augustine's famous formula, *Dei Verbum* says that because God is the "inspirer and author" (*inspirator et auctor*) of both Testaments, he "wisely arranged that the New Testament be hidden in the Old and the Old be made manifest in the New."

CHAPTER V
The New Testament

17. The word of God, which is the power of God for the salvation of all who believe (see Rom. 1:16), is set forth and shows its power in a most excellent way in the writings of the New Testament. For when the fullness of time arrived (see Gal. 4:4), the Word was made flesh and dwelt among us in His fullness of graces and truth (see John 1:14). Christ established the kingdom of God on earth, manifested His Father and Himself by deeds and words, and completed His work by His death, resurrection, and glorious Ascension and by the sending of the Holy Spirit. Having been lifted up from the earth, He draws all men to Himself (see John 12:32, Greek text), He who alone has the words of eternal life (see John 6:68). This mystery had not been manifested to other generations as it was now revealed to His holy Apostles and prophets in the Holy Spirit (see Eph. 3:4–6, Greek text), so that they might preach the Gospel, stir up faith in Jesus, Christ and Lord, and gather together the Church. Now the writings of the New Testament stand as a perpetual and divine witness to these realities.

The Meaning of the Gospels
Dei Verbum 18

**Pope
St. John Paul II**

—

Fides et Ratio 94

The truth of the biblical texts, and of the Gospels in particular, is certainly not restricted to the narration of simple historical events or the statement of neutral facts, as historicist positivism would claim. Beyond simple historical occurrence, the truth of the events which these texts relate lies rather in the meaning they have *in* and *for* the history of salvation. This truth is elaborated fully in the Church's constant reading of these texts over the centuries, a reading which preserves intact their original meaning. There is a pressing need, therefore, that the relationship between fact and meaning, a relationship which constitutes the specific sense of history, be examined also from the philosophical point of view.

18. It is common knowledge that among all the Scriptures, even those of the New Testament, the Gospels have a special preeminence, and rightly so, for they are the principal witness for the life and teaching of the incarnate Word, our savior.

The Church has always and everywhere held and continues to hold that the four Gospels are of apostolic origin. For what the Apostles preached in fulfillment of the commission of Christ, afterwards they themselves and apostolic men, under the inspiration of the divine Spirit, handed on to us in writing: the foundation of faith, namely, the fourfold Gospel, according to Matthew, Mark, Luke, and John.[1]

19. Holy Mother Church has firmly and with absolute constancy held, and continues to hold, that the four Gospels just named, whose historical character the Church unhesitatingly asserts, faithfully hand on what Jesus Christ, while living among men, really did and taught for their eternal salvation until the day He was taken up into heaven (see Acts 1:1). Indeed, after the Ascension of the Lord the Apostles handed on to their hearers what He had said and done. This they did with that clearer understanding which they enjoyed[2] after they had been instructed by the glorious events of Christ's life and taught by the light of the Spirit of truth.[3] The sacred authors wrote the four Gospels, selecting some things from the many which had been handed on by word of mouth or in writing, reducing some of them to a synthesis, explaining some things in view of the situation of their churches and preserving the form of proclamation but always in such fashion that they told us the honest truth about Jesus.[4] For their intention in writing was that either from their own memory and recollections, or from the witness of those who "themselves from the beginning were eyewitnesses and ministers of the Word" we might know "the truth" concerning those matters about which we have been instructed (see Luke 1:2–4).

20. Besides the four Gospels, the canon of the New Testament also contains the epistles of St. Paul and other apostolic writings, composed under the inspiration of the Holy Spirit, by which, according to the wise plan of God, those matters which concern Christ the Lord are confirmed, His true teaching is more and more fully stated, the saving power of the divine work of Christ is preached, the story is told of the beginnings of the Church and its marvelous growth, and its glorious fulfillment is foretold.

For the Lord Jesus was with His apostles as He had promised (see Matt. 28:20) and sent them the advocate Spirit who would lead them into the fullness of truth (see John 16:13).

CHAPTER VI
Sacred Scripture in the Life of the Church

21. The Church has always venerated the divine Scriptures just as she venerates the body of the Lord, since, especially in the sacred liturgy, she unceasingly receives and offers to the faithful the bread of life from the table both of God's word and of Christ's body. She has always maintained them, and continues to do so, together with sacred tradition, as the supreme rule of faith, since, as inspired by God and committed once and for all to writing, they impart the word of God Himself without change, and make the voice of the Holy Spirit resound in the words of the prophets and Apostles. Therefore, like the Christian religion itself, all the preaching of the Church must be nourished and regulated by Sacred Scripture. For in the sacred books, the Father who is in heaven meets His children with great love and speaks with them; and the force and power in the word of God is so great that it stands as the support and energy of the Church, the

---

Easy Access to Scripture

Dei Verbum 21–22 | Bishop Barron

In the sixth and final chapter of *Dei Verbum*, we find a discussion of the role of Scripture in the life of the Church today. The council fathers couldn't be clearer as to the importance of the Bible: "The Church has always venerated the divine Scriptures just as she venerates the body of the Lord, since, especially in the sacred liturgy, she unceasingly receives and offers to the faithful the bread of life from the table both of God's word and of Christ's body." The Bible is "food of the soul, the pure and everlasting source of spiritual life."

Therefore, "easy access to Sacred Scripture should be provided for all the Christian faithful." The emphasis of the Vatican II fathers on making the Scriptures available to all, especially through "correct translations" in "different languages," offers a resounding answer to the old Protestant charge that the Catholic Church does not want to offer the Bible to the people of God.

strength of faith for her sons, the food of the soul, the pure and everlasting source of spiritual life. Consequently these words are perfectly applicable to Sacred Scripture: "For the word of God is living and active" (Heb. 4:12) and "it has power to build you up and give you your heritage among all those who are sanctified" (Acts 20:32; see 1 Thess. 2:13).

Bringing the Scripture to Life
Dei Verbum 21

Pope Benedict XVI
———
Verbum Domini 59

In the Apostolic Exhortation *Sacramentum Caritatis*, I pointed out that "given the importance of the word of God, the quality of homilies needs to be improved. The homily 'is part of the liturgical action' and is meant to foster a deeper understanding of the word of God, so that it can bear fruit in the lives of the faithful." The homily is a means of bringing the scriptural message to life in a way that helps the faithful to realize that God's word is present and at work in their everyday lives. It should lead to an understanding of the mystery being celebrated, serve as a summons to mission, and prepare the assembly for the profession of faith, the universal prayer, and the Eucharistic liturgy. Consequently, those who have been charged with preaching by virtue of a specific ministry ought to take this task to heart. Generic and abstract homilies which obscure the directness of God's word should be avoided, as well as useless digressions which risk drawing greater attention to the preacher than to the heart of the Gospel message. The faithful should be able to perceive clearly that the preacher has a compelling desire to present Christ, who must stand at the center of every homily. For this reason preachers need to be in close and constant contact with the sacred text; they should prepare for the homily by meditation and prayer, so as to preach with conviction and passion.

22. Easy access to Sacred Scripture should be provided for all the Christian faithful. That is why the Church from the very beginning accepted as her own that very ancient Greek translation; of the Old Testament which is called the septuagint; and she has always given a place of honor to other Eastern translations and Latin ones especially the Latin translation known as the vulgate. But since the word of God should be accessible at all times, the Church by her authority and with maternal concern sees to it that suitable and correct translations are made into different languages, especially from the original texts of the sacred books. And should the opportunity arise and the Church authorities approve, if these translations are produced in cooperation with the separated brethren as well, all Christians will be able to use them.

23. The bride of the incarnate Word, the Church taught by the Holy Spirit, is concerned to move ahead toward a deeper understanding of the Sacred Scriptures so that she may increasingly feed her sons with the divine words. Therefore, she also encourages the study of the holy Fathers of both East and West and of sacred liturgies. Catholic exegetes then and other students

---

The Church Fathers

Dei Verbum 23 | Bishop Barron

The council fathers explicitly recommend the study of the Church Fathers, both East and West, as a privileged way of coming to know the meaning of Scripture. We don't just pick up the Bible and read it; rather, we read the sacred texts within the tradition and through the liturgy.

Like so many of the other texts of Vatican II, *Dei Verbum* itself is best read under the rubric of *ressourcement* (or "return to the sources"), the recovery of the biblical and patristic roots of the Christian faith. The great *ressourcement* theologians of the twentieth century, many of whom were *periti* at the council, tended to engage modernity in an oblique manner. Unlike their liberal colleagues who endeavored to present Christian theology in a straightforwardly modern form, the *ressourcement* masters—de Lubac, Balthasar, Ratzinger, Daniélou—attempted to assimilate the best of modernity to the patristic form of the faith. They took modernity in, but they adapted and corralled it, making it ancillary to classical Christianity.

---

of sacred theology, working diligently together and using appropriate means, should devote their energies, under the watchful care of the sacred teaching office of the Church, to an exploration and exposition of the divine writings. This should be so done that as many ministers of the divine word as possible will be able effectively to provide the nourishment of the Scriptures for the people of God, to enlighten their minds, strengthen their wills, and set men's hearts on fire with the love of God.[1] The sacred synod encourages the sons of the Church and Biblical scholars to continue energetically, following the mind of the Church, with the work they have so well begun, with a constant renewal of vigor.[2]

24. Sacred theology rests on the written word of God, together with sacred tradition, as its primary and perpetual foundation. By scrutinizing in the light of faith all truth stored up in the mystery of Christ, theology is most powerfully strengthened and constantly rejuvenated by that word. For the Sacred Scriptures contain the word of God and since they are inspired really are the word of God; and so the study of the sacred page is, as it were, the soul of sacred theology.[3] By the same word of Scripture the ministry of the word also, that is, pastoral preaching, catechetics, and all Christian instruction, in which the liturgical homily must hold the foremost place, is nourished in a healthy way and flourishes in a holy way.

The Soul of Sacred Theology

Dei Verbum 24 | Bishop Barron

The Vatican II fathers call for a sort of *circumincessio* of biblical exegesis and theology, each one conditioning and informing the other. When they speak of the Bible as "the soul of sacred theology," they imply that Scripture animates theology and that theology instantiates and gives concrete expression to the meaning of Scripture.

---

25. Therefore, all the clergy must hold fast to the Sacred Scriptures through diligent sacred reading and careful study, especially the priests of Christ and others, such as deacons and catechists who are legitimately active in

the ministry of the word. This is to be done so that none of them will become "an empty preacher of the word of God outwardly, who is not a listener to it inwardly"[4] since they must share the abundant wealth of the divine word with the faithful committed to them, especially in the sacred liturgy. The sacred synod also earnestly and especially urges all the Christian faithful, especially Religious, to learn by frequent reading of the divine Scriptures the "excellent knowledge of Jesus Christ" (Phil. 3:8). "For ignorance of the Scriptures is ignorance of Christ."[5] Therefore, they should gladly put themselves in touch with the sacred text itself, whether it be through the liturgy, rich in the divine word, or through devotional reading, or through instructions suitable for the purpose and other aids which, in our time, with approval and active support of the shepherds of the Church, are commendably spread everywhere. And let them remember that prayer should accompany the reading of Sacred Scripture, so that God and man may talk together; for "we speak to Him when we pray; we hear Him when we read the divine saying."[6]

It devolves on sacred bishops "who have the apostolic teaching"[7] to give the faithful entrusted to them suitable instruction in the right use of the divine books, especially the New Testament and above all the Gospels. This can be done through translations of the sacred texts, which are to be provided with the necessary and really adequate explanations so that the children of the Church may safely and profitably become conversant with the Sacred Scriptures and be penetrated with their spirit.

Furthermore, editions of the Sacred Scriptures, provided with suitable footnotes, should be prepared also for the use of non-Christians and adapted to their situation. Both pastors of souls and Christians generally should see to the wise distribution of these in one way or another.

26. In this way, therefore, through the reading and study of the sacred books "the word of God may spread rapidly and be glorified" (2 Thess. 3:1) and the treasure of revelation, entrusted to the Church, may more and more fill the hearts of men. Just as the life of the Church is strengthened through more frequent celebration of the Eucharistic mystery, similarly we may hope for a new stimulus for the life of the Spirit from a growing reverence for the word of God, which "lasts forever" (Isa. 40:8; see 1 Pet. 1:23–25).

A Call to All the Faithful

Dei Verbum 25–26 | Bishop Barron

The final paragraphs of *Dei Verbum* affirm that the clergy "must hold fast to the Sacred Scriptures through diligent sacred reading and careful study, especially the priests of Christ and others, such as deacons and catechists who are legitimately active in the ministry of the word."

But we also hear that "all the Christian faithful" are to be immersed in the Bible, whether through the liturgy or devotional reading or careful study.

The bishops, we are also told, have a prime responsibility here in instructing the faithful.

Dei Verbum concludes: "Just as the life of the Church is strengthened through more frequent celebration of the Eucharistic mystery, similarly we may hope for a new stimulus for the life of the Spirit from a growing reverence for the word of God, which 'lasts forever.'" Given this strongly worded conclusion, it is fair to ask: Have either of these revivals envisioned by the council, Eucharistic or scriptural, happened yet?

NOTES

PREFACE

1   See St. Augustine, "De Catechizandis Rudibus," C.IV 8: PL. 40, 316.

CHAPTER I

2   See Matt. 11:27; John 1:14 and 17; 14:6; 17:1–3; 2 Cor. 3:16 and 4:6; Eph. 1:3–14.

3   Epistle to Diognetus, c. VII, 4: Funk, Apostolic Fathers, I, p. 403.

4   First Vatican Council, Dogmatic Constitution on the Catholic Faith, Chap. 3, "On Faith": Denzinger 1789 (3008).

5   Second Council of Orange, Canon 7: Denzinger 180 (377); First Vatican Council, loc. cit.: Denzinger 1791 (3010).

6   First Vatican Council, Dogmatic Constitution on the Catholic Faith, Chap. 2, "On Revelation:" Denzinger 1786 (3005).

7   Ibid.: Denzinger 1785 and 1786 (3004 and 3005).

CHAPTER II

1   See Matt. 28:19–20, and Mark 16:15; Council of Trent, session IV, Decree on Scriptural Canons: Denzinger 783 (1501).

2   See Council of Trent, loc. cit.; First Vatican Council, session III, Dogmatic Constitution on the Catholic Faith, Chap. 2, "On revelation:" Denzinger 1787 (3005).

3   St. Irenaeus, "Against Heretics" III, 3, 1: PG 7, 848; Harvey, 2, p. 9.

4   See Second Council of Nicea: Denzinger 303 (602); Fourth Council of Constance, session X, Canon 1: Denzinger 336 (650–652).

5   See First Vatican Council, Dogmatic Constitution on the Catholic Faith, Chap. 4, "On Faith and Reason:" Denzinger 1800 (3020).

6   See Council of Trent, session IV, loc. cit.: Denzinger 783 (1501).

7   See Pius XII, apostolic constitution, "Munificentissimus Deus," Nov. 1, 1950: A.A.S. 42 (1950) p. 756; Collected Writings of St. Cyprian, Letter 66, 8: Hartel, III, B, p. 733: "The Church [is] people united with the priest and the pastor together with his flock."

8   See First Vatican Council, Dogmatic Constitution on the Catholic Faith, Chap. 3 "On Faith:" Denzinger 1792 (3011).

9   See Pius XII, encyclical "Humani Generis," Aug. 12, 1950: A.A.S. 42 (1950) pp. 568–69: Denzinger 2314 (3886).

CHAPTER III

1   See First Vatican Council, Dogmatic Constitution on the Catholic Faith, Chap. 2 "On Revelation:" Denzinger 1787 (3006); Biblical Commission, Decree of June 18, 1915: Denzinger 2180 (3629): EB 420; Holy Office, Epistle of Dec. 22, 1923: EB 499.

2   See Pius XII, encyclical "Divino Afflante Spiritu," Sept. 30, 1943: A.A.S. 35 (1943) p. 314; Enchiridion Bible. (EB) 556.

3   "In" and "for" man: see Heb. 1, and 4:7; ("in"): 2 Sam. 23:2; Matt. 1:22 and various places; ("for"): First Vatican Council, Schema on Catholic Doctrine, note 9: Coll. Lac. VII, 522.

4   Leo XIII, encyclical "Providentissimus Deus," Nov. 18, 1893: Denzinger 1952 (3293); EB 125.

5   See St. Augustine, "Gen. ad Litt." 2, 9, 20: PL 34, 270–271; Epistle 82, 3: PL 33, 277: CSEL 34, 2, p. 354. St. Thomas, "On Truth," Q. 12, A. 2, C. Council of Trent, session IV, Scriptural Canons: Denzinger 783 (1501). Leo XIII, encyclical "Providentissimus Deus:" EB 121, 124, 126–127. Pius XII, encyclical "Divino Afflante Spiritu:" EB 539.

6   St. Augustine, "City of God" XVII, 6, 2 PL 41, 537: CSEL. XL, 2, 228.

7   St. Augustine, "On Christian Doctrine" III, 18, 26; PL 34, 75–76.

8   Pius XII, loc. cit. Denzinger 2294 (3829–3830); EB 557–562.

9   See Benedict XV, encyclical "Spiritus Paraclitus," Sept. 15, 1920: EB 469. St. Jerome, "In Galatians' 5, 19–20: PL 26, 417 A.

10   See First Vatican Council, Dogmatic Constitution on the Catholic Faith, Chapter 2, "On Revelation:" Denzinger 1788 (3007).

11   St. John Chrysostom "In Genesis" 3, 8 (Homily 17, 1): PG 53, 134; "Attemperatio" [in English "Suitable adjustment"] in Greek "synkatabasis."

CHAPTER IV

1   Pius XI, encyclical "Mit Brennender Sorge," March 14, 1937: A.A.S. 29 (1937) p. 51.

2   St. Augustine, "Quest. in Hept." 2,73: PL 34,623.

3   St. Irenaeus, "Against Heretics" III, 21,3: PG 7,950; (Same as 25,1: Harvey 2, p. 115). St. Cyril of Jerusalem, "Catech." 4,35; PG 33,497. Theodore of Mopsuestia, "In Soph." 1, 4–6: PG 66, 452D–453A.

CHAPTER V

1   See St. Irenaeus, "Against Heretics" III, 11, 8: PG 7,885, Sagnard Edition, p. 194.

2   See John 14:26; 16:13.

3   John 2:22; 12:16; see 14:26; 16:12–13; 7:39.

4   See instruction "Holy Mother Church" edited by Pontifical Consilium for Promotion of Bible Studies; A.A.S. 56 (1964) p. 715.

CHAPTER VI

1   See Pius XII, encyclical "Divino Afflante Spiritu:" EB 551, 553, 567. Pontifical Biblical Commission, Instruction on Proper Teaching of Sacred Scripture in Seminaries and Religious Colleges, May 13, 1950: A.A.S. 42 (1950) pp. 495–505.

2   See Pius XII, ibid.: EB 569.

3   See Leo XIII, encyclical "Providentissmus Deus:" EB 114; Benedict XV, encyclical "Spiritus Paraclitus": EB 483.

4   St. Augustine Sermons, 179, 1: PL 38, 966.

5   St. Jerome, Commentary on Isaiah, Prol.: PL 24, 17. see Benedict XV, encyclical "Spiritus Paraclitus": EB 475–480; Pius XII, encyclical "Divino Afflante Spiritu": EB 544.

6   St. Ambrose, On the Duties of Ministers I, 20, 88: PL l6, 50.

7   St. Irenaeus, "Against Heretics" IV, 32,1: PG 7, 1071; (Same as 49,2) Harvey, 2, p. 255.

LUMEN GENTIUM

Dogmatic Constitution on
the Church

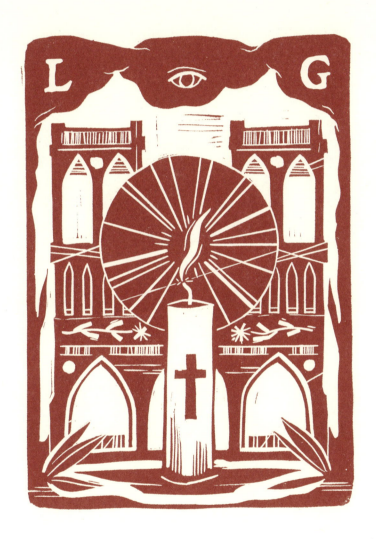

SOLEMNLY PROMULGATED *by* HIS HOLINESS
POPE PAUL VI
on NOVEMBER 21, 1964

The Light of the Nations

Introduction to *Lumen Gentium* by Bishop Robert Barron

There is a photograph of Pope St. John XXIII, taken not long after he summoned the Second Vatican Council, in which the pope stands next to an enormous globe. He spoke of his hopes for the council and used a phrase that eventually became the title of the most significant of the conciliar documents, *Lumen Gentium*. (The same speech, many have said, was the inspiration also behind *Gaudium et Spes*.) The *lumen* (light) in question is not the Church, but Christ Jesus. And the task, mission, and entire purpose of the Church is to bring the *lumen* to the *gentes*, to the nations.

Hans Urs von Balthasar, though he himself was not present at Vatican II, had an outsize influence on many who were: Ratzinger, de Lubac, Congar, Wojtyła, and others. And in 1952, Balthasar wrote a short book that had an enormous impact. It was called *Schleifung der Bastionen* (*Razing the Bastions*). His argument, simply put, was that the Church was crouching too defensively behind its medieval walls and was not living up to its missionary mandate to evangelize the world. Its treasures, which are meant for the world, were not being shared, since they were couched too often in language, style, and conceptuality that was alien to contemporary audiences. Balthasar didn't think for a moment that the project was to allow modernity, with all of its intellectual and moral ambiguity, simply to come rushing through the broken walls. In fact, he was throughout his career a sharp critic of modernity. The project was to let the life of the Church *out*, somewhat in the manner of Noah opening the windows and doors of the ark.

The members of the Church become holy precisely in the measure that they bring holiness to the world—and this, quite obviously, involves the laity, who share the missionary purpose (see LG 30–38). The clergy are appreciated as those who teach and sanctify and shepherd the laity for their work of transforming the world. Hence, to use the cliché, the laity are not to "pray, pay, and obey," but rather to carry the light of Christ into the ordinary circumstances of their lives.

The ultimate purpose of the Church is not to turn in on itself, fussing primarily with its own inner life; it is, as *Lumen Gentium* teaches, to go *out*, proclaiming and spreading Christ's kingdom "among all peoples" (LG 5) and becoming the vehicle by which God draws the world to himself.

LUMEN GENTIUM

Dogmatic Constitution
on the Church

CHAPTER I

The Mystery of the Church

1. Christ is the Light of nations. Because this is so, this Sacred Synod gathered together in the Holy Spirit eagerly desires, by proclaiming the Gospel to every creature,[1] to bring the light of Christ to all men, a light brightly visible on the countenance of the Church. Since the Church is in Christ like a sacrament or as a sign and instrument both of a very closely knit union with God and of the unity of the whole human race, it desires now to unfold more fully to the faithful of the Church and to the whole world its own inner nature and universal mission. This it intends to do following faithfully the teaching of previous councils. The present-day conditions of the world add greater urgency to this work of the Church so that all men, joined more closely today by various social, technical, and cultural ties, might also attain fuller unity in Christ.

2. The eternal Father, by a free and hidden plan of His own wisdom and goodness, created the whole world. His plan was to raise men to a participation of the divine life. Fallen in Adam, God the Father did not leave men to themselves, but ceaselessly offered helps to salvation, in view of Christ, the Redeemer "who is the image of the invisible God, the firstborn of every creature."[2] All the elect, before time began, the Father "foreknew

and pre-destined to become conformed to the image of His Son, that he should be the firstborn among many brethren."[3] He planned to assemble in the holy Church all those who would believe in Christ. Already from the beginning of the world the foreshadowing of the Church took place. It was prepared in a remarkable way throughout the history of the people of Israel and by means of the Old Covenant.[1*] In the present era of time the Church was constituted and, by the outpouring of the Spirit, was made manifest. At the end of time it will gloriously achieve completion, when, as is read in the Fathers, all the just, from Adam and "from Abel, the just one, to the last of the elect,"[2*] will be gathered together with the Father in the universal Church.

3. The Son, therefore, came, sent by the Father. It was in Him, before the foundation of the world, that the Father chose us and predestined us to become adopted sons, for in Him it pleased the Father to re-establish all things.[4] To carry out the will of the Father, Christ inaugurated the Kingdom of heaven on earth and revealed to us the mystery of that kingdom. By His obedience He brought about redemption. The Church, or, in other words, the kingdom of Christ now present in mystery, grows visibly through the power of God in the world. This inauguration and this growth are both symbolized by the blood and water which flowed from the open side of a crucified Jesus,[5] and are foretold in the words of the Lord referring to His death on the Cross: "And I, if I be lifted up from the earth, will draw all things to myself."[6] As often as the sacrifice of the cross in which Christ our Passover was sacrificed[7], is celebrated on the altar, the work of our redemption is carried on, and, in the sacrament of the eucharistic bread, the unity of all believers who form one body in Christ[8] is both expressed and brought about. All men are called to this union with Christ, who is the light of the world, from whom we go forth, through whom we live, and toward whom our whole life strains.

4. When the work which the Father gave the Son to do on earth[9] was accomplished, the Holy Spirit was sent on the day of Pentecost in order that He might continually sanctify the Church, and thus, all those who believe would have access through Christ in one Spirit to the Father.[10] He is the Spirit of Life, a fountain of water springing up to life eternal.[11] To men, dead in sin, the Father gives life through Him, until, in Christ, He brings to life their mortal bodies.[12] The Spirit dwells in the Church

and in the hearts of the faithful, as in a temple.[13] In them He prays on their behalf and bears witness to the fact that they are adopted sons.[14] The Church, which the Spirit guides in the way of all truth[15] and which He unified in communion and in works of ministry, He both equips and directs with hierarchical and charismatic gifts and adorns with His fruits.[16] By the power of the Gospel He makes the Church keep the freshness of youth. Uninterruptedly He renews it and leads it to perfect union with its Spouse.[3*] The Spirit and the Bride both say to Jesus, the Lord, "Come!"[17]

Thus, the Church has been seen as "a people made one with the unity of the Father, the Son, and the Holy Spirit."[4*]

5. The mystery of the holy Church is manifest in its very foundation. The Lord Jesus set it on its course by preaching the Good News, that is, the coming of the Kingdom of God, which, for centuries, had been promised in the Scriptures: "The time is fulfilled, and the kingdom of God is at hand."[18] In the word, in the works, and in the presence of Christ, this kingdom was clearly open to the view of men. The Word of the Lord is compared to a seed which is sown in a field;[19] those who hear the Word with faith and become part of the little flock of Christ,[20] have received the Kingdom itself. Then, by its own power the seed sprouts and grows until harvest time.[21] The Miracles of Jesus also confirm that the Kingdom has already arrived on earth: "If I cast out devils by the finger of God, then the kingdom of God has come upon you."[22] Before all things, however, the Kingdom is clearly visible in the very Person of Christ, the Son of God and the Son of Man, who came "to serve and to give His life as a ransom for many."[23]

When Jesus, who had suffered the death of the cross for mankind, had risen, He appeared as the one constituted as Lord, Christ, and eternal Priest,[24] and He poured out on His disciples the Spirit promised by the Father.[25] From this source the Church, equipped with the gifts of its Founder and faithfully guarding His precepts of charity, humility, and self-sacrifice, receives the mission to proclaim and to spread among all peoples the Kingdom of Christ and of God and to be, on earth, the initial budding forth of that kingdom. While it slowly grows, the Church strains toward the completed Kingdom and, with all its strength, hopes, and desires to be united in glory with its King.

6. In the old Testament the revelation of the Kingdom is often conveyed

by means of metaphors. In the same way the inner nature of the Church is now made known to us in different images taken either from tending sheep or cultivating the land, from building or even from family life and betrothals; the images receive preparatory shaping in the books of the Prophets.

The Church is a sheepfold whose one and indispensable door is Christ.[26] It is a flock of which God Himself foretold He would be the shepherd,[27] and whose sheep, although ruled by human shepherds; are nevertheless continuously led and nourished by Christ Himself, the Good Shepherd and the Prince of the shepherds,[28] who gave His life for the sheep.[29] The Church is a piece of land to be cultivated, the tillage of God.[30] On that land the ancient olive tree grows whose holy roots were the Prophets and in which the reconciliation of Jews and Gentiles has been brought about and will be brought about.[31] That land, like a choice vineyard, has been planted by the heavenly Husbandman.[32] The true vine is Christ who gives life and the power to bear abundant fruit to the branches, that is, to us, who through the Church remain in Christ without whom we can do nothing.[33]

Often the Church has also been called the building of God.[34] The Lord Himself compared Himself to the stone which the builders rejected, but which was made into the cornerstone.[35] On this foundation the Church is built by the apostles,[36] and from it the Church receives durability and consolidation. This edifice has many names to describe it: the house of God[37] in which dwells His family; the household of God in the Spirit;[38] the dwelling place of God among men;[39] and, especially, the holy temple. This Temple, symbolized in places of worship built out of stone, is praised by the Holy Fathers and, not without reason, is compared in the liturgy to the Holy City, the New Jerusalem.[5*] As living stones we here on earth are built into it.[40] John contemplates this holy city coming down from heaven at the renewal of the world as a bride made ready and adorned for her husband.[41]

The Church, further, "that Jerusalem which is above" is also called "our mother."[42] It is described as the spotless spouse of the spotless Lamb,[43] whom Christ "loved and for whom He delivered Himself up that He might sanctify her,"[44] whom He unites to Himself by an unbreakable covenant, and whom He unceasingly "nourishes and cherishes,"[45] and whom, once purified, He willed to be cleansed and joined to Himself, subject to Him in love and fidelity,[46] and whom, finally, He filled with heavenly gifts for all eternity, in order that we may know the love of God and of Christ for us, a love which surpasses all knowledge.[47] The Church, while on earth it journeys in a foreign land away from the Lord,[48] is like in exile. It seeks and experiences those things which are above, where Christ is seated at the right-hand of God, where the life of the Church is hidden with Christ in God until it appears in glory with its Spouse.[49]

7. In the human nature united to Himself the Son of God, by overcoming death through His own death and resurrection, redeemed man and re-molded him into a new creation.[50] By communicating His Spirit, Christ made His brothers, called together from all nations, mystically the components of His own Body.

In that Body the life of Christ is poured into the believers who, through the sacraments, are united in a hidden and real way to Christ who suffered and was glorified.[6'] Through Baptism we are formed in the likeness of Christ: "For in one Spirit we were all baptized into one body."[51] In this sacred rite a oneness with Christ's death and resurrection is both symbolized and brought about: "For we were buried with Him by means of Baptism into death"; and if "we have been united with Him in the likeness of His death, we shall be so in the likeness of His resurrection also."[52] Really partaking of the body of the Lord in the breaking of the Eucharistic bread, we are taken up into communion with Him and with one another. "Because the bread is one, we though many, are one body, all of us who partake of the one bread."[53] In this way all of us are made members of His Body,[54] "but severally members one of another."[55]

As all the members of the human body, though they are many, form one body, so also are the faithful in Christ.[56] Also, in the building up of Christ's Body various members and functions have their part to play. There is only one Spirit who, according to His own richness and the needs of the ministries, gives His different gifts for the welfare of the Church.[57] What has a special place among these gifts is the grace of the apostles to whose authority the Spirit Himself subjected even those who were endowed with charisms.[58] Giving the body unity through Himself and through His power and inner joining of the members, this same Spirit produces and urges love among the believers. From all this it follows that if one member endures anything, all the members co-endure it, and if one member is honored, all the members together rejoice.[59]

The Head of this Body is Christ. He is the image of the invisible God and in Him all things came into being. He is before all creatures and in Him all things hold together. He is the head of the Body which is the Church.[7*] He is the beginning, the firstborn from the dead, that in all things He might have the first place.[60] By the greatness of His power He rules the things in heaven and the things on earth, and with His all-surpassing perfection and way of acting He fills the whole body with the riches of His glory.[61]

All the members ought to be molded in the likeness of Him, until Christ be formed in them.[62] For this reason we, who have been made to conform with Him, who have died with Him and risen with Him, are taken up into the mysteries of His life, until we will reign together with Him.[63] On earth, still as pilgrims in a strange land, tracing in trial and in oppression the paths He trod, we are made one with His sufferings like the body is one with the Head, suffering with Him, that with Him we may be glorified.[64]

From Him "the whole body, supplied and built up by joints and ligaments, attains a growth that is of God."[65] He continually distributes in His body, that is, in the Church, gifts of ministries in which, by His own power, we serve each other unto salvation so that, carrying out the truth in love, we might through all things grow unto Him who is our Head.[66]

In order that we might be unceasingly renewed in Him,[67] He has shared with us His Spirit who, existing as one and the same being in the Head and in the members, gives life to, unifies, and moves through the whole body. This He does in such a way that His work could be compared by the holy Fathers with the function which the principle of life, that is, the soul, fulfills in the human body.[8*]

Christ loves the Church as His bride, having become the model of a man loving his wife as his body;[68] the Church, indeed, is subject to its Head.[69] "Because in Him dwells all the fullness of the Godhead bodily,"[70] He fills the Church, which is His body and His fullness, with His divine gifts[71] so that it may expand and reach all the fullness of God.[72]

8. Christ, the one Mediator, established and continually sustains here on earth His holy Church, the community of faith, hope, and charity, as an entity with visible delineation[9*] through which He communicated truth and grace to all. But, the society structured with hierarchical organs and the Mystical Body of Christ, are not to be considered as two realities, nor are the visible assembly and the spiritual community, nor the earthly

Church and the Church enriched with heavenly things; rather they form one complex reality which coalesces from a divine and a human element.[10*] For this reason, by no weak analogy, it is compared to the mystery of the incarnate Word. As the assumed nature inseparably united to Him, serves the divine Word as a living organ of salvation, so, in a similar way, does the visible social structure of the Church serve the Spirit of Christ, who vivifies it, in the building up of the body.[73] [11*]

This is the one Church of Christ which in the Creed is professed as one, holy, catholic, and apostolic,[12*] which our Savior, after His Resurrection, commissioned Peter to shepherd,[74] and him and the other apostles to extend and direct with authority,[75] which He erected for all ages as "the pillar and mainstay of the truth."[76] This Church constituted and organized in the world as a society, subsists in the Catholic Church, which is governed by the successor of Peter and by the Bishops in communion with him,[13*] although many elements of sanctification and of truth are found outside of its visible structure. These elements, as gifts belonging to the Church of Christ, are forces impelling toward catholic unity.

Just as Christ carried out the work of redemption in poverty and persecution, so the Church is called to follow the same route that it might communicate the fruits of salvation to men. Christ Jesus, "though He was by nature God . . . emptied Himself, taking the nature of a slave,"[77] and "being rich, became poor"[78] for our sakes. Thus, the Church, although it needs human resources to carry out its mission, is not set up to seek earthly glory, but to proclaim, even by its own example, humility and self-sacrifice. Christ was sent by the Father "to bring good news to the poor, to heal the contrite of heart,"[79] "to seek and to save what was lost."[80] Similarly, the Church encompasses with love all who are afflicted with human suffering and in the poor and afflicted sees the image of its poor and suffering Founder. It does all it can to relieve their need and in them it strives to serve Christ. While Christ, holy, innocent, and undefiled[81] knew nothing of sin,[82] but came to expiate only the sins of the people,[83] the Church, embracing in its bosom sinners, at the same time holy and always in need of being purified, always follows the way of penance and renewal. The Church, "like a stranger in a foreign land, presses forward amid the persecutions of the world and the consolations of God,"[14*] announcing the cross and death of the Lord until He comes.[84] By the power of the risen Lord it is given strength that it might, in patience and in love, overcome its sorrows and its challenges, both within itself and from without, and that it might reveal to the world, faithfully though darkly, the mystery of its Lord until, in the end, it will be manifested in full light.

Christ's Church Subsists in the Catholic Church

Lumen Gentium 8

Congregation for the Doctrine of the Faith
(under Pope St. John Paul II)
———
Dominus Iesus 16

The Lord Jesus, the only Savior, did not only establish a simple community of disciples, but constituted the Church as a *salvific mystery:* he himself is in the Church and the Church is in him (see John 15:1ff.; Gal. 3:28; Eph. 4:15–16; Acts 9:5). Therefore, the fullness of Christ's salvific mystery belongs also to the Church, inseparably united to her Lord. Indeed, Jesus Christ continues his presence and his work of salvation in the Church and by means of the Church (see Col. 1:24–27), which is his body (see 1 Cor. 12:12–13, 27; Col. 1:18). And thus, just as the head and members of a living body, though not identical, are inseparable, so too Christ and the Church can neither be confused nor separated, and constitute a single "whole Christ." This same inseparability is also expressed in the New Testament by the analogy of the Church as the *Bride* of Christ (see 2 Cor. 11:2; Eph. 5:25–29; Rev. 21:2, 9).

Therefore, in connection with the unicity and universality of the salvific mediation of Jesus Christ, the unicity of the Church founded by him must be *firmly believed* as a truth of Catholic faith. Just as there is one Christ, so there exists a single body of Christ, a single Bride of Christ: "a single Catholic and apostolic Church." Furthermore, the promises of the Lord that he would not abandon his Church (see Matt. 16:18; 28:20) and that he would guide her by his Spirit (see John 16:13) mean, according to Catholic faith, that the unicity and the unity of the

Church—like everything that belongs to the Church's integrity—will never be lacking.

The Catholic faithful *are required to profess* that there is an historical continuity—rooted in the apostolic succession—between the Church founded by Christ and the Catholic Church: "This is the one Church of Christ . . . which our Savior, after His Resurrection, commissioned Peter to shepherd, and him and the other apostles to extend and direct with authority, which He erected for all ages as 'the pillar and mainstay of the truth.' This Church constituted and organized in the world as a society, subsists in [*subsistit in*] the Catholic Church, which is governed by the successor of Peter and by the Bishops in communion with him." With the expression *subsistit in*, the Second Vatican Council sought to harmonize two doctrinal statements: on the one hand, that the Church of Christ, despite the divisions which exist among Christians, continues to exist fully only in the Catholic Church, and on the other hand, that "many elements of sanctification and of truth are found outside of its visible structure," that is, in those Churches and ecclesial communities which are not yet in full communion with the Catholic Church.[1] But with respect to these, it needs to be stated that "they derive their efficacy from the very fullness of grace and truth entrusted to the Catholic Church."

1. The interpretation of those who would derive from the formula *subsistit in* the thesis that the one Church of Christ could subsist also in non-Catholic Churches and ecclesial communities is therefore contrary to the authentic meaning of *Lumen Gentium*.

CHAPTER II
On the People of God

9. At all times and in every race God has given welcome to whosoever fears Him and does what is right.[85] God, however, does not make men holy and save them merely as individuals, without bond or link between one another. Rather has it pleased Him to bring men together as one people, a people which acknowledges Him in truth and serves Him in holiness. He therefore chose the race of Israel as a people unto Himself. With it

He set up a covenant. Step by step He taught and prepared this people, making known in its history both Himself and the decree of His will and making it holy unto Himself. All these things, however, were done by way of preparation and as a figure of that new and perfect covenant, which was to be ratified in Christ, and of that fuller revelation which was to be given through the Word of God Himself made flesh. "Behold the days shall come saith the Lord, and I will make a new covenant with the House of Israel, and with the house of Judah. . . . I will give my law in their bowels, and I will write it in their heart, and I will be their God, and they shall be my people. . . . For all of them shall know Me, from the least of them even to the greatest, saith the Lord."[86] Christ instituted this new covenant, the new testament, that is to say, in His Blood,[87] calling together a people made up of Jew and gentile, making them one, not according to the flesh but in the Spirit. This was to be the new People of God. For those who believe in Christ, who are reborn not from a perishable but from an imperishable seed through the word of the living God,[88] not from the flesh but from water and the Holy Spirit,[89] are finally established as "a chosen race, a royal priesthood, a holy nation, a purchased people . . . who in times past were not a people, but are now the people of God."[90]

That messianic people has Christ for its head, "Who was delivered up for our sins, and rose again for our justification,"[91] and now, having won a name which is above all names, reigns in glory in heaven. The state of this people is that of the dignity and freedom of the sons of God, in whose hearts the Holy Spirit dwells as in His temple. Its law is the new commandment to love as Christ loved us.[92] Its end is the kingdom of God, which has been begun by God Himself on earth, and which is to be further extended until it is brought to perfection by Him at the end of time, when Christ, our life,[93] shall appear, and "creation itself will be delivered from its slavery to corruption into the freedom of the glory of the sons of God."[94] So it is that that messianic people, although it does not actually include all men, and at times may look like a small flock, is nonetheless a lasting and sure seed of unity, hope, and salvation for the whole human race. Established by Christ as a communion of life, charity, and truth, it is also used by Him as an instrument for the redemption of all, and is sent forth into the whole world as the light of the world and the salt of the earth.[95]

Israel according to the flesh, which wandered as an exile in the desert, was already called the Church of God.[96] So likewise the new Israel which while living in this present age goes in search of a future and abiding city[97] is called the Church of Christ.[98] For He has bought it for Himself with His blood,[99] has filled it with His Spirit and provided it with those means which befit it as a visible and social union. God gathered together as one all those who in faith look upon Jesus as the author of salvation and the source of unity and peace, and established them as the Church that for each and all it may be the visible sacrament of this saving unity.[1*] While it transcends all limits of time and confines of race, the Church is destined to extend to all regions of the earth and so enters into the history of mankind. Moving forward through trial and tribulation, the Church is strengthened by the power of God's grace, which was promised to her by the Lord, so that in the weakness of the flesh she may not waver from perfect fidelity, but remain a bride worthy of her Lord, and moved by the Holy Spirit may never cease to renew herself, until through the Cross she arrives at the light which knows no setting.

10. Christ the Lord, High Priest taken from among men,[100] made the new people "a kingdom and priests to God the Father."[101] The baptized, by regeneration and the anointing of the Holy Spirit, are consecrated as a spiritual house and a holy priesthood, in order that through all those works which are those of the Christian man they may offer spiritual sacrifices and proclaim the power of Him who has called them out of darkness into His marvelous light.[102] Therefore all the disciples of Christ, persevering in prayer and praising God,[103] should present themselves as a living sacrifice, holy and pleasing to God.[104] Everywhere on earth they must bear witness to Christ and give an answer to those who seek an account of that hope of eternal life which is in them.[105]

Though they differ from one another in essence and not only in degree, the common priesthood of the faithful and the ministerial or hierarchical priesthood are nonetheless interrelated: each of them in its own special way is a participation in the one priesthood of Christ.[2*] The ministerial priest, by the sacred power he enjoys, teaches and rules the priestly people; acting in the person of Christ, he makes present the Eucharistic sacrifice, and offers it to God in the name of all the people. But the faithful, in virtue of their royal priesthood, join in the offering of the Eucharist.[3*] They likewise exercise that priesthood in receiving the sacraments, in prayer and thanksgiving, in the witness of a holy life, and by self-denial and active charity.

The Priesthood of All Believers

Lumen Gentium 10 | Bishop Barron

Lumen Gentium says that every baptized person is a priest—that is to say, someone capable of entering into the sacrificial dynamic of the liturgy. Though the ordained priest alone can preside at the Mass and effect the Eucharistic change, all of the baptized participate in the Mass in a priestly way. They do this through their prayers and responses but also, the document specifies, by uniting their personal sacrifices and sufferings to the great sacrifice of Christ. So a father witnesses the agony of his son in the hospital; a mother endures the rebellion of a teenage daughter; a young man receives news of his brother's death in battle; an elderly man tosses on his bed in anxiety as he contemplates his unsure financial situation; a graduate student struggles to complete his doctoral thesis; a child experiences for the first time the breakup of a close friendship; an idealist confronts the stubborn resistance of a cynical opponent.

These people could see their pain as simply dumb suffering, the offscourings of an indifferent universe. Or they could see them through the lens provided by the sacrificial death of Jesus, appreciating them as the means by which God is drawing them closer to himself. Suffering, once joined to the cross of Jesus, can become a vehicle for the reformation of the sinful self, the turning of the soul in the direction of love. Mind you, I am not suggesting a simplistic causal correlation between sin and suffering (indeed, the book of Job rules out such a move); but I am suggesting that pain, consciously aligned to the sacrifice of Jesus, can be spiritually transfiguring. Thus, the sufferer becomes, not simply a person in pain, but Abraham giving away what he loves the most, Moses enduring the long discipline of the desert, David confronting Goliath and being pursued by Saul, or the crucified Messiah wondering why he has been forsaken by the Father. The place where this alignment happens is the liturgy, for the liturgy is the re-presentation of the sacrifice of the Lord in all of its richness and multivalence. Consequently, those who gather, with intentionality and focus, at the altar of Jesus are not simply witnessing the event of the cross; they are sharing in it. And this participation changes fundamentally the manner in which they experience and interpret their own pain.

11. It is through the sacraments and the exercise of the virtues that the sacred nature and organic structure of the priestly community is brought into operation. Incorporated in the Church through baptism, the faithful are destined by the baptismal character for the worship of the Christian religion; reborn as sons of God they must confess before men the faith which they have received from God through the Church.[4*] They are more perfectly bound to the Church by the sacrament of Confirmation, and the Holy Spirit endows them with special strength so that they are more strictly obliged to spread and defend the faith, both by word and by deed, as true witnesses of Christ.[5*] Taking part in the Eucharistic sacrifice, which is the fount and apex of the whole Christian life, they offer the Divine Victim to God, and offer themselves along with It.[6*] Thus both by reason of the offering and through Holy Communion all take part in this liturgical service, not indeed, all in the same way but each in that way which is proper to himself. Strengthened in Holy Communion by the Body of Christ, they then manifest in a concrete way that unity of the people of God which is suitably signified and wondrously brought about by this most august sacrament.

Those who approach the sacrament of Penance obtain pardon from the mercy of God for the offence committed against Him and are at the same time reconciled with the Church, which they have wounded by their sins, and which by charity, example, and prayer seeks their conversion. By the sacred anointing of the sick and the prayer of her priests the whole Church commends the sick to the suffering and glorified Lord, asking that He may lighten their suffering and save them;[106] she exhorts them, moreover, to contribute to the welfare of the whole people of God by associating themselves freely with the passion and death of Christ.[107] Those of the faithful who are consecrated by Holy Orders are appointed to feed the Church in Christ's name with the word and the grace of God. Finally, Christian spouses, in virtue of the sacrament of Matrimony, whereby they signify and partake of the mystery of that unity and fruitful love which exists between Christ and His Church,[108] help each other to attain to holiness in their married life and in the rearing and education of their children. By reason of their state and rank in life they have their own special gift among the people of God.[109] [7*] From the wedlock of Christians there comes the family, in which new citizens of human society are born, who by the grace of the Holy Spirit received in baptism are made children of God, thus perpetuating the people of God through the centuries. The family is, so to speak, the domestic church. In it parents should, by their word and example, be the first preachers of the faith to their children; they

The Source and Summit of the Christian Life

Lumen Gentium 11 | Bishop Barron

In the spring of 2007, I was privileged to be a scholar in residence at the North American College in Rome. During that period, I had the opportunity, on three occasions, to distribute communion at Mass in St. Peter's Square. Standing on one side of a partition, I watched as scores of people came forward to receive the Eucharist. In the typically Italian style, things were a tad disorganized, and the faithful were compelled, in the press of the crowd, to stretch out their hands toward me. I saw all sorts of hands—old and young, dirty and clean, lined and unlined—reaching out for the Bread of Life. When I would move along the partition, some would cry out to me plaintively, "Padre, Padre, per favore" (Father, Father, please). Never before in my priesthood, though I had distributed Communion to thousands, had I had the sense of carrying food to those who were desperate for it. Those faithful in St. Peter's Square embodied a truth that is deep in our Catholic tradition, though too infrequently stated: the Eucharist is not a luxury but a necessity, for without it, we would, in the spiritual sense, starve to death.

The fathers of the Second Vatican Council expressed this truth in a lyrical and oft-repeated phrase from *Lumen Gentium*: the Eucharistic sacrifice is "the fount and apex" (or, as another translation has it, "the source and summit") of the whole Christian life. It is both the fountain from which life in Christ flows and the goal toward which it tends; it is the alpha and the omega of Christian discipleship; it is the energy without which authentic Christianity runs down. Without the Eucharist, we could be a pious congregation of like-minded people or a society dedicated to the memory and teaching of Jesus, but we couldn't possibly be the Church. As John Paul II argued in what was, fittingly enough, his last encyclical, *Ecclesia de Eucharistia* (the Church comes from the Eucharist), the Body and Blood of Jesus are not simply the sacred objects at the center of the Church's concern; they *are* the Church, its lifeblood and raison d'être.

should encourage them in the vocation which is proper to each of them, fostering with special care vocation to a sacred state.

Fortified by so many and such powerful means of salvation, all the faithful, whatever their condition or state, are called by the Lord, each in his own way, to that perfect holiness whereby the Father Himself is perfect.

12. The holy people of God shares also in Christ's prophetic office; it spreads abroad a living witness to Him, especially by means of a life of faith and charity and by offering to God a sacrifice of praise, the tribute of lips which give praise to His name.[110] The entire body of the faithful, anointed as they are by the Holy One,[111] cannot err in matters of belief. They manifest this special property by means of the whole people's supernatural discernment in matters of faith when "from the Bishops down to the last of the lay faithful"[8*] they show universal agreement in matters of faith and morals. That discernment in matters of faith is aroused and sustained by the Spirit of truth. It is exercised under the guidance of the sacred teaching authority, in faithful and respectful obedience to which the people of God accepts that which is not just the word of men but truly the word of God.[112] Through it, the people of God adheres unwaveringly to the faith given once and for all to the saints,[113] penetrates it more deeply with right thinking, and applies it more fully in its life.

It is not only through the sacraments and the ministries of the Church that the Holy Spirit sanctifies and leads the people of God and enriches it with virtues, but, "allotting his gifts to everyone according as He wills,"[114] He distributes special graces among the faithful of every rank. By these gifts He makes them fit and ready to undertake the various tasks and offices which contribute toward the renewal and building up of the Church, according to the words of the Apostle: "The manifestation of the Spirit is given to everyone for profit."[115] These charisms, whether they be the more outstanding or the more simple and widely diffused, are to be received with thanksgiving and consolation for they are perfectly suited to and useful for the needs of the Church. Extraordinary gifts are not to be sought after, nor are the fruits of apostolic labor to be presumptuously expected from their use; but judgment as to their genuinity and proper use belongs to those who are appointed leaders in the Church, to whose special competence it belongs, not indeed to extinguish the Spirit, but to test all things and hold fast to that which is good.[116]

Sensus Fidei

Lumen Gentium 12

Congregation for the Doctrine of the Faith
(under Pope St. John Paul II)

———

Donum Veritatis 35

The opinions of the faithful cannot be purely and simply identified with the "sensus fidei." The sense of the faith is a property of theological faith; and, as God's gift which enables one to adhere personally to the Truth, it cannot err. This personal faith is also the faith of the Church since God has given guardianship of the Word to the Church. Consequently, what the believer believes is what the Church believes. The "sensus fidei" implies then by its nature a profound agreement of spirit and heart with the Church, "sentire cum Ecclesia" [to think with the Church].

Although theological faith as such then cannot err, the believer can still have erroneous opinions since all his thoughts do not spring from faith. Not all the ideas which circulate among the People of God are compatible with the faith. This is all the more so given that people can be swayed by a public opinion influenced by modern communications media. Not without reason did the Second Vatican Council emphasize the indissoluble bond between the "sensus fidei" and the guidance of God's People by the magisterium of the Pastors. These two realities cannot be separated. Magisterial interventions serve to guarantee the Church's unity in the truth of the Lord. They aid her to "abide in the truth" in face of the arbitrary character of changeable opinions and are an expression of obedience to the Word of God (see DV 10). Even when it might seem that they limit the freedom of theologians, these actions, by their fidelity to the faith which has been handed on, establish a deeper freedom which can only come from unity in truth.

13. All men are called to belong to the new people of God. Wherefore this people, while remaining one and only one, is to be spread throughout the

whole world and must exist in all ages, so that the decree of God's will may be fulfilled. In the beginning God made human nature one and decreed . that all His children, scattered as they were, would finally be gathered together as one.[117] It was for this purpose that God sent His Son, whom He appointed heir of all things,[118] that he might be teacher, king, and priest of all, the head of the new and universal people of the sons of God. For this too God sent the Spirit of His Son as Lord and Life-giver. He it is who brings together the whole Church and each and every one of those who believe, and who is the well-spring of their unity in the teaching of the apostles and in fellowship, in the breaking of bread and in prayers.[119]

It follows that though there are many nations there is but one people of God, which takes its citizens from every race, making them citizens of a kingdom which is of a heavenly rather than of an earthly nature. All the faithful, scattered though they be throughout the world, are in communion with each other in the Holy Spirit, and so, "he who dwells in Rome knows that the people of India are his members."[9*] Since the kingdom of Christ is not of this world[120] the Church or people of God in establishing that kingdom takes nothing away from the temporal welfare of any people. On the contrary it fosters and takes to itself, insofar as they are good, the ability, riches, and customs in which the genius of each people expresses itself. Taking them to itself it purifies, strengthens, elevates, and ennobles them. The Church in this is mindful that she must bring together the nations for that king to whom they were given as an inheritance,[121] and to whose city they bring gifts and offerings.[122] This characteristic of universality which adorns the people of God is a gift from the Lord Himself. By reason of it, the Catholic Church strives constantly and with due effect to bring all humanity and all its possessions back to its source in Christ, with Him as its head and united in His Spirit.[10*]

In virtue of this catholicity each individual part contributes through its special gifts to the good of the other parts and of the whole Church. Through the common sharing of gifts and through the common effort to attain fullness in unity, the whole and each of the parts receive increase. Not only, then, is the people of God made up of different peoples but in its inner structure also it is composed of various ranks. This diversity among its members arises either by reason of their duties, as is the case with those who exercise the sacred ministry for the good of their brethren, or by reason of their condition and state of life, as is the case with those many who enter the religious state and, tending toward holiness by a narrower path, stimulate their brethren by their example. Moreover, within the Church particular Churches hold a rightful place; these Churches retain their own traditions, without in any way opposing the primacy of the Chair of Peter, which presides over the whole assembly of charity[11*] and protects legitimate differences, while at the same time assuring that such differences do not hinder unity but rather contribute toward it. Between all the parts of the Church there remains a bond of close communion whereby they share spiritual riches, apostolic workers, and temporal resources. For the members of the people of God are called to share these goods in common, and of each of the Churches the words of the Apostle hold good: "According to the gift that each has received, administer it to one another as good stewards of the manifold grace of God."[123]

All men are called to be part of this catholic unity of the people of God which in promoting universal peace presages it. And there belong to or are related to it in various ways, the Catholic faithful, all who believe in Christ, and indeed the whole of mankind, for all men are called by the grace of God to salvation.

14. This Sacred Council wishes to turn its attention firstly to the Catholic faithful. Basing itself upon Sacred Scripture and Tradition, it teaches that the Church, now sojourning on earth as an exile, is necessary for salvation. Christ, present to us in His Body, which is the Church, is the one Mediator and the unique way of salvation. In explicit terms He Himself affirmed the necessity of faith and baptism[124] and thereby affirmed also the necessity of the Church, for through baptism as through a door men enter the Church. Whosoever, therefore, knowing that the Catholic Church was made necessary by Christ, would refuse to enter or to remain in it, could not be saved.

They are fully incorporated in the society of the Church who, possessing the Spirit of Christ accept her entire system and all the means of salvation given to her, and are united with her as part of her visible bodily structure and through her with Christ, who rules her through the Supreme Pontiff and the bishops. The bonds which bind men to the Church in a visible way are profession of faith, the sacraments, and ecclesiastical government and communion. He is not saved, however, who, though part of the body of the Church, does not persevere in charity. He remains indeed in the bosom of the Church, but, as it were, only in a "bodily" manner and not "in his heart."[12*] All the Church's children should remember that their exalted status is to be attributed not to their own merits but to the special grace of Christ. If they fail moreover to respond to that grace in thought, word, and deed, not only shall they not be saved but they will be the more severely judged.[13*]

Catechumens who, moved by the Holy Spirit, seek with explicit intention to be incorporated into the Church are by that very intention joined with her. With love and solicitude Mother Church already embraces them as her own.

Pope St. John Paul II

———

Redemptoris Missio 9

The Mystery of Salvation

Lumen Gentium 13–14

The Council makes frequent reference to the Church's role in the salvation of mankind. While acknowledging that God loves all people and grants them the possibility of being saved (see 1 Tim. 2:4), the Church believes that God has established Christ as the one mediator and that she herself has been established as the universal sacrament of salvation. "All men are called to be part of this catholic unity of the people of God. . . . And there belong to or are related to it in various ways, the Catholic faithful, all who believe in Christ, and indeed the whole of mankind, for all men are called by the grace of God to salvation." It is necessary to keep these two truths together, namely, the real possibility of salvation in Christ for all mankind and the necessity of the Church for salvation. Both these truths help us to understand the *one mystery of salvation*, so that we can come to know God's mercy and our own responsibility. Salvation, which always remains a gift of the Holy Spirit, requires man's cooperation, both to save himself and to save others. This is God's will, and this is why he established the Church and made her a part of his plan of salvation. Referring to "this messianic people," the Council says: "Established by Christ as a communion of life, charity and truth, it is also used by Him as an instrument for the redemption of all, and is sent forth into the whole world as the light of the world and the salt of the earth" (LG 9).

15. The Church recognizes that in many ways she is linked with those who, being baptized, are honored with the name of Christian, though they do not profess the faith in its entirety or do not preserve unity of communion with the successor of Peter.[14*] For there are many who honor Sacred Scripture, taking it as a norm of belief and a pattern of life, and who show a sincere zeal. They lovingly believe in God the Father Almighty and in Christ, the Son of God and Savior.[15*] They are consecrated by baptism, in which they are united with Christ. They also recognize and accept other sacraments within their own Churches or ecclesiastical communities. Many of them rejoice in the episcopate, celebrate the Holy Eucharist, and cultivate devotion toward the Virgin Mother of God.[16*] They also share with us in prayer and other spiritual benefits. Likewise we can say that in some real way they are joined with us in the Holy Spirit, for to them too He gives His gifts and graces whereby He is operative among them with His sanctifying power. Some indeed He has strengthened to the extent of the shedding of their blood. In all of Christ's disciples the Spirit arouses the desire to be peacefully united, in the manner determined by Christ, as one flock under one shepherd, and He prompts them to pursue this end.[17*] Mother Church never ceases to pray, hope, and work that this may come about. She exhorts her children to purification and renewal so that the sign of Christ may shine more brightly over the face of the earth.

16. Finally, those who have not yet received the Gospel are related in various ways to the people of God.[18*] In the first place we must recall the people to whom the testament and the promises were given and from whom Christ was born according to the flesh.[125] On account of their fathers this people remains most dear to God, for God does not repent of the gifts He makes nor of the calls He issues.[126] But the plan of salvation also includes those who acknowledge the Creator. In the first place amongst these there are the Mohammedans, who, professing to hold the faith of Abraham, along with us adore the one and merciful God, who on the last day will judge mankind. Nor is God far distant from those who in shadows and images seek the unknown God, for it is He who gives to all men life and breath and all things,[127] and as Savior wills that all men be saved.[128] Those also can attain to salvation who through no fault of their own do not know the Gospel of Christ or His Church, yet sincerely seek God and moved by grace strive by their deeds to do His will as it is known to them through the dictates of conscience.[19*] Nor does Divine Providence deny the helps

necessary for salvation to those who, without blame on their part, have not yet arrived at an explicit knowledge of God and with His grace strive to live a good life. Whatever good or truth is found amongst them is looked upon by the Church as a preparation for the Gospel.[20*] She knows that it is given by Him who enlightens all men so that they may finally have life. But often men, deceived by the Evil One, have become vain in their reasonings and have exchanged the truth of God for a lie, serving the creature rather than the Creator.[129] Or some there are who, living and dying in this world without God, are exposed to final despair. Wherefore to promote the glory of God and procure the salvation of all of these, and mindful of the command of the Lord, "Preach the Gospel to every creature,"[130] the Church fosters the missions with care and attention.

Catholics and Muslims

Lumen Gentium 16

Pope Benedict XVI

———

Verbum Domini 118

Among the various religions the Church also looks with respect to Muslims, who adore the one God. They look to Abraham and worship God above all through prayer, almsgiving, and fasting. We acknowledge that the Islamic tradition includes countless biblical figures, symbols, and themes. Taking up the efforts begun by the Venerable John Paul II, I express my hope that the trust-filled relationships established between Christians and Muslims over the years will continue to develop in a spirit of sincere and respectful dialogue. In this dialogue the Synod [on the Word of God] asked for a deeper reflection on respect for life as a fundamental value, the inalienable rights of men and women, and their equal dignity. Taking into account the important distinction to be made between the socio-political order and the religious order, the various religions must make their specific contribution to the common good.

Can Non-Christians and Nonbelievers Be Saved?

Lumen Gentium 16 | Bishop Barron

Lumen Gentium speaks here of the possibility that non-Christians—even nonbelievers—*can* be saved. This does not amount to saying that they *will* be saved and that evangelization is therefore unnecessary; in fact, as the conclusion of the paragraph indicates, just the contrary. If they are saved, *Lumen Gentium* argues, they are saved through some participation in the grace of Christ, some light that comes from Jesus, though they might not be aware of it. In the case of nonbelievers, it would happen through following, honestly and courageously, the dictates of the conscience, which John Henry Newman helpfully described as the "aboriginal Vicar of Christ" in the soul. The great English master was anticipating the teaching of Vatican II by insisting that the voice of conscience is, in point of fact, the voice of Christ, though anonymously so. If Jesus were but one spiritual teacher among many, this would not hold, but since he is, in person, the very Word of the Father, the dictate of conscience is his dictate.

17. As the Son was sent by the Father,[131] so He too sent the Apostles, saying: "Go, therefore, make disciples of all nations, baptizing them in the name of the Father and of the Son and of the Holy Spirit, teaching them to observe all things whatsoever I have commanded you. And behold I am with you all days even to the consummation of the world."[132] The Church has received this solemn mandate of Christ to proclaim the saving truth from the apostles and must carry it out to the very ends of the earth.[133] Wherefore she makes the words of the Apostle her own: "Woe to me, if I do not preach the Gospel,"[134] and continues unceasingly to send heralds of the Gospel until such time as the infant churches are fully established and can themselves continue the work of evangelizing. For the Church is compelled by the Holy Spirit to do her part that God's plan may be fully realized, whereby He has constituted Christ as the source of salvation for the whole world. By the proclamation of the Gospel she prepares her hearers to receive and profess the faith. She gives them the dispositions necessary for baptism, snatches them from the slavery of error and of idols, and

incorporates them in Christ so that through charity they may grow up into full maturity in Christ. Through her work, whatever good is in the minds and hearts of men, whatever good lies latent in the religious practices and cultures of diverse peoples, is not only saved from destruction but is also cleansed, raised up, and perfected unto the glory of God, the confusion of the devil, and the happiness of man. The obligation of spreading the faith is imposed on every disciple of Christ, according to his state.[21*] Although, however, all the faithful can baptize, the priest alone can complete the building up of the Body in the eucharistic sacrifice. Thus are fulfilled the words of God, spoken through His prophet: "From the rising of the sun until the going down thereof my name is great among the gentiles, and in every place a clean oblation is sacrificed and offered up in my name."[135] [(22*)] In this way the Church both prays and labors in order that the entire world may become the People of God, the Body of the Lord, and the Temple of the Holy Spirit, and that in Christ, the Head of all, all honor and glory may be rendered to the Creator and Father of the Universe.

The Evangelizing Church

Lumen Gentium 17

Pope Francis

—

Evangelii Gaudium
24

The Church which "goes forth" is a community of missionary disciples who take the first step, who are involved and supportive, who bear fruit and rejoice. An evangelizing community knows that the Lord has taken the initiative, he has loved us first (see 1 John 4:19), and therefore we can move forward, boldly take the initiative, go out to others, seek those who have fallen away, stand at the crossroads and welcome the outcast. Such a community has an endless desire to show mercy, the fruit of its own experience of the power of the Father's infinite mercy. Let us try a little harder to take the first step and to become involved. Jesus washed the feet of his disciples. The Lord gets involved and he involves his own, as he kneels to wash their feet. He tells his disciples: "You will be blessed if you do this" (John 13:17). An evangelizing community gets involved by word and deed in people's daily lives; it bridges distances, it is willing to abase itself if necessary, and it embraces human life, touching the suffering flesh of Christ in others. Evangelizers thus take on the "smell of the sheep" and the sheep are willing to hear their voice. An evangelizing community is also supportive, standing by people at every step of the way, no matter how difficult or lengthy this may prove to be. It is familiar with patient expectation and apostolic endurance. Evangelization consists mostly of patience and disregard for constraints of time. Faithful to the Lord's gift, it also bears fruit. An evangelizing community is always concerned with fruit, because the Lord wants her to be fruitful. It cares for the grain and does not grow impatient at the weeds. The sower, when he sees weeds sprouting among the grain does not grumble or overreact. He or she finds a way to let the word take flesh in a particular situation and bear fruits of new life, however imperfect or incomplete these may appear. The disciple is ready to put his or her whole life on the line, even to accepting martyrdom, in bearing witness to Jesus Christ, yet the goal is not to make enemies but to see God's word accepted and its capacity for liberation and renewal revealed. Finally an evangelizing community is filled with joy; it knows how to rejoice always. It celebrates every small victory, every step forward in the work of evangelization.

CHAPTER III

On the Hierarchical Structure of the Church and
In Particular on the Episcopate

18. For the nurturing and constant growth of the People of God, Christ the Lord instituted in His Church a variety of ministries, which work for the good of the whole body. For those ministers, who are endowed with sacred power, serve their brethren, so that all who are of the People of God, and therefore enjoy a true Christian dignity, working toward a common goal freely and in an orderly way, may arrive at salvation.

This Sacred Council, following closely in the footsteps of the First Vatican Council, with that Council teaches and declares that Jesus Christ, the eternal Shepherd, established His holy Church, having sent forth the apostles as He Himself had been sent by the Father;[136] and He willed that their successors, namely the bishops, should be shepherds in His Church even to the consummation of the world. And in order that the episcopate itself might be one and undivided, He placed Blessed Peter over the other apostles, and instituted in him a permanent and visible source and foundation of unity of faith and communion.[1*] And all this teaching about the institution, the perpetuity, the meaning and reason for the sacred primacy of the Roman Pontiff and of his infallible magisterium, this Sacred Council again proposes to be firmly believed by all the faithful. Continuing in that same undertaking, this Council is resolved to declare and proclaim before all men the doctrine concerning bishops, the successors of the apostles, who together with the successor of Peter, the Vicar of Christ,[2*] the visible Head of the whole Church, govern the house of the living God.

19. The Lord Jesus, after praying to the Father, calling to Himself those whom He desired, appointed twelve to be with Him, and whom He would send to preach the Kingdom of God;[137] and these apostles[138] He formed after the manner of a college or a stable group, over which He placed Peter chosen from among them.[139] He sent them first to the children of Israel and then to all nations,[140] so that as sharers in His power they might make all peoples His disciples, and sanctify and govern them,[141] and thus spread His Church, and by ministering to it under the guidance of the Lord, direct it all days even to the consummation of the world.[142] And in this mission they were fully confirmed on the day of Pentecost[143] in accordance

with the Lord's promise: "You shall receive power when the Holy Spirit comes upon you, and you shall be witnesses for me in Jerusalem, and in all Judea and in Samaria, and even to the very ends of the earth."[144] And the apostles, by preaching the Gospel everywhere,[145] and it being accepted by their hearers under the influence of the Holy Spirit, gather together the universal Church, which the Lord established on the apostles and built upon blessed Peter, their chief, Christ Jesus Himself being the supreme cornerstone.[146] (3*)

20. That divine mission, entrusted by Christ to the apostles, will last until the end of the world,[147] since the Gospel they are to teach is for all time the source of all life for the Church. And for this reason the apostles, appointed as rulers in this society, took care to appoint successors.

For they not only had helpers in their ministry,[4*] but also, in order that the mission assigned to them might continue after their death, they passed on to their immediate cooperators, as it were, in the form of a testament, the duty of confirming and finishing the work begun by themselves,[5*] recommending to them that they attend to the whole flock in which the Holy Spirit placed them to shepherd the Church of God.[148] They therefore appointed such men, and gave them the order that, when they should have died, other approved men would take up their ministry.[6*] Among those various ministries which, according to tradition, were exercised in the Church from the earliest times, the chief place belongs to the office of those who, appointed to the episcopate, by a succession running from the beginning,[7*] are passers-on of the apostolic seed.[8*] Thus, as St. Irenaeus testifies, through those who were appointed bishops by the apostles, and through their successors down in our own time, the apostolic tradition is manifested[9*] and preserved.[10*]

Bishops, therefore, with their helpers, the priests and deacons, have taken up the service of the community,[11*] presiding in place of God over the flock,[12*] whose shepherds they are, as teachers for doctrine, priests for sacred worship, and ministers for governing.[13*] And just as the office granted individually to Peter, the first among the apostles, is permanent and is to be transmitted to his successors, so also the apostles' office of nurturing the Church is permanent, and is to be exercised without interruption by the sacred order of bishops.[14*] Therefore, the Sacred Council teaches that bishops by divine institution have succeeded to the place of the apostles,[15*] as shepherds of the Church, and he who hears them, hears Christ, and he who rejects them, rejects Christ and Him who sent Christ.[149] (16*)

Permanent Mission

Lumen Gentium 20 | Bishop Barron

"That divine mission, entrusted by Christ to the apostles, will last until the end of the world." The Church is called ultimately into the fullness of life and love that will obtain in heaven, but for the historical moment, it is called into permanent mission. Perhaps the central insight of Pope St. Paul VI's apostolic exhortation *Evangelii Nuntiandi* is that the Church doesn't have a mission alongside of myriad other projects; rather, it *is* a mission, by its very nature: "Evangelizing is in fact the grace and vocation proper to the Church, her deepest identity. She exists in order to evangelize, that is to say, in order to preach and teach, to be the channel of the gift of grace, to reconcile sinners with God, and to perpetuate Christ's sacrifice in the Mass, which is the memorial of His death and glorious resurrection."

21. In the bishops, therefore, for whom priests are assistants, Our Lord Jesus Christ, the Supreme High Priest, is present in the midst of those who believe. For sitting at the right hand of God the Father, He is not absent from the gathering of His high priests,[17*] but above all through their excellent service He is preaching the word of God to all nations, and constantly administering the sacraments of faith to those who believe, by their paternal functioning.[150] He incorporates new members in His Body by a heavenly regeneration, and finally by their wisdom and prudence He directs and guides the People of the New Testament in their pilgrimage toward eternal happiness. These pastors, chosen to shepherd the Lord's flock of the elect, are servants of Christ and stewards of the mysteries of God,[151] to whom has been assigned the bearing of witness to the Gospel of the grace of God,[152] and the ministration of the Spirit and of justice in glory.[153]

For the discharging of such great duties, the apostles were enriched by Christ with a special outpouring of the Holy Spirit coming upon them,[154] and they passed on this spiritual gift to their helpers by the imposition of hands,[155] and it has been transmitted down to us in Episcopal consecration.[18*] And the Sacred Council teaches that by Episcopal consecration the fullness of the sacrament of Orders is conferred, that fullness of power, namely, which both in the Church's liturgical practice and in the language of the Fathers of the Church is called the high priesthood, the supreme power of the sacred ministry.[19*] But Episcopal consecration, together with the office of sanctifying, also confers the office of teaching and of governing, which, however, of its very nature, can be exercised only in hierarchical communion with the head and the members of the college. For from the tradition, which is expressed especially in liturgical rites and in the practice of both the Church of the East and of the West, it is clear that, by means of the imposition of hands and the words of consecration, the grace of the Holy Spirit is so conferred,[20*] and the sacred character so impressed,[21*] that bishops in an eminent and visible way sustain the roles of Christ Himself as Teacher, Shepherd, and High Priest, and that they act in His person.[22*] Therefore it pertains to the bishops to admit newly elected members into the Episcopal body by means of the sacrament of Orders.

22. Just as in the Gospel, the Lord so disposing, St. Peter and the other apostles constitute one apostolic college, so in a similar way the Roman Pontiff, the successor of Peter, and the bishops, the successors of the apostles, are joined together. Indeed, the very ancient practice whereby bishops duly established in all parts of the world were in communion with one another and with the Bishop of Rome in a bond of unity, charity, and peace,[23*] and also the councils assembled together,[24*] in which more profound issues were settled in common,[25*] the opinion of the many having been prudently considered,[26*] both of these factors are already an indication of the collegiate character and aspect of the Episcopal order; and the ecumenical councils held in the course of centuries are also manifest proof of that same character. And it is intimated also in the practice, introduced in ancient times, of summoning several bishops to take part in the elevation of the newly elected to the ministry of the high priesthood. Hence, one is constituted a member of the Episcopal body in virtue of sacramental consecration and hierarchical communion with the head and members of the body.

But the college or body of bishops has no authority unless it is understood together with the Roman Pontiff, the successor of Peter as its head. The pope's power of primacy over all, both pastors and faithful, remains whole and intact. In virtue of his office, that is as Vicar of Christ and pastor of the whole Church, the Roman Pontiff has full, supreme, and universal power over the Church. And he is always free to exercise this power. The order of bishops, which succeeds to the college of apostles and gives this apostolic body continued existence, is also the subject of supreme and full power over the universal Church, provided we understand this body together with its head the Roman Pontiff and never without this head.[27*] This power can be exercised only with the consent of the Roman Pontiff. For our Lord placed Simon alone as the rock and the bearer of the keys of the Church,[156] and made him shepherd of the whole flock;[157] it is evident, however, that the power of binding and loosing, which was given to Peter,[158] was granted also to the college of apostles, joined with their head.[159] [(28*)] This college, insofar as it is composed of many, expresses the variety and universality of the People of God, but insofar as it is assembled under one head, it expresses the unity of the flock of Christ. In it, the bishops, faithfully recognizing the primacy and pre-eminence of their head, exercise their own authority for the good of their own faithful, and indeed of the whole Church, the Holy Spirit supporting its organic structure and harmony with moderation. The supreme power in the universal Church, which this college enjoys, is exercised in a solemn way in an ecumenical council. A council is never ecumenical unless it is confirmed or at least accepted as such by the successor of Peter; and it is prerogative of the Roman Pontiff to convoke these councils, to preside over them, and to confirm them.[29*] This same collegiate power can be exercised together with the pope by the bishops living in all parts of the world, provided that the head of the college calls them to collegiate action, or at least approves of or freely accepts the united action of the scattered bishops, so that it is thereby made a collegiate act.

23. This collegial union is apparent also in the mutual relations of the individual bishops with particular churches and with the universal Church. The Roman Pontiff, as the successor of Peter, is the perpetual and visible principle and foundation of unity of both the bishops and of the faithful.[30*] The individual bishops, however, are the visible principle and foundation of unity in their particular churches,[31*] fashioned after the model of the universal Church, in and from which churches comes into being the one and only Catholic Church.[32*] For this reason the individual bishops represent each his own church, but all of them together and with

The Mission of the Bishop of Rome
Lumen Gentium 22

**Pope
St. John Paul II**

—

Ut Unum Sint
94–95

[The] service of unity, rooted in the action of divine mercy, is entrusted within the College of Bishops to one among those who have received from the Spirit the task, not of exercising power over the people—as the rulers of the Gentiles and their great men do (see Matt. 20:25; Mark 10:42)—but of leading them towards peaceful pastures. This task can require the offering of one's own life (see John 10:11–18). Saint Augustine, after showing that Christ is "the one Shepherd, in whose unity all are one," goes on to exhort: "May all shepherds thus be one in the one Shepherd; may they let the one voice of the Shepherd be heard; may the sheep hear this voice and follow their Shepherd, not this shepherd or that, but the only one; in him may they all let one voice be heard and not a babble of voices . . . the voice free of all division, purified of all heresy, that the sheep hear." The mission of the Bishop of Rome within the College of all the Pastors consists precisely in "keeping watch" (*episkopein*), like a sentinel, so that, through the efforts of the Pastors, the true voice of Christ the Shepherd may be heard in all the particular Churches. In this way, in each of the particular Churches entrusted to those Pastors, the *una, sancta, catholica et apostolica Ecclesia* [one, holy, catholic, and apostolic Church] is made present. All the Churches are in full· and visible communion, because all the Pastors are in communion with Peter and therefore united in Christ.

With the power and the authority without which such an office would be illusory, the Bishop of Rome must ensure the communion of all the Churches. For this reason, he is the first servant of unity. This primacy is exercised on various levels, including vigilance over the handing down of the Word, the celebration of the Liturgy and the Sacraments, the Church's mission, discipline and the Christian life. It is the responsibility of the Successor of Peter to recall the requirements of the common good of the Church, should anyone be tempted to overlook it in the pursuit of personal interests. He has the duty to admonish, to caution, and to declare at times that this or that opinion being circulated is irreconcilable with the unity of faith. When circumstances require it, he speaks in the name of all the Pastors in communion with him. He can also—under very specific conditions clearly laid down by the First Vatican Council—declare *ex cathedra* that a certain doctrine belongs to the deposit of faith. By thus bearing witness to the truth, he serves unity.

All this however must always be done in communion. When the Catholic Church affirms that the office of the Bishop of Rome corresponds to the will of Christ, she does not separate this office from the mission entrusted to the whole body of Bishops, who are also "vicars and ambassadors of Christ" (LG 27). The Bishop of Rome is a member of the "College," and the Bishops are his brothers in the ministry.

the Pope represent the entire Church in the bond of peace, love, and unity. The individual bishops, who are placed in charge of particular churches, exercise their pastoral government over the portion of the People of God committed to their care, and not over other churches nor over the universal Church. But each of them, as a member of the episcopal college and legitimate successor of the apostles, is obliged by Christ's institution and command to be solicitous for the whole Church,[33*] and this solicitude, though it is not exercised by an act of jurisdiction, contributes greatly to the advantage of the universal Church. For it is the duty of all bishops to promote and to safeguard the unity of faith and the discipline common to the whole Church, to instruct the faithful to love for the whole mystical body of Christ, especially for its poor and sorrowing members and for those who are suffering persecution for justice's sake,[160] and finally to promote every activity that is of interest to the whole Church, especially that the faith may take increase and the light of full truth appear to all men. And this also is important, that by governing well their own church as a portion of the universal Church, they themselves are effectively contributing to the welfare of the whole Mystical Body, which is also the body of the churches.[34*]

The task of proclaiming the Gospel everywhere on earth pertains to the body of pastors, to all of whom in common Christ gave His command, thereby imposing upon them a common duty, as Pope Celestine in his time recommended to the Fathers of the Council of Ephesus.[35*] From this it follows that the individual bishops, insofar as their own discharge of their duty permits, are obliged to enter into a community of work among themselves and with the successor of Peter, upon whom was imposed in a special way the great duty of spreading the Christian name.[36*] With all their energy, therefore, they must supply to the missions both workers for the harvest and also spiritual and material aid, both directly and on their own account, as well as by arousing the ardent cooperation of the faithful. And finally, the bishops, in a universal fellowship of charity, should gladly extend their fraternal aid to other churches, especially to neighboring and more needy dioceses in accordance with the venerable example of antiquity. By divine Providence it has come about that various churches, established in various places by the apostles and their successors, have in the course of time coalesced into several groups, organically united, which, preserving the unity of faith and the unique divine constitution of the universal Church, enjoy their own discipline, their own liturgical usage, and their own theological and spiritual heritage. Some of these churches, notably the ancient patriarchal churches, as parent-stocks of the Faith, so to speak, have begotten others as daughter churches, with which they are connected down to our own time by a close bond of charity in their sacramental life and in their mutual respect for their rights and duties.[37*] This variety of local churches with one common aspiration is splendid evidence of the catholicity of the undivided Church. In like manner the Episcopal bodies of today are in a position to render a manifold and fruitful assistance, so that this collegiate feeling may be put into practical application.

24. Bishops, as successors of the apostles, receive from the Lord, to whom was given all power in heaven and on earth, the mission to teach all nations and to preach the Gospel to every creature, so that all men may attain to salvation by faith, baptism, and the fulfilment of the commandments.[161] To fulfill this mission, Christ the Lord promised the Holy Spirit to the Apostles, and on Pentecost day sent the Spirit from heaven, by whose power they would be witnesses to Him before the nations and peoples

and kings even to the ends of the earth.[162] And that duty, which the Lord committed to the shepherds of His people, is a true service, which in sacred literature is significantly called "diakonia" or ministry.[163]

Pope Francis

⸻

Lumen Fidei 48

The Unity of Faith

Lumen Gentium 23

Since faith is one, it must be professed in all its purity and integrity. Precisely because all the articles of faith are interconnected, to deny one of them, even of those that seem least important, is tantamount to distorting the whole. Each period of history can find this or that point of faith easier or harder to accept: hence the need for vigilance in ensuring that the deposit of faith is passed on in its entirety (see 1 Tim. 6:20) and that all aspects of the profession of faith are duly emphasized. Indeed, inasmuch as the unity of faith is the unity of the Church, to subtract something from the faith is to subtract something from the veracity of communion. The Fathers described faith as a body, the body of truth composed of various members, by analogy with the body of Christ and its prolongation in the Church. The integrity of the faith was also tied to the image of the Church as a virgin and her fidelity in love for Christ her spouse; harming the faith means harming communion with the Lord. The unity of faith, then, is the unity of a living body; this was clearly brought out by Blessed John Henry Newman when he listed among the characteristic notes for distinguishing the continuity of doctrine over time its power to assimilate everything that it meets in the various settings in which it becomes present and in the diverse cultures which it encounters, purifying all things and bringing them to their finest expression. Faith is thus shown to be universal, catholic, because its light expands in order to illumine the entire cosmos and all of history.

The canonical mission of bishops can come about by legitimate customs that have not been revoked by the supreme and universal authority of the Church, or by laws made or recognized by that the authority, or directly through the successor of Peter himself; and if the latter refuses or denies apostolic communion, such bishops cannot assume any office.[38*]

25. Among the principal duties of bishops the preaching of the Gospel occupies an eminent place.[39*] For bishops are preachers of the faith, who lead new disciples to Christ, and they are authentic teachers, that is, teachers endowed with the authority of Christ, who preach to the people committed to them the faith they must believe and put into practice, and by the light of the Holy Spirit illustrate that faith. They bring forth from the treasury of Revelation new things and old,[164] making it bear fruit and vigilantly warding off any errors that threaten their flock.[165] Bishops, teaching in communion with the Roman Pontiff, are to be respected by all as witnesses to divine and Catholic truth. In matters of faith and morals, the bishops speak in the name of Christ and the faithful are to accept their teaching and adhere to it with a religious assent. This religious submission of mind and will must be shown in a special way to the authentic magisterium of the Roman Pontiff, even when he is not speaking ex cathedra; that is, it must be shown in such a way that his supreme magisterium is acknowledged with reverence, the judgments made by him are sincerely adhered to, according to his manifest mind and will. His mind and will in the matter may be known either from the character of the documents, from his frequent repetition of the same doctrine, or from his manner of speaking.

Although the individual bishops do not enjoy the prerogative of infallibility, they nevertheless proclaim Christ's doctrine infallibly whenever, even though dispersed through the world, but still maintaining the bond of communion among themselves and with the successor of Peter, and authentically teaching matters of faith and morals, they are in agreement on one position as definitively to be held.[40*] This is even more clearly verified when, gathered together in an ecumenical council, they are teachers and judges of faith and morals for the universal Church, whose definitions must be adhered to with the submission of faith.[41*]

And this infallibility with which the Divine Redeemer willed His Church to be endowed in defining doctrine of faith and morals, extends as far as the deposit of Revelation extends, which must be religiously guarded and faithfully expounded. And this is the infallibility which the Roman Pontiff, the head of the college of bishops, enjoys in virtue of his office, when, as the supreme shepherd and teacher of all the faithful, who confirms his brethren in their faith,[166] by a definitive act he proclaims a doctrine of faith or morals.[42*] And therefore his definitions, of themselves, and not from the consent of the Church, are justly styled irreformable, since they are pronounced with the assistance of the Holy Spirit, promised to him in blessed Peter, and therefore they need no approval of others, nor do they allow an appeal to any other judgment. For then the Roman Pontiff is not pronouncing judgment as a private person, but as the supreme teacher of the universal Church, in whom the charism of infallibility of the Church itself is individually present, he is expounding or defending a doctrine of Catholic faith.[43*] The infallibility promised to the Church resides also in the body of Bishops, when that body exercises the supreme magisterium with the successor of Peter. To these definitions the assent of the Church can never be wanting, on account of the activity of that same Holy Spirit, by which the whole flock of Christ is preserved and progresses in unity of faith.[44*]

But when either the Roman Pontiff or the Body of Bishops together with him defines a judgment, they pronounce it in accordance with Revelation itself, which all are obliged to abide by and be in conformity with, that is, the Revelation which as written or orally handed down is transmitted in its entirety through the legitimate succession of bishops and especially in care of the Roman Pontiff himself, and which under the guiding light of the Spirit of truth is religiously preserved and faithfully expounded in the Church.[45*] The Roman Pontiff and the bishops, in view of their office and the importance of the matter, by fitting means diligently strive to inquire properly into that revelation and to give apt expression to its contents;[46*] but a new public revelation they do not accept as pertaining to the divine deposit of faith.[47*]

26. A bishop marked with the fullness of the sacrament of Orders, is "the steward of the grace of the supreme priesthood,"[48*] especially in the Eucharist, which he offers or causes to be offered,[49*] and by which the Church continually lives and grows. This Church of Christ is truly present in all legitimate local congregations of the faithful which, united with their

The Charism of Infallibility

Lumen Gentium 25

Catechism of the Catholic Church
(promulgated by Pope St. John Paul II)
—
890–892

The mission of the Magisterium is linked to the definitive nature of the covenant established by God with his people in Christ. It is this Magisterium's task to preserve God's people from deviations and defections and to guarantee them the objective possibility of professing the true faith without error. Thus, the pastoral duty of the Magisterium is aimed at seeing to it that the People of God abides in the truth that liberates. To fulfill this service, Christ endowed the Church's shepherds with the charism of infallibility in matters of faith and morals. The exercise of this charism takes several forms:

"The Roman Pontiff, the head of the college of bishops, enjoys [this infallibility] in virtue of his office, when, as the supreme shepherd and teacher of all the faithful, who confirms his brethren in their faith, by a definitive act he proclaims a doctrine of faith or morals. . . . The infallibility promised to the Church resides also in the body of Bishops, when that body exercises the supreme magisterium with the successor of Peter," above all in an Ecumenical Council. When the Church through its supreme Magisterium proposes a doctrine "for belief as divinely revealed" (DV 10), and as the teaching of Christ, the definitions "must be adhered to with the submission of faith." This infallibility extends as far as the deposit of divine Revelation itself.

Divine assistance is also given to the successors of the apostles, teaching in communion with the successor of Peter, and, in a particular way, to the bishop of Rome, pastor of the whole Church, when, without arriving at an infallible definition and without pronouncing in a "definitive manner," they propose in the exercise of the ordinary Magisterium a teaching that leads to better understanding of Revelation in matters of faith and morals. To this ordinary teaching the faithful "are to . . . adhere to it with a religious assent" which, though distinct from the assent of faith, is nonetheless an extension of it.

pastors, are themselves called churches in the New Testament.[50*] For in their locality these are the new People called by God, in the Holy Spirit and in much fullness.[167] In them the faithful are gathered together by the preaching of the Gospel of Christ, and the mystery of the Lord's Supper is celebrated, that by the food and blood of the Lord's body the whole brotherhood may be joined together.[51*] In any community of the altar, under the sacred ministry of the bishop,[52*] there is exhibited a symbol of that charity and "unity of the mystical Body, without which there can be no salvation."[53*] In these communities, though frequently small and poor, or living in the Diaspora, Christ is present, and in virtue of His presence there is brought together one, holy, catholic, and apostolic Church.[54*] For "the partaking of the body and blood of Christ does nothing other than make us be transformed into that which we consume."[55*]

Every legitimate celebration of the Eucharist is regulated by the bishop, to whom is committed the office of offering the worship of Christian religion to the Divine Majesty and of administering it in accordance with the Lord's commandments and the Church's laws, as further defined by his particular judgment for his diocese.

Bishops thus, by praying and laboring for the people, make outpourings in many ways and in great abundance from the fullness of Christ's holiness. By the ministry of the word they communicate God's power to those who believe unto salvation[168] and through the sacraments, the regular and fruitful distribution of which they regulate by their authority,[56*] they sanctify the faithful. They direct the conferring of baptism, by which a sharing in the kingly priesthood of Christ is granted. They are the original ministers of confirmation, dispensers of sacred Orders, and the moderators of penitential discipline, and they earnestly exhort and instruct their people to carry out with faith and reverence their part in the liturgy and especially in the holy sacrifice of the Mass. And lastly, by the example of their way of life they must be an influence for good to those over whom they preside, refraining from all evil and, as far as they are able with God's help, exchanging evil for good, so that together with the flock committed to their care they may arrive at eternal life.[57*]

27. Bishops, as vicars and ambassadors of Christ, govern the particular churches entrusted to them[58*] by their counsel, exhortations, example, and even by their authority and sacred power, which indeed they use only for the edification of their flock in truth and holiness, remembering that he who is greater should become as the lesser and he who is the chief become as the servant.[169] This power, which they personally exercise in Christ's name, is proper, ordinary, and immediate, although its exercise is ultimately regulated by the supreme authority of the Church, and can be circumscribed by certain limits, for the advantage of the Church or of the faithful. In virtue of this power, bishops have the sacred right and the duty before the Lord to make laws for their subjects, to pass judgment on them, and to moderate everything pertaining to the ordering of worship and the apostolate.

The pastoral office or the habitual and daily care of their sheep is entrusted to them completely; nor are they to be regarded as vicars of the Roman Pontiffs, for they exercise an authority that is proper to them, and are quite correctly called "prelates," heads of the people whom they govern.[59*] Their power, therefore, is not destroyed by the supreme and universal power, but on the contrary it is affirmed, strengthened, and vindicated by it,[60*] since the Holy Spirit unfailingly preserves the form of government established by Christ the Lord in His Church.

A bishop, since he is sent by the Father to govern his family, must keep before his eyes the example of the Good Shepherd, who came not to be ministered unto but to minister,[170] and to lay down his life for his sheep.[171] Being taken from among men, and himself beset with weakness, he is able to have compassion on the ignorant and erring.[172] Let him not refuse to listen to his subjects, whom he cherishes as his true sons and exhorts to cooperate readily with him. As having one day to render an account for their souls,[173] he takes care of them by his prayer, preaching, and all the works of charity, and not only of them but also of those who are not yet of the one flock, who also are commended to him in the Lord. Since, like Paul the Apostle, he is debtor to all men, let him be ready to preach the Gospel to all,[174] and to urge his faithful to apostolic and missionary activity. But the faithful must cling to their bishop, as the Church does to Christ, and

Jesus Christ to the Father, so that all may be of one mind through unity,[61*] and abound to the glory of God.[175]

28. Christ, whom the Father has sanctified and sent into the world,[176] has through His apostles, made their successors, the bishops, partakers of His consecration and His mission.[62*] They have legitimately handed on to different individuals in the Church various degrees of participation in this ministry. Thus the divinely established ecclesiastical ministry is exercised on different levels by those who from antiquity have been called bishops, priests, and deacons.[63*] Priests, although they do not possess the highest degree of the priesthood, and although they are dependent on the bishops in the exercise of their power, nevertheless they are united with the bishops in sacerdotal dignity.[64*] By the power of the sacrament of Orders,[65*] in the image of Christ the eternal high Priest,[177] they are consecrated to preach the Gospel and shepherd the faithful and to celebrate divine worship, so that they are true priests of the New Testament.[66*] Partakers of the function of Christ the sole Mediator,[178] on their level of ministry, they announce the divine word to all. They exercise their sacred function especially in the Eucharistic worship or the celebration of the Mass by which acting in the person of Christ[67*] and proclaiming His Mystery they unite the prayers of the faithful with the sacrifice of their Head and renew and apply[68*] in the sacrifice of the Mass until the coming of the Lord[179] the only sacrifice of the New Testament, namely that of Christ offering Himself once for all a spotless Victim to the Father.[180] For the sick and the sinners among the faithful, they exercise the ministry of alleviation and reconciliation and they present the needs and the prayers of the faithful to God the Father.[181] Exercising within the limits of their authority the function of Christ as Shepherd and Head,[69*] they gather together God's family as a brotherhood all of one mind,[70*] and lead them in the Spirit, through Christ, to God the Father. In the midst of the flock they adore Him in spirit and in truth.[182] Finally, they labor in word and doctrine,[183] believing what they have read and meditated upon in the law of God, teaching what they have believed, and putting in practice in their own lives what they have taught.[71*]

Priests, prudent cooperators with the Episcopal order,[72*] its aid and instrument, called to serve the people of God, constitute one priesthood[73*] with their bishop although bound by a diversity of duties. Associated with their bishop in a spirit of trust and generosity, they make him present in a certain sense in the individual local congregations, and take upon themselves, as far as they are able, his duties and the burden of his care, and discharge them with a daily interest. And as they sanctify and govern under the bishop's authority, that part of the Lord's flock entrusted to them they make the universal Church visible in their own locality and bring an efficacious assistance to the building up of the whole body of Christ.[184] Intent always upon the welfare of God's children, they must strive to lend their effort to the pastoral work of the whole diocese, and even of the entire Church. On account of this sharing in their priesthood and mission, let priests sincerely look upon the bishop as their father and reverently obey him. And let the bishop regard his priests as his co-workers and as sons and friends, just as Christ called His disciples now not servants but friends.[185] All priests, both diocesan and religious, by reason of Orders and ministry, fit into this body of bishops and priests, and serve the good of the whole Church according to their vocation and the grace given to them.

The Eucharist and Holy Orders

Lumen Gentium 26–29

Pope Benedict XVI

—

Sacramentum Caritatis 23

The intrinsic relationship between the Eucharist and the sacrament of Holy Orders clearly emerges from Jesus' own words in the Upper Room: "Do this in memory of me" (Luke 22:19). On the night before he died, Jesus instituted the Eucharist and at the same time established the *priesthood of the New Covenant*. He is priest, victim, and altar: the mediator between God the Father and his people (see Heb. 5:5–10), the victim of atonement (see 1 John 2:2, 4:10) who offers himself on the altar of the Cross. No one can say "this is my body" and "this is the cup of my blood" except in the name and in the person of Christ, the one high priest of the new and eternal Covenant (see Heb. 8–9). . . . I consider it important to recall several important points about the relationship between the sacrament of the Eucharist and Holy Orders. First of all, we need to stress once again that the connection between *Holy Orders and the Eucharist* is seen most clearly at Mass, when the Bishop or priest presides *in the person of Christ the Head.*

The Church teaches that priestly ordination is the indispensable condition for the valid celebration of the Eucharist. Indeed, "in the ecclesial service of the ordained minister, it is Christ himself who is present to his Church as Head of his Body, Shepherd of his flock, High Priest of the redemptive sacrifice." Certainly the ordained minister also acts "in the name of the whole Church, when presenting to God the prayer of the Church, and above all when offering the eucharistic sacrifice." As a result, priests should be conscious of the fact that in their ministry they must never put themselves or their personal opinions in first place, but Jesus Christ. Any attempt to make themselves the center of the liturgical action contradicts their very identity as priests. The priest is above all a servant of others, and he must continually work at being a sign pointing to Christ, a docile instrument in the Lord's hands. This is seen particularly in his humility in leading the liturgical assembly, in obedience to the rite, uniting himself to it in mind and heart, and avoiding anything that might give the impression of an inordinate emphasis on his own personality. I encourage the clergy always to see their eucharistic ministry as a humble service offered to Christ and his Church. The priesthood, as Saint Augustine said, is *amoris officium* [the office of love], it is the office of the good shepherd, who offers his life for his sheep (see John 10:14–15).

In virtue of their common sacred ordination and mission, all priests are bound together in intimate brotherhood, which naturally and freely manifests itself in mutual aid, spiritual as well as material, pastoral as well as personal, in their meetings and in communion of life, of labor, and charity.

Let them, as fathers in Christ, take care of the faithful whom they have begotten by baptism and their teaching.[186] Becoming from the heart a pattern to the flock,[187] let them so lead and serve their local community that it may worthily be called by that name, by which the one and entire people of God is signed, namely, the Church of God.[188] Let them remember that by their daily life and interests they are showing the face of a truly sacerdotal and pastoral ministry to the faithful and the infidel, to Catholics and non-Catholics, and that to all they bear witness to the truth and life, and as good shepherds go after those also,[189] who though baptized in the Catholic Church have fallen away from the use of the sacraments, or even from the faith.

Because the human race today is joining more and more into a civic, economic, and social unity, it is that much the more necessary that priests, by combined effort and aid, under the leadership of the bishops and the Supreme Pontiff, wipe out every kind of separateness, so that the whole human race may be brought into the unity of the family of God.

29. At a lower level of the hierarchy are deacons, upon whom hands are imposed "not unto the priesthood, but unto a ministry of service."[74*] For strengthened by sacramental grace, in communion with the bishop and his group of priests they serve in the diaconate of the liturgy, of the word, and of charity to the people of God. It is the duty of the deacon, according as it shall have been assigned to him by competent authority, to administer baptism solemnly, to be custodian and dispenser of the Eucharist, to assist at and bless marriages in the name of the Church, to bring Viaticum to the dying, to read the Sacred Scripture to the faithful, to instruct and exhort the people, to preside over the worship and prayer of the faithful, to administer sacramentals, to officiate at funeral and burial services. Dedicated to duties of charity and of administration, let deacons be mindful of the admonition of Blessed Polycarp: "Be merciful, diligent, walking according to the truth of the Lord, who became the servant of all."[75*]

Since these duties, so very necessary to the life of the Church, can be fulfilled only with difficulty in many regions in accordance with the discipline of the Latin Church as it exists today, the diaconate can in the future be restored as a proper and permanent rank of the hierarchy. It pertains to the competent territorial bodies of bishops, of one kind or another, with the approval of the Supreme Pontiff, to decide whether and where it is opportune for such deacons to be established for the care of souls. With the consent of the Roman Pontiff, this diaconate can, in the future, be conferred upon men of more mature age, even upon those living in the married state. It may also be conferred upon suitable young men, for whom the law of celibacy must remain intact.

CHAPTER IV
The Laity

30. Having set forth the functions of the hierarchy, the Sacred Council gladly turns its attention to the state of those faithful called the laity. Everything that has been said above concerning the People of God is intended for the laity, religious, and clergy alike. But there are certain things which pertain in a special way to the laity, both men and women, by reason of their condition and mission. Due to the special circumstances of our time the foundations of this doctrine must be more thoroughly examined. For their pastors know how much the laity contribute to the welfare of the entire Church. They also know that they were not ordained by Christ to take upon themselves alone the entire salvific mission of the Church toward the world. On the contrary they understand that it is their noble duty to shepherd the faithful and to recognize their ministries and charisms, so that all according to their proper roles may cooperate in this common undertaking with one mind. For we must all "practice the truth in love, and so grow up in all things in Him who is head, Christ. For from Him the whole body, being closely joined and knit together through every joint of the system, according to the functioning in due measure of each single part, derives its increase to the building up of itself in love."[190]

31. The term laity is here understood to mean all the faithful except those in holy orders and those in the state of religious life specially approved by the Church. These faithful are by baptism made one body with Christ and are constituted among the People of God; they are in their own way made sharers in the priestly, prophetical, and kingly functions of Christ; and they carry out for their own part the mission of the whole Christian people in the Church and in the world.

What specifically characterizes the laity is their secular nature. It is true that those in holy orders can at times be engaged in secular activities, and even have a secular profession. But they are by reason of their particular vocation especially and professedly ordained to the sacred ministry. Similarly, by their state in life, religious give splendid and striking testimony that the world cannot be transformed and offered to God without the spirit of the beatitudes. But the laity, by their very vocation, seek the kingdom of God by engaging in temporal affairs and by ordering them according to the plan of God. They live in the world, that is, in each and in all of the secular professions and occupations. They live in the ordinary circumstances of family and social life, from which the very web of their existence is woven. They are called there by God that by exercising their proper function and led by the spirit of the Gospel they may work for the sanctification of the world from within as a leaven. In this way they may make Christ known to others, especially by the testimony of a life resplendent in faith, hope, and charity. Therefore, since they are tightly bound up in all types of temporal affairs it is their special task to order and to throw light upon these affairs in such a way that they may come into being and then continually increase according to Christ to the praise of the Creator and the Redeemer.

Priests, Prophets, and Kings

Lumen Gentium 31 | Bishop Barron

According to the documents of Vatican II, the clergy are, by ordination, priests, prophets, and kings. As priests, they sanctify the people of God through the sacraments; as prophets, they speak the divine word and form the minds and hearts of their flocks; and as kings, they order the charisms of the community toward the realization of the kingdom of God. Accordingly, the immediate area of concern for bishops and priests is the Church—that is to say, the community of the baptized.

Now, the laity, by virtue of their baptism, are also priests, prophets, and kings—but their sanctifying, teaching, and governing work is directed not so much inwardly to the Church but outwardly to the world. For the Vatican II fathers, the proper arena of the laity is the *saeculum* (the secular order), and their task is the Christification of that realm. They are charged to take the teaching, direction, and sanctification that they have received from the priests and bishops and then go forth, equipped to transform the world and thereby find their own path to holiness.

Every Catholic layperson, each in his or her special area of competence, is meant to bring Christ to the society and the culture. And when I say "Catholic" here, I don't mean incidentally so or merely privately so, but rather vibrantly and publicly so. This Christification of the culture ought never, of course, to be done aggressively, for as John Paul II said, the Church never imposes but only proposes; but it is indeed to be done confidently, boldly, and through concrete action.

32. By divine institution Holy Church is ordered and governed with a wonderful diversity. "For just as in one body we have many members, yet all the members have not the same function, so we, the many, are one body in Christ, but severally members one of another."[191] Therefore, the chosen People of God is one: "one Lord, one faith, one baptism";[192] sharing a common dignity as members from their regeneration in Christ, having the same filial grace and the same vocation to perfection; possessing in common one salvation, one hope, and one undivided charity. There is, therefore, in Christ and in the Church no inequality on the basis of race or nationality, social condition or sex, because "there is neither Jew nor Greek; there is neither bond nor free; there is neither male nor female. For you are all 'one' in Christ Jesus."[193]

If therefore in the Church everyone does not proceed by the same path, nevertheless all are called to sanctity and have received an equal privilege of faith through the justice of God.[194] And if by the will of Christ some are made teachers, pastors, and dispensers of mysteries on behalf of others, yet all share a true equality with regard to the dignity and to the activity common to all the faithful for the building up of the Body of Christ. For the distinction which the Lord made between sacred ministers and the rest of the People of God bears within it a certain union, since pastors and the other faithful are bound to each other by a mutual need. Pastors of the Church, following the example of the Lord, should minister to one another and to the other faithful. These in their turn should enthusiastically lend their joint assistance to their pastors and teachers. Thus in their diversity all bear witness to the wonderful unity in the Body of Christ. This very diversity of graces, ministries, and works gathers the children of God into one, because "all these things are the work of one and the same Spirit."[195]

Therefore, from divine choice the laity have Christ for their brother who though He is the Lord of all, came not to be served but to serve.[196] They also have for their brothers those in the sacred ministry who by teaching, by sanctifying, and by ruling with the authority of Christ feed the family of God so that the new commandment of charity may be fulfilled by all. St. Augustine puts this very beautifully when he says: "What I am for you terrifies me; what I am with you consoles me. For you I am a bishop; but with you I am a Christian. The former is a duty; the latter a grace. The former is a danger; the latter, salvation."[1*]

33. The laity are gathered together in the People of God and make up the Body of Christ under one head. Whoever they are they are called upon, as living members, to expend all their energy for the growth of the Church and its continuous sanctification, since this very energy is a gift of the Creator and a blessing of the Redeemer.

The lay apostolate, however, is a participation in the salvific mission of the Church itself. Through their baptism and confirmation all are commissioned to that apostolate by the Lord Himself. Moreover, by the sacraments, especially holy Eucharist, that charity toward God and man which is the soul of the apostolate is communicated and nourished. Now the laity are called in a special way to make the Church present and operative in those places and circumstances where only through them can it become the salt of the earth.[2*] Thus every layman, in virtue of the very gifts bestowed upon him, is at the same time a witness and a living instrument of the mission of the Church itself "according to the measure of Christ's bestowal."[197]

The Mission of the Lay Faithful
Lumen Gentium 33

**Pope
Benedict XVI**

———

Deus Caritas Est
29

The direct duty to work for a just ordering of society . . . is proper to the lay faithful. As citizens of the State, they are called to take part in public life in a personal capacity. So they cannot relinquish their participation "in the many different economic, social, legislative, administrative, and cultural areas, which are intended to promote organically and institutionally the *common good.*" The mission of the lay faithful is therefore to configure social life correctly, respecting its legitimate autonomy and cooperating with other citizens according to their respective competences and fulfilling their own responsibility. Even if the specific expressions of ecclesial charity can never be confused with the activity of the State, it still remains true that charity must animate the entire lives of the lay faithful and therefore also their political activity, lived as "social charity."

Besides this apostolate which certainly pertains to all Christians, the laity can also be called in various ways to a more direct form of cooperation in the apostolate of the Hierarchy.[3*] This was the way certain men and women assisted Paul the Apostle in the Gospel, laboring much in the Lord.[198] Further, they have the capacity to assume from the Hierarchy certain ecclesiastical functions, which are to be performed for a spiritual purpose.

Upon all the laity, therefore, rests the noble duty of working to extend the divine plan of salvation to all men of each epoch and in every land. Consequently, may every opportunity be given them so that, according to their abilities and the needs of the times, they may zealously participate in the saving work of the Church.

34. The supreme and eternal Priest, Christ Jesus, since he wills to continue his witness and service also through the laity, vivifies them in this Spirit and increasingly urges them on to every good and perfect work.

For besides intimately linking them to His life and His mission, He also gives them a sharing in His priestly function of offering spiritual worship for the glory of God and the salvation of men. For this reason the laity, dedicated to Christ and anointed by the Holy Spirit, are marvelously called and wonderfully prepared so that ever more abundant fruits of the Spirit may be produced in them. For all their works, prayers, and apostolic endeavors, their ordinary married and family life, their daily occupations, their physical and mental relaxation, if carried out in the Spirit, and even the hardships of life, if patiently borne—all these become "spiritual sacrifices acceptable to God through Jesus Christ."[199] Together with the offering of the Lord's body, they are most fittingly offered in the celebration of the Eucharist. Thus, as those everywhere who adore in holy activity, the laity consecrate the world itself to God.

Agents of the Sanctification of the World

Lumen Gentium 31–36 | Bishop Barron

Prior to Vatican II, there were a number of theologians and activists who were calling for a greater awareness of the role of the laity in the transformation of the world. One of the leading figures in this group was a priest from Chicago named Reynold Hillenbrand, who was rector of Mundelein Seminary during the 1930s and early 40s and who helped to form a generation of socially active priests. He was instrumental in the Catholic Action movement and in relating liturgy to the political and economic realms. The views of Hillenbrand and his colleagues in this regard were largely adopted at the Second Vatican Council.

But then in the years following the council, this great teaching was not propagated. Catholics tended to understand "lay involvement" as getting lay people into the sanctuary and into the administrative and ministerial structures of the Church. While these roles are not, in themselves, bad things, they are not primarily what the council was talking about.

Let's look at some of the passages from this section of *Lumen Gentium*: "They are called there by God that by exercising their proper function and led by the spirit of the Gospel they may work for the sanctification of the world from within as a leaven." The laity are to be the agents of the sanctification of the world, to use their expertise in business, finance, law, government, communications, healthcare, and entertainment in order to make those realms holier places.

A few paragraphs later we read: "Now the laity are called in a special way to make the Church present and operative in those places and circumstances where only through them can it become the salt of the earth." Priests and religious cannot reach deeply into the secular world, for they don't know it adequately. But the laity can, and hence they can work as salt, enhancing what is good and putting to death what is evil.

And then this beautiful quotation: "The faithful, therefore, must learn the deepest meaning and the value of all creation, as well as its role in the harmonious praise of God. They must assist each other to live holier lives even in their daily occupations. In this way the world may be permeated by the spirit of Christ." How is the spirit of Christ brought to bear in the secular world? Through the laity and by means of their special expertise.

Though modernity has taught us to separate the sacred and the secular, the holy and the profane, that distinction does not make sense on biblical grounds. God is not a being, one thing among many, but rather *ipsum esse subsistens*, the sheer act of to-be itself. Therefore, God impinges on everything; God has to do with everything. And therefore, Christ's spirit must penetrate everything. You cannot think therefore of a secular aspect of your life alongside of the sacred; rather, everything that you do must be grounded in and related to the holy.

35. Christ, the great Prophet, who proclaimed the Kingdom of His Father both by the testimony of His life and the power of His words, continually fulfills His prophetic office until the complete manifestation of glory. He does this not only through the hierarchy who teach in His name and with His authority, but also through the laity whom He made His witnesses and to whom He gave understanding of the faith (*sensu fidei*) and an attractiveness in speech[200] so that the power of the Gospel might shine forth in their daily social and family life. They conduct themselves as children of the promise, and thus strong in faith and in hope they make the most of the present,[201] and with patience await the glory that is to come.[202] Let them not, then, hide this hope in the depths of their hearts, but even in the program of their secular life let them express it by a continual conversion and by wrestling "against the world-rulers of this darkness, against the spiritual forces of wickedness."[203]

Just as the sacraments of the New Law, by which the life and the apostolate of the faithful are nourished, prefigure a new heaven and a new earth,[204] so too the laity go forth as powerful proclaimers of a faith in things to be hoped for,[205] when they courageously join to their profession of faith a life springing from faith. This evangelization, that is, this announcing of Christ by a living testimony as well as by the spoken word, takes on a specific quality and a special force in that it is carried out in the ordinary surroundings of the world.

In connection with the prophetic function is that state of life which is sanctified by a special sacrament obviously of great importance, namely, married and family life. For where Christianity pervades the entire mode of family life, and gradually transforms it, one will find there both the practice and an excellent school of the lay apostolate. In such a home husbands and wives find their proper vocation in being witnesses of the faith and love of Christ to one another and to their children. The Christian family loudly proclaims both the present virtues of the Kingdom of God and the hope of a blessed life to come. Thus by its example and its witness it accuses the world of sin and enlightens those who seek the truth.

Consequently, even when preoccupied with temporal cares, the laity can and must perform a work of great value for the evangelization of the world. For even if some of them have to fulfill their religious duties on their own, when there are no sacred ministers or in times of persecution; and even if many of them devote all their energies to apostolic work; still it remains for each one of them to cooperate in the external spread and the dynamic growth of the Kingdom of Christ in the world. Therefore, let the laity devotedly strive to acquire a more profound grasp of revealed truth, and let them insistently beg of God the gift of wisdom.

36. Christ, becoming obedient even unto death and because of this exalted by the Father,[206] entered into the glory of His kingdom. To Him all things are made subject until He subjects Himself and all created things to the Father that God may be all in all.[207] Now Christ has communicated this royal power to His disciples that they might be constituted in royal freedom and that by true penance and a holy life they might conquer the reign of sin in themselves.[208] Further, He has shared this power so that serving Christ in their fellow men they might by humility and patience lead their brethren to that King for whom to serve is to reign. But the Lord wishes to spread His kingdom also by means of the laity, namely, a kingdom of truth and life, a kingdom of holiness and grace, a kingdom of justice, love, and peace.[4*] In this kingdom creation itself will be delivered from its slavery to corruption into the freedom of the glory of the sons of God.[209] Clearly then a great promise and a great trust is committed to the disciples: "All things are yours, and you are Christ's, and Christ is God's."[210]

The faithful, therefore, must learn the deepest meaning and the value of all creation, as well as its role in the harmonious praise of God. They must assist each other to live holier lives even in their daily occupations. In this way the world may be permeated by the spirit of Christ and it may more effectively fulfill its purpose in justice, charity, and peace. The laity have the principal role in the overall fulfillment of this duty. Therefore, by their competence in secular training and by their activity, elevated from within by the grace of Christ, let them vigorously contribute their effort, so that created goods may be perfected by human labor, technical skill, and civic culture for the benefit of all men according to the design of the Creator and the light of His Word. May the goods of this world be more equitably distributed among all men, and may they in their own way be conducive to universal progress in human and Christian freedom. In this manner, through the members of the Church, will Christ progressively illumine the whole of human society with His saving light.

Moreover, let the laity also by their combined efforts remedy the customs and conditions of the world, if they are an inducement to sin, so that they all may be conformed to the norms of justice and may favor the practice of virtue rather than hinder it. By so doing they will imbue culture and human activity with genuine moral values; they will better prepare the field of the world for the seed of the Word of God; and at the same time they will open wider the doors of the Church by which the message of peace may enter the world.

Because of the very economy of salvation the faithful should learn how to distinguish carefully between those rights and duties which are theirs as members of the Church, and those which they have as members of human society. Let them strive to reconcile the two, remembering that in every temporal affair they must be guided by a Christian conscience, since even in secular business there is no human activity which can be withdrawn from God's dominion. In our own time, however, it is most urgent that this distinction and also this harmony should shine forth more clearly than ever in the lives of the faithful, so that the mission of the Church may correspond more fully to the special conditions of the world today. For it must be admitted that the temporal sphere is governed by its own principles, since it is rightly concerned with the interests of this world. But that ominous doctrine which attempts to build a society with no regard whatever for religion, and which attacks and destroys the religious liberty of its citizens, is rightly to be rejected.[5*]

Lay Missionaries
Lumen Gentium 34–36

**Pope
St. John Paul II**
———
*Redemptoris
Missio* 71–72

It is clear that from the very origins of Christianity, the laity—as individuals, families, and entire communities—shared in spreading the faith. Pope Pius XII recalled this fact in his first encyclical on the missions, in which he pointed out some instances of lay missions. In modern times, this active participation of lay men and women missionaries has not been lacking. How can we forget the important role played by women: their work in the family, in schools, in political, social, and cultural life, and especially their teaching of Christian doctrine? Indeed, it is necessary to recognize—and it is a title of honor—that some churches owe their origins to the activity of lay men and women missionaries.

The Second Vatican Council confirmed this tradition in its description of the missionary character of the entire People of God and of the apostolate of the laity in particular, emphasizing the specific contribution to missionary activity which they are called to make. The need for all the faithful to share in this responsibility is not merely a matter of making the apostolate more effective, it is a right and duty based on their baptismal dignity, whereby "the faithful participate, for their part, in the threefold mission of Christ as Priest, Prophet, and King." Therefore, "they are bound by the general obligation and they have the right, whether as individuals or in associations, to strive so that the divine message of salvation may be known and accepted by all people throughout the world. This obligation is all the more insistent in circumstances in which only through them are people able to hear the Gospel and to know Christ." Furthermore, because of their secular character, they especially are called to "seek the kingdom of God by engaging in temporal affairs and by ordering them according to the plan of God" (LG 31).

The sphere in which lay people are present and active as missionaries is very extensive. "Their own field . . . is the vast and complicated world of politics, society, and economics . . ." on the local, national, and international levels. Within the Church, there are various types of services, functions, ministries, and ways of promoting the Christian life. I call to mind, as a new development occurring in many churches in recent times, the rapid growth of "ecclesial movements" filled with missionary dynamism. When these movements humbly seek to become part of the life of local churches and are welcomed by bishops and priests within diocesan and parish structures, they represent a true gift of God both for new evangelization and for missionary activity properly so-called. I therefore recommend that they be spread, and that they be used to give fresh energy, especially among young people, to the Christian life and to evangelization, within a pluralistic view of the ways in which Christians can associate and express themselves.

37. The laity have the right, as do all Christians, to receive in abundance from their spiritual shepherds the spiritual goods of the Church, especially the assistance of the word of God and of the sacraments.[6*] They should openly reveal to them their needs and desires with that freedom and confidence which is fitting for children of God and brothers in Christ. They are, by reason of the knowledge, competence, or outstanding ability which they may enjoy, permitted and sometimes even obliged to express their opinion on those things which concern the good of the Church.[7*] When occasions arise, let this be done through the organs erected by the Church for this purpose. Let it always be done in truth, in courage, and in prudence, with reverence and charity toward those who by reason of their sacred office represent the person of Christ.

The laity should, as all Christians, promptly accept in Christian obedience decisions of their spiritual shepherds, since they are representatives of Christ as well as teachers and rulers in the Church. Let them follow the example of Christ, who by His obedience even unto death, opened to all men the blessed way of the liberty of the children of God. Nor should they omit to pray for those placed over them, for they keep watch as having to render an account of their souls, so that they may do this with joy and not with grief.[211]

Let the spiritual shepherds recognize and promote the dignity as well as the responsibility of the laity in the Church. Let them willingly employ their prudent advice. Let them confidently assign duties to them in the service of the Church, allowing them freedom and room for action. Further, let them encourage lay people so that they may undertake tasks on their own initiative. Attentively in Christ, let them consider with fatherly love the projects, suggestions, and desires proposed by the laity.[8*] However, let the shepherds respectfully acknowledge that just freedom which belongs to everyone in this earthly city.

A great many wonderful things are to be hoped for from this familiar dialogue between the laity and their spiritual leaders: in the laity a strengthened sense of personal responsibility; a renewed enthusiasm; a more ready application of their talents to the projects of their spiritual leaders. The latter, on the other hand, aided by the experience of the laity, can more clearly and more incisively come to decisions regarding both spiritual and temporal matters. In this way, the whole Church, strengthened by each one of its members, may more effectively fulfill its mission for the life of the world.

38. Each individual layman must stand before the world as a witness to the resurrection and life of the Lord Jesus and a symbol of the living God. All the laity as a community and each one according to his ability must nourish the world with spiritual fruits.[212] They must diffuse in the world that spirit which animates the poor, the meek, the peace makers—whom the Lord in the Gospel proclaimed as blessed.[213] In a word, "Christians must be to the world what the soul is to the body."[9*]

CHAPTER V
The Universal Call to Holiness in the Church

39. The Church, whose mystery is being set forth by this Sacred Synod, is believed to be indefectibly holy. Indeed Christ, the Son of God, who with the Father and the Spirit is praised as "uniquely holy,"[1*] loved the Church as His bride, delivering Himself up for her. He did this that He might sanctify her.[214] He united her to Himself as His own body and brought it to perfection by the gift of the Holy Spirit for God's glory. Therefore in the Church, everyone whether belonging to the hierarchy, or being cared for by it, is called to holiness, according to the saying of the Apostle: "For this is the will of God, your sanctification."[215] However, this holiness of the Church is unceasingly manifested, and must be manifested, in the fruits of grace which the Spirit produces in the faithful; it is expressed in many ways in individuals, who in their walk of life, tend toward the perfection of charity, thus causing the edification of others; in a very special way this holiness appears in the practice of the counsels, customarily called "evangelical." This practice of the counsels, under the impulsion of the Holy Spirit, undertaken by many Christians, either privately or in a Church-approved condition or state of life, gives and must give in the world an outstanding witness and example of this same holiness.

We Are All Called to Be Holy
Lumen Gentium 39–42

Pope Francis

———

Gaudete et
Exsultate 14–16

To be holy does not require being a bishop, a priest, or a religious. We are frequently tempted to think that holiness is only for those who can withdraw from ordinary affairs to spend much time in prayer. That is not the case. We are all called to be holy by living our lives with love and by bearing witness in everything we do, wherever we find ourselves. Are you called to the consecrated life? Be holy by living out your commitment with joy. Are you married? Be holy by loving and caring for your husband or wife, as Christ does for the Church. Do you work for a living? Be holy by laboring with integrity and skill in the service of your brothers and sisters. Are you a parent or grandparent? Be holy by patiently teaching the little ones how to follow Jesus. Are you in a position of authority? Be holy by working for the common good and renouncing personal gain.

Let the grace of your baptism bear fruit in a path of holiness. Let everything be open to God; turn to him in every situation. Do not be dismayed, for the power of the Holy Spirit enables you to do this, and holiness, in the end, is the fruit of the Holy Spirit in your life (see Gal. 5:22–23). When you feel the temptation to dwell on your own weakness, raise your eyes to Christ crucified and say: "Lord, I am a poor sinner, but you can work the miracle of making me a little bit better." In the Church, holy yet made up of sinners, you will find everything you need to grow towards holiness. The Lord has bestowed on the Church the gifts of scripture, the sacraments, holy places, living communities, the witness of the saints, and a multifaceted beauty that proceeds from God's love, "like a bride bedecked with jewels" (Isa. 61:10).

This holiness to which the Lord calls you will grow through small gestures. Here is an example: a woman goes shopping, she meets a neighbor and they begin to speak, and the gossip starts. But she says in her heart: "No, I will not speak badly of anyone." This is a step forward in holiness. Later, at home, one of her children wants to talk to her about his hopes and dreams, and even though she is tired, she sits down and listens with patience and love. That is another sacrifice that brings holiness. Later she experiences some anxiety, but recalling the love of the Virgin Mary, she takes her rosary and prays with faith. Yet another path of holiness. Later still, she goes out onto the street, encounters a poor person, and stops to say a kind word to him. One more step.

40. The Lord Jesus, the divine Teacher and Model of all perfection, preached holiness of life to each and every one of His disciples of every condition. He Himself stands as the author and consummator of this holiness of life: "Be you therefore perfect, even as your heavenly Father is perfect."[216] [(2*)] Indeed He sent the Holy Spirit upon all men that He might move them inwardly to love God with their whole heart and their whole soul, with all their mind and all their strength[217] and that they might love each other as Christ loves them.[218] The followers of Christ are called by God, not because of their works, but according to His own purpose and grace. They are justified in the Lord Jesus, because in the baptism of faith they truly become sons of God and sharers in the divine nature. In this way they are really made holy. Then too, by God's gift, they must hold on to and complete in their lives this holiness they have received. They are warned by the Apostle to live "as becomes saints,"[219] and to put on "as God's chosen ones, holy and beloved a heart of mercy, kindness, humility, meekness, patience,"[220] and to possess the fruit of the Spirit in holiness.[221] Since truly we all offend in many things[222] we all need God's mercies continually and we all must daily pray: "Forgive us our debts."[223] [(3*)]

Thus it is evident to everyone, that all the faithful of Christ of whatever rank or status, are called to the fullness of the Christian life and to the perfection of charity;[4*] by this holiness as such a more human manner of living is promoted in this earthly society. In order that the faithful may reach this perfection, they must use their strength accordingly as they have received it, as a gift from Christ. They must follow in His footsteps and conform themselves to His image seeking the will of the Father in all things. They must devote themselves with all their being to the glory of God and the service of their neighbor. In this way, the holiness of the People of God will grow into an abundant harvest of good, as is admirably shown by the life of so many saints in Church history.

41. The classes and duties of life are many, but holiness is one—that sanctity which is cultivated by all who are moved by the Spirit of God, and who obey the voice of the Father and worship God the Father in spirit and in truth. These people follow the poor Christ, the humble and cross-bearing Christ in order to be worthy of being sharers in His glory. Every person must walk unhesitatingly according to his own personal gifts and duties in the path of living faith, which arouses hope and works through charity.

In the first place, the shepherds of Christ's flock must holily and eagerly, humbly and courageously carry out their ministry, in imitation of the eternal high Priest, the Shepherd and Guardian of our souls. They ought to fulfill this duty in such a way that it will be the principal means also of their own sanctification. Those chosen for the fullness of the priesthood are granted the ability of exercising the perfect duty of pastoral charity by the grace of the sacrament of Orders. This perfect duty of pastoral charity[5*] is exercised in every form of episcopal care and service, prayer, sacrifice, and preaching. By this same sacramental grace, they are given the courage necessary to lay down their lives for their sheep, and the ability of promoting greater holiness in the Church by their daily example, having become a pattern for their flock.[224]

Priests, who resemble bishops to a certain degree in their participation of the sacrament of Orders, form the spiritual crown of the bishops.[6*] They participate in the grace of their office and they should grow daily in their love of God and their neighbor by the exercise of their office through Christ, the eternal and unique Mediator. They should preserve the bond of priestly communion, and they should abound in every spiritual good and thus present to all men a living witness to God.[7*] All this they should do in emulation of those priests who often, down through the course of the centuries, left an outstanding example of the holiness of humble and hidden service. Their praise lives on in the Church of God. By their very office of praying and offering sacrifice for their own people and the entire people of God, they should rise to greater holiness. Keeping in mind what they are doing and imitating what they are handling,[8*] these priests, in their apostolic labors, rather than being ensnared by perils and hardships, should rather rise to greater holiness through these perils and hardships. They should ever nourish and strengthen their action from an abundance of contemplation, doing all this for the comfort of the entire Church of God. All priests, and especially those who are called "diocesan priests," due to the special title of their ordination, should keep continually before their minds the fact that their faithful loyalty toward and their generous cooperation with their bishop is of the greatest value in their growth in holiness.

Ministers of lesser rank are also sharers in the mission and grace of the Supreme Priest. In the first place among these ministers are deacons, who, in as much as they are dispensers of Christ's mysteries and servants of the Church,[9*] should keep themselves free from every vice and stand before men as personifications of goodness and friends of God.[225] Clerics, who are called by the Lord and are set aside as His portion in order to prepare themselves for the various ministerial offices under the watchful eye of spiritual shepherds, are bound to bring their hearts and minds into accord with this special election which is theirs. They will accomplish this by their constancy in prayer, by their burning love, and by their unremitting recollection of whatever is true, just, and of good repute. They will accomplish all this for the glory and honor of God. Besides these already named, there are also laymen, chosen of God and called by the bishop. These laymen spend themselves completely in apostolic labors, working the Lord's field with much success.[10*]

Furthermore, married couples and Christian parents should follow their own proper path to holiness by faithful love. They should sustain one another in grace throughout the entire length of their lives. They should embue their offspring, lovingly welcomed as God's gift, with Christian doctrine and the evangelical virtues. In this manner, they offer all men the example of unwearying and generous love; in this way they build up the brotherhood of charity; in so doing, they stand as the witnesses and cooperators in the fruitfulness of Holy Mother Church; by such lives, they are a sign and a participation in that very love, with which Christ loved His Bride and for which He delivered Himself up for her.[11*] A like example, but one given in a different way, is that offered by widows and single people, who are able to make great contributions toward holiness and apostolic endeavor in the Church. Finally, those who engage in labor—and frequently it is of a heavy nature—should better themselves by their human labors. They should be of aid to their fellow citizens. They should raise all of society, and even creation itself, to a better mode of existence. Indeed, they should imitate by their lively charity, in their joyous hope, and by their voluntary sharing of each other's burdens, the very Christ who plied His hands with carpenter's tools and Who in union with His Father, is continually working for the salvation of all men. In this, then, their daily work they should climb to the heights of holiness and apostolic activity.

May all those who are weighed down with poverty, infirmity, and sickness, as well as those who must bear various hardships or who suffer persecution for justice's sake—may they all know they are united with the suffering Christ in a special way for the salvation of the world. The Lord called them blessed in His Gospel and they are those whom "the God of all graces, who has called us unto His eternal glory in Christ Jesus, will Himself, after we have suffered a little while, perfect, strengthen, and establish."[226]

Finally all Christ's faithful, whatever be the conditions, duties, and circumstances of their lives—and indeed through all these, will daily increase in holiness, if they receive all things with faith from the hand of their heavenly Father and if they cooperate with the divine will. In this temporal service, they will manifest to all men the love with which God loved the world.

42. "God is love, and he who abides in love, abides in God and God in Him."[227] But, God pours out his love into our hearts through the Holy Spirit, Who has been given to us;[228] thus the first and most necessary gift is love, by which we love God above all things and our neighbor because of God. Indeed, in order that love, as good seed may grow and bring forth fruit in the soul, each one of the faithful must willingly hear the Word of God and accept His Will, and must complete what God has begun by their own actions with the help of God's grace. These actions consist in the use of the sacraments and in a special way the Eucharist, frequent participation in the sacred action of the Liturgy, application of oneself to prayer, self-abnegation, lively fraternal service, and the constant exercise of all the virtues. For charity, as the bond of perfection and the fullness of the law,[229] rules over all the means of attaining holiness and gives life to these same means.[12*] It is charity which guides us to our final end. It is the love of God and the love of one's neighbor which points out the true disciple of Christ.

Since Jesus, the Son of God, manifested His charity by laying down His life for us, so too no one has greater love than he who lays down his life for Christ and His brothers.[230] From the earliest times, then, some Christians have been called upon—and some will always be called upon—to give the supreme testimony of this love to all men, but especially to persecutors. The Church, then, considers martyrdom as an exceptional gift and as the fullest proof of love. By martyrdom a disciple is transformed into an image of his Master by freely accepting death for the salvation of the world—as well as his conformity to Christ in the shedding of his blood. Though few are presented such an opportunity, nevertheless all must be prepared to confess Christ before men. They must be prepared to make this profession of faith even in the midst of persecutions, which will never be lacking to the Church, in following the way of the cross.

Likewise, the holiness of the Church is fostered in a special way by the observance of the counsels proposed in the Gospel by Our Lord to His disciples.[13*] An eminent position among these is held by virginity or the celibate state.[231] This is a precious gift of divine grace given by the Father to certain souls,[232] whereby they may devote themselves to God alone the more easily, due to an undivided heart.[14*] This perfect continency, out of desire for the kingdom of heaven, has always been held in particular honor in the Church. The reason for this was and is that perfect continency for the love of God is an incentive to charity, and is certainly a particular source of spiritual fecundity in the world.

The Church continually keeps before it the warning of the Apostle which moved the faithful to charity, exhorting them to experience personally what Christ Jesus had known within Himself. This was the same Christ Jesus, who "emptied Himself, taking the nature of a slave . . . becoming obedient to death,"[233] and because of us, "being rich, he became poor."[234] Because the disciples must always offer an imitation of and a testimony to the charity and humility of Christ, Mother Church rejoices at finding within her bosom men and women who very closely follow their Savior who debased Himself to our comprehension. There are some who, in their freedom as sons of God, renounce their own wills and take upon themselves the state of poverty. Still further, some become subject of their own accord to another man, in the matter of perfection for love of God. This is beyond the measure of the commandments, but is done in order to become more fully like the obedient Christ.[15*]

Therefore, all the faithful of Christ are invited to strive for the holiness and perfection of their own proper state. Indeed they have an obligation to so strive. Let all then have care that they guide aright their own deepest sentiments of soul. Let neither the use of the things of this world nor attachment to riches, which is against the spirit of evangelical poverty, hinder them in their quest for perfect love. Let them heed the admonition of the Apostle to those who use this world; let them not come to terms with this world; for this world, as we see it, is passing away.[235] [16*]

CHAPTER VI
Religious

43. The evangelical counsels of chastity dedicated to God, poverty, and obedience are based upon the words and examples of the Lord. They were further commanded by the apostles and Fathers of the Church, as well as

The Summons of All the Baptized

Lumen Gentium 39–42 | Bishop Barron

Lumen Gentium speaks of the universal call to holiness—that is, the summons of all the baptized to be a transforming leaven in the wider society. The Vatican II fathers wanted to inspire a generation of great Catholic lawyers, great Catholic business leaders, great Catholic nurses and physicians, great Catholic teachers and writers, in the hopes that such people would carry the holiness they learned in the Church out to their areas of specialization in the secular world. This biblically based vision runs counter, of course, to our modern preference for the privatization of religion, the sequestering of the faith within the interiority of the individual conscience. In terms of the Noah story, the contemporary approach is tantamount to keeping the animals on the ark. But the life of the Church is not meant to hunker down permanently behind the walls of the ship; it is meant to invade the world.

by the doctors and pastors of souls. The counsels are a divine gift, which the Church received from its Lord and which it always safeguards with the help of His grace. Church authority has the duty, under the inspiration of the Holy Spirit, of interpreting these evangelical counsels, of regulating their practice, and finally to build on them stable forms of living. Thus it has come about, that, as if on a tree which has grown in the field of the Lord, various forms of solidarity and community life, as well as various religious families have branched out in a marvelous and multiple way from this divinely given seed. Such a multiple and miraculous growth augments both the progress of the members of these various religious families themselves and the welfare of the entire Body of Christ.[1*] These religious families give their members the support of a more firm stability in their way of life and a proven doctrine of acquiring perfection. They further offer their members the support of fraternal association in the militia of Christ and of liberty strengthened by obedience. Thus these religious are able to tranquilly fulfill and faithfully observe their religious profession and so spiritually rejoicing make progress on the road of charity.[2*]

From the point of view of the divine and hierarchical structure of the Church, the religious state of life is not an intermediate state between the clerical and lay states. But, rather, the faithful of Christ are called by God from both these states of life so that they might enjoy this particular gift in the life of the Church and thus each in one's own way, may be of some advantage to the salvific mission of the Church.[3*]

The Evangelical Counsels
Lumen Gentium 43

Pope St. John Paul II

—

Mulieris Dignitatem 20

The Gospel puts forward *the ideal of the consecration of the person,* that is, the person's exclusive dedication to God by virtue of the evangelical counsels: in particular, chastity, poverty, and obedience. Their perfect incarnation is Jesus Christ himself. Whoever wishes to follow him in a radical way chooses to live according to these counsels. They are distinct from the commandments and show the Christian the radical way of the Gospel. From the very beginning of Christianity men and women have set out on this path, since the evangelical ideal is addressed to human beings without any distinction of sex.

44. The faithful of Christ bind themselves to the three aforesaid counsels either by vows, or by other sacred bonds, which are like vows in their purpose. By such a bond, a person is totally dedicated to God, loved beyond all things. In this way, that person is ordained to the honor and service of God under a new and special title. Indeed through Baptism a person dies to sin and is consecrated to God. However, in order that he may be capable of deriving more abundant fruit from this baptismal grace, he intends, by the profession of the evangelical counsels in the Church, to free himself from those obstacles, which might draw him away from the fervor of charity and the perfection of divine worship. By his profession of the evangelical counsels, then, he is more intimately consecrated to divine service.[4*] This consecration will be the more perfect, in as much as the indissoluble bond of the union of Christ and His bride, the Church, is represented by firm and more stable bonds.

The evangelical counsels which lead to charity[5*] join their followers to the Church and its mystery in a special way. Since this is so, the spiritual life of these people should then be devoted to the welfare of the whole Church. From this arises their duty of working to implant and strengthen the Kingdom of Christ in souls and to extend that Kingdom to every clime. This duty is to be undertaken to the extent of their capacities and in keeping with the proper type of their own vocation. This can be realized through prayer or active works of the apostolate. It is for this reason that the Church preserves and fosters the special character of her various religious institutes.

The profession of the evangelical counsels, then, appears as a sign which can and ought to attract all the members of the Church to an effective and prompt fulfillment of the duties of their Christian vocation. The people of God have no lasting city here below, but look forward to one that is to come. Since this is so, the religious state, whose purpose is to free its members from earthly cares, more fully manifests to all believers the presence of heavenly goods already possessed here below. Furthermore, it not only witnesses to the fact of a new and eternal life acquired by the redemption of Christ, but it foretells the future resurrection and the glory of the heavenly kingdom. Christ proposed to His disciples this form of life, which He, as the Son of God, accepted in entering this world to do the will of the Father. This same state of life is accurately exemplified and perpetually made present in the Church. The religious state clearly manifests that the Kingdom of God and its needs, in a very special way, are raised above all earthly considerations. Finally it clearly shows all men both the unsurpassed breadth of the strength of Christ the King and the infinite power of the Holy Spirit marvelously working in the Church.

Thus, the state which is constituted by the profession of the evangelical counsels, though it is not the hierarchical structure of the Church, nevertheless, undeniably belongs to its life and holiness.

45. It is the duty of the ecclesiastical hierarchy to regulate the practice of the evangelical counsels by law, since it is the duty of the same hierarchy to care for the People of God and to lead them to most fruitful pastures.[236] The importance of the profession of the evangelical counsels is seen in the fact that it fosters the perfection of love of God and love of neighbor in an outstanding manner and that this profession is strengthened by vows.[6*] Furthermore, the hierarchy, following with docility the prompting of the

Holy Spirit, accepts the rules presented by outstanding men and women and authentically approves these rules after further adjustments. It also aids by its vigilant and safeguarding authority those institutes variously established for the building up of Christ's Body in order that these same institutes may grow and flourish according to the spirit of the founders.

Any institute of perfection and its individual members may be removed from the jurisdiction of the local Ordinaries by the Supreme Pontiff and subjected to himself alone. This is done in virtue of his primacy over the entire Church in order to more fully provide for the necessities of the entire flock of the Lord and in consideration of the common good.[7*] In like manner, these institutes may be left or committed to the charge of the proper patriarchical authority. The members of these institutes, in fulfilling their obligation to the Church due to their particular form of life, ought to show reverence and obedience to bishops according to the sacred canons. The bishops are owed this respect because of their pastoral authority in their own churches and because of the need of unity and harmony in the apostolate.[8*]

The Church not only raises the religious profession to the dignity of a canonical state by her approval, but even manifests that this profession is a state consecrated to God by the liturgical setting of that profession. The Church itself, by the authority given to it by God, accepts the vows of the newly professed. It begs aid and grace from God for them by its public prayer. It commends them to God, imparts a spiritual blessing on them, and accompanies their self-offering by the Eucharistic sacrifice.

46. Religious should carefully keep before their minds the fact that the Church presents Christ to believers and non-believers alike in a striking manner daily through them. The Church thus portrays Christ in contemplation on the mountain, in His proclamation of the kingdom of God to the multitudes, in His healing of the sick and maimed, in His work of converting sinners to a better life, in His solicitude for youth and His goodness to all men, always obedient to the will of the Father who sent Him.[9*]

All men should take note that the profession of the evangelical counsels, though entailing the renunciation of certain values which are to be undoubtedly esteemed, does not detract from a genuine development of the human person, but rather by its very nature is most beneficial to that development. Indeed the counsels, voluntarily undertaken according to each one's personal vocation, contribute a great deal to the purification of heart and spiritual liberty. They continually stir up the fervor of charity. But especially they are able to more fully mold the Christian man to that type of chaste and detached life, which Christ the Lord chose for Himself and which His Mother also embraced. This is clearly proven by the example of so many holy founders. Let no one think that religious have become strangers to their fellowmen or useless citizens of this earthly city by their consecration. For even though it sometimes happens that religious do not directly mingle with their contemporaries, yet in a more profound sense these same religious are united with them in the heart of Christ and spiritually cooperate with them. In this way the building up of the earthly city may have its foundation in the Lord and may tend toward Him, lest perhaps those who build this city shall have labored in vain.[10*]

Therefore, this Sacred Synod encourages and praises the men and women, Brothers and Sisters, who in monasteries, or in schools and hospitals, or in the missions, adorn the Bride of Christ by their unswerving and humble faithfulness in their chosen consecration and render generous services of all kinds to mankind.

47. Let each of the faithful called to the profession of the evangelical counsels, therefore, carefully see to it that he persevere and ever grow in that vocation God has given him. Let him do this for the increased holiness of the Church, for the greater glory of the one and undivided Trinity, which in and through Christ is the fount and the source of all holiness.

CHAPTER VII

The Eschatological Nature of the Pilgrim Church
and its Union with the Church in Heaven

48. The Church, to which we are all called in Christ Jesus, and in which we acquire sanctity through the grace of God, will attain its full perfection only in the glory of heaven, when there will come the time of the restoration of all things.[237] At that time the human race as well as the entire world, which is intimately related to man and attains to its end through him, will be perfectly re-established in Christ.[238]

Christ, having been lifted up from the earth has drawn all to Himself.[239] Rising from the dead[240] He sent His life-giving Spirit upon His disciples and through Him has established His Body which is the Church as the universal sacrament of salvation. Sitting at the right hand of the Father, He is continually active in the world that He might lead men to the Church and through it join them to Himself and that He might make them partakers of His glorious life by nourishing them with His own Body and Blood. Therefore the promised restoration which we are awaiting has already begun in Christ, is carried forward in the mission of the Holy Spirit, and through Him continues in the Church in which we learn the meaning of our terrestrial life through our faith, while we perform with hope in the future the work committed to us in this world by the Father, and thus work out our salvation.[241]

Already the final age of the world has come upon us[242] and the renovation of the world is irrevocably decreed and is already anticipated in some kind of a real way; for the Church already on this earth is signed with a sanctity which is real although imperfect. However, until there shall be new heavens and a new earth in which justice dwells,[243] the pilgrim Church in her sacraments and institutions, which pertain to this present time, has the appearance of this world which is passing and she herself dwells among creatures who groan and travail in pain until now and await the revelation of the sons of God.[244]

Joined with Christ in the Church and signed with the Holy Spirit "who is the pledge of our inheritance,"[245] truly we are called and we are sons of God[246] but we have not yet appeared with Christ in glory,[247] in which we shall be like to God, since we shall see Him as He is.[248] And therefore "while we are in the body, we are exiled from the Lord[249] and having the first-fruits of the Spirit we groan within ourselves[250] and we desire to be with Christ."[251] By that same charity however, we are urged to live more for Him, who died for us and rose again.[252] We strive therefore to please God in all things[253] and we put on the armor of God, that we may be able to stand against the wiles of the devil and resist in the evil day.[254] Since however we know not the day nor the hour, on Our Lord's advice we must be constantly vigilant so that, having finished the course of our earthly life,[255] we may merit to enter into the marriage feast with Him and to be numbered among the blessed[256] and that we may not be ordered to go into eternal fire[257] like the wicked and slothful servant,[258] into the exterior darkness where "there will be the weeping and the gnashing of teeth."[259]

For before we reign with Christ in glory, all of us will be made manifest "before the tribunal of Christ, so that each one may receive what he has won through the body, according to his works, whether good or evil"[260] and at the end of the world "they who have done good shall come forth unto resurrection of life; but those who have done evil unto resurrection of judgment."[261] Reckoning therefore that "the sufferings of the present time are not worthy to be compared with the glory to come that will be revealed in us,"[262] strong in faith we look for the "blessed hope and the glorious coming of our great God and Savior, Jesus Christ"[263] "who will refashion the body of our lowliness, conforming it to the body of His glory,"[264] and who will come "to be glorified in His saints and to be marveled at in all those who have believed."[265]

The Pilgrim Church
Lumen Gentium 48

**Pope
St. John Paul II**

———

*Redemptoris
Mater* 25

The Second Vatican Council speaks of the pilgrim Church, establishing an analogy with the Israel of the Old Covenant journeying through the desert. The journey also has an external character, visible in the time and space in which it historically takes place. For the Church "is destined to extend to all regions of the earth and so enters into the history of mankind," but at the same time "it transcends all limits of time and confines of race" (LG 9). And yet the essential character of her pilgrimage is interior: it is a question of a pilgrimage through faith, by "the power of the risen Lord" (LG 8), a pilgrimage in the Holy Spirit, given to the Church as the invisible Comforter (*parakletos*) (see John 14:26; 15:26; 16:7): "Moving forward through trial and tribulation, the Church is strengthened by the power of God's grace, which was promised to her by the Lord, so that . . . moved by the Holy Spirit [she] may never cease to renew herself, until through the Cross she arrives at the light which knows no setting" (LG 9).

49. Until the Lord shall come in His majesty, and all the angels with Him[266] and death being destroyed, all things are subject to Him,[267] some of His disciples are exiles on earth, some having died are purified, and others are in glory beholding "clearly God Himself triune and one, as He is";[1*] but all in various ways and degrees are in communion in the same charity of God and neighbor and all sing the same hymn of glory to our God. For all who are in Christ, having His Spirit, form one Church and cleave together in Him.[268] Therefore the union of the wayfarers with the brethren who have gone to sleep in the peace of Christ is not in the least weakened or interrupted, but on the contrary, according to the perpetual faith of the Church, is strengthened by communication of spiritual goods.[2*] For by reason of the fact that those in heaven are more closely united with Christ, they establish the whole Church more firmly in holiness, lend nobility to the worship which the Church offers to God here on earth, and in many ways contribute to its greater edification.[269] [(3*)] For after they have been received into their heavenly home and are present to the Lord,[270] through Him and with Him and in Him they do not cease to intercede with the Father for us,[4*] showing forth the merits which they won on earth through the one Mediator between God and man,[271] serving God in all things and filling up in their flesh those things which are lacking of the sufferings of Christ for His Body which is the Church.[272] [(5*)] Thus by their brotherly interest our weakness is greatly strengthened.

50. Fully conscious of this communion of the whole Mystical Body of Jesus Christ, the pilgrim Church from the very first ages of the Christian religion has cultivated with great piety the memory of the dead,[6*] and "because it is a holy and wholesome thought to pray for the dead that they may be loosed from their sins,"[273] also offers suffrages for them. The Church has always believed that the apostles and Christ's martyrs who had given the supreme witness of faith and charity by the shedding of their blood, are closely joined with us in Christ, and she has always venerated them with special devotion, together with the Blessed Virgin Mary and the holy angels.[7*] The Church has piously implored the aid of their intercession. To these were soon added also those who had more closely imitated Christ's virginity and poverty,[8*] and finally others whom the outstanding practice of the Christian virtues[9*] and the divine charisms recommended to the pious devotion and imitation of the faithful.[10*]

When we look at the lives of those who have faithfully followed Christ, we are inspired with a new reason for seeking the City that is to come[274] and at the same time we are shown a most safe path by which among the vicissitudes of this world, in keeping with the state in life and condition proper to each of us, we will be able to arrive at perfect union with Christ, that is, perfect holiness.[11*] In the lives of those who, sharing in our humanity, are however more perfectly transformed into the image of Christ,[275] God vividly manifests His presence and His face to men. He speaks to us in them, and gives us a sign of His Kingdom,[12*] to which we are strongly drawn, having so great a cloud of witnesses over us[276] and such a witness to the truth of the Gospel.

Nor is it by the title of example only that we cherish the memory of those in heaven, but still more in order that the union of the whole Church may be strengthened in the Spirit by the practice of fraternal charity.[277] For just as Christian communion among wayfarers brings us closer to Christ, so our companionship with the saints joins us to Christ, from Whom as from its Fountain and Head issues every grace and the very life of the people of God.[13*] It is supremely fitting, therefore, that we love those friends and coheirs of Jesus Christ, who are also our brothers and extraordinary benefactors, that we render due thanks to God for them[14*] and "suppliantly invoke them and have recourse to their prayers, their power and help in obtaining benefits from God through His Son, Jesus Christ, who is our Redeemer and Savior."[15*] For every genuine testimony of love shown by us to those in heaven, by its very nature tends toward and terminates in Christ who is the "crown of all saints,"[16*] and through Him, in God Who is wonderful in his saints and is magnified in them.[17*]

Our union with the Church in heaven is put into effect in its noblest manner especially in the sacred Liturgy, wherein the power of the Holy Spirit acts upon us through sacramental signs. Then, with combined rejoicing we celebrate together the praise of the divine majesty;[18*] then all those from every tribe and tongue and people and nation[278] who have been redeemed by the blood of Christ and gathered together into one Church, with one song of praise magnify the one and triune God. Celebrating the Eucharistic sacrifice therefore, we are most closely united to the Church in heaven in communion with and venerating the memory first of all of the glorious ever-Virgin Mary, of Blessed Joseph and the blessed apostles and martyrs, and of all the saints.[19*]

51. This Sacred Council accepts with great devotion this venerable faith of our ancestors regarding this vital fellowship with our brethren who are in heavenly glory or who having died are still being purified; and it proposes again the decrees of the Second Council of Nicea,[20*] the Council of Florence,[21*] and the Council of Trent.[22*] And at the same time, in conformity with our own pastoral interests, we urge all concerned, if any abuses, excesses, or defects have crept in here or there, to do what is in their power to remove or correct them, and to restore all things to a fuller praise of Christ and of God. Let them therefore teach the faithful that the authentic cult of the saints consists not so much in the multiplying of external acts, but rather in the greater intensity of our love, whereby, for our own greater good and that of the whole Church, we seek from the saints "example in their way of life, fellowship in their communion, and aid by their intercession."[23*] On the other hand, let them teach the faithful that our communion with those in heaven, provided that it is understood in the fuller light of faith according to its genuine nature, in no way weakens, but conversely, more thoroughly enriches the latreutic worship we give to God the Father, through Christ, in the Spirit.[24*]

For all of us, who are sons of God and constitute one family in Christ,[279] as long as we remain in communion with one another in mutual charity and in one praise of the most holy Trinity, are corresponding with the intimate vocation of the Church and partaking in foretaste the liturgy of consummate glory.[25*] For when Christ shall appear and the glorious resurrection of the dead will take place, the glory of God will light up the heavenly City and the Lamb will be the lamp thereof.[280] Then the whole Church of the saints in the supreme happiness of charity will adore God and "the Lamb who was slain,"[281] proclaiming with one voice: "To Him who sits upon the throne, and to the Lamb blessing, and honor, and glory, and dominion forever and ever."[282]

Models of Holiness
Lumen Gentium 50–51

Pope St. John Paul II
—
Veritatis Splendor
107

Just as it does in proclaiming the truths of faith, and even more so in presenting the foundations and content of Christian morality, the new evangelization will show its authenticity and unleash all its missionary force when it is carried out through the gift not only of the word proclaimed but also of the word lived. In particular, *the life of holiness* which is resplendent in so many members of the People of God, humble and often unseen, constitutes the simplest and most attractive way to perceive at once the beauty of truth, the liberating force of God's love, and the value of unconditional fidelity to all the demands of the Lord's law, even in the most difficult situations. For this reason, the Church, as a wise teacher of morality, has always invited believers to seek and to find in the Saints, and above all in the Virgin Mother of God "full of grace" and "all-holy," the model, the strength, and the joy needed to live a life in accordance with God's commandments and the Beatitudes of the Gospel.

The lives of the saints, as a reflection of the goodness of God—the One who "alone is good" (Mark 10:18; see Luke 18:19)—constitute not only a genuine profession of faith and an incentive for sharing it with others, but also a glorification of God and his infinite holiness. The life of holiness thus brings to full expression and effectiveness the threefold and unitary *munus propheticum, sacerdotale et regale* [prophetic, priestly, and kingly office] which every Christian receives as a gift by being born again "of water and the Spirit" (John 3:5) in Baptism. His moral life has the value of a "spiritual worship" (Rom. 12:1; see Phil. 3:3), flowing from and nourished by that inexhaustible source of holiness and glorification of God which is found in the Sacraments, especially in the Eucharist: by sharing in the sacrifice of the Cross, the Christian partakes of Christ's self-giving love and is equipped and committed to live this same charity in all his thoughts and deeds. In the moral life the Christian's royal service is also made evident and effective: with the help of grace, the more one obeys the new law of the Holy Spirit, the more one grows in the freedom to which he or she is called by the service of truth, charity, and justice.

CHAPTER VIII

The Blessed Virgin Mary, Mother of God,
in the Mystery of Christ and the Church

I. Introduction

52. Wishing in His supreme goodness and wisdom to effect the redemption of the world, "when the fullness of time came, God sent His Son, born of a woman . . . that we might receive the adoption of sons."[283] "He for us men, and for our salvation, came down from heaven, and was incarnate by the Holy Spirit from the Virgin Mary."[1*] This divine mystery of salvation is revealed to us and continued in the Church, which the Lord established as His body. Joined to Christ the Head and in the unity of fellowship with all His saints, the faithful must in the first place reverence the memory "of the glorious ever Virgin Mary, Mother of our God and Lord Jesus Christ."[2*]

53. The Virgin Mary, who at the message of the angel received the Word of God in her heart and in her body and gave Life to the world, is acknowledged and honored as being truly the Mother of God and Mother of the Redeemer. Redeemed by reason of the merits of her Son and united to Him by a close and indissoluble tie, she is endowed with the high office and dignity of being the Mother of the Son of God, by which account she is also the beloved daughter of the Father and the temple of the Holy Spirit. Because of this gift of sublime grace she far surpasses all creatures, both in heaven and on earth. At the same time, however, because she belongs to the offspring of Adam she is one with all those who are to be saved. She is "the mother of the members of Christ . . . having cooperated by charity that the faithful might be born in the Church, who are members of that Head."[3*] Wherefore she is hailed as a pre-eminent and singular member of the Church, and as its type and excellent exemplar in faith and charity. The Catholic Church, taught by the Holy Spirit, honors her with filial affection and piety as a most beloved mother.

54. Wherefore this Holy Synod, in expounding the doctrine on the Church, in which the divine Redeemer works salvation, intends to describe with diligence both the role of the Blessed Virgin in the mystery of the Incarnate Word and the Mystical Body, and the duties of redeemed mankind toward the Mother of God, who is mother of Christ and mother

of men, particularly of the faithful. It does not, however, have it in mind to give a complete doctrine on Mary, nor does it wish to decide those questions which the work of theologians has not yet fully clarified. Those opinions therefore may be lawfully retained which are propounded in Catholic schools concerning her, who occupies a place in the Church which is the highest after Christ and yet very close to us.[4*]

II. The Role of the Blessed Mother in the Economy of Salvation

55. The Sacred Scriptures of both the Old and the New Testament, as well as ancient Tradition show the role of the Mother of the Savior in the economy of salvation in an ever clearer light and draw attention to it. The books of the Old Testament describe the history of salvation, by which the coming of Christ into the world was slowly prepared. These earliest documents, as they are read in the Church and are understood in the light of a further and full revelation, bring the figure of the woman, Mother of the Redeemer, into a gradually clearer light. When it is looked at in this way, she is already prophetically foreshadowed in the promise of victory over the serpent which was given to our first parents after their fall into sin.[284] Likewise she is the Virgin who shall conceive and bear a son, whose name will be called Emmanuel.[285] She stands out among the poor and humble of the Lord, who confidently hope for and receive salvation from Him. With her the exalted Daughter of Sion, and after a long expectation of the promise, the times are fulfilled and the new Economy established, when the Son of God took a human nature from her, that He might in the mysteries of His flesh free man from sin.

56. The Father of mercies willed that the incarnation should be preceded by the acceptance of her who was predestined to be the mother of His Son, so that just as a woman contributed to death, so also a woman should contribute to life. That is true in outstanding fashion of the mother of Jesus, who gave to the world Him who is Life itself and who renews all things, and who was enriched by God with the gifts which befit such a role. It is no wonder therefore that the usage prevailed among the Fathers whereby they called the mother of God entirely holy and free from all stain of sin, as though fashioned by the Holy Spirit and formed as a new creature.[5*] Adorned from the first instant of her conception with the radiance of an entirely unique holiness, the Virgin of Nazareth is greeted,

on God's command, by an angel messenger as "full of grace,"[286] and to the heavenly messenger she replies: "Behold the handmaid of the Lord, be it done unto me according to thy word."[287] Thus Mary, a daughter of Adam, consenting to the divine Word, became the mother of Jesus, the one and only Mediator. Embracing God's salvific will with a full heart and impeded by no sin, she devoted herself totally as a handmaid of the Lord to the person and work of her Son, under Him and with Him, by the grace of almighty God, serving the mystery of redemption. Rightly therefore the holy Fathers see her as used by God not merely in a passive way, but as freely cooperating in the work of human salvation through faith and obedience. For, as St. Irenaeus says, she "being obedient, became the cause of salvation for herself and for the whole human race."[6*] Hence not a few of the early Fathers gladly assert in their preaching, "The knot of Eve's disobedience was untied by Mary's obedience; what the virgin Eve bound through her unbelief, the Virgin Mary loosened by her faith."[7*] Comparing Mary with Eve, they call her "the Mother of the living,"[8*] and still more often they say: "death through Eve, life through Mary."[9*]

57. This union of the Mother with the Son in the work of salvation is made manifest from the time of Christ's virginal conception up to His death. It is shown first of all when Mary, arising in haste to go to visit Elizabeth, is greeted by her as blessed because of her belief in the promise of salvation and the precursor leaped with joy in the womb of his mother.[288] This union is manifest also at the birth of Our Lord, who did not diminish His mother's virginal integrity but sanctified it,[10*] when the Mother of God joyfully showed her firstborn Son to the shepherds and Magi. When she presented Him to the Lord in the temple, making the offering of the poor, she heard Simeon foretelling at the same time that her Son would be a sign of contradiction and that a sword would pierce the mother's soul, that out of many hearts thoughts might be revealed.[289] When the Child Jesus was lost and they had sought Him sorrowing, His parents found Him in the temple, taken up with the things that were His Father's business; and they did not understand the word of their Son. His Mother indeed kept these things to be pondered over in her heart.[290]

58. In the public life of Jesus, Mary makes significant appearances. This is so even at the very beginning, when at the marriage feast of Cana, moved with pity, she brought about by her intercession the beginning of miracles

of Jesus the Messiah.[291] In the course of her Son's preaching she received the words whereby in extolling a kingdom beyond the calculations and bonds of flesh and blood, He declared blessed[292] those who heard and kept the word of God, as she was faithfully doing.[293] After this manner the Blessed Virgin advanced in her pilgrimage of faith, and faithfully persevered in her union with her Son unto the cross, where she stood, in keeping with the divine plan,[294] grieving exceedingly with her only begotten Son, uniting herself with a maternal heart with His sacrifice, and lovingly consenting to the immolation of this Victim which she herself had brought forth. Finally, she was given by the same Christ Jesus dying on the cross as a mother to His disciple with these words: "Woman, behold thy son."[295] [(11*)]

59. But since it has pleased God not to manifest solemnly the mystery of the salvation of the human race before He would pour forth the Spirit promised by Christ, we see the apostles before the day of Pentecost "persevering with one mind in prayer with the women and Mary the Mother of Jesus, and with His brethren,"[296] and Mary by her prayers imploring the gift of the Spirit, who had already overshadowed her in the Annunciation. Finally, the Immaculate Virgin, preserved free from all guilt of original sin,[12*] on the completion of her earthly sojourn, was taken up body and soul into heavenly glory,[13*] and exalted by the Lord as Queen of the universe, that she might be the more fully conformed to her Son, the Lord of lords[297] and the conqueror of sin and death.[14*]

III. On the Blessed Virgin and the Church

60. There is but one Mediator as we know from the words of the apostle, "for there is one God and one mediator of God and men, the man Christ Jesus, who gave himself a redemption for all."[298] The maternal duty of Mary toward men in no wise obscures or diminishes this unique mediation of Christ, but rather shows His power. For all the salvific influence of the Blessed Virgin on men originates, not from some inner necessity, but from the divine pleasure. It flows forth from the superabundance of the merits of Christ, rests on His mediation, depends entirely on it and draws all its power from it. In no way does it impede, but rather does it foster the immediate union of the faithful with Christ.

61. Predestined from eternity by that decree of divine providence which

determined the incarnation of the Word to be the Mother of God, the Blessed Virgin was on this earth the virgin Mother of the Redeemer, and above all others and in a singular way the generous associate and humble handmaid of the Lord. She conceived, brought forth, and nourished Christ. She presented Him to the Father in the temple, and was united with Him by compassion as He died on the Cross. In this singular way she cooperated by her obedience, faith, hope, and burning charity in the work of the Savior in giving back supernatural life to souls. Wherefore she is our mother in the order of grace.

62. This maternity of Mary in the order of grace began with the consent which she gave in faith at the Annunciation and which she sustained without wavering beneath the cross, and lasts until the eternal fulfillment of all the elect. Taken up to heaven she did not lay aside this salvific duty, but by her constant intercession continued to bring us the gifts of eternal salvation.[15*] By her maternal charity, she cares for the brethren of her Son, who still journey on earth surrounded by dangers and cultics, until they are led into the happiness of their true home. Therefore the Blessed Virgin is invoked by the Church under the titles of Advocate, Auxiliatrix, Adjutrix, and Mediatrix.[16*] This, however, is to be so understood that it neither takes away from nor adds anything to the dignity and efficaciousness of Christ the one Mediator.[17*]

For no creature could ever be counted as equal with the Incarnate Word and Redeemer. Just as the priesthood of Christ is shared in various ways both by the ministers and by the faithful, and as the one goodness of God is really communicated in different ways to His creatures, so also the unique mediation of the Redeemer does not exclude but rather gives rise to a manifold cooperation which is but a sharing in this one source.

The Church does not hesitate to profess this subordinate role of Mary. It knows it through unfailing experience of it and commends it to the hearts of the faithful, so that encouraged by this maternal help they may the more intimately adhere to the Mediator and Redeemer.

63. By reason of the gift and role of divine maternity, by which she is united with her Son, the Redeemer, and with His singular graces and functions, the Blessed Virgin is also intimately united with the Church. As St. Ambrose taught, the Mother of God is a type of the Church in the order of faith, charity, and perfect union with Christ.[18*] For in the

mystery of the Church, which is itself rightly called mother and virgin, the Blessed Virgin stands out in eminent and singular fashion as exemplar both of virgin and mother.[19*] By her belief and obedience, not knowing man but overshadowed by the Holy Spirit, as the new Eve she brought forth on earth the very Son of the Father, showing an undefiled faith, not in the word of the ancient serpent, but in that of God's messenger. The Son whom she brought forth is He whom God placed as the firstborn among many brethren,[299] namely the faithful, in whose birth and education she cooperates with a maternal love.

64. The Church indeed, contemplating her hidden sanctity, imitating her charity, and faithfully fulfilling the Father's will, by receiving the word of God in faith becomes herself a mother. By her preaching she brings forth to a new and immortal life the sons who are born to her in baptism, conceived of the Holy Spirit and born of God. She herself is a virgin, who keeps the faith given to her by her Spouse whole and entire. Imitating the mother of her Lord, and by the power of the Holy Spirit, she keeps with virginal purity an entire faith, a firm hope, and a sincere charity.[20*]

65. But while in the most holy Virgin the Church has already reached that perfection whereby she is without spot or wrinkle, the followers of Christ still strive to increase in holiness by conquering sin.[300] And so they turn their eyes to Mary who shines forth to the whole community of the elect as the model of virtues. Piously meditating on her and contemplating her in the light of the Word made man, the Church with reverence enters more intimately into the great mystery of the Incarnation and becomes more and more like her Spouse. For Mary, who since her entry into salvation history unites in herself and re-echoes the greatest teachings of the faith as she is proclaimed and venerated, calls the faithful to her Son and His sacrifice and to the love of the Father. Seeking after the glory of Christ, the Church becomes more like her exalted Type, and continually progresses in faith, hope, and charity, seeking and doing the will of God in all things. Hence the Church, in her apostolic work also, justly looks to her, who, conceived of the Holy Spirit, brought forth Christ, who was born of the Virgin that through the Church He may be born and may increase in the hearts of the faithful also. The Virgin in her own life lived an example of that maternal love, by which it behooves that all should be animated who cooperate in the apostolic mission of the Church for the regeneration of men.

Mary's Pilgrimage of Faith

Lumen Gentium 63–65

Pope St. John Paul II

Redemptoris Mater 5–6

The Second Vatican Council, by presenting Mary in the mystery of Christ, also finds the path to a deeper understanding of the mystery of the Church. Mary, as the Mother of Christ, is in a particular way united with the Church, "which the Lord established as His body" (LG 52). It is significant that the conciliar text places this truth about the Church as the Body of Christ (according to the teaching of the Pauline Letters) in close proximity to the truth that the Son of God "through the power of the Holy Spirit was born of the Virgin Mary." The reality of the Incarnation finds a sort of extension in the mystery of the Church—the Body of Christ. And one cannot think of the reality of the Incarnation without referring to Mary, the Mother of the Incarnate Word. . . .

I wish to consider primarily that "pilgrimage of faith" in which "the Blessed Virgin advanced," faithfully preserving her union with Christ (see LG 58). In this way the "twofold bond" which unites the Mother of God with Christ and with the Church takes on historical significance. Nor is it just a question of the Virgin Mother's life-story, of her personal journey of faith and "the better part" which is hers in the mystery of salvation; it is also a question of the history of the whole People of God, of all those who take part in the same "pilgrimage of faith."

The Council expresses this when it states in another passage that Mary "has gone before," becoming "a type of the Church in the order of faith, charity, and perfect union with Christ." This "going before" as a figure or model is in reference to the intimate mystery of the Church, as she actuates and accomplishes her own saving mission by uniting in herself—as Mary did—the qualities of mother and virgin. She is a virgin who "keeps the faith given to her by her Spouse whole and entire" and "becomes herself a mother," for "she brings forth to a new and immortal life the sons who are . . . conceived of the Holy Spirit and born of God."

All this is accomplished in a great historical process, comparable "to a journey." The pilgrimage of faith indicates the interior history, that is, the story of souls. But it is also the story of all human beings, subject here on earth to transitoriness, and part of the historical dimension. . . . We wish to concentrate first of all on the present, which in itself is not yet history, but which nevertheless is constantly forming it, also in the sense of the history of salvation. Here there opens up a broad prospect, within which the Blessed Virgin Mary continues to "go before" the People of God. Her exceptional pilgrimage of faith represents a constant point of reference for the Church, for individuals and for communities, for peoples and nations and, in a sense, for all humanity. It is indeed difficult to encompass and measure its range.

The Council emphasizes that the Mother of God is already the eschatological fulfillment of the Church: "In the most holy Virgin the Church has already reached that perfection whereby she is without spot or wrinkle"; and at the same time the Council says that "the followers of Christ still strive to increase in holiness by conquering sin. And so they turn their eyes to Mary who shines forth to the whole community of the elect as the model of virtues." The pilgrimage of faith no longer belongs to the Mother of the Son of God: glorified at the side of her Son in heaven, Mary has already crossed the threshold between faith and that vision which is "face to face" (1 Cor. 13:12). At the same time, however, in this eschatological fulfillment, Mary does not cease to be the "Star of the Sea" (*Maris Stella*) for all those who are still on the journey of faith. If they lift their eyes to her from their earthly existence, they do so because "the Son whom she brought forth is He whom God placed as the firstborn among many brethren," and also because in the "birth and education" of these brothers and sisters "she cooperates with a maternal love."

IV. The Cult of the Blessed Virgin in the Church

66. Placed by the grace of God, as God's Mother, next to her Son, and exalted above all angels and men, Mary intervened in the mysteries of Christ and is justly honored by a special cult in the Church. Clearly from earliest times the Blessed Virgin is honored under the title of Mother of God, under whose protection the faithful took refuge in all their dangers and necessities.[21*] Hence after the Synod of Ephesus the cult of the people of God toward Mary wonderfully increased in veneration and love, in invocation and imitation, according to her own prophetic words: "All generations shall call me blessed, because He that is mighty hath done great things to me."[301] This cult, as it always existed, although it is altogether singular, differs essentially from the cult of adoration which is offered to the Incarnate Word, as well to the Father and the Holy Spirit, and it is most favorable to it. The various forms of piety toward the Mother of God, which the Church within the limits of sound and orthodox doctrine, according to the conditions of time and place, and the nature and ingenuity of the faithful has approved, bring it about that while the Mother is honored, the Son, through whom all things have their being[302] and in whom it has pleased the Father that all fullness should dwell,[303] is rightly known, loved, and glorified and that all His commands are observed.

67. This most Holy Synod deliberately teaches this Catholic doctrine and at the same time admonishes all the sons of the Church that the cult, especially the liturgical cult, of the Blessed Virgin, be generously fostered, and the practices and exercises of piety, recommended by the magisterium of the Church toward her in the course of centuries be made of great moment, and those decrees, which have been given in the early days regarding the cult of images of Christ, the Blessed Virgin, and the saints, be religiously observed.[22*] But it exhorts theologians and preachers of the divine word to abstain zealously both from all gross exaggerations as well as from petty narrow-mindedness in considering the singular dignity of the Mother of God.[23*] Following the study of Sacred Scripture, the Holy Fathers, the doctors, and liturgies of the Church, and under the guidance of the Church's magisterium, let them rightly illustrate the duties and privileges of the Blessed Virgin which always look to Christ, the source of all truth, sanctity, and piety. Let them assiduously keep away from whatever, either by word or deed, could lead separated brethren or

any other into error regarding the true doctrine of the Church. Let the faithful remember moreover that true devotion consists neither in sterile or transitory affection, nor in a certain vain credulity, but proceeds from true faith, by which we are led to know the excellence of the Mother of God, and we are moved to a filial love toward our mother and to the imitation of her virtues.

The Mother of the Church

Lumen Gentium 66–67

**Pope
St. John Paul II**

*Redemptor
Hominis 22*

Mary is Mother of the Church because, on account of the Eternal Father's ineffable choice (see LG 56) and due to the Spirit of Love's special action, she gave human life to the Son of God, "for whom and by whom all things exist" (1 Cor. 8:6) and from whom the whole of the People of God receives the grace and dignity of election. Her Son explicitly extended his Mother's maternity in a way that could easily be understood by every soul and every heart by designating, when he was raised on the Cross, his beloved disciple as her son. The Holy Spirit inspired her to remain in the Upper Room, after our Lord's Ascension, recollected in prayer and expectation, together with the Apostles, until the day of Pentecost, when the Church was to be born in visible form, coming forth from darkness. Later, all the generations of disciples, of those who confess and love Christ, like the Apostle John, spiritually took this Mother to their own homes, and she was thus included in the history of salvation and in the Church's mission from the very beginning, that is from the moment of the Annunciation. Accordingly, we who form today's generation of disciples of Christ all wish to unite ourselves with her in a special way. We do so with all our attachment to our ancient tradition and also with full respect and love for the members of all the Christian Communities.

We do so at the urging of the deep need of faith, hope, and charity. For if we feel a special need, in this difficult and responsible phase of the history of the Church and of mankind, to turn to Christ, who is Lord of the Church and Lord of man's history on account of the mystery of the Redemption, we believe that nobody else can bring us as Mary can into the divine and human dimension of this mystery. Nobody has been brought into it by God himself as Mary has. It is in this that the exceptional character of the grace of the divine Motherhood consists. Not only is the dignity of this Motherhood unique and unrepeatable in the history of the human race, but Mary's participation, due to this Maternity, in God's plan for man's salvation through the mystery of the Redemption is also unique in profundity and range of action.

V. Mary the sign of created hope and solace to the wandering people of God

68. In the interim just as the Mother of Jesus, glorified in body and soul in heaven, is the image and beginning of the Church as it is to be perfected in the world to come, so too does she shine forth on earth, until the day of the Lord shall come,[304] as a sign of sure hope and solace to the people of God during its sojourn on earth.

69. It gives great joy and comfort to this holy and general Synod that even among the separated brethren there are some who give due honor to the Mother of our Lord and Savior, especially among the Orientals, who with devout mind and fervent impulse give honor to the Mother of God, ever virgin.[24*] The entire body of the faithful pours forth instant supplications to the Mother of God and Mother of men that she, who aided the beginnings of the Church by her prayers, may now, exalted as she is above all the angels and saints, intercede before her Son in the fellowship of all the saints, until all families of people, whether they are honored with the title of Christian or whether they still do not know the Savior, may be happily gathered together in peace and harmony into one people of God, for the glory of the Most Holy and Undivided Trinity.

Each and all these items which are set forth in this dogmatic Constitution have met with the approval of the Council Fathers. And We by the apostolic power given Us by Christ together with the Venerable Fathers in the Holy Spirit, approve, decree, and establish it and command that what has thus been decided in the Council be promulgated for the glory of God.

—*Given in Rome at St. Peter's on November 21, 1964.*

APPENDIX

'Notificationes' Given by the Secretary General of the Council at the 123rd General Congrergation, November 16, 1964

A question has arisen regarding the precise theological note which should be attached to the doctrine that is set forth in the Schema de Ecclesia and is being put to a vote.

The Theological Commission has given the following response regarding the Modi that have to do with Chapter III of the de Ecclesia Schema: "As is self-evident, the Council's text must always be interpreted in accordance with the general rules that are known to all."

On this occasion the Theological Commission makes reference to its Declaration of March 6, 1964, the text of which we transcribe here:

"Taking conciliar custom into consideration and also the pastoral purpose of the present Council, the sacred Council defines as binding on the Church only those things in matters of faith and morals which it shall openly declare to be binding. The rest of the things which the sacred Council sets forth, inasmuch as they are the teaching of the Church's supreme magisterium, ought to be accepted and embraced by each and every one of Christ's faithful according to the mind of the sacred Council. The mind of the Council becomes known either from the matter treated or from its manner of speaking, in accordance with the norms of theological interpretation."

The following was published as an appendix to the official Latin version of the Constitution on the Church.

A preliminary note of explanation is being given to the Council Fathers from higher-authority, regarding the Modi bearing on Chapter III of the Schema de Ecclesia; the doctrine set forth in Chapter III ought to be explained and understood in accordance with the meaning and intent of this explanatory note.

Preliminary Note of Explanation

The Commission has decided to preface the assessment of the Modi with the following general observations.

1. "College" is not understood in a strictly juridical sense, that is as a group of equals who entrust their power to their president, but as a stable group whose structure and authority must be learned from Revelation. For this reason, in reply to Modus 12 it is expressly said of the Twelve that the Lord set them up "as a college or stable group." See also Modus 53, c.

For the same reason, the words "Ordo" or "Corpus" are used throughout with reference to the College of bishops. The parallel between Peter and the rest of the Apostles on the one hand, and between the Supreme Pontiff and the bishops on the other hand, does not imply the transmission of the Apostles' extraordinary power to their successors; nor does it imply, as is obvious, equality between the head of the College and its members, but only a proportionality between the first relationship (Peter-Apostles) and the second (Pope-bishops). Thus the Commission decided to write "pari ratione," not "eadem ratione," in n. 22. See Modus 57.

2. A person becomes a member of the College by virtue of Episcopal consecration and by hierarchical communion with the head of the College and with its members. See n. 22, end of 11.

In his consecration a person is given an ontological participation in the sacred functions [munera]; this is absolutely clear from Tradition, liturgical tradition included. The word "functions [munera]" is used deliberately instead of the word "powers [potestates]," because the latter word could be understood as a power fully ready to act. But for this power to be fully ready to act, there must be a further canonical or juridical determination through the hierarchical authority. This determination of power can consist in the granting of a particular office or in the allotment of subjects, and it is done according to the norms approved by the supreme authority. An additional norm of this sort is required by the very nature of the case, because it involves functions [munera] which must be exercised by many subjects cooperating in a hierarchical manner in accordance with Christ's will. It is evident that this "communion" was applied in the Church's life according to the circumstances of the time, before it was codified as law.

For this reason it is clearly stated that hierarchical communion with the head and members of the church is required. Communion is a notion which is held in high honor in the ancient Church (and also today, especially in the East). However, it is not understood as some kind of vague disposition, but as an organic reality which requires a juridical form and is animated by charity. Hence the Commission, almost unanimously, decided that this wording should be used: "in hierarchical communion." See Modus 40 and the statements on canonical mission (n. 24).

The documents of recent Pontiffs regarding the jurisdiction of bishops must be interpreted in terms of this necessary determination of powers.

3. The College, which does not exist without the head, is said "to exist also as the subject of supreme and full power in the universal Church." This must be admitted of necessity so that the fullness of power belonging to the Roman Pontiff is not called into question. For the College, always and of necessity, includes its head, because in the college he preserves unhindered his function as Christ's Vicar and as Pastor of the universal Church. In other words, it is not a distinction between the Roman Pontiff and the bishops taken collectively, but a distinction between the Roman Pontiff taken separately and the Roman Pontiff together with the bishops. Since the Supreme Pontiff is head of the College, he alone is able to perform certain actions which are not at all within the competence of the bishops, e.g., convoking the College and directing it, approving norms of action, etc. See Modus 81. It is up to the judgment of the Supreme Pontiff, to whose care Christ's whole flock has been entrusted, to determine, according to the needs of the Church as they change over the course of centuries, the way in which this care may best be exercised—whether in a personal or a collegial way. The Roman Pontiff, taking account of the Church's welfare, proceeds according to his own discretion in arranging, promoting, and approving the exercise of collegial activity.

4. As Supreme Pastor of the Church, the Supreme Pontiff can always exercise his power at will, as his very office demands. Though it is always in existence, the College is not as a result permanently engaged in strictly collegial activity; the Church's Tradition makes this clear. In other words, the College is not always "fully active [in actu pleno]"; rather, it acts as a college in the strict sense only from time to time and only with the consent of its head. The phrase "with the consent of its head" is used to avoid the idea of dependence on some kind of outsider; the term "consent" suggests rather communion between the head and the members, and implies the need for an act which belongs properly to the competence of the head. This is explicitly affirmed in n. 22, 12, and is explained at the end of that section. The word "only" takes in all cases. It is evident from this that the

norms approved by the supreme authority must always be observed. See Modus 84.

It is clear throughout that it is a question of the bishops acting in conjunction with their head, never of the bishops acting independently of the Pope. In the latter instance, without the action of the head, the bishops are not able to act as a College: this is clear from the concept of "College." This hierarchical communion of all the bishops with the Supreme Pontiff is certainly firmly established in Tradition.

N.B. Without hierarchical communion the ontologico-sacramental function [munus], which is to be distinguished from the juridico-canonical aspect, cannot be exercised. However, the Commission has decided that it should not enter into question of liceity and validity. These questions are left to theologians to discuss—specifically the question of the power exercised de facto among the separated Eastern Churches, about which there are various explanations.

+ PERICLE FELICI

Titular Archbishop of Samosata
Secretary General of the Second Vatican Ecumenical Council

NOTES

CHAPTER I

1   See Mark 16:15.
2   Col. 1:15.
3   Rom. 8:29.
4   See Eph. 1:4–5 and 10.
5   See John 19:34.
6   John 12:32.
7   1 Cor. 5:7.
8   See 1 Cor. 10:17.
9   See John 17:4.
10   See Eph. 1:18.
11   See John 4:14; 7:38–39.
12   See Rom. 8:10–11.
13   See Cor. 3:16; 6:19.
14   See Gal. 4:6; Rom. 8:15–16 and 26.
15   See John 16:13.
16   See Eph. 1:11–12; 1 Cor. 12:4; Gal. 5:22.
17   Rev. 22:17.
18   Mark 1:15; see Matt. 4:17.
19   Mark 4:14.
20   Luke 12:32.
21   See Mark 4:26–29.
22   Luke 11:20; see Matt. 12:28.
23   Mark 10:45.
24   See Acts 2:36; Heb. 5:6; 7:17–21.
25   See Acts 2:33.
26   John 10:1–10.
27   See Isa. 40:11; Exod. 34:11ff.
28   See John 10:11; 1 Pet. 5:4.
29   See John 10:11–15.
30   1 Cor. 3:9.
31   1 Rom. 11:13–26.
32   Matt. 21:33–43; see Isa. 5:1 ff.
33   John 15:1–5.
34   1 Cor. 3:9.
35   Matt. 21:42; see Acts 4:11; 1 Pet. 2:7; Ps. 117:2.
36   See 1 Cor. 3:11.
37   1 Tim. 3:15.
38   Eph. 2:19–22.
39   Rev. 21:3.
40   1 Pet. 2:5.
41   Rev. 21:16.

42   Gal. 4:26; see Rev. 12:17.

43   Rev. 19:7; 21:2 and 9; 22:17

44   Eph. 5:26.

45   Eph. 5:29.

46   See Eph. 5:24.

47   See Eph. 3:19.

48   See 2 Cor. 5:6.

49   See Col. 3:1–4.

50   See Gal. 6:15; 2 Cor. 5:17.

51   1 Cor. 12:13.

52   Rom. 6:15.

53   1 Cor. 10:17.

54   See 1 Cor. 12:27.

55   Rom. 12:5.

56   See 1 Cor. 12:12.

57   See 1 Cor. 12:1–11.

58   See 1 Cor. 14.

59   See 1 Cor. 12:26.

60   See Col. 1:15–18.

61   See Eph. 1:18–23.

62   See Gal. 4:19.

63   See Phil. 3:21; 2 Tim. 2:11; Eph. 2:6; Col. 2:12; etc.

64   See Rom. 8:17.

65   Col. 2:19.

66   See Eph. 4:11–16.

67   See Eph. 4:23.

68   See Eph. 5:25–28.

69   Ibid. 23–24.

70   Col. 2:9.

71   See Eph. 1:22–23.

72   See Eph. 3:19.

73   See Eph. 4:16.

74   John 21:17.

75   See Matt. 28:18f.

76   1 Tim. 3:15.

77   Phil. 2:6.

78   2 Cor. 8:9.

79   Luke 4:18.

80   Luke 19:10.

81   Heb. 7:26.

82   2 Cor. 5:21.

83   See Heb. 2:17.

84   See 1 Cor. 11:26.

CHAPTER II

85   See Acts 10:35.

86   Jer. 31:31–34.

87   See 1 Cor. 11:25.

88   See 1 Pet. 1:23.

89   See John 3:5–6.

90   1 Pet. 2:9–10.

91   Rom. 4:25.

92   See John 13:34.

93   See Col. 3:4.

94   Rom. 8:21.

95   See Matt. 5:13–16.

96   Neh. 13:1; see Deut. 23:1 ff; Num. 20:4.

97   See Heb. 13:14.

98   See Matt. 16:18.

99   See Acts 20:28.

100   See Heb. 5:1–5.

101   See Rev. 6:1; see 5:9–10.

102   See 1 Pet. 2:4–10.

103   See Acts 2:42–47.

104   See Rom. 12:1.

105   See 1 Pet. 3:15.

106   See James 5:14–16.

107   See Rom. 8:17; Col. 1:24; 2 Tim. 2:11–12; 1 Pet. 4:13.

108   See Eph. 5:32.

109   See 1 Cor. 7:7.

110   See Heb. 13:15.

111   See 1 John 2:20, 21

112   See 1 Thess. 2:13.

113   See Jude 3.

114   1 Cor. 12:11.

115   1 Cor. 12:7.

116   See 1 Thess. 5:12, 19–21.

117   See John 11:52.

118   See Heb. 1:2.

119   See Acts 2:42.

120   See John 18:36

121   See Ps. 2:8.

122   See Ps. 71 (72):10; Isa. 60:4–7; Rev. 21:24.

123   1 Pet. 4:10.

124   See Mark 16:16; John 3:5.

125   See Rom. 9:4–5.

126   See Rom. 11:28–29.

127   See Acts 17:25–28.

128   See 1 Tim. 2:4.

129 See Rom. 1:21, 25.

130 Mark 16:15.

131 See John 20:21.

132 Matt. 28:18–20.

133 See Acts 1:8.

134 1 Cor. 9:16.

135 Mal. 1:11.

CHAPTER III

136 John 20:21.

137 Mark 3:13–19; Matt. 10:1–42.

138 See Luke 6:13.

139 See John 21:15–17.

140 Rom. 1:16.

141 See Matt. 28:16–20; Mark 16:15; Luke 24:45–48; John 20:21–23.

142 See Matt. 28:20.

143 See Acts 2:1–26.

144 Acts 1:8.

145 See Mark 16:20.

146 See Rev. 21:14; Matt. 16:18; Eph. 2:20

147 See Matt. 28:20.

148 See Acts 20:28.

149 See Luke 10:16.

150 See 1 Cor. 4:15.

151 See 1 Cor. 4:1.

152 See Rom. 15:16; Acts 20:24.

153 See 2 Cor. 3:8–9.

154 See Acts 1:8, 2:4, John 20:22–23.

155 See 1 Tim. 4:14; 2 Tim. 1:6–7.

156 See Matt. 16:18–19.

157 See John 21:15 ff.

158 Matt. 16:19.

159 Matt. 18:18, 28:16–20.

160 See Matt. 5:10.

161 See Matt. 28:18; Mark 16:15–16; Acts 26:17 ff..

162 See Acts 1:8–2:1 ff, 9:15.

163 See Acts 1:17, 25; 21:19; Rom. 11:13; 1 Tim. 1:12.

164 See Matt. 13:52.

165 See 2 Tim. 4:1–4.

166 See Luke 22:32.

167 See 1. Thess. 1:5.

168 See Rom. 1:16.

169 See Luke 22:26–27.

170 See Matt. 20:28; Mark 10:45.

171 See John 10:11.

172 See Heb. 5:1–2.

173   See Heb. 13:17.

174   See Rom. 1:14–15.

175   See 1 Cor. 4:15.

176   John 10:36.

177   Heb. 5:1–10, 7:24, 9:11–28.

178   1 Tim. 2:5.

179   See 1 Cor. 11:26.

180   See Heb. 9:11–28.

181   Heb. 5:1–4.

182   John 4:24.

183   See 1 Tim. 5:17.

184   See Eph. 4:12.

185   See John 15:15.

186   See 1 Cor. 4:15; 1 Pet. 1:23.

187   1 Pet. 5:3.

188   See 1 Cor. 1:2; 2 Cor. 1:1

189   See Luke 15:4–7.

CHAPTER IV

190   Eph. 4:15–16.

191   Rom. 12:4–5.

192   See Eph. 4:5.

193   Gal. 3:28; see Col. 3:11.

194   See 2 Pet. 1:1.

195   1 Cor. 12:11.

196   See Matt. 20:28.

197   Eph. 4:7.

198   See Phil. 4:3; Rom. 16:3ff.

199   1 Pet. 2:5.

200   See Acts 2:17–18; Rev. 19:10.

201   See Eph. 5:16; Col. 4:5.

202   See Rom. 8:25.

203   Eph. 6:12

204   See Rev. 21:1.

205   See Heb. 11:1.

206   See Phil. 2:8–9.

207   See 1 Cor. 15:27

208   See Rom. 6:12.

209   See Rom. 8:21.

210   1 Cor. 3:23.

211   See Heb. 13:17.

212   See Gal. 5:12.

213   See Matt. 5:3–9.

214   See Eph. 5:25–26.

CHAPTER V

215 1 Thess. 4:3; see Eph. 1:4.

216 Matt. 5:48.

217 See Mark 12:30.

218 See John 13:34; 15:12.

219 Eph. 5:3.

220 Col. 3:12.

221 See Gal. 5:22; Rom. 6:22.

222 See James 3:2.

223 1 Matt. 6:12.

224 See 1 Pet. 5:3.

225 See 1 Tim. 3:8–10 and 12–13.

226 1 Pet. 5:10.

227 1 John 4:16.

228 See Rom. 5:5.

229 See Col. 3:14; Rom. 13:10.

230 See 1 John 3:16; John 15:13.

231 See 1 Cor. 7:32–34.

232 See Matt. 19:11; 1 Cor. 7:7.

233 Phil. 2:7–8.

234 2 Cor. 8:9.

235 See 1. Cor. 7:31ff.

CHAPTER VI

236 Ezek. 34:14.

CHAPTER VII

237 Acts 3:21.

238 See Eph. 1:10; Col. 1:20; 2 Pet. 3:10–13.

239 See John 12:32.

240 See Rom. 6:9.

241 See Phil. 2:12.

242 See 1 Cor. 10:11.

243 See 2 Pet. 3:13.

244 See Rom. 8:19–22.

245 Eph. 1:14.

246 See 1 John 3:1.

247 See Col. 3:4.

248 See 1 John 3:2.

249 2 Cor. 5:6.

250 See Rom. 8:23.

251 See Phil. 1:23.

252 See 2 Cor. 5:15.

253 See 2 Cor. 5:9.

254 See Eph. 6:11–13.

255 See Heb. 9:27.

256 See Matt. 25:31–46.

257 See Matt. 25:41.

258 See Matt. 25:26.

259 Matt. 22:13 and 25:30.

260 2 Cor. 5:10.

261 John 5:29; see Matt. 25:46.

262 Rom. 8:18; see 2 Tim. 2:11–12.

263 Titus 2:13.

264 Phil. 3:21.

265 2 Thess. 1:10.

266 See Matt. 25:31.

267 See 1 Cor. 15:26–27.

268 See Eph. 4:16.

269 See 1 Cor. 12:12–27.

270 See 2 Cor. 5:8.

271 See 1 Tim. 2:5.

272 See Col. 1:24.

273 2 Macc. 12:46.

274 See Heb. 13:14; 11:10.

275 See 2 Cor. 3:18.

276 See Heb. 12:1.

277 See Eph. 4:1–6.

278 See Rev. 5:9.

279 See Heb. 3:6.

280 See Rev. 21:24.

281 Rev. 5:12.

282 Rev. 5:13–14.

CHAPTER VIII

283 Gal. 4:4–5.

284 See Gen. 3:15.

285 See Isa. 7:14; see Mic. 5:2–3; Matt. 1:22–23.

286 See Luke 1:28.

287 Luke 1:38.

288 See Luke 1:41–45.

289 See Luke 2:34–35.

290 See Luke 2:41–51.

291 See John 2:1–11.

292 See Mark 3:35; Luke 11:27–28.

293 See Luke 2:19, 51.

294 See John 19:25.

295 See John 19:26–27.

296 Acts 1:14.

297 See Rev. 19:16.

298 1 Tim. 2:5–6.

299 Rom. 8:29.

300 See Eph. 5:27.

301 Luke 1:48.

302 See Col. 1:15–16.

303 Col. 1:19.

304 See 2 Pet. 3:10.

SUPPLEMENTARY NOTES

CHAPTER I

1* See S. Cyprianus, Epist. 64, 4: PL 3, 1017. CSEL (Hartcl), III B p. 720. S. Hilarius Pict., In Mt 23:6: PL 9, 1047. S. Augustinus, passim. S. Cyrillus Alex., Glaph in Gen. 2:10: PG 69, 110 A.

2* See S. Gregorius M., Hom in Evang. 19, 1: PL 76, 1154 B. S Augustinus, Serm. 341, 9, 11: PL 39, 1499 s. S. Io. Damascenus, Adv. Iconocl. 11: PG 96, 1357.

3* See Irenaeus, adv. Haer, III 24, 1: PG 7, 966 B; Harvey 2, 13i, ed. Sagnard, Sources Chr., p 398.

4* S. Cyprianus, De Orat Dom. 23: PL 4, 5S3, Hartel, III A, p. 28S. S. Augustinus, Serm. 71, 20, 33: PL 38, 463 s. S. Io. Damascenus, Adv. Iconocl. 12: PG 96, 1358 D.

5* See Origenes, In Matth. 16, 21: PG 13, 1443 C, Tertullianus Adv. Marc. 3, 7: PL 2, 357 C, CSEL 47, 3 p. 386. Pro documentis liturgicis, see Sacramentarium Gregorianum: PL 78, 160 B. Vel C. Mohlberg, Liber Sactamentorum romanae ecclesiae, Romao 1950, p. 111, XC:. fsDeus, qui ex omni coaptacione sanctorum aeternum tibi condis habitaculum. . . . Hymnus Urbs Ierusalem beata in Breviario monastico, et Coclest urbs Ierusalem in Breviario Romano.

6* See S. Thomas, Summa Theol. III, q. 62, a. 5, ad 1.

7* See Pius XII, Litt. Encycl Mystici Corporis, 29 iun. 1943 AAS 35 (1943), p. 208.

8* See Leo XIII, Epist. Encycl Divinum illud, 9 maii 1897: AAS 29 (1896–97) p. 6S0. Pius XII, Litt Encyl. Mystici Corporis, 1. c., pp 219–220; Denz. 2288 (3808).S. Augustinus, Serm. 268, 2: PL 38 232, ct alibi. S. Io. Chrysostomus n Eph. Hom. 9, 3: PG 62, 72. idymus Alex., Trin. 2, 1: PG 39 49 s. S. Thomas, In Col. 1:18 cet. 5 ed. Marietti, II, n. 46 Sieut constituitur unum eorpus ex nitate animae, ita Ecelesia ex unil atc Spiritus. . . .

9* Leo XIII, Litt. Encycl. Sapientiae christianae, 10 ian. 1890 AAS 22 (1889–90) p. 392. Id., Epist. Encycl. Satis cognitium, 29 iun. 1896; AAS 28 (1895–96) pp. 710 ct 724 ss. Pius XII, Litt. Encycl. Mystici Corporis, 1. c., pp. 199–200.

10* See Pius XII, Litt. Encycl. Mystici Corporis, 1. c., p. 221 ss. Id., Lin. Encycl. Humani genesis, 12 Aug. 1950: AAS 42 (1950) p. 571. 73 See Eph. 4:16.

11* Leo XIII, Epist. Encycl. Satis cognitum, 1. c., p. 713.

12* See Symbolum Apostolicum: Denz. 6–9 (10–13); Symb. Nic.-Const.: Denz. 86 (150), coll. Prof. fidei Trid.: Denz. 994 et 999 (1862 et 1868).

13* Dieitur. Saneta (catholica apostolica) Romana Ecelesia.: in Prof. fidei Trid., 1. c. et Concl. Vat. I, Sess. III, Const. dogm. de fide cath.: Denz. 1782 (3001).

14* S. Augustinus, Civ. Dei, XVIII, 51, 2: PL 41, 614.

CHAPTER II

1*   See S. Cyprianus, Epist. 69, 6: PL 3, 1142 B; Hartel 3 B, p. 754: inseparabile unitatis sacramentum.

2*   See Pius XII, Alloc. Magnificate Dominum, 2 nov. 1954: AAS 46 (1954) p. 669. Litt. Encycl. Mediator Dei, 20 nov. 1947: AAS 39 (1947) p. 555.

3*   See Pius XI, Litt. Encycl. Miserentissimus Redemptor, 8 maii 1928: AAS 20 (1928) p. 171 s. Pius XII Alloc. Vous nous avez, 22 sept. 1956: AAS 48 (1956) p. 714.

4*   See S. Thomas, Summa Theol. III, q. 63, a. 2.

5*   See S. Cyrillus Hieros., Catech. 17, de Spiritu Sancto, II, 35–37: PG 33, 1009–1012. Nic. Cabasilas, De vita in Christo, lib. III, de utilitate chrismatis: PG 150, 569–580. S. Thomas, Summa Theol. III, q. 65, a. 3 et q. 72, a. 1 et 5.

6*   See Pius XII, Litt. Encycl. Mediator Dei 20 nov. 1947: AAS 39 (1947), paesertim p. 552 s.

7*   1 Cor. 7:7:. Unusquisque proprium donum (idion charisma) habet ex Deo: alius quidem sic alius vero sic . . . See S. Augustinus, De Dono Persev. 14, 37: PL 45, 1015 s.: Non tantum continenti Dei donum est, sed coniugatorum etiam castitas.

8*   See S. Augustinus, De Praed. Sanct. 14, 27: PL 44, 980.

9*   See S. Io. Chrysostomus, In Io. Hom. 65, 1: PG 59, 361.

10*   See S. Irenaeus, Adv. Haer. III, 16, 6; III, 22, 1–3: PG 7, 925 C–926 Aet 955 C–958 A; Harvey 2, 87 s. et 120–123; Sagnard, Ed. Sources Chret., pp. 290–292 et 372 ss.

11*   See S. Ignatius M., Ad Rom., Praef.: Ed. Funk, I, p. 252.

12*   See S. Augustinus, Bapt. c. Donat. V, 28, 39; PL 43, 197: Certe manifestum est, id quod dicitur, in Ecdesia intus et foris, in corde, non in corpore cogitandum. See ib., III, 19, 26: col. 152; V, 18, 24: col. 189; In Io. Tr. 61, 2: PL 35, 1800, et alibi saepe.

13*   See Lc. 12:48: Omni autem, cui multum datum est, multum quaeretur ab eo. See etiam Matt. 5:19–20; 7:21–22; 25:41–46; Iac., 2:14.

14*   See Leo XIII, Epist. Apost. Praeclara gratulationis, 20 iun. 1894; AAS 26 (1893–94) p. 707.

15*   See Leo XIII, Epist. Encycl. Satis cognitum, 29 iun. 1896: ASS 28 (1895–96) p. 738. Epist. Encycl. Caritatis studium, 25 iul. 1898: ASS 31 (1898–99) p. 11. Pius XII, Nuntius radioph. Nell'alba, 24 dec. 1941: AAS 34 (1942) p. 21.

16*   See Pius XI, Litt. Encycl. Rerum Orientalium, 8 sept. 1928: AAS 20 (1928) p. 287. Pius XII, Litt. Encycl Orientalis Ecclesiae, 9 apr. 1944: AAS 36 (1944) p. 137

17*   See Inst. S.S.C.S. Officii 20 dec. 1949: AAS 42 (1950) p.142.

18*   See S. Thomas, Summa Theol. III, q. 8, a. 3, ad 1.

19*   See Epist. S.S.C.S. Officii ad Archiep. Boston.: Denz. 3869–72.

20*   See Eusebius Caes., Praeparatio Evangelica, 1, 1: PG 2128 AB.

21*   See Benedictus XV, Epist. Apost. Maximum illud: AAS 11 (1919) p. 440, praesertim p. 451 ss. Pius XI, Litt. Encycl. Rerum Ecclesiae: AAS 18 (1926) p. 68–69. Pius XII, Litt. Encycl. Fidei Donum, 21 apr. 1957: AAS 49 (1957) pp. 236–237. 135 Mal. 1:11.

22*   See Didache, 14: ed. Funk I, p. 32. S. Iustinus, Dial. 41: PG 6, 564. S. Irenaeus, Adv. Haer. IV 17, 5; PG 7, 1023; Harvey, 2, p. 199 s. Conc. Trid., Sess. 22, cap. 1; Denz. 939 (1742).

CHAPTER III

1*   See Conc. Vat. I, Sess. IV, Const. Dogm. Pastor aeternus. Denz. 1821 (3050 s.).

2*   See Conc. Flor., Decretum pro Graecis: Denz. 694 (1307) et Conc. Vat. I, ib.: Denz. 1826 (3059).

3*   See Liber sacramentorum S. Gregorii, Praefatio in Cathedra S. Petri, in natali S. Mathiae et S. Thomas: PL 78, 50, 51 et 152. S. Hilarius, In Ps. 67, 10: PL 9, 4S0; CSEL 22, p. 286. S. Hieronymus, Adv. Iovin. 1, 26: PL 23, 247 A. S. Augustinus, In Ps. 86, 4: PL 37, 1103. S. Gregorius M., Mor. in Iob, XXVIII, V: PL 76, 455–456. Primasius, Comm. in Apoc. V: PL 68, 924 BC. Paschasius Radb., In Matth. L. VIII, cap. 16: PL 120, 561 C. See Leo XIII, Epist. Et sane, 17 dec. 1888: AAS 21 (1888) p. 321. 147 See Matt. 28:20.

4*   See Act 6:2–6; 11:30; 13:1, 14, 23; 20:17; 1 Thess. 5:12–13; Phil. 1:1; Col. 4:11, et passim.

5*   See Act. 20:25–27; 2 Tim. 4:6 s. coll. c. 1 Tim. 5:22; 2 Tim. 2:2; Titus 1:5; S. Clem. Rom., Ad Cor. 44, 3; ed. Funk, 1, p. 156. 148 See Acts 20:28.

6*   S. Clem. Rom., ad Cor. 44, 2; ed. Funk, I, p. 154 s.

7*   See Tertull., Praescr. Haer. 32; PL 2, 52 s.; S. Ignatius M., passim.

8*   See Tertull., Praescr. Haer. 32; PL 2, 53.

9*   See S. Irenaeus, Adv. Haer. III, 3, 1; PG 7, 848 A; Harvey 2, 8; Sagnard, p. 100 s.: manifestatam.

10*   See S. Irenaeus, Adv. Haer. III, 2, 2; PG 7, 847; Harvey 2, 7; Sagnard, p. 100:. custoditur., see ib. IV, 26, 2; col. 1053, Harvey 2, 236, necnon IV, 33, 8; col. 1077; Harvey 2, 262.

11*   S. Ign. M., Philad., Praef.; ed. Funk, I, p. 264.

12*   S. Ign. M., Philad., 1, 1; Magn. 6, 1; Ed. Funk, I, pp. 264 et 234.

13*   S. Clem. Rom., 1. c., 42, 3–4, 44, 3–4; 57, 1–2; Ed. Funk. I, 152, 156, 171 s. S. Ign. M., Philad. 2; Smyrn. 8; Magn. 3; Trall. 7; Ed. Funk, I, p. 265 s.; 282; 232 246 s. etc.; S. Iustinus, Apol., 1, 65 PG 6, 428; S. Cyprianus, Epist. assim.

14*   See Leo XIII, Epist. Encycl. Satis cognitum, 29 iun. 896: ASS 28 (1895–96) p. 732.

15*   See Conc. Trid., Sess. 23, ecr. de sacr. Ordinis, cap. 4; Denz. 960 (1768); Conc. Vat. I, ess. 4 Const. Dogm. I De Ecclesia Christi, cap. 3: Denz. 1828 (3061). Pius XII, Litt. Encycl. Mystici Corporis, 29 iun. 1943: ASS 35 (1943) p. 209 et 212. Cod. Iur. Can., c. 291.

16*   See Leo XIII, Epist. Et sane, 17 dec. 1888: ASS 21 (1888) p. 321 s.

17*   S. Leo M., Serm. 5, 3: PL 54, 154.

18*   Conc. Trid., Sess. 23, cap. 3, citat verba 2 Tim. 1:6–7, ut demonstret Ordinem esse verum sacramentum: Denz. 959 (1766).

19*   In Trad. Apost. 3, ed. Botte, Sources Chr., pp. 27–30, Episcopo tribuitur primatus sacerdotii. See Sacramentarium Leonianum, ed. C. Mohlberg, Sacramentarium Veronense, Romae, 195S, p. 119: ad summi sacerdotii ministerium . . . Comple in sacerdotibus tuis mysterii tui summam. . . . Idem, Liber Sacramentorum Romanae Ecclesiae Romae, 1960, pp. 121–122: Tribuas eis, Domine, cathedram episcopalem ad regendam Ecclesiam tuam et plebem universam . . . See PL 78, 224.

20*   Trad. Apost. 2, ed. Botte, p. 27.

21*   Conc. Trid., Sess. 23, cap. 4, docet Ordinis sacramentum imprimere characterem indelebilem: Denz. 960 (1767). See Ioannes XXIII, Alloc. Iubilate Deo, 8 maii 1960: AAS S2 (1960) p. 466. Pall us VI, Homelia in Bas, Vaticana, 20 oct. 1963: AAS 55 (1963) p. 1014.

22* S. Cyprianus, Epist. 63, 14: PL 4, 386; Hartel, III B, p. 713: Saccrdos vice Christi vere fungitur . . . S. Io. Chrysostomus, In 2 Tim. Hom. 2, 4: PG 62, 612: Saccrdos est symbolon. Christi. S. Ambrosius, In Ps. 38:25–26: PL 14, 105 1–52: CSEL 64, 203–204. Ambrosiascr In 1 Tim. 5:19: PL 17, 479 C ct in Eph. 4:1–12; col. 387. C. Theodorus Mops., from. Catech. XV, 21 ct 24: ed. Tonneau, pp. 497 et 503. Hesychiu Hieros., In Lcv. L. 2, 9, 23: PG 93, 894 B.

23* See Eusebius, Hist. ecl., V, 24, 10: GCS II, 1, p. 49S; ed. Bardy, Sources Chr. II, p. 69 Dionysius, apud Eusebium, ib. VII 5, 2: GCS 11, 2, p. 638 s.; Bardy, II, p. 168 s.

24* See de antiquis Conciliis, Eusebius, Hist. Eccl. V, 23–24: GCS 1, 1, p. 488 ss.; Bardy, 11, p. 66 ss. et. passim. Conc. Nicaenum. Can. S: Conc. Oec. Decr. p. 7.

25* Tertullianus, de Ieiunio, 13: PL 2, 972 B; CSFL 20, p. 292, lin. 13–16.

26* S. Cyprianus, Epist. 56, 3: Hartel, 111 B, p. 650; Bayard, p. 154.

27* See Relatio officialis Zinelli, in Conc. Vat. I: Mansi S2,1 109 C.

28* See Conc. Vat. 1, Schema Const. dogm. 11, de Ecclesia Christi, c. 4: Mansi S3, 310. See Relatio Kleutgen de Schemate reformato: Mansi S3, 321 B–322 B et declaratio Zinelli: Mansi 52 1110 A. Vide etiam S. Leonem M. Serm. 4, 3: PL 54, 151 A.

29* See Cod. Iur. Can., c. 227.

30* See Conc. Vat. I, Const.Dogm. Pastor aeternis: Denz. 1821 (3050 s.).

31* See S. Cyprianus, Epist. 66, 8: Hartel 111, 2, p. 733: Episcopus in Ecclesia et Ecclesia in Episcopo.

32* See S. Cyprianus, Epist. 55, 24: Hartel, p. 642, line. 13:. Una Ecclesia per totum mundum in multa membra divisa . . . Epist. 36, 4: Hartel, p. 575, lin. 20–21.

33* See Pius XII, Litt. Encycl. Fidei Donum, 21 apr. 1957: AAS 49 (1957) p. 237.

34* See S. Hilarius Pict., In Ps. 14:3: PL 9, 206; CSEL 22, p. 86. S. Gregorius M., Moral, IV, 7, 12: PL 75, 643 C. Ps. Basilius, In Is. 15, 296: PG 30, 637 C.

35* S. Coelestinus, Epist. 18:1–2, ad Conc. Maximum illud: AAS 11 (1919) p. 440, Pius XI. Litt. Encycl. Rerum Ecclesiae, 28 febr. 1926: AAS 18 (1926) p. 69. Pius XII, Litt. Encycl. Fidei Donum, 1. c.

36* Leo XIII, Litt. Encycl. I Grande munus, 30 sept. 1880: ASS 13 (1880) p. 14S. See Cod. Iur. | Can., c. 1327; c. 13S02.

37* De iuribus Sedium patriarchalium, see Conc. Nicaenum, I can. 6 de Alexandria et Antiochia, et can. 7 de Hierosolymis: Conc. I Oec. Decr., p. 8. Conc. Later. IV, anno 1215, Constit. V: De dignigate Patriarcharum: ibid. p. 212.| Conc. Ferr. Flor.: ibid. p. 504.

38* See Cod. Iuris pro Eccl. I Orient., c. 216–314: de Patriarchis; c. 324–399: de Archiepiscopis I maioribus; c. 362–391: de aliis dignitariis; in specie, c. 238 3; 216; 240; 251; 255: de Episcopis a Patriarch nominandis.

39* See Conc. Trid., Decr. de I reform., Sess. V, c. 2, n. 9; et Sess. I XXIV, can. 4; Conc. Oec. Decr. pp. 645 et 739.

40* See Conc. Vat. I, Const. dogm. Dei Filius, 3: Denz. 1712 (3011). See nota adiecta ad Schema I de Eccl. (desumpta ex.S. Rob. Bellarmino): Mansi 51, I 579 C, necnon Schema reformatum I Const. II de Ecclesia Christi, cum I commentario Kleutgen: Mansi 53, 313 AB. Pius IX, Epist. Tuas libener: Denz. 1683 (2879).

41* See Cod. Iur. Can., c. 1322–1323.

42* See Conc. Vat. I, Const. dogm. Pastor Aeternus: Denz. 1839 (3074).

43* See explicatio Gasser in Conc. Vat. I: Mansi 52, 1213 AC.

44* Gasser, ib.: Mansi 1214 A.

45* Gasser, ib.: Mansi 1215 CD, 1216–1217 A.

46*   Gasser, ib.: Mansi 1213.

47*   Conc. Vat. I, Const. dogm. Pastor Aeternus, 4: Denz. 1836 (3070) no. 26.

48*   Oratio consecrationis cpiscopalis in ritu byzantino: Euchologion to mega, Romae, 1873, p. 139.

49*   See S. Ignatius M. Smyrn 8, 1: ed. Funk, 1, p. 282.

50*   See Act. 8:1; 14:22–23; 20:17, et passim.

51*   Oratio mozarabica: PL 96 7S9 B.

52*   See S. Ignatius M., Smyrn 8, 1: ed. Funk, I, p. 282.

53*   S. Thomas, Summa Theol. III, q. 73, a. 3.

54*   See S. Augustinus, C. Faustum, 12, 20: PL 42, 26S Serm. 57, 7: PL 38, 389, etc.

55*   S. Leo M., Serm. 63, 7: PL 54, 3S7 C.

56*   Traditio A postolica Hippolyti, 2–3: ed. Botte, pp. 26–30.

57*   See textus examinis in initio consecrationis episcopalis, et Oratio in fine vissae eiusdem consecrationis, post Te Deum.

58*   Benedictus XIV, Br. Romana Ecclesia, 5 oct. 1752, p 1: Bullarium Benedicti XIV, t. IV, Romae, 1758, 21:. Episcopus Christi typum gerit, Eiusque munere fungitur. Pius XII, Litt. Encycl. Mystici Corporis, 1. c., p. 211:. Assignatos sibi greges singuli singulos Christi nomine pascunt et regunt.

59*   Leo XIII, Epist. Encycl. Satis cognitum, 29 iun. 1896: ASS 28 (1895–96) p. 732. Idem, Epist. Officio sanctissimo, 22 dec. 1887: AAS 20 (1887) p. 264. Pius IX itt. Apost. ad Episcopol Geraniae, 12 mart. 1875, et alloc. onsist., 15 mart. 187S: Denz. 112–3117, in nova ed. tantum.

60*   Conc. Vat. I, Const. dogm. Pastor aeternus, 3: Denz. 1828 (3061). See Relatio Zinelli: Mand 1 2, 1114 D.

61*   See S. Ignatius M., ad ephes. 5, 1: ed. Funk, I, p. 216.

62*   See S. Ignatius M., ad ephes. 6, 1: ed. Funk, I, p. 218.

63*   See Conc. Trid., Sess. 23, sacr. Ordinis, cap. 2: Denz. 958 (1765), et can. 6: Denz. 966 (1776).

64*   See Innocentius I, Epist. ad Decentium: PL 20, 554 A; sansi 3, 1029; Denz. 98 (215): Presbyteri, licet secundi sint sa erdotcs, pontificatus tamen api em non habent . . . S. Cyprianus, Epist. 61, 3: ed. Hartel, p. 696.

65*   See Conc. Trid., l. c., Denz. 962–968 (1763–1778), et in specie l an. 7: Denz. 967 (1777). Pius l II, Const. Apost. Sacramentum ordinis: Denz. 2301 (38S7–61).

66*   See Innocentius I, 1. c. S. Gregorius Naz., Apol. II, 22: PGS, 432 B. Ps.-Dionysius, Eccl. ier., 1, 2: PG 3, 372 D.

67*   See Conc. Trid., Sess. 22: Denz. 940 (1743). Pius XII, Litt. Encycl. Mediator Dei, 20 nov. 1947: AAS 39 (1947) p. 553; Denz. 2300 (3850).

68*   See Conc. Trid. Sess. 22: Denz. 938 (1739–40). Conc. Vat. II, Const. De Sacra Liturgia, n. 7 et n. 47.

69*   See Pius XII, Litt. Encycl. Mediator Dei, 1. c., sub. n. 67.

70*   See S. Cyprianus, Epist. 11, 3: PL 4, 242 B; Hartel, II, 2, p. 497.

71*   Ordo consecrationis sacerdotalis, in impositione vestimentorum.

72*   Ordo consecrationis sacerdotalis in praefatione.

73*   See S. Ignatius M. Philad. 4: ed. Funk, I, p. 266. S. Cornelius I, apud S. Cyprianum, Epist. 48, 2: Hartel, III, 2, p. 610.

74*   Constitutiones Ecclesiac aegyptiacae, III, 2: ed. Funk, Didascalia, II, p. 103. Statuta Eccl. Ant. 371: Mansi 3, 954.

75* S. Polycarpus, Ad Phil. 5, 2: ed. Funk, I, p. 300: Christus dicitur. omnium diaconus factus . . . See Didache, 15, 1: ib., p. 32. S.Ignatius M. Trall. 2, 3: ib., p. 242. Constitutiones Apostolorum, 8, 28, 4: ed. Funk, Didascalia, I, p. 530.

CHAPTER IV

1* S. Augustinus, Serm. 340, 1: PL 38, 1483.

2* See Pius XI, Litt. Encycl. Quadragesimo anno 15 maii 1931: AAS 23 (1931) p. 121 s. Pius XII, Alloc. De quelle consolation, 14 oct. 1951: AAS 43 (1951) p. 790 s.

3* See Pius XII, Alloc. Six ans se sont ecoules, 5 oct. 19S7: AAS 49 (19S7) p. 927. De mandato et missione canonica, see Decretum De Apostolatu laicorum, cap. IV, n. 16, cum notis 12 et 15.

4* Ex Praefatione festi Christi Regis.

5* See Leo XIII, Epist. Encycl. Immortale Dei, 1 nov. 188S: ASS 18 (188S) p. 166 ss. Idem, Litt. Encycl. Sapientae christianae, 10 ian. 1890: ASS 22 (1889–90) p. 397 ss. Pius XII, Alloc. Alla vostra filfale. 23 mart. 19S8: AAS S0 (145R) p. 220: Ia Iegittima sana laicita dello Stato.

6* Cod. Iur. Can., can. 682.

7* See Pius XII, Alloc. De quelle consolation, 1. c., p. 789: Dans les batailles decisives, c'est parfois du front que partent les plus heureuses initiatives . . . Idem Alloc. L'importance de la presse catholique, 17 febr. 1950: AAS 42 (1950) p. 256.

8* See 1 Thess. 5:19 et 1 Io. 4:1.

9* Epist. ad Diognetum, 6: ed. Funk, I, p. 400. See S. Io. Chrysostomus, In Matth. Hom. 46 (47) 2: PG 58, 78, de fermento in massa.

CHAPTER V

1* Missale Romanum, Gloria in excelsis. See Lc. 1:35; Mc. 1:24, Lc. 4:34; Io. 6:69 (ho hagios tou theou); Acts 3:14; 4:27, 30; Heb. 7:26, 1 John 2:20; Rev. 3:7.

2* See Origenes, Comm. Rom. 7:7: PG 14, 1122 B. Ps. Macarius, De Oratione, 11: PG 34, 861 AB. S. Thomas, Summa Theol. II–II, q. 184, a. 3.

3* See S. Augustinus Retract. II, 18: PL 32, 637 s. Pius XII Litt. Encycl. Mystici Corporis, 29 iun. 1943: AAS 35 (1943) p. 225.

4* See Pius XI, Litt. Encycl. Rerum omnium, 26 ian. 1923: AAS 15 (1923) p. 50 ct pp. 59–60. Litt. Encycl. Casti Connubii, 31 dec. 1930: AAS 22 (1930) p. 548. Pius XII, Const. Apost. Provida Mater, 2 febr. 1947: AAS 39 (1947) p. 117. Alloc. Annus sacer, 8 dec. 1950: AAS 43 (1951) pp. 27–28. Alloc. Nel darvi, 1 iul. 1956: AAS 48 (1956) p. 574 s.

5* See S. Thomas, Summa Theol. II–II, q. 184, a. 5 et 6. De perf. vitae spir., c. 18. Origenes, In Is. Hom. 6, 1: PG 13, 239.

6* See S. Ignatius M., Magn. 13, 1: ed. Funk, I, p. 241.

7* See S. Pius X, Exhort. Haerent animo, 4 aug. 1908: ASS 41 (1908) p. 560 s. Cod. Iur. Can., can. 124. Pius XI, Litt. Encycl. Ad catholici sacerdotii, 20 dec. 1935: AAS 28 (1936) p. 22 s.

8* Ordo consecrationis sacerdotalis, in Exhortatione initiali.

9* See S. Ignatius M., Trall. 2, 3: ed. Funk, l, p. 244.

10* See Pius XII, Alloc. Sous la maternclle protection, 9 dec. 1957: AAS 50 (19S8) p. 36.

11* Pius XI, Litt. Encycl. Castf Connubii, 31 dec. 1930. AAS 22 (1930) p. 548 s. See S. Io Chrysostomus, In Ephes. Hom. 20, 2: P. 62, 136 ss.

12* See S. Augustinus, Enchir. 121, 32: PL 40 288. S. Thomas Summa Theol. II–II, q. 184, a. 1. Pius XII, Adhort. Apost. Menti nostrae, 23 sept. 1950: AAS 42 (1950) p. 660.

13* De consiliis in genere, see Origenes, Comm. Rom. 10:14: PG 14 127S B. S. Augustinus, De S. Virginitate, 15, 15: PL 40, 403. S. Thomas, Summa Theol. I–II, q. 100, a. 2 C (in fine); II–II, q. 44, a. 4 ad 3.

14* De praestantia sacrae virginitatis, see Tertullianus, Exhort. Cast. 10: PL 2, 925 C. S. Cyprianus, Hab. Virg. 3 et 22: PL 4, 443 B et 461 A. A. S. Athanasius (?), De Virg.: PG 28, 252 ss. S. Io. Chrysostomus, De Virg.: PG 48, 533 u.

15* De spirituali paupertate et oboedientia testimonia praccipua S.Scripturae et Patrum afferuntur in Relatione pp. 152–153.

16* De praxi effectiva consiliorum quae non omnibus imponitur, see S. Io. Chrysostomus, In Matth. Hom. 7, 7: PG S7, 8 I s. 5. Ambrosius, De Vidu s, 4, 23: PL 16, 241 s.

CHAPTER VI

1* See Rosweydus, Viqae Patrum, Antwerpiae 1628. Apophtegmata Patrum: PG 65. Palladius, Historia Lausiaca: PG 34, 995 ss.; ed. C. Butler, Cambridge 1898 (1904). Pius XI, Const. Apost. Umbratilem, 8 iul. 1924: AAS 16 (1924) pp. 386–387. Pius XII, Alloc. Nous sommes heureux, 11 apr. 1958: AAS 50 (1958) p. 283.

2* Paulus VI, Alloc. Magno gaudio, 23 maii 1964: AAS 56 (1964) p. 566.

3* See Cod. Iur. Can., c. 487 et 488, 40. Pius XII, Alloc. Annus sacer, 8 dec. 1950, AAS 43 (1951) p. 27 s. Pius XII, Cons. Apost. Provida Mater, 2 Febr. 1947: AAS 39 (1947) p. 120 ss.

4* Paulus VI, 1. c., p. S67.

5* See S. Thomas, Summa Theol. II–II, q. 184, a. 3 et q. 188, a. 2. S. Bonaventura, Opusc. X, Apologia Pauperum, c. 3, 3: ed. Opera, Quaracchi, t. 8, 1898, p. 245 a.

6* See Conc. Vat. I. Schema De Ecclesia Christi, cap. XV, et Adnot. 48: Mansi 51, 549 s. et 619 s. Leo XIII, Epist. Au milieu des consolations, 23 dec. 1900: AAS 33 (1900–01) p. 361. Pius XII, Const. Apost. Provida Mater, 1. c., p. 1145.

7* See Leo XIII, Const. Romanos Pontifices, 8 maii 1881: AAS 13 (1880–81) p. 483. Pius XII, Alloc. Annus sacer, 8 dec. 1950: AAS 43 (1951) p. 288.

8* See Pius XII, Alloc. Annus sacer, 1. c., p. 28. Pius XII, Const. Apost. Sedes Sapientiae, 31 Maii 19S6: AAS 48 (1956) p. 355. Paulus VI, 1. c., pp. 570–571.

9* See Pius XII Litt. Encycl. Mystici Corporis, 19 iun. 1943: AAS 35 (1943) p. 214 s.

10* See Pius XII, Alloc. Annus sacer, 1. c., p. 30. Alloc. Sous la maternelle protecrion, 9 dec. 19S7: AAS 50 (19S8) p. 39 s.

CHAPTER VII

1* Conc. Florentinum, Decretum pro Graecis: Denz. 693 (1305).

2* Praeter documenta antiquiora contra quamlibet formam evocationis spirituum inde ab Alexandro IV (27 sept. 1958), cfr Encycl. S.S.C.S. Officii, De magne tismi abusu, 4 aug. 1856: AAS (1865) pp. 177–178, Denz. 1653–1654 (2823–2825); responsioner S.S.C.S. Offici, 24 apr. 1917: 9 (1917) p. 268, Denz. 218 (3642).

3* Videatur synthetiea espositi huius doctrinae paulinae in: Piu XII, Litt. Encycl. Mystici Corporis AAS 35 (1943) p. 200 et passilr.

4* See, i. a., S. Augustinus, Enarr. in Ps. 85, 24: PL 37, 1095 S. Hieronymus, Liber contra Vigl lantium, b: PL 23, 344. S. Thomas In 4m Sent., d. 45, q. 3, a. 2. Bonaventura, In 4m Sent., d. 45, a. 3, q. 2; etc.

5* See Pius XII, Litt. Encycl. Mystici Corporis: AAS 35 (1943) p. 245.

6* See Plurimae inseriptione in Catacumbis romanis.

7* See Gelasius I, Decretalis De libris recipiendis, 3: PL 59, 160, Denz. 165 (353).

8* See S. Methodius, Symposion, VII, 3: GCS (Bodwetseh), p. 74.

9* See Benedictus XV, Decretum approbationis virtutum in Causa beatificationis et canonizationis Servi Dei Ioannis Nepomuecni Neumann: AAS 14 (1922) p. 23; plures Allocutiones Pii X de Sanetis: Inviti all'croismo Diseorsit. I–III, Romae 1941–1942, passim; Pius XII, Discorsi Radiomessagi, t. 10, 1949, pp 37–43.

10* See Pius XII, Litt. Encycl: Mediator Dei: AAS 39 (1947) p. 581.

11* See Hebr. 13:7: Eccli 44–50, Nebr. 11, 340. See etia Pius XII, Litt. Encycl. Mediati Dei: AAS 39 (1947) pp. 582–583.

12* See Conc. Vaticanum Const. De fide catholica, cap. 3 Denz. 1794 (3013).

13* See Pius XII, Litt. Encycl. Mystici Corporis: AAS 35 (1943) p. 216.

14* Quoad gratitudinem erga ipsos Sanctos, see E. Diehl, Inscriptiones latinae christianae vereres, 1, Berolini, 1925, nn. 2008 2382 et passim.

15* Conc. Tridentinum, Sess. 25, De invocatione . . . Sanctorum: Denz. 984 (1821).

16* Breviarium Romanum, Invitatorium infesto Sanctorum Omnium.

17* See v. g., 2 Thess. 1:10.

18* Conc. Vaticanum II, Const. De Sacra Liturgia, cap. 5, n. 104.

19* Canon Missae Romanae.

20* Conc. Nicaenum II, Act. VII: Denz. 302 (600).

21* Conc. Florentinum, Decretum pro Graecis: Denz. 693 (1304).

22* Conc. Tridentinum Sess. 35, De invocatione, veneratione et reliquiis Sanctorum et sacris imaginibus: Denz. 984–988 (1821–1824); Sess. 25, Decretum de Purgatorio: Denz. 983 (1820); Sess. 6, Decretum de iustificatione, can. 30: Denz. 840 (1580).

23* Ex Praefatione, aliquious dioecesibus concessa.

24* See S. Petrus Canisius, Catechismus Maior seu Summa Doctrinae christianae, cap. III (ed. crit. F. Streicher) pas I, pp. 15–16, n. 44 et pp. 100–101, n. 49.

25* See Conc. Vaticanum II Const. De Sacra Liturgia, cap. 1 n. 8.

CHAPTER VIII

1* Credo in Missa Romana: Symbolum Constantinopolitanum: Mansi 3, 566. See Conc. Ephesinum, ib. 4, 1130 (necnon ib. 2, 665 et 4, 1071); Conc. Chalcedonense, ib. 7, 111–116; Cow. Constantinopolitanum II, ib. 9, 375–396.

2* Canon Missae Romanae.

3* S. Augustine, De S. Virginitate. 6: PL 40, 399.

4* See Paulus Pp. VI, allocutio in Concilio, die 4 dec. 1963: AAS 56 (1964) p. 37.

5* See S. Germanus Const., Nom. in annunt. Deiparae: PG 98, 328 A; In Dorm. 2: col. 357. Anastasius Antioch., Serm. 2 de Annunt., 2: PG 89, 1377 AB; Serm. 3, 2: col. 1388 C. S. Andrcas Cret. Can. in B. V. Nat. 4: PG 97, 1321 B. In B. V. Nat., 1: col. 812 A. Hom. in dorm. 1: col. 1068 C. S. Sophronius, Or. 2 in Annunt., 18: PG 87 (3), 3237 BD.

6* S. Irenaeus, Adv. Haer. III, 22, 4: PG 7, 9S9 A; Harvey, 2, 123.

7* S. Irenaeus, ib.; Harvey, 2, 124.

8* S. Epiphanius, Nacr. 78, 18: PG 42, 728 CD; 729 AB.

9* S. Hieronymus, Epist. 22, 21: PL 22, 408. See S. Augwtinus, Serm. S1, 2, 3: PL 38, 33S; Serm. 232, 2: col. 1108. S. Cyrillus Hieros., Catech. 12, 15: PG 33, 741 AB. S. Io. Chrysostomus, In Ps. 44, 7: PG SS, 193. S. Io. Damascenus, Nom. 2 in dorm. B.M.V., 3: PG 96, 728.

10* See Conc. Lateranense anni 649, Can. 3: Mansi 10, 1151. S. Leo M., Epist. ad Flav.: PL S4, 7S9. Conc. Chalcedonense: Mansi 7, 462. S. Ambrosius, De inst. virg.: PL 16, 320.

11* See Pius XII, Litt. Encycl. Mystici Corporis, 29 iun. 1943: AAS 35 (1943) pp. 247–248.

12* See Pius IX, Bulla Ineffabilis 8 dec. 1854: acta Pii IX, I, I, p. 616; Denz. 1641 (2803).

13* See Pius XII, Const. Apost. Munificensissimus, 1 no. 1950: AAS 42 (1950): Denz. 2333 (3903). See S. Io. Damascenus, Enc. in dorm. Dei gcnitricis, Hom. 2 et 3: PG 96, 721–761, speciatim col. 728 B. S. Germanus Constantinop., in S. Dei gen. dorm. Serm. 1: PG 98 (6), 340–348; Serm. 3: col. 361. S. Modestus Hier., In dorm. SS. Deiparae: PG 86 (2), 3277–3312.

14* See Pius XII Litt. Encycl. Ad coeli Reginam, 11 Oct. 1954: AAS 46 (1954), pp. 633–636; Denz. 3913 ss. See S. Andreas Cret., Hom. 3 in dorm. SS. Deiparae: PG 97, 1089–1109. S. Io. Damascenus, De fide orth., IV, 14: PG 94, 1153–1161.

15* See Kleutgen, textus reformstus De mysterio Verbi incarnati, cap. IV: Mansi 53, 290. See S. Andreas Cret., In nat. Mariac, sermo 4: PG 97, 865 A. S. Germanus Constantinop., In annunt. Deiparae: PG 98, 321 BC. In dorm. Deiparae, III: col. 361 D. S. Io. Damascenus, In dorm. B. V. Mariae, Hom. 1, 8: PG 96, 712 BC–713 A.

16* See Leo XIII, Litt. Encycl. Adiutricem populi, 5 sept. 1895: ASS 15 (1895–96), p. 303. S. Pius X, Litt. Encycl. Ad diem illum, 2 febr. 1904: Acta, I, p. 154 Denz. 1978 a (3370). Pius XI, Litt. Encycl. Miserentissimus, 8 maii 1928: AAS 20 (1928) p. 178. Pius XII, Nuntius Radioph., 13 maii 1946: AAS 38 (1946) p. 266.

17* S. Ambrosius, Epist. 63: PL 16, 1218.

18* S. Ambrosius, Expos. Lc. II, 7: PL 15, 1555.

19* See Ps. Petrus Dam. Serm. 63: PL 144, 861 AB. Godefridus a S. Victore. In nat. B. M., Ms. Paris, Mazarine, 1002, fol. 109 r. Gerhohus Reich., De gloria ct honore Filii hominis, 10: PL 194, 1105AB.

20* S. Ambrosius, l. c. et Expos. Lc. X, 24–25: PL 15, 1810. S.Augustinus, In lo. Tr. 13, 12: PL 35 1499. See Serm. 191, 2, 3: PL 38 1010; etc. See ctiam Ven. Beda, In Lc. Expos. I, cap. 2: PL 92, 330. Isaac de Stella, Serm. 51. PL 194, 1863 A.

21* Sub tuum praesidium.

22* Conc. Nicaenum II, anno 787: Mansi 13. 378–379; Denz. 302 (600–601). Conc. Trident., sess. 2S: Mansi 33, 171–172.

23* See Pius XII, Nunius radioph., 24 oct. 1954: AAS 46 (1954) p. 679. Litt. Encycl. Ad coeli Reginam, 11 oct. 1954: AAS 46 (1954) p. 637.

24* See Pius XI, Litt. Encycl. Ecclesiam Dei, 12 nov. 1923: AAS 15 (1923) p. 581. Pius XII, Litt. Encycl. Fulgens corona, 8 sept. 1953: AAS 45 (1953) pp. 590–591.

SACROSANCTUM CONCILIUM

Constitution
on the Sacred Liturgy

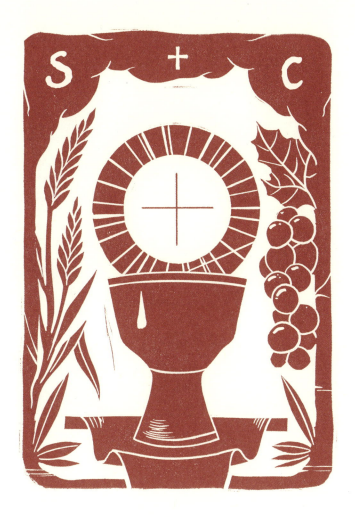

SOLEMNLY PROMULGATED *by* HIS HOLINESS
POPE PAUL VI
on DECEMBER 4, 1963

Revitalizing Right Praise

Introduction to *Sacrosanctum Concilium* by Bishop Robert Barron

If the Scriptures are right, the single greatest problem today is what it has always been throughout human history: lack of orthodoxy, a suspension of right praise. Like the woman at the well, most of us are looking for love in all of the wrong places. Like the priests of Baal, most of us hop around the altars to gods that cannot, even in principle, satisfy us. Following the prompt of Thomas Aquinas, we might imagine that well and those altars to the Baals as symbolic of our quest for the four great substitutes for God—namely, wealth, pleasure, power, and honor. The more we order our infinite longing for God toward one of these finite objects, the more addicted we become, even to the point of doing damage to ourselves, which is powerfully suggested by the priests of Baal slashing themselves as they supplicate their false gods (1 Kings 18:28). The elegant liturgical formula "Glory to God in the highest and on earth peace to people of good will" functions as a sort of prescription: in the measure that our worship is rightly directed, order obtains both in ourselves and in the wider society.

This is precisely why the great theologians of the Liturgical Movement and the fathers of Vatican II called for a revival of the Mass, including the "fully conscious and active participation" of the laity (SC 14). Awakening the people of God to a keener awareness of right worship would, they wagered, shape Catholics more fully for their work of mission and evangelization. As Benedict XVI commented in *Sacramentum Caritatis*, the concluding words of the Mass, *Ite, missa est*, "succinctly express the missionary nature of the Church." Dorothy Day and Peter Maurin, the cofounders of the Catholic Worker Movement, never tired of saying "cult, culture, cultivation"—in other words, that cult (liturgy and prayer) cultivates the culture. When he came to Gethsemani Abbey for a Holy Week retreat in 1941, the young Thomas Merton said, "This is the only real city in America—in a desert. It is the axle around which the whole country blindly turns." Any remaking of the culture undertaken without reference to rightness of praise will founder.

But how have Catholics been doing in this regard since the council? The statistics tell a disturbing story. In the United States, over 60% of baptized Catholics regularly stay away from what Vatican II called the source and summit of the Christian life (see LG 11; SC 10), and the numbers in Australia and Europe are far worse. Moreover, the numbers of Catholics who are having their babies baptized or who seek out marriage in the Church are plummeting. If you had told Romano Guardini, Henri de Lubac, Yves Congar, or Reynold Hillenbrand—all great leaders of the preconciliar Liturgical Movement—that today, the overwhelming majority of Catholics in the West rarely attend Mass, they would have seen their work as a failure.

But this is not what the Vatican II fathers wanted! Turning to *Sacrosanctum Concilium*, we see a vision of a revitalized liturgy cultivating a vibrant Catholic culture that will draw the world to itself—and the vital importance of that vision to the life of the Church today.

SACROSANCTUM CONCILIUM

Constitution
on the Sacred Liturgy

INTRODUCTION

1. This sacred Council has several aims in view: it desires to impart an ever increasing vigor to the Christian life of the faithful; to adapt more suitably to the needs of our own times those institutions which are subject to change; to foster whatever can promote union among all who believe in Christ; to strengthen whatever can help to call the whole of mankind into the household of the Church. The Council therefore sees particularly cogent reasons for undertaking the reform and promotion of the liturgy.

2. For the liturgy, "through which the work of our redemption is accomplished,"[1] most of all in the divine sacrifice of the Eucharist, is the outstanding means whereby the faithful may express in their lives, and manifest to others, the mystery of Christ and the real nature of the true Church. It is of the essence of the Church that she be both human and divine, visible and yet invisibly equipped, eager to act and yet intent on contemplation, present in this world and yet not at home in it; and she is all these things in such wise that in her the human is directed and subordinated to the divine, the visible likewise to the invisible, action to contemplation, and this present world to that city yet to come, which we seek.[2] While the liturgy daily builds up those who are within into a holy temple of the Lord, into a dwelling place for God in the Spirit,[3] to the mature measure of the fullness of Christ,[4] at the same time it marvelously strengthens their power to preach Christ, and thus shows forth the Church

to those who are outside as a sign lifted up among the nations[5] under which the scattered children of God may be gathered together,[6] until there is one sheepfold and one shepherd.[7]

3. Wherefore the sacred Council judges that the following principles concerning the promotion and reform of the liturgy should be called to mind, and that practical norms should be established.

Among these principles and norms there are some which can and should be applied both to the Roman rite and also to all the other rites. The practical norms which follow, however, should be taken as applying only to the Roman rite, except for those which, in the very nature of things, affect other rites as well.

4. Lastly, in faithful obedience to tradition, the sacred Council declares that holy Mother Church holds all lawfully acknowledged rites to be of equal right and dignity; that she wishes to preserve them in the future and to foster them in every way. The Council also desires that, where necessary, the rites be revised carefully in the light of sound tradition, and that they be given new vigor to meet the circumstances and needs of modern times.

CHAPTER I
General Principles for the Restoration and Promotion of the Sacred Liturgy

I. The Nature of the Sacred Liturgy and Its Importance in the Church's Life

5. God who "wills that all men be saved and come to the knowledge of the truth" (1 Tim. 2:4), "who in many and various ways spoke in times past to the fathers by the prophets" (Heb. 1:1), when the fullness of time had come sent His Son, the Word made flesh, anointed by the Holy Spirit, to preach the gospel to the poor, to heal the contrite of heart,[8] to be a "bodily and spiritual medicine,"[9] the Mediator between God and man.[10] For His humanity, united with the person of the Word, was the instrument of our salvation. Therefore in Christ "the perfect achievement of our reconciliation came forth, and the fullness of divine worship was given to us."[11]

The wonderful works of God among the people of the Old Testament were but a prelude to the work of Christ the Lord in redeeming mankind and giving perfect glory to God. He achieved His task principally by the paschal mystery of His blessed passion, resurrection from the dead, and the glorious ascension, whereby "dying, he destroyed our death and, rising, he restored our life."[12] For it was from the side of Christ as He slept the sleep of death upon the cross that there came forth "the wondrous sacrament of the whole Church."[13]

6. Just as Christ was sent by the Father, so also He sent the apostles, filled with the Holy Spirit. This He did that, by preaching the gospel to every creature,[14] they might proclaim that the Son of God, by His death and resurrection, had freed us from the power of Satan[15] and from death, and brought us into the kingdom of His Father. His purpose also was that they might accomplish the work of salvation which they had proclaimed, by means of sacrifice and sacraments, around which the entire liturgical life revolves. Thus by baptism men are plunged into the paschal mystery of Christ: they die with Him, are buried with Him, and rise with Him;[16] they receive the spirit of adoption as sons "in which we cry: Abba, Father" (Rom. 8:15), and thus become true adorers whom the Father seeks.[17] In like manner, as often as they eat the supper of the Lord they proclaim the death of the Lord until He comes.[18] For that reason, on the very day of Pentecost, when the Church appeared before the world, "those who received the word" of Peter "were baptized." And "they continued steadfastly in the teaching of the apostles and in the communion of the breaking of bread and in prayers . . . praising God and being in favor with all the people" (Acts 2:41–47). From that time onwards the Church has never failed to come together to celebrate the paschal mystery: reading those things "which were in all the scriptures concerning him" (Luke 24:27), celebrating the eucharist in which "the victory and triumph of his death are again made present,"[19] and at the same time giving thanks "to God for his unspeakable gift" (2 Cor. 9:15) in Christ Jesus, "in praise of his glory" (Eph. 1:12), through the power of the Holy Spirit.

7. To accomplish so great a work, Christ is always present in His Church, especially in her liturgical celebrations. He is present in the sacrifice of the Mass, not only in the person of His minister, "the same now offering, through the ministry of priests, who formerly offered himself on the cross,"[20] but especially under the Eucharistic species. By His power He is present in the sacraments, so that when a man baptizes it is really Christ

Himself who baptizes.[21] He is present in His word, since it is He Himself who speaks when the holy scriptures are read in the Church. He is present, lastly, when the Church prays and sings, for He promised: "Where two or three are gathered together in my name, there am I in the midst of them" (Matt. 18:20).

Christ indeed always associates the Church with Himself in this great work wherein God is perfectly glorified and men are sanctified. The Church is His beloved Bride who calls to her Lord, and through Him offers worship to the Eternal Father.

Rightly, then, the liturgy is considered as an exercise of the priestly office of Jesus Christ. In the liturgy the sanctification of the man is signified by signs perceptible to the senses, and is effected in a way which corresponds with each of these signs; in the liturgy the whole public worship is performed by the Mystical Body of Jesus Christ, that is, by the Head and His members.

From this it follows that every liturgical celebration, because it is an action of Christ the priest and of His Body which is the Church, is a sacred action surpassing all others; no other action of the Church can equal its efficacy by the same title and to the same degree.

The Liturgy of the Eucharist

Sacrosanctum Concilium 7 | Bishop Barron

Though Vatican II placed a renewed stress on the Liturgy of the Word, it would not be correct to say that the two principal sections of the Mass are coequal in importance. For at the heart of the liturgy of the Eucharist is the realization of the "substantial" presence of Jesus Christ, a presence that is qualitatively different than those realized in the gathering of the people, the person of the priest, or the proclamation of the Scriptures. We might say that the Liturgy of the Eucharist focuses and fully expresses what is inchoately present in the first part of the Mass.

8. In the earthly liturgy we take part in a foretaste of that heavenly liturgy which is celebrated in the holy city of Jerusalem toward which we journey as pilgrims, where Christ is sitting at the right hand of God, a minister of

the holies and of the true tabernacle;[22] we sing a hymn to the Lord's glory with all the warriors of the heavenly army; venerating the memory of the saints, we hope for some part and fellowship with them; we eagerly await the Savior, Our Lord Jesus Christ, until He, our life, shall appear and we too will appear with Him in glory.[23]

Joining Heaven and Earth

Sacrosanctum Concilium 8

Pope Francis

Laudato Si' 236

It is in the Eucharist that all that has been created finds its greatest exaltation. Grace, which tends to manifest itself tangibly, found unsurpassable expression when God himself became man and gave himself as food for his creatures. The Lord, in the culmination of the mystery of the Incarnation, chose to reach our intimate depths through a fragment of matter. He comes not from above, but from within, he comes that we might find him in this world of ours. In the Eucharist, fullness is already achieved; it is the living center of the universe, the overflowing core of love and of inexhaustible life. Joined to the incarnate Son, present in the Eucharist, the whole cosmos gives thanks to God. Indeed the Eucharist is itself an act of cosmic love: "Yes, cosmic! Because even when it is celebrated on the humble altar of a country church, the Eucharist is always in some way celebrated on the altar of the world." The Eucharist joins heaven and earth; it embraces and penetrates all creation. The world which came forth from God's hands returns to him in blessed and undivided adoration: in the bread of the Eucharist, "creation is projected towards divinization, towards the holy wedding feast, towards unification with the Creator himself." Thus, the Eucharist is also a source of light and motivation for our concerns for the environment, directing us to be stewards of all creation.

9. The sacred liturgy does not exhaust the entire activity of the Church. Before men can come to the liturgy they must be called to faith and to conversion: "How then are they to call upon him in whom they have not yet believed? But how are they to believe him whom they have not heard? And how are they to hear if no one preaches? And how are men to preach unless they be sent?" (Rom. 10:14–15).

Therefore the Church announces the good tidings of salvation to those who do not believe, so that all men may know the true God and Jesus Christ whom He has sent, and may be converted from their ways, doing penance.[24] To believers also the Church must ever preach faith and penance, she must prepare them for the sacraments, teach them to observe all that Christ has commanded,[25] and invite them to all the works of charity, piety, and the apostolate. For all these works make it clear that Christ's faithful, though not of this world, are to be the light of the world and to glorify the Father before men.

10. Nevertheless the liturgy is the summit toward which the activity of the Church is directed; at the same time it is the font from which all her power flows. For the aim and object of apostolic works is that all who are made sons of God by faith and baptism should come together to praise God in the midst of His Church, to take part in the sacrifice, and to eat the Lord's supper.

The liturgy in its turn moves the faithful, filled with "the paschal sacraments," to be "one in holiness";[26] it prays that "they may hold fast in their lives to what they have grasped by their faith";[27] the renewal in the Eucharist of the covenant between the Lord and man draws the faithful into the compelling love of Christ and sets them on fire. From the liturgy, therefore, and especially from the Eucharist, as from a font, grace is poured forth upon us; and the sanctification of men in Christ and the glorification of God, to which all other activities of the Church are directed as toward their end, is achieved in the most efficacious possible way.

11. But in order that the liturgy may be able to produce its full effects, it is necessary that the faithful come to it with proper dispositions, that their minds should be attuned to their voices, and that they should cooperate with divine grace lest they receive it in vain.[28] Pastors of souls must therefore realize that, when the liturgy is celebrated, something more is required than the mere observation of the laws governing valid and licit

The Central Prayer of the Church

Sacrosanctum Concilium **10** | Bishop Barron

The council fathers say that the liturgy is "the summit toward which the activity of the Church is directed" and "the font from which all her power flows," implying that the Mass is the place where the "Catholic thing" is most thoroughly displayed and realized. If we want to understand who God is, who Christ is, who we are in relation to God, and what our mission and purpose might be, we look to the Eucharistic liturgy.

This is, furthermore, precisely why the liturgy is so crucial in regard to the conversation with the culture. The central prayer of the Church radiates outward and shapes the worlds of art, politics, economics, and so on. Both the rabbis of the intertestamental period and the Fathers of the Church interpreted Adam before the fall as the prototypical priest and the Garden of Eden as a kind of primordial temple. The right praise offered by Adam was meant to infiltrate every aspect of life, coming in time to "Edenize" the world.

celebration; it is their duty also to ensure that the faithful take part fully aware of what they are doing, actively engaged in the rite, and enriched by its effects.

12. The spiritual life, however, is not limited solely to participation in the liturgy. The Christian is indeed called to pray with his brethren, but he must also enter into his chamber to pray to the Father, in secret;[29] yet more, according to the teaching of the Apostle, he should pray without ceasing.[30] We learn from the same Apostle that we must always bear about in our body the dying of Jesus, so that the life also of Jesus may be made manifest in our bodily frame.[31] This is why we ask the Lord in the sacrifice of the Mass that, "receiving the offering of the spiritual victim," he may fashion us for himself "as an eternal gift."[32]

13. Popular devotions of the Christian people are to be highly commended, provided they accord with the laws and norms of the Church, above all when they are ordered by the Apostolic See.

Devotions proper to individual Churches also have a special dignity if they are undertaken by mandate of the bishops according to customs or books lawfully approved.

But these devotions should be so drawn up that they harmonize with the liturgical seasons, accord with the sacred liturgy, are in some fashion derived from it, and lead the people to it, since, in fact, the liturgy by its very nature far surpasses any of them.

II. The Promotion of Liturgical Instruction and Active Participation

14. Mother Church earnestly desires that all the faithful should be led to that fully conscious and active participation in liturgical celebrations which is demanded by the very nature of the liturgy. Such participation by the Christian people as "a chosen race, a royal priesthood, a holy nation, a redeemed people" (1 Pet. 2:9; see 2:4–5), is their right and duty by reason of their baptism.

In the restoration and promotion of the sacred liturgy, this full and active participation by all the people is the aim to be considered before all else; for it is the primary and indispensable source from which the faithful are to derive the true Christian spirit; and therefore pastors of souls must zealously strive to achieve it, by means of the necessary instruction, in all their pastoral work.

Yet it would be futile to entertain any hopes of realizing this unless the pastors themselves, in the first place, become thoroughly imbued with the spirit and power of the liturgy, and undertake to give instruction about it. A prime need, therefore, is that attention be directed, first of all, to the liturgical instruction of the clergy. Wherefore the sacred Council has decided to enact as follows:

Fully Conscious and Active Participation

Sacrosanctum Concilium **14** | Bishop Barron

Prior to the council, both in Europe and this country, there were a number of theologians placing an emphasis on the idea of the Mystical Body of Christ. On this reading, rooted of course in St. Paul, the Church is not so much a club or a society as an organism, a body made up of interdependent cells, molecules, and organs, drawing its life from Christ's grace.

Nowhere is this organic sense of the Church on fuller display than in the liturgy—and this is why it bothered these theologians so much that most of the laity saw themselves as spectators at a clerical show. They wanted to demonstrate that, through their posture, gesture, singing, responding, processing, etc., the people of God are intimately involved in the Mass. And the laity are essential, these thinkers insisted, because they are meant to carry the grace of the Mass out into the world.

All of this theologizing came to full expression in *Sacrosanctum Concilium*, in which the council fathers famously said that all the faithful should be led to a "fully conscious and active participation" in the Mass. This happens through their gathering; their listening and responding; their common prayer; their sitting, standing, and kneeling; their reverent silence; their processing; their receiving; their greeting of those around them; etc.

The Mass is a great call and response between Christ the Head and his Mystical Body. As Christians, we are called to relationship with Jesus, and there is no more intense, privileged way to relate to him than at the Mass. It's the great prayer, the supreme form of adoration, and the most powerful way that we encounter the living Christ. The Mass is not a lecture or performance that we witness from a distance. That is why we are called to fully conscious and active participation in it.

---

15. Professors who are appointed to teach liturgy in seminaries, religious houses of study, and theological faculties must be properly trained for their work in institutes which specialize in this subject.

16. The study of sacred liturgy is to be ranked among the compulsory and major courses in seminaries and religious houses of studies; in theological faculties it is to rank among the principal courses. It is to be taught under its theological, historical, spiritual, pastoral, and juridical aspects. Moreover, other professors, while striving to expound the mystery of Christ and the history of salvation from the angle proper to each of their own subjects, must nevertheless do so in a way which will clearly bring out the connection between their subjects and the liturgy, as also the unity which underlies all priestly training. This consideration is especially important for professors of dogmatic, spiritual, and pastoral theology and for those of holy scripture.

17. In seminaries and houses of religious, clerics shall be given a liturgical formation in their spiritual life. For this they will need proper direction, so that they may be able to understand the sacred rites and take part in them wholeheartedly; and they will also need personally to celebrate the sacred mysteries, as well as popular devotions which are imbued with the spirit of the liturgy. In addition they must learn how to observe the liturgical laws, so that life in seminaries and houses of religious may be thoroughly influenced by the spirit of the liturgy.

18. Priests, both secular and religious, who are already working in the Lord's vineyard are to be helped by every suitable means to understand ever more fully what it is that they are doing when they perform sacred rites; they are to be aided to live the liturgical life and to share it with the faithful entrusted to their care.

19. With zeal and patience, pastors of souls must promote the liturgical instruction of the faithful, and also their active participation in the liturgy both internally and externally, taking into account their age and condition, their way of life, and standard of religious culture. By so doing, pastors will be fulfilling one of the chief duties of a faithful dispenser of the mysteries of God; and in this matter they must lead their flock not only in word but also by example.

20. Transmissions of the sacred rites by radio and television shall be done with discretion and dignity, under the leadership and direction of a suitable person appointed for this office by the bishops. This is especially important when the service to be broadcast is the Mass.

III. The Reform of the Sacred Liturgy

21. In order that the Christian people may more certainly derive an abundance of graces from the sacred liturgy, holy Mother Church desires to undertake with great care a general restoration of the liturgy itself. For the liturgy is made up of immutable elements divinely instituted, and of elements subject to change. These not only may but ought to be changed with the passage of time if they have suffered from the intrusion of anything out of harmony with the inner nature of the liturgy or have become unsuited to it.

In this restoration, both texts and rites should be drawn up so that they express more clearly the holy things which they signify; the Christian people, so far as possible, should be enabled to understand them with ease and to take part in them fully, actively, and as befits a community.

Wherefore the sacred Council establishes the following general norms:

A) GENERAL NORMS

22. §1. Regulation of the sacred liturgy depends solely on the authority of the Church, that is, on the Apostolic See and, as laws may determine, on the bishop.

§2. In virtue of power conceded by the law, the regulation of the liturgy within certain defined limits belongs also to various kinds of competent territorial bodies of bishops legitimately established.

§3. Therefore no other person, even if he be a priest, may add, remove, or change anything in the liturgy on his own authority.

Liturgy Is Never Anyone's Private Property
Sacrosanctum Concilium 22

Pope St. John Paul II

Ecclesia de Eucharistia 52

I consider it my duty . . . to appeal urgently that the liturgical norms for the celebration of the Eucharist be observed with great fidelity. These norms are a concrete expression of the authentically ecclesial nature of the Eucharist; this is their deepest meaning. Liturgy is never anyone's private property, be it of the celebrant or of the community in which the mysteries are celebrated. The Apostle Paul had to address fiery words to the community of Corinth because of grave shortcomings in their celebration of the Eucharist resulting in divisions (*schismata*) and the emergence of factions (*haireseis*) (see 1 Cor. 11:17–34). Our time, too, calls for a renewed awareness and appreciation of liturgical norms as a reflection of, and a witness to, the one universal Church made present in every celebration of the Eucharist. Priests who faithfully celebrate Mass according to the liturgical norms, and communities which conform to those norms, quietly but eloquently demonstrate their love for the Church.

23. That sound tradition may be retained, and yet the way remain open to legitimate progress, careful investigation is always to be made into each part of the liturgy which is to be revised. This investigation should be theological, historical, and pastoral. Also the general laws governing the structure and meaning of the liturgy must be studied in conjunction with the experience derived from recent liturgical reforms and from the indults conceded to various places. Finally, there must be no innovations unless the good of the Church genuinely and certainly requires them; and care must be taken that any new forms adopted should in some way grow organically from forms already existing.

As far as possible, notable differences between the rites used in adjacent regions must be carefully avoided.

24. Sacred scripture is of the greatest importance in the celebration of the liturgy. For it is from scripture that lessons are read and explained in the homily, and psalms are sung; the prayers, collects, and liturgical songs are scriptural in their inspiration and their force, and it is from the scriptures that actions and signs derive their meaning. Thus to achieve the restoration, progress, and adaptation of the sacred liturgy, it is essential to promote that warm and living love for scripture to which the venerable tradition of both eastern and western rites gives testimony.

The Soul of the Mass

Sacrosanctum Concilium 24 | Bishop Barron

In *Sacrosanctum Concilium* 24, we find the frank assertion that "sacred scripture is of the greatest importance in the celebration of the liturgy." The council fathers remind us that the readings at Mass are derived from Scripture, as are the Psalms and, more indirectly, the prayers that are recited and the liturgical songs that are sung. The Bible is the soul of the Mass as it is of theology (see DV 24). When in *Sacrosanctum Concilium* 35 the fathers say that "there is to be more reading from holy scripture, and it is to be more varied and suitable," they are not asking simply for more of the Bible but for the integral, organic, richly typological reading that we saw advocated in *Dei Verbum*. The proof of this is in the practical norms that followed the council, according to which a patristically flavored typological relationship is meant typically to obtain between the Old Testament reading and the Gospel at Mass. The liturgy is, in a very real sense, the proper home of the

Bible, the place where the Scriptures are most effectively presented and understood. This is in no sense to gainsay the importance of more technical exegesis, even of a modern sort, but to insist, in the spirit of Irenaeus and the other Church Fathers, that the Bible is above all God's Word, God's story told according to his intention and for his purpose.

25. The liturgical books are to be revised as soon as possible; experts are to be employed on the task, and bishops are to be consulted, from various parts of the world.

B) NORMS DRAWN FROM THE HIERARCHIC AND COMMUNAL NATURE OF THE LITURGY

26. Liturgical services are not private functions, but are celebrations of the Church, which is the "sacrament of unity," namely, the holy people united and ordered under their bishops.[33]

Therefore liturgical services pertain to the whole body of the Church; they manifest it and have effects upon it; but they concern the individual members of the Church in different ways, according to their differing rank, office, and actual participation.

Lex Orandi, Lex Credendi

Sacrosanctum Concilium 26

**Pope
St. John Paul II**

—

*Vicesimus Quintus
Annus* 10

Since liturgical celebrations are not private acts but "celebrations of the Church, which is the 'sacrament of unity,'" their regulation is dependent solely upon the hierarchical authority of the Church (see SC 22). The Liturgy belongs to the whole body of the Church. It is for this reason that it is not permitted to anyone, even the priest, or any group, to subtract or change anything whatsoever on their own initiative (see SC 22). Fidelity to the rites and to the authentic texts of the Liturgy is a requirement of the *Lex orandi* [the law of what is prayed], which must always be in conformity with the *Lex credendi* [the law of what is believed]. A lack of fidelity on this point may even affect the very validity of the sacraments.

27. It is to be stressed that whenever rites, according to their specific nature, make provision for communal celebration involving the presence and active participation of the faithful, this way of celebrating them is to be preferred, so far as possible, to a celebration that is individual and quasi-private.

This applies with special force to the celebration of Mass and the administration of the sacraments, even though every Mass has of itself a public and social nature.

28. In liturgical celebrations each person, minister or layman, who has an office to perform, should do all of, but only, those parts which pertain to his office by the nature of the rite and the principles of liturgy.

29. Servers, lectors, commentators, and members of the choir also exercise a genuine liturgical function. They ought, therefore, to discharge their office with the sincere piety and decorum demanded by so exalted a ministry and rightly expected of them by God's people.

Consequently they must all be deeply imbued with the spirit of the liturgy, each in his own measure, and they must be trained to perform their functions in a correct and orderly manner.

30. To promote active participation, the people should be encouraged to take part by means of acclamations, responses, psalmody, antiphons, and songs, as well as by actions, gestures, and bodily attitudes. And at the proper times all should observe a reverent silence.

31. The revision of the liturgical books must carefully attend to the provision of rubrics also for the people's parts.

32. The liturgy makes distinctions between persons according to their liturgical function and sacred Orders, and there are liturgical laws providing for due honors to be given to civil authorities. Apart from these instances, no special honors are to be paid in the liturgy to any private persons or classes of persons, whether in the ceremonies or by external display.

C) NORMS BASED UPON THE DIDACTIC AND PASTORAL NATURE OF THE LITURGY

33. Although the sacred liturgy is above all things the worship of the divine Majesty, it likewise contains much instruction for the faithful.[34] For in the liturgy God speaks to His people and Christ is still proclaiming His gospel. And the people reply to God both by song and prayer.

Moreover, the prayers addressed to God by the priest who presides over the assembly in the person of Christ are said in the name of the entire holy people and of all present. And the visible signs used by the liturgy to signify invisible divine things have been chosen by Christ or the Church. Thus not only when things are read "which were written for our instruction" (Rom. 15:4), but also when the Church prays or sings or acts, the faith of those taking part is nourished and their minds are raised to God, so that they may offer Him their rational service and more abundantly receive His grace.

Wherefore, in the revision of the liturgy, the following general norms should be observed:

A Noble and Expressive Simplicity
Sacrosanctum Concilium 34

Pope St. John Paul II

—

Vicesimus Quintus Annus 10

Since the Liturgy has great pastoral value, the liturgical books have provided for a certain degree of adaptation to the assembly and to individuals, with the possibility of openness to the traditions and cultures of different peoples. The revision of the rites has sought a noble simplicity and signs that are easily understood, but the desired simplicity must not degenerate into an impoverishment of the signs. On the contrary, the signs, above all the sacramental signs, must be easily grasped but carry the greatest possible expressiveness. Bread and wine, water and oil, and also incense, ashes, fire, and flowers, and indeed almost all the elements of creation have their place in the Liturgy as gifts to the Creator and as a contribution to the dignity and beauty of the celebration.

34. The rites should be distinguished by a noble simplicity; they should be short, clear, and unencumbered by useless repetitions; they should be within the people's powers of comprehension, and normally should not require much explanation.

35. That the intimate connection between words and rites may be apparent in the liturgy:

1. In sacred celebrations there is to be more reading from holy scripture, and it is to be more varied and suitable.

2. Because the sermon is part of the liturgical service, the best place for it is to be indicated even in the rubrics, as far as the nature of the rite will allow; the ministry of preaching is to be fulfilled with exactitude and fidelity. The sermon, moreover, should draw its content mainly from scriptural and liturgical sources, and its character should be that of a proclamation of God's wonderful works in the history of salvation, the mystery of Christ, ever made present and active within us, especially in the celebration of the liturgy.

3. Instruction which is more explicitly liturgical should also be given in a variety of ways; if necessary, short directives to be spoken by the priest or proper minister should be provided within the rites themselves. But they should occur only at the more suitable moments, and be in prescribed or similar words.

4. Bible services should be encouraged, especially on the vigils of the more solemn feasts, on some weekdays in Advent and Lent, and on Sundays and feast days. They are particularly to be commended in places where no priest is available; when this is so, a deacon or some other person authorized by the bishop should preside over the celebration.

36. §1. Particular law remaining in force, the use of the Latin language is to be preserved in the Latin rites.

§2. But since the use of the mother tongue, whether in the Mass, the administration of the sacraments, or other parts of the liturgy, frequently may be of great advantage to the people, the limits of its employment may be extended. This will apply in the first place to the readings and directives, and to some of the prayers and chants, according to the regulations on this matter to be laid down separately in subsequent chapters.

§3. These norms being observed, it is for the competent territorial ecclesiastical authority mentioned in Art. 22, 2, to decide whether, and to what extent, the vernacular language is to be used; their decrees are to be approved, that is, confirmed, by the Apostolic See. And, whenever it seems to be called for, this authority is to consult with bishops of neighboring regions which have the same language.

§4. Translations from the Latin text into the mother tongue intended for use in the liturgy must be approved by the competent territorial ecclesiastical authority mentioned above.

Preserving Latin

Sacrosanctum Concilium 36

Pope Benedict XVI

Sacramentum Caritatis 61–62

[The Eleventh Ordinary General Assembly of the Synod of Bishops] considered the quality of participation in the case of large-scale celebrations held on special occasions and involving not only a great number of the lay faithful, but also many concelebrating priests. . . .

In order to express more clearly the unity and universality of the Church, I wish to endorse the proposal made by the Synod of Bishops, in harmony with the directives of the Second Vatican Council, that, with the exception of the readings, the homily, and the prayer of the faithful, it is fitting that such liturgies be celebrated in Latin. Similarly, the better-known prayers of the Church's tradition should be recited in Latin and, if possible, selections of Gregorian chant should be sung. Speaking more generally, I ask that future priests, from their time in the seminary, receive the preparation needed to understand and to celebrate Mass in Latin, and also to use Latin texts and execute Gregorian chant; nor should we forget that the faithful can be taught to recite the more common prayers in Latin, and also to sing parts of the liturgy to Gregorian chant.

D) NORMS FOR ADAPTING THE LITURGY TO THE CULTURE AND TRADITIONS OF PEOPLES

37. Even in the liturgy, the Church has no wish to impose a rigid uniformity in matters which do not implicate the faith or the good of the whole community; rather does she respect and foster the genius and talents of the various races and peoples. Anything in these peoples' way of life which is not indissolubly bound up with superstition and error she studies with sympathy and, if possible, preserves intact. Sometimes in fact she admits such things into the liturgy itself, so long as they harmonize with its true and authentic spirit.

38. Provisions shall also be made, when revising the liturgical books, for legitimate variations and adaptations to different groups, regions, and peoples, especially in mission lands, provided that the substantial unity of the Roman rite is preserved; and this should be borne in mind when drawing up the rites and devising rubrics.

39. Within the limits set by the typical editions of the liturgical books, it shall be for the competent territorial ecclesiastical authority mentioned in Art. 22, 2, to specify adaptations, especially in the case of the administration of the sacraments, the sacramentals, processions, liturgical language, sacred music, and the arts, but according to the fundamental norms laid down in this Constitution.

40. In some places and circumstances, however, an even more radical adaptation of the liturgy is needed, and this entails greater difficulties. Wherefore:

1. The competent territorial ecclesiastical authority mentioned in Art. 22, 2, must, in this matter, carefully and prudently consider which elements from the traditions and culture of individual peoples might appropriately be admitted into divine worship. Adaptations which are judged to be useful or necessary should then be submitted to the Apostolic See, by whose consent they may be introduced.

2. To ensure that adaptations may be made with all the circumspection which they demand, the Apostolic See will grant power to this same territorial ecclesiastical authority to permit

and to direct, as the case requires, the necessary preliminary experiments over a determined period of time among certain groups suited for the purpose.

3. Because liturgical laws often involve special difficulties with respect to adaptation, particularly in mission lands, men who are experts in these matters must be employed to formulate them.

Inculturation of the Liturgy
Sacrosanctum Concilium 37–40

Pope Francis
—
Querida Amazonia
82

"Encountering God does not mean fleeing from this world or turning our back on nature." It means that we can take up into the liturgy many elements proper to the experience of indigenous peoples in their contact with nature, and respect native forms of expression in song, dance, rituals, gestures, and symbols. The Second Vatican Council called for this effort to inculturate the liturgy among indigenous peoples; over fifty years have passed and we still have far to go along these lines.

E) PROMOTION OF LITURGICAL LIFE IN DIOCESE AND PARISH

41. The bishop is to be considered as the high priest of his flock, from whom the life in Christ of his faithful is in some way derived and dependent.

Therefore all should hold in great esteem the liturgical life of the diocese centered around the bishop, especially in his cathedral church; they must be convinced that the pre-eminent manifestation of the Church consists in the full active participation of all God's holy people in these liturgical celebrations, especially in the same eucharist, in a single prayer, at one altar, at which there presides the bishop surrounded by his college of priests and by his ministers.[35]

42. But because it is impossible for the bishop always and everywhere to preside over the whole flock in his Church, he cannot do other than establish lesser groupings of the faithful. Among these the parishes, set up locally under a pastor who takes the place of the bishop, are the

most important: for in some manner they represent the visible Church constituted throughout the world.

And therefore the liturgical life of the parish and its relationship to the bishop must be fostered theoretically and practically among the faithful and clergy; efforts also must be made to encourage a sense of community within the parish, above all in the common celebration of the Sunday Mass.

F) THE PROMOTION OF PASTORAL-LITURGICAL ACTION

43. Zeal for the promotion and restoration of the liturgy is rightly held to be a sign of the providential dispositions of God in our time, as a movement of the Holy Spirit in His Church. It is today a distinguishing mark of the Church's life, indeed of the whole tenor of contemporary religious thought and action.

So that this pastoral-liturgical action may become even more vigorous in the Church, the sacred Council decrees:

Movement of the Spirit, Abuse of the Reform

Sacrosanctum Concilium 43

Pope St. John Paul II

———

Vicesimus Quintus Annus 12–13

The vast majority of the pastors and the Christian people have accepted the liturgical reform in a spirit of obedience and indeed joyful fervor. For this we should give thanks to God for that movement of the Holy Spirit in the Church which the liturgical renewal represents; for the fact that the table of the word of God is now abundantly furnished for all; for the immense effort undertaken throughout the world to provide the Christian people with translations of the Bible, the Missal, and other liturgical books; for the increased participation of the faithful by prayer and song, gesture and silence, in the Eucharist and the other sacraments; for the ministries exercised by lay people and the responsibilities that they have assumed in virtue of the common priesthood into which they have been initiated through Baptism and Confirmation; for the radiant vitality of so many Christian communities, a vitality drawn from the wellspring of the Liturgy.

These are all reasons for holding fast to the teaching of the Constitution *Sacrosanctum Concilium* and to the reforms which it has made possible: "the liturgical renewal is the most visible fruit of the whole work of the Council." For many people the message of the Second Vatican Council has been experienced principally through the liturgical reform.

Side by side with these benefits of the liturgical reform, one has to acknowledge with regret deviations of greater or lesser seriousness in its application.

On occasion there have been noted illicit omissions or additions, rites invented outside the framework of established norms; postures or songs which are not conducive to faith or to a sense of the sacred; abuses in the practice of general absolution; confusion between the ministerial priesthood, linked with Ordination, and the common priesthood of the faithful, which has its foundation in Baptism.

It cannot be tolerated that certain priests should take upon themselves the right to compose Eucharistic Prayers or to substitute profane readings for texts from Sacred Scripture. Initiatives of this sort, far from being linked with the liturgical reform as such, or with the books which have issued from it, are in direct contradiction to it, disfigure it, and deprive the Christian people of the genuine treasures of the Liturgy of the Church.

It is for the bishops to root out such abuses, because the regulation of the Liturgy depends on the bishop within the limits of the law and because "from [him] the life in Christ of his faithful is in some way derived and dependent" (SC 41)

44. It is desirable that the competent territorial ecclesiastical authority mentioned in Art. 22, 2, set up a liturgical commission, to be assisted by experts in liturgical science, sacred music, art, and pastoral practice. So far as possible the commission should be aided by some kind of Institute for Pastoral Liturgy, consisting of persons who are eminent in these matters, and including laymen as circumstances suggest. Under the direction of the above-mentioned territorial ecclesiastical authority the commission

is to regulate pastoral-liturgical action throughout the territory, and to promote studies and necessary experiments whenever there is question of adaptations to be proposed to the Apostolic See.

45. For the same reason every diocese is to have a commission on the sacred liturgy under the direction of the bishop, for promoting the liturgical apostolate.

Sometimes it may be expedient that several dioceses should form between them one single commission which will be able to promote the liturgy by common consultation.

46. Besides the commission on the sacred liturgy, every diocese, as far as possible, should have commissions for sacred music and sacred art.

These three commissions must work in closest collaboration; indeed it will often be best to fuse the three of them into one single commission.

CHAPTER II
The Most Sacred Mystery of the Eucharist

47. At the Last Supper, on the night when He was betrayed, our Savior instituted the eucharistic sacrifice of His Body and Blood. He did this in order to perpetuate the sacrifice of the Cross throughout the centuries

The Sacrifice of the Cross Perpetuated
Sacrosanctum Concilium 47

Pope St. John Paul II

—

Ecclesia de Eucharistia 11

"The Lord Jesus on the night he was betrayed" (1 Cor. 11:23) instituted the Eucharistic Sacrifice of his body and his blood. The words of the Apostle Paul bring us back to the dramatic setting in which the Eucharist was born. The Eucharist is indelibly marked by the event of the Lord's passion and death, of which it is not only a reminder but the sacramental re-presentation. It is the sacrifice of the Cross perpetuated down the ages. This truth is well expressed by the words with which the assembly in the Latin rite responds to the priest's proclamation of the "Mystery of Faith": "*We announce your death, O Lord.*"

until He should come again, and so to entrust to His beloved spouse, the Church, a memorial of His death and resurrection: a sacrament of love, a sign of unity, a bond of charity,[36] a paschal banquet in which Christ is eaten, the mind is filled with grace, and a pledge of future glory is given to us.[37]

48. The Church, therefore, earnestly desires that Christ's faithful, when present at this mystery of faith, should not be there as strangers or silent spectators; on the contrary, through a good understanding of the rites and prayers they should take part in the sacred action conscious of what they are doing, with devotion and full collaboration. They should be instructed by God's word and be nourished at the table of the Lord's body; they should give thanks to God; by offering the Immaculate Victim, not only through the hands of the priest, but also with him, they should learn also

Participants in the Sacred Action

Sacrosanctum Concilium 48

Pope Benedict XVI

———

Sacramentum Caritatis 52

The Second Vatican Council rightly emphasized the active, full, and fruitful participation of the entire People of God in the eucharistic celebration (see SC 14–20; 30ff.). Certainly, the renewal carried out in these past decades has made considerable progress towards fulfilling the wishes of the Council Fathers. Yet we must not overlook the fact that some misunderstanding has occasionally arisen concerning the precise meaning of this participation. It should be made clear that the word "participation" does not refer to mere external activity during the celebration. In fact, the active participation called for by the Council must be understood in more substantial terms, on the basis of a greater awareness of the mystery being celebrated and its relationship to daily life. The conciliar Constitution *Sacrosanctum Concilium* encouraged the faithful to take part in the eucharistic liturgy not "as strangers or silent spectators," but as participants "in the sacred action conscious of what they are doing, with devotion and full collaboration." This exhortation has lost none of its force.

to offer themselves; through Christ the Mediator,[38] they should be drawn day by day into ever more perfect union with God and with each other, so that finally God may be all in all.

49. For this reason the sacred Council, having in mind those Masses which are celebrated with the assistance of the faithful, especially on Sundays and feasts of obligation, has made the following decrees in order that the sacrifice of the Mass, even in the ritual forms of its celebration, may become pastorally efficacious to the fullest degree.

50. The rite of the Mass is to be revised in such a way that the intrinsic nature and purpose of its several parts, as also the connection between them, may be more clearly manifested, and that devout and active participation by the faithful may be more easily achieved.

For this purpose the rites are to be simplified, due care being taken to preserve their substance; elements which, with the passage of time, came to be duplicated, or were added with but little advantage, are now to be discarded; other elements which have suffered injury through accidents of history are now to be restored to the vigor which they had in the days of the holy Fathers, as may seem useful or necessary.

51. The treasures of the bible are to be opened up more lavishly, so that richer fare may be provided for the faithful at the table of God's word. In this way a more representative portion of the holy scriptures will be read to the people in the course of a prescribed number of years.

The Treasures of Scripture in the Lectionary
Sacrosanctum Concilium 51

**Pope
Benedict XVI**
———
Verbum Domini 57

The reform [of the lectionary] called for by the Second Vatican Council (see SC 107–108) has borne fruit in a richer access to sacred Scripture, which is now offered in abundance, especially at Sunday Mass. The present structure of the Lectionary not only presents the more important texts of Scripture with some frequency, but also helps us to understand the unity of God's plan thanks to the interplay of the Old and New Testament readings, an interplay "in which Christ is the central figure, commemorated in his paschal mystery." Any remaining difficulties in seeing the relationship between those readings should be approached in the light of canonical interpretation, that is to say, by referring to the inherent unity of the Bible as a whole. . . .

Nor should we overlook the fact that the current Lectionary of the Latin rite has ecumenical significance, since it is used and valued also by communities not yet in full communion with the Catholic Church.

52. By means of the homily the mysteries of the faith and the guiding principles of the Christian life are expounded from the sacred text, during the course of the liturgical year; the homily, therefore, is to be highly esteemed as part of the liturgy itself; in fact, at those Masses which are celebrated with the assistance of the people on Sundays and feasts of obligation, it should not be omitted except for a serious reason.

The Homily Is a Liturgical Act

Sacrosanctum Concilium 52 | Bishop Barron

One of the most powerful presentations of Jesus' speech is the story, found in the fourth chapter of St. John's Gospel, of the encounter with the Samaritan woman at the well. Although Jesus speaks intimately with one person, homilists can learn a great deal by apprenticing to the style and content of the Master's words on this occasion.

For the homily is a proposal of marriage; in the liturgical sermon, Christ the Bridegroom is seeking his Bride. And those who listen to a homily are, consciously or not, seeking communion with the Lord. Two thirsts meet therefore in every sermon: God's thirst for us and ours for God. And the preacher functions as a kind of mediator of this encounter. He must above all articulate the divine longing for us—for grace always comes first— but he also has the responsibility of naming and stirring up our longing for God. Beyond all of the proximate yearnings and concerns of a human being, there lies an ultimate concern, a hunger and thirst for perfect truth, goodness, and beauty. The woman at the well is every man and every woman who seeks after God with holy longing. In this sense, she is a sister to Nicodemus, Bartimaeus, Zacchaeus, Simon the Pharisee, Mary Magdalene, Peter, Pontius Pilate, the centurion at the cross—all those who encountered Christ at the level of the heart. Every homily should be a meeting of thirst and fulfillment. If only questions are entertained, the homily becomes diffuse and unfocused; and if only answers are given, it becomes strident or dry. The preacher should be so deft at awakening the questions and thirsts of the heart that his listeners will be eager for the answers he gives and will echo the woman at the well: "Give me this water, so that I may never be thirsty" (John 4:15).

Moral challenges—even those dealing with the delicate issues of sex, marriage, and relationships—can be offered and can be heard, provided that they are made in the context of the promise of grace. The woman at the well was not put off by Jesus' willingness to name her dysfunction; indeed, it drew from her a word of praise: "Sir, I see that you are a prophet" (John 4:19). And it led her to ask the most searching question of all, the one dealing with the worship of the true God.

One of the most important teachings of Vatican II in regard to preaching was the insistence that the homily is not a pious talk that happens to take place during the liturgy, but is instead an integral part of the liturgy itself. Jesus' conversation with the woman at the well led her, finally, to right praise. So the homily at the Sunday liturgy—involving inspiration, information, moral instruction, etc.—is meant to lead finally to the right praise of God, to the true "thanksgiving" that is at the heart of the Liturgy of the Eucharist. In fact, one might even say that the homilist connects the two sections of the Mass, as he looks back at the readings and looks ahead to the sacrificial meal.

---

53. Especially on Sundays and feasts of obligation there is to be restored, after the Gospel and the homily, "the common prayer" or "the prayer of the faithful." By this prayer, in which the people are to take part, intercession will be made for holy Church, for the civil authorities, for those oppressed by various needs, for all mankind, and for the salvation of the entire world.[39]

54. In Masses which are celebrated with the people, a suitable place may be allotted to their mother tongue. This is to apply in the first place to the readings and "the common prayer," but also, as local conditions may warrant, to those parts which pertain to the people, according to the norm laid down in Art. 36 of this Constitution.

Nevertheless steps should be taken so that the faithful may also be able to say or to sing together in Latin those parts of the Ordinary of the Mass which pertain to them.

And wherever a more extended use of the mother tongue within the Mass appears desirable, the regulation laid down in Art. 40 of this Constitution is to be observed.

55. That more perfect form of participation in the Mass whereby the faithful, after the priest's communion, receive the Lord's body from the same sacrifice, is strongly commended.

The dogmatic principles which were laid down by the Council of Trent remaining intact,[40] communion under both kinds may be granted when the bishops think fit, not only to clerics and religious, but also to the laity, in cases to be determined by the Apostolic See, as, for instance, to the newly ordained in the Mass of their sacred ordination, to the newly professed in the Mass of their religious profession, and to the newly baptized in the Mass which follows their baptism.

56. The two parts which, in a certain sense, go to make up the Mass, namely, the liturgy of the word and the eucharistic liturgy, are so closely connected with each other that they form but one single act of worship. Accordingly this sacred Synod strongly urges pastors of souls that, when instructing the faithful, they insistently teach them to take their part in the entire Mass, especially on Sundays and feasts of obligation.

57. §1. Concelebration, whereby the unity of the priesthood is appropriately manifested, has remained in use to this day in the Church both in the east and in the west. For this reason it has seemed good to the Council to extend permission for concelebration to the following cases:

1.   a) on the Thursday of the Lord's Supper, not only at the Mass of the Chrism, but also at the evening Mass.
    b) at Masses during councils, bishops' conferences, and synods;
    c) at the Mass for the blessing of an abbot.

2. Also, with permission of the ordinary, to whom it belongs to decide whether concelebration is opportune:

    a) at conventual Mass, and at the principal Mass in churches when the needs of the faithful do not require that all priests available should celebrate individually;

    b) at Masses celebrated at any kind of priests' meetings, whether the priests be secular clergy or religious.

§2.

1. The regulation, however, of the discipline of concelebration in the diocese pertains to the bishop.

2. Nevertheless, each priest shall always retain his right to celebrate Mass individually, though not at the same time in the same church as a concelebrated Mass, nor on Thursday of the Lord's Supper.

58. A new rite for concelebration is to be drawn up and inserted into the Pontifical and into the Roman Missal.

CHAPTER III
The Other Sacraments and the Sacramentals

59. The purpose of the sacraments is to sanctify men, to build up the body of Christ, and, finally, to give worship to God; because they are signs they also instruct. They not only presuppose faith, but by words and objects they also nourish, strengthen, and express it; that is why they are called "sacraments of faith." They do indeed impart grace, but, in addition, the very act of celebrating them most effectively disposes the faithful to receive this grace in a fruitful manner, to worship God duly, and to practice charity.

It is therefore of the highest importance that the faithful should easily understand the sacramental signs, and should frequent with great eagerness those sacraments which were instituted to nourish the Christian life.

60. Holy Mother Church has, moreover, instituted sacramentals. These are sacred signs which bear a resemblance to the sacraments: they signify effects, particularly of a spiritual kind, which are obtained through the Church's intercession. By them men are disposed to receive the chief effect of the sacraments, and various occasions in life are rendered holy.

61. Thus, for well-disposed members of the faithful, the liturgy of the sacraments and sacramentals sanctifies almost every event in their lives; they are given access to the stream of divine grace which flows from the paschal mystery of the passion, death, and resurrection of Christ, the font from which all sacraments and sacramentals draw their power. There is hardly any proper use of material things which cannot thus be directed toward the sanctification of men and the praise of God.

62. With the passage of time, however, there have crept into the rites of the sacraments and sacramentals certain features which have rendered their nature and purpose far from clear to the people of today; hence some changes have become necessary to adapt them to the needs of our own times. For this reason the sacred Council decrees as follows concerning their revision.

63. Because of the use of the mother tongue in the administration of the sacraments and sacramentals can often be of considerable help to the people, this use is to be extended according to the following norms:

    a) The vernacular language may be used in administering the sacraments and sacramentals, according to the norm of Art. 36.

    b) In harmony with the new edition of the Roman Ritual, particular rituals shall be prepared without delay by the competent territorial ecclesiastical authority mentioned in Art. 22, 2, of this Constitution. These rituals, which are to be adapted, also as regards the language employed, to the needs of the different regions, are to be reviewed by the Apostolic See and then introduced into the regions for which they have been prepared. But in drawing up these rituals or particular collections of rites, the instructions prefixed to the individual rites in the Roman Ritual, whether they be pastoral and rubrical or whether they have special social import, shall not be omitted.

64. The catechumenate for adults, comprising several distinct steps, is to be restored and to be taken into use at the discretion of the local ordinary. By this means the time of the catechumenate, which is intended as a period of suitable instruction, may be sanctified by sacred rites to be celebrated at successive intervals of time.

The Road of Preparation for Baptism
Sacrosanctum Concilium 64

Pope Francis
—
Lumen Fidei 42

Water is at once a symbol of death, inviting us to pass through self-conversion to a new and greater identity, and a symbol of life, of a womb in which we are reborn by following Christ in his new life. In this way, through immersion in water, baptism speaks to us of the incarnational structure of faith. Christ's work penetrates the depths of our being and transforms us radically, making us adopted children of God and sharers in the divine nature. It thus modifies all our relationships, our place in this world and in the universe, and opens them to God's own life of communion. This change which takes place in baptism helps us to appreciate the singular importance of the catechumenate—whereby growing numbers of adults, even in societies with ancient Christian roots, now approach the sacrament of baptism—for the new evangelization. It is the road of preparation for baptism, for the transformation of our whole life in Christ.

65. In mission lands it is found that some of the peoples already make use of initiation rites. Elements from these, when capable of being adapted to Christian ritual, may be admitted along with those already found in Christian tradition, according to the norm laid down in Art. 37–40, of this Constitution.

66. Both the rites for the baptism of adults are to be revised: not only the simpler rite, but also the more solemn one, which must take into account the restored catechumenate. A special Mass "for the conferring of baptism" is to be inserted into the Roman Missal.

67. The rite for the baptism of infants is to be revised, and it should be adapted to the circumstance that those to be baptized are, in fact, infants. The roles of parents and godparents, and also their duties, should be brought out more clearly in the rite itself.

68. The baptismal rite should contain variants, to be used at the discretion of the local ordinary, for occasions when a very large number are to be baptized together. Moreover, a shorter rite is to be drawn up, especially for mission lands, to be used by catechists, but also by the faithful in general when there is danger of death, and neither priest nor deacon is available.

69. In place of the rite called the "Order of supplying what was omitted in the baptism of an infant," a new rite is to be drawn up. This should manifest more fittingly and clearly that the infant, baptized by the short rite, has already been received into the Church.

And a new rite is to be drawn up for converts who have already been validly baptized; it should indicate that they are now admitted to communion with the Church.

70. Except during Eastertide, baptismal water may be blessed within the rite of baptism itself by an approved shorter formula.

71. The rite of confirmation is to be revised and the intimate connection which this sacrament has with the whole of Christian initiation is to be more clearly set forth; for this reason it is fitting for candidates to renew their baptismal promises just before they are confirmed.

Confirmation may be given within the Mass when convenient; when it is given outside the Mass, the rite that is used should be introduced by a formula to be drawn up for this purpose.

72. The rite and formulas for the sacrament of penance are to be revised so that they more clearly express both the nature and effect of the sacrament.

73. "Extreme unction," which may also and more fittingly be called "anointing of the sick," is not a sacrament for those only who are at the point of death. Hence, as soon as any one of the faithful begins to be in danger of death from sickness or old age, the fitting time for him to receive this sacrament has certainly already arrived.

74. In addition to the separate rites for anointing of the sick and for viaticum, a continuous rite shall be prepared according to which the sick man is anointed after he has made his confession and before he receives viaticum.

75. The number of the anointings is to be adapted to the occasion, and the prayers which belong to the rite of anointing are to be revised so as to correspond with the varying conditions of the sick who receive the sacrament.

76. Both the ceremonies and texts of the ordination rites are to be revised. The address given by the bishop at the beginning of each ordination or consecration may be in the mother tongue.

When a bishop is consecrated, the laying of hands may be done by all the bishops present.

77. The marriage rite now found in the Roman Ritual is to be revised and enriched in such a way that the grace of the sacrament is more clearly signified and the duties of the spouses are taught.

"If any regions are wont to use other praiseworthy customs and ceremonies when celebrating the sacrament of matrimony, the sacred Synod earnestly desires that these by all means be retained."[41]

Moreover the competent territorial ecclesiastical authority mentioned in Art. 22, 2, of this Constitution is free to draw up its own rite suited to the usages of place and people, according to the provision of Art. 63. But the rite must always conform to the law that the priest assisting at the marriage must ask for and obtain the consent of the contracting parties.

78. Matrimony is normally to be celebrated within the Mass, after the reading of the gospel and the homily, and before "the prayer of the faithful." The prayer for the bride, duly amended to remind both spouses of their equal obligation to remain faithful to each other, may be said in the mother tongue.

But if the sacrament of matrimony is celebrated apart from Mass, the epistle and gospel from the nuptial Mass are to be read at the beginning of the rite, and the blessing should always be given to the spouses.

79. The sacramentals are to undergo a revision which takes into account the primary principle of enabling the faithful to participate intelligently, actively, and easily; the circumstances of our own days must also be considered. When rituals are revised, as laid down in Art. 63, new sacramentals may also be added as the need for these becomes apparent.

Reserved blessings shall be very few; reservations shall be in favor of bishops or ordinaries.

Let provision be made that some sacramentals, at least in special circumstances and at the discretion of the ordinary, may be administered by qualified lay persons.

80. The rite for the consecration of virgins at present found in the Roman Pontifical is to be revised.

Moreover, a rite of religious profession and renewal of vows shall be drawn up in order to achieve greater unity, sobriety, and dignity. Apart from exceptions in particular law, this rite should be adopted by those who make their profession or renewal of vows within the Mass.

Religious profession should preferably be made within the Mass.

81. The rite for the burial of the dead should express more clearly the paschal character of Christian death, and should correspond more closely to the circumstances and traditions found in various regions. This holds good also for the liturgical color to be used.

82. The rite for the burial of infants is to be revised, and a special Mass for the occasion should be provided.

CHAPTER IV
The Divine Office

83. Christ Jesus, high priest of the new and eternal covenant, taking human nature, introduced into this earthly exile that hymn which is sung throughout all ages in the halls of heaven. He joins the entire community of mankind to Himself, associating it with His own singing of this canticle of divine praise.

For he continues His priestly work through the agency of His Church, which is ceaselessly engaged in praising the Lord and interceding for the salvation of the whole world. She does this, not only by celebrating the eucharist, but also in other ways, especially by praying the divine office.

84. By tradition going back to early Christian times, the divine office is devised so that the whole course of the day and night is made holy by the praises of God. Therefore, when this wonderful song of praise is rightly

performed by priests and others who are deputed for this purpose by the Church's ordinance, or by the faithful praying together with the priest in the approved form, then it is truly the voice of the bride addressed to her bridegroom; it is the very prayer which Christ Himself, together with His body, addresses to the Father.

85. Hence all who render this service are not only fulfilling a duty of the Church, but also are sharing in the greatest honor of Christ's spouse, for by offering these praises to God they are standing before God's throne in the name of the Church their Mother.

86. Priests who are engaged in the sacred pastoral ministry will offer the praises of the hours with greater fervor the more vividly they realize that they must heed St. Paul's exhortation: "Pray without ceasing" (1 Thess. 5:17). For the work in which they labor will effect nothing and bring forth no fruit except by the power of the Lord who said: "Without me you can do nothing" (John 15:5). That is why the apostles, instituting deacons, said: "We will devote ourselves to prayer and to the ministry of the word" (Acts 6:4).

87. In order that the divine office may be better and more perfectly prayed in existing circumstances, whether by priests or by other members of the Church, the sacred Council, carrying further the restoration already so happily begun by the Apostolic See, has seen fit to decree as follows concerning the office of the Roman rite.

88. Because the purpose of the office is to sanctify the day, the traditional sequence of the hours is to be restored so that once again they may be genuinely related to the time of the day when they are prayed, as far as this may be possible. Moreover, it will be necessary to take into account the modern conditions in which daily life has to be lived, especially by those who are called to labor in apostolic works.

89. Therefore, when the office is revised, these norms are to be observed:
   a) By the venerable tradition of the universal Church, Lauds as morning prayer and Vespers as evening prayer are the two hinges on which the daily office turns; hence they are to be considered as the chief hours and are to be celebrated as such.

   b) Compline is to be drawn up so that it will be a suitable prayer for the end of the day.

   c) The hour known as Matins, although it should retain the character of nocturnal praise when celebrated in choir, shall be adapted so that it may be recited at any hour of the day; it shall be made up of fewer psalms and longer readings.

   d) The hour of Prime is to be suppressed.

   e) In choir the hours of Terce, Sext, and None are to be observed. But outside choir it will be lawful to select any one of these three, according to the respective time of the day.

90. The divine office, because it is the public prayer of the Church, is a source of piety, and nourishment for personal prayer. And therefore priests and all others who take part in the divine office are earnestly exhorted in the Lord to attune their minds to their voices when praying it. The better to achieve this, let them take steps to improve their understanding of the liturgy and of the bible, especially of the psalms.

   In revising the Roman office, its ancient and venerable treasures are to be so adapted that all those to whom they are handed on may more extensively and easily draw profit from them.

Sharing in the Greatest Honor of Christ's Spouse

Sacrosanctum Concilium 83–90

Pope Benedict XVI

Verbum Domini 62

Among the forms of prayer which emphasize sacred Scripture, the Liturgy of the Hours has an undoubted place. [The Fathers of the Synod on the Word of God] called it "a privileged form of hearing the word of God, inasmuch as it brings the faithful into contact with Scripture and the living Tradition of the Church." Above all, we should reflect on the profound theological and ecclesial dignity of this prayer. "In the Liturgy of the Hours, the Church, exercising the priestly office of her Head, offers 'incessantly' (1 Thess. 5:17) to God the sacrifice of praise, that is, the fruit of lips that confess his name (see Heb. 13:15). This prayer is 'the voice of a bride speaking to her bridegroom, it is the very prayer that Christ himself, together with his Body, addressed to the Father.'" The Second Vatican Council stated in this regard that "all who render this service are not only fulfilling a duty of the Church, but also are sharing in the greatest honor of Christ's spouse, for by offering these praises to God they are standing before God's throne in the name of the Church their Mother." The Liturgy of the Hours, as the public prayer of the Church, sets forth the Christian ideal of the sanctification of the entire day, marked by the rhythm of hearing the word of God and praying the Psalms; in this way every activity can find its point of reference in the praise offered to God.

Those who by virtue of their state in life are obliged to pray the Liturgy of the Hours should carry out this duty faithfully for the benefit of the whole Church. Bishops, priests, and deacons aspiring to the priesthood, all of whom have been charged by the Church to celebrate this liturgy, are obliged to pray all the Hours daily. As for the obligation of celebrating this liturgy in the Eastern Catholic Churches *sui iuris* [autonomous], the prescriptions of their proper law are to be followed. I also encourage communities of consecrated life to be exemplary in the celebration of the Liturgy of the Hours, and thus to become a point of reference and an inspiration for the spiritual and pastoral life of the whole Church.

The Synod [on the Word of God] asked that this prayer become more widespread among the People of God, particularly the recitation of Morning Prayer and Evening Prayer. This could only lead to greater familiarity with the word of God on the part of the faithful. Emphasis should also be placed on the value of the Liturgy of the Hours for the First Vespers of Sundays and Solemnities, particularly in the Eastern Catholic Churches. To this end I recommend that, wherever possible, parishes and religious communities promote this prayer with the participation of the lay faithful.

91. So that it may really be possible in practice to observe the course of the hours proposed in Art. 89, the psalms are no longer to be distributed throughout one week, but through some longer period of time.

The work of revising the psalter, already happily begun, is to be finished as soon as possible, and is to take into account the style of Christian Latin, the liturgical use of psalms, also when sung, and the entire tradition of the Latin Church.

92. As regards the readings, the following shall be observed: a) Readings from sacred scripture shall be arranged so that the riches of God's word may be easily accessible in more abundant measure.

b) Readings excerpted from the works of the fathers, doctors, and ecclesiastical writers shall be better selected.

c) The accounts of martyrdom or the lives of the saints are to accord with the facts of history.

93. To whatever extent may seem desirable, the hymns are to be restored to their original form, and whatever smacks of mythology or ill accords with Christian piety is to be removed or changed. Also, as occasion may arise, let other selections from the treasury of hymns be incorporated.

94. That the day may be truly sanctified, and that the hours themselves may be recited with spiritual advantage, it is best that each of them be prayed at a time which most closely corresponds with its true canonical time.

95. Communities obliged to choral office are bound to celebrate the office in choir every day in addition to the conventual Mass. In particular:

a) Orders of canons, of monks, and of nuns, and of other regulars bound by law or constitutions to choral office must celebrate the entire office.

b) Cathedral or collegiate chapters are bound to recite those parts of the office imposed on them by general or particular law.

c) All members of the above communities who are in major orders or who are solemnly professed, except for lay brothers, are bound to recite individually those canonical hours which they do not pray in choir.

96. Clerics not bound to office in choir, if they are in major orders, are bound to pray the entire office every day, either in common or individually, as laid down in Art. 89.

97. Appropriate instances are to be defined by the rubrics in which a liturgical service may be substituted for the divine office.

In particular cases, and for a just reason, ordinaries can dispense their subjects wholly or in part from the obligation of reciting the divine office, or may commute the obligation.

98. Members of any institute dedicated to acquiring perfection who, according to their constitutions, are to recite any parts of the divine office are thereby performing the public prayer of the Church.

They too perform the public prayer of the Church who, in virtue of their constitutions, recite any short office, provided this is drawn up after the pattern of the divine office and is duly approved.

99. Since the divine office is the voice of the Church, that is of the whole mystical body publicly praising God, those clerics who are not obliged to office in choir, especially priests who live together or who assemble for any purpose, are urged to pray at least some part of the divine office in common.

All who pray the divine office, whether in choir or in common, should fulfill the task entrusted to them as perfectly as possible: this refers not only to the internal devotion of their minds but also to their external manner of celebration.

It is, moreover, fitting that the office, both in choir and in common, be sung when possible.

100. Pastors of souls should see to it that the chief hours, especially Vespers, are celebrated in common in church on Sundays and the more solemn feasts. And the laity, too, are encouraged to recite the divine office, either with the priests, or among themselves, or even individually.

101. §1. In accordance with the centuries-old tradition of the Latin rite, the Latin language is to be retained by clerics in the divine office. But in individual cases the ordinary has the power of granting the use of a vernacular translation to those clerics for whom the use of Latin constitutes a grave obstacle to their praying the office properly. The vernacular version, however, must be one that is drawn up according to the provision of Art. 36.

§2. The competent superior has the power to grant the use of the vernacular in the celebration of the divine office, even in choir, to nuns and to members of institutes dedicated to acquiring perfection, both men who are not clerics and women. The version, however, must be one that is approved.

§3. Any cleric bound to the divine office fulfills his obligation if he prays the office in the vernacular together with a group of the faithful or with those mentioned in 52 above provided that the text of the translation is approved.

CHAPTER V
The Liturgical Year

102. Holy Mother Church is conscious that she must celebrate the saving work of her divine Spouse by devoutly recalling it on certain days throughout the course of the year. Every week, on the day which she has called the Lord's day, she keeps the memory of the Lord's resurrection, which she also celebrates once in the year, together with His blessed passion, in the most solemn festival of Easter.

Within the cycle of a year, moreover, she unfolds the whole mystery of Christ, from the incarnation and birth until the ascension, the day of Pentecost, and the expectation of blessed hope and of the coming of the Lord.

Recalling thus the mysteries of redemption, the Church opens to the faithful the riches of her Lord's powers and merits, so that these are in some way made present for all time, and the faithful are enabled to lay hold upon them and become filled with saving grace.

The Reenactment of the Paschal Mystery
Sacrosanctum Concilium 102

Pope St. John Paul II

———

Vicesimus Quintus Annus 5–6

The guiding principles of the Constitution which were the basis of the reform, remain fundamental in the task of leading the faithful to an active celebration of the mysteries, "the primary and indispensable source . . . [of] the true Christian spirit" (SC 14). . . .

The first principle is the reenactment of the Paschal Mystery of Christ in the Liturgy of the Church, based on the fact that "it was from the side of Christ as He slept the sleep of death upon the cross that there came forth 'the wondrous sacrament of the whole Church'" (SC 5). The whole of liturgical life gravitates about the Eucharistic Sacrifice and the other sacraments in which we draw upon the living springs of salvation (see Isa. 13:3). Hence we must have a sufficient awareness that through the "Paschal Mystery we have been buried with Christ in Baptism, so that we may rise with him to new life." When the faithful participate in the Eucharist they must understand that truly "each time we offer this memorial sacrifice the work of our redemption is accomplished," and to this end bishops must carefully train the faithful to celebrate every Sunday the marvelous work that Christ has wrought in the mystery of his Passover, in order that they likewise may proclaim it to the world. In the hearts of all, bishops and faithful, Easter must regain its unique importance in the liturgical year, so that it really is the Feast of feasts.

Since Christ's Death on the Cross and his Resurrection constitute the content of the daily life of the Church and the pledge of his eternal Passover, the Liturgy has as its first task to lead us untiringly back to the Easter pilgrimage initiated by Christ, in which we accept death in order to enter into life.

103. In celebrating this annual cycle of Christ's mysteries, holy Church honors with special love the Blessed Mary, Mother of God, who is joined by an inseparable bond to the saving work of her Son. In her the Church holds up and admires the most excellent fruit of the redemption, and joyfully contemplates, as in a faultless image, that which she herself desires and hopes wholly to be.

104. The Church has also included in the annual cycle days devoted to the memory of the martyrs and the other saints. Raised up to perfection by the manifold grace of God, and already in possession of eternal salvation, they sing God's perfect praise in heaven and offer prayers for us. By celebrating the passage of these saints from earth to heaven the Church proclaims the paschal mystery achieved in the saints who have suffered and been glorified

with Christ; she proposes them to the faithful as examples drawing all to the Father through Christ, and through their merits she pleads for God's favors.

105. Finally, in the various seasons of the year and according to her traditional discipline, the Church completes the formation of the faithful by means of pious practices for soul and body, by instruction, prayer, and works of penance and of mercy.

Accordingly the sacred Council has seen fit to decree as follows.

106. By a tradition handed down from the apostles which took its origin from the very day of Christ's resurrection, the Church celebrates the paschal mystery every seventh day; with good reason this, then, bears the name of the Lord's day or Sunday. For on this day Christ's faithful are bound to come together into one place so that, by hearing the word of God and taking part in the eucharist, they may call to mind the passion, the resurrection, and the glorification of the Lord Jesus, and may thank God who "has begotten them again, through the resurrection of Jesus Christ from the dead, unto a living hope" (1 Pet. 1:3). Hence the Lord's day is the original feast day, and it should be proposed to the piety of the faithful and taught to them so that it may become in fact a day of joy and of freedom from work. Other celebrations, unless they be truly of greatest importance, shall not have precedence over the Sunday which is the foundation and kernel of the whole liturgical year.

107. The liturgical year is to be revised so that the traditional customs and discipline of the sacred seasons shall be preserved or restored to suit the conditions of modern times; their specific character is to be retained, so that they duly nourish the piety of the faithful who celebrate the mysteries of Christian redemption, and above all the paschal mystery. If certain adaptations are considered necessary on account of local conditions, they are to be made in accordance with the provisions of Art. 39 and 40.

108. The minds of the faithful must be directed primarily toward the feasts of the Lord whereby the mysteries of salvation are celebrated in the course of the year. Therefore, the proper of the time shall be given the preference which is its due over the feasts of the saints, so that the entire cycle of the mysteries of salvation may be suitably recalled.

109. The season of Lent has a twofold character: primarily by recalling or preparing for baptism and by penance, it disposes the faithful, who more diligently hear the word of God and devote themselves to prayer, to celebrate the paschal mystery. This twofold character is to be brought into greater prominence both in the liturgy and by liturgical catechesis. Hence:

a) More use is to be made of the baptismal features proper to the Lenten liturgy; some of them, which used to flourish in bygone days, are to be restored as may seem good.

b) The same is to apply to the penitential elements. As regards instruction it is important to impress on the minds of the faithful not only the social consequences of sin but also that essence of the virtue of penance which leads to the detestation of sin as an offence against God; the role of the Church in penitential practices is not to be passed over, and the people must be exhorted to pray for sinners.

110. During Lent penance should not be only internal and individual, but also external and social. The practice of penance should be fostered in ways that are possible in our own times and in different regions, and according to the circumstances of the faithful; it should be encouraged by the authorities mentioned in Art. 22.

Nevertheless, let the paschal fast be kept sacred. Let it be celebrated everywhere on Good Friday and, where possible, prolonged throughout Holy Saturday, so that the joys of the Sunday of the resurrection may be attained with uplifted and clear mind.

111. The saints have been traditionally honored in the Church and their authentic relics and images held in veneration. For the feasts of the saints proclaim the wonderful works of Christ in His servants, and display to the faithful fitting examples for their imitation.

Lest the feasts of the saints should take precedence over the feasts which commemorate the very mysteries of salvation, many of them should be left to be celebrated by a particular Church or nation or family of religious; only those should be extended to the universal Church which commemorate saints who are truly of universal importance.

CHAPTER VI
Sacred Music

112. The musical tradition of the universal Church is a treasure of inestimable value, greater even than that of any other art. The main reason for this pre-eminence is that, as sacred song united to the words, it forms a necessary or integral part of the solemn liturgy.

Holy Scripture, indeed, has bestowed praise upon sacred song,[42] and the same may be said of the fathers of the Church and of the Roman pontiffs who in recent times, led by St. Pius X, have explained more precisely the ministerial function supplied by sacred music in the service of the Lord.

Therefore sacred music is to be considered the more holy in proportion as it is more closely connected with the liturgical action, whether it adds delight to prayer, fosters unity of minds, or confers greater solemnity upon the sacred rites. But the Church approves of all forms of true art having the needed qualities, and admits them into divine worship.

Accordingly, the sacred Council, keeping to the norms and precepts of ecclesiastical tradition and discipline, and having regard to the purpose of sacred music, which is the glory of God and the sanctification of the faithful, decrees as follows.

113. Liturgical worship is given a more noble form when the divine offices are celebrated solemnly in song, with the assistance of sacred ministers and the active participation of the people.

As regards the language to be used, the provisions of Art. 36 are to be observed; for the Mass, Art. 54; for the sacraments, Art. 63; for the divine office, Art. 101.

114. The treasure of sacred music is to be preserved and fostered with great care. Choirs must be diligently promoted, especially in cathedral churches; but bishops and other pastors of souls must be at pains to ensure that, whenever the sacred action is to be celebrated with song, the whole body of the faithful may be able to contribute that active participation which is rightly theirs, as laid down in Art. 28 and 30.

115. Great importance is to be attached to the teaching and practice of music in seminaries, in the novitiates and houses of study of religious of both sexes, and also in other Catholic institutions and schools. To impart

this instruction, teachers are to be carefully trained and put in charge of the teaching of sacred music.

It is desirable also to found higher institutes of sacred music whenever this can be done.

Composers and singers, especially boys, must also be given a genuine liturgical training.

116. The Church acknowledges Gregorian chant as specially suited to the Roman liturgy: therefore, other things being equal, it should be given pride of place in liturgical services.

But other kinds of sacred music, especially polyphony, are by no means excluded from liturgical celebrations, so long as they accord with the spirit of the liturgical action, as laid down in Art. 30.

117. The typical edition of the books of Gregorian chant is to be completed; and a more critical edition is to be prepared of those books already published since the restoration by St. Pius X.

It is desirable also that an edition be prepared containing simpler melodies, for use in small churches.

118. Religious singing by the people is to be intelligently fostered so that in devotions and sacred exercises, as also during liturgical services, the voices of the faithful may ring out according to the norms and requirements of the rubrics.

119. In certain parts of the world, especially mission lands, there are peoples who have their own musical traditions, and these play a great part in their religious and social life. For this reason due importance is to be attached to their music, and a suitable place is to be given to it, not only in forming their attitude toward religion, but also in adapting worship to their native genius, as indicated in Art. 39 and 40.

Therefore, when missionaries are being given training in music, every effort should be made to see that they become competent in promoting the traditional music of these peoples, both in schools and in sacred services, as far as may be practicable.

120. In the Latin Church the pipe organ is to be held in high esteem, for it is the traditional musical instrument which adds a wonderful splendor to

the Church's ceremonies and powerfully lifts up man's mind to God and to higher things.

But other instruments also may be admitted for use in divine worship, with the knowledge and consent of the competent territorial authority, as laid down in Art. 22, 2, 37, and 40. This may be done, however, only on condition that the instruments are suitable, or can be made suitable, for sacred use, accord with the dignity of the temple, and truly contribute to the edification of the faithful.

121. Composers, filled with the Christian spirit, should feel that their vocation is to cultivate sacred music and increase its store of treasures.

Let them produce compositions which have the qualities proper to genuine sacred music, not confining themselves to works which can be sung only by large choirs, but providing also for the needs of small choirs and for the active participation of the entire assembly of the faithful.

The texts intended to be sung must always be in conformity with Catholic doctrine; indeed they should be drawn chiefly from holy scripture and from liturgical sources.

Pope Benedict XVI

———

Sacramentum Caritatis 42

Singing the Praises of God
Sacrosanctum Concilium 112–121

In the *ars celebrandi,* liturgical song has a pre-eminent place. Saint Augustine rightly says in a famous sermon that "the new man sings a new song. Singing is an expression of joy and, if we consider the matter, an expression of love." The People of God assembled for the liturgy sings the praises of God. In the course of her two-thousand-year history, the Church has created, and still creates, music and songs which represent a rich patrimony of faith and love. This heritage must not be lost. Certainly as far as the liturgy is concerned, we cannot say that one song is as good as another. Generic improvisation or the introduction of musical genres which fail to respect the meaning of the liturgy should be avoided. As an element of the liturgy, song should be well integrated into the overall celebration. Consequently everything—texts, music, execution—ought to correspond to the meaning of the mystery being celebrated, the structure of the rite, and the liturgical seasons. Finally, while respecting various styles and different and highly praiseworthy traditions, I desire, in accordance with the request advanced by [the Fathers of the Eleventh Ordinary General Assembly of the Synod of Bishops], that Gregorian chant be suitably esteemed and employed as the chant proper to the Roman liturgy.

CHAPTER VII
Sacred Art and Sacred Furnishings

122. Very rightly the fine arts are considered to rank among the noblest activities of man's genius, and this applies especially to religious art and to its highest achievement, which is sacred art. These arts, by their very nature, are oriented toward the infinite beauty of God which they attempt in some way to portray by the work of human hands; they achieve their purpose of redounding to God's praise and glory in proportion as they are directed the more exclusively to the single aim of turning men's minds devoutly toward God.

Holy Mother Church has therefore always been the friend of the fine arts and has ever sought their noble help, with the special aim that all things set apart for use in divine worship should be truly worthy, becoming, and beautiful, signs and symbols of the supernatural world, and for this purpose she has trained artists. In fact, the Church has, with good reason, always reserved to herself the right to pass judgment upon the arts, deciding which of the works of artists are in accordance with faith, piety, and cherished traditional laws, and thereby fitted for sacred use.

The Church has been particularly careful to see that sacred furnishings should worthily and beautifully serve the dignity of worship, and has admitted changes in materials, style, or ornamentation prompted by the progress of the technical arts with the passage of time.

Wherefore it has pleased the Fathers to issue the following decrees on these matters.

123. The Church has not adopted any particular style of art as her very own; she has admitted styles from every period according to the natural talents and circumstances of peoples, and the needs of the various rites. Thus, in the course of the centuries, she has brought into being a treasury of art which must be very carefully preserved. The art of our own days, coming from every race and region, shall also be given free scope in the Church, provided that it adorns the sacred buildings and holy rites with due reverence and honor; thereby it is enabled to contribute its own voice to that wonderful chorus of praise in honor of the Catholic faith sung by great men in times gone by.

A Variety of Cultural Styles
Sacrosanctum Concilium 123

Pope St. John Paul II

———

Ecclesia de Eucharistia 51

The development of sacred art and liturgical discipline which took place in lands of ancient Christian heritage is also taking place *on continents where Christianity is younger.* This was precisely the approach supported by the Second Vatican Council on the need for sound and proper "inculturation." In my numerous Pastoral Visits I have seen, throughout the world, the great vitality which the celebration of the Eucharist can have when marked by the forms, styles, and sensibilities of different cultures. By adaptation to the changing conditions of time and place, the Eucharist offers sustenance not only to individuals but to entire peoples, and it shapes cultures inspired by Christianity.

It is necessary, however, that this important work of adaptation be carried out with a constant awareness of the ineffable mystery against which every generation is called to measure itself. The "treasure" is too important and precious to risk impoverishment or compromise through forms of experimentation or practices introduced without a careful review on the part of the competent ecclesiastical authorities. Furthermore, the centrality of the Eucharistic mystery demands that any such review must be undertaken in close association with the Holy See. As I wrote in my Post-Synodal Apostolic Exhortation *Ecclesia in Asia*, "such cooperation is essential because the Sacred Liturgy expresses and celebrates the one faith professed by all and, being the heritage of the whole Church, cannot be determined by local Churches in isolation from the universal Church."

124. Ordinaries, by the encouragement and favor they show to art which is truly sacred, should strive after noble beauty rather than mere sumptuous display. This principle is to apply also in the matter of sacred vestments and ornaments.

Let bishops carefully remove from the house of God and from other sacred places those works of artists which are repugnant to faith, morals, and Christian piety, and which offend true religious sense either by depraved forms or by lack of artistic worth, mediocrity and pretense.

And when churches are to be built, let great care be taken that they be suitable for the celebration of liturgical services and for the active participation of the faithful.

The Evangelizing Beauty of the Liturgy

Sacrosanctum Concilium 124

Pope Francis

———

Evangelii Gaudium
24

Evangelization with joy becomes beauty in the liturgy, as part of our daily concern to spread goodness. The Church evangelizes and is herself evangelized through the beauty of the liturgy, which is both a celebration of the task of evangelization and the source of her renewed self-giving.

125. The practice of placing sacred images in churches so that they may be venerated by the faithful is to be maintained. Nevertheless their number should be moderate and their relative positions should reflect right order. For otherwise they may create confusion among the Christian people and foster devotion of doubtful orthodoxy.

126. When passing judgment on works of art, local ordinaries shall give a hearing to the diocesan commission on sacred art and, if needed, also to others who are especially expert, and to the commissions referred to in Art. 44, 45, and 46.

Ordinaries must be very careful to see that sacred furnishings and works of value are not disposed of or dispersed; for they are the ornaments of the house of God.

127. Bishops should have a special concern for artists, so as to imbue them with the spirit of sacred art and of the sacred liturgy. This they may do in person or through suitable priests who are gifted with a knowledge and love of art.

It is also desirable that schools or academies of sacred art should be founded in those parts of the world where they would be useful, so that artists may be trained.

All artists who, prompted by their talents, desire to serve God's glory in holy Church, should ever bear in mind that they are engaged in a kind of sacred imitation of God the Creator, and are concerned with works destined to be used in Catholic worship, to edify the faithful, and to foster their piety and their religious formation.

128. Along with the revision of the liturgical books, as laid down in Art. 25, there is to be an early revision of the canons and ecclesiastical statutes which govern the provision of material things involved in sacred worship. These laws refer especially to the worthy and well planned construction of sacred buildings, the shape and construction of altars, the nobility, placing, and safety of the eucharistic tabernacle, the dignity and suitability of the baptistery, the proper ordering of sacred images, embellishments, and vestments. Laws which seem less suited to the reformed liturgy are to be brought into harmony with it, or else abolished; and any which are helpful are to be retained if already in use, or introduced where they are lacking.

According to the norm of Art. 22 of this Constitution, the territorial bodies of bishops are empowered to adapt such things to the needs and customs of their different regions; this applies especially to the materials and form of sacred furnishings and vestments.

129. During their philosophical and theological studies, clerics are to be

taught about the history and development of sacred art, and about the sound principles governing the production of its works. In consequence they will be able to appreciate and preserve the Church's venerable monuments, and be in a position to aid, by good advice, artists who are engaged in producing works of art.

130. It is fitting that the use of pontificals be reserved to those ecclesiastical persons who have episcopal rank or some particular jurisdiction.

A Sublime Expression of God's Glory

Sacrosanctum Concilium 122–130

Pope Benedict XVI

—

Sacramentum Caritatis 35, 41

Like the rest of Christian Revelation, the liturgy is inherently linked to beauty: it is *veritatis splendor*. The liturgy is a radiant expression of the paschal mystery, in which Christ draws us to himself and calls us to communion. As Saint Bonaventure would say, in Jesus we contemplate beauty and splendor at their source. This is no mere aestheticism, but the concrete way in which the truth of God's love in Christ encounters us, attracts us, and delights us, enabling us to emerge from ourselves and drawing us towards our true vocation, which is love (see GS 22). God allows himself to be glimpsed first in creation, in the beauty and harmony of the cosmos (see Wis. 13:5; Rom. 1:19–20). In the Old Testament we see many signs of the grandeur of God's power as he manifests his glory in his wondrous deeds among the Chosen People (see Exod. 14; 16:10; 24:12–18; Num. 14:20–23). In the New Testament this epiphany of beauty reaches definitive fulfilment in God's revelation in Jesus Christ (see DV 2, 4): Christ is the full manifestation of the glory of God. In the glorification of the Son, the Father's glory shines forth and is communicated (see John 1:14; 8:54; 12:28; 17:1). Yet this beauty is not simply a harmony of proportion and form; "the fairest of the sons of men" (Ps. 45[44]:3) is also, mysteriously, the one "who had no form or comeliness that we should look at him, and no beauty that we should desire him" (Isa. 53:2). Jesus Christ shows us how the truth of love can transform even the dark mystery of death into the radiant light of the resurrection. Here the splendor of God's glory surpasses all worldly beauty. The truest beauty is the love of God, who definitively revealed himself to us in the paschal mystery.

The beauty of the liturgy is part of this mystery; it is a sublime expression of God's glory and, in a certain sense, a glimpse of heaven on earth. The memorial of Jesus' redemptive sacrifice contains something of that beauty which Peter, James, and John beheld when the Master, making his way to Jerusalem, was transfigured before their eyes (see Mark 9:2). Beauty, then, is not mere decoration, but rather an essential element of the liturgical action, since it is an attribute of God himself and his revelation. These considerations should make us realize the care which is needed, if the liturgical action is to reflect its innate splendor. . . .

The profound connection between beauty and the liturgy should make us attentive to every work of art placed at the service of the celebration. Certainly an important element of sacred art is church architecture, which should highlight the unity of the furnishings of the sanctuary, such as the altar, the crucifix, the tabernacle, the ambo, and the celebrant's chair. Here it is important to remember that the purpose of sacred architecture is to offer the Church a fitting space for the celebration of the mysteries of faith, especially the Eucharist. The very nature of a Christian church is defined by the liturgy, which is an assembly of the faithful (ecclesia) who are the living stones of the Church (see 1 Pet. 2:5).

This same principle holds true for sacred art in general, especially painting and sculpture, where religious iconography should be directed to sacramental mystagogy. A solid knowledge of the history of sacred art can be advantageous for those responsible for commissioning artists and architects to create works of art for the liturgy. Consequently it is essential that the education of seminarians and priests include the study of art history, with special reference to sacred buildings and the corresponding liturgical norms. Everything related to the Eucharist should be marked by beauty. Special respect and care must also be given to the vestments, the furnishings, and the sacred vessels, so that by their harmonious and orderly arrangement they will foster awe for the mystery of God, manifest the unity of the faith, and strengthen devotion.

The Emptying Out of Our Churches

Sacrosanctum Concilium 122–130 |
Bishop Barron

Much of Catholic sacramental theology in the immediate wake of the Second Vatican Council presented the Eucharist almost exclusively as a fellowship meal and as a merely symbolic manifestation of Jesus' presence. Witness the number of altars that became "tables" during that time, as well as the sharply reduced sense of devotion to the Blessed Sacrament. This dramatic emptying out of our churches—the destruction of altars, statues, pictures, stained glass, reredos, etc.—finds an antecedent in·Martin Luther's revolutionary text *On the Babylonian Captivity of the Church*: "We must be careful to begin by setting aside all the later additions to the first, simple institution . . . such things as vestments, ornaments, chants, prayers, organs, candles, and the whole pageantry of things visible."

Even as it calls for a simplification of the liturgy, *Sacrosanctum Concilium* puts a special emphasis on art, beauty, music, and the visual dimension of the Mass. But in the popular implementation of Vatican II, Luther seemed more an inspiration than the Constitution on the Sacred Liturgy itself.

APPENDIX

A Declaration of the Second Ecumenical Council of the Vatican on Revision of the Calendar

The Second Ecumenical Sacred Council of the Vatican, recognizing the importance of the wishes expressed by many concerning the assignment of the feast of Easter to a fixed Sunday and concerning an unchanging calendar, having carefully considered the effects which could result from the introduction of a new calendar, declares as follows:

1. The Sacred Council would not object if the feast of Easter were assigned to a particular Sunday of the Gregorian Calendar, provided that those whom it may concern, especially the brethren who are not in communion with the Apostolic See, give their assent.

2. The sacred Council likewise declares that it does not oppose efforts designed to introduce a perpetual calendar into civil society.

But among the various systems which are being suggested to stabilize a perpetual calendar and to introduce it into civil life, the Church has no objection only in the case of those systems which retain and safeguard a seven-day week with Sunday, without the introduction of any days outside the week, so that the succession of weeks may be left intact, unless there is question of the most serious reasons. Concerning these the Apostolic See shall judge.

NOTES

INTRODUCTION

1   Secret of the ninth Sunday after Pentecost.

2   See Heb. 13:14.

3   See Eph. 2:21–22.

4   See Eph. 4:13.

5   See Isa. 11:12.

6   See John 11:52.

7   See John 10:16.

CHAPTER I

8   See Isa. 61:1; Luke 4:18.

9   St. Ignatius of Antioch, *To the Ephesians*, 7, 2.

10   See 1 Tim. 2:5.

11   *Sacramentarium Veronese* (ed. Mohlberg), n. 1265; see also n. 1241, 1248.

12   Easter Preface of the Roman Missal.

13   Prayer before the second lesson for Holy Saturday, as it was in the Roman Missal before the restoration of Holy Week.

14   See Mark 16:15.

15   See Acts 26:18.

16   See Rom. 6:4; Eph. 2:6; Col. 3:1; 2 Tim. 2:11.

17   See John 4:23.

18   See 1 Cor. 11:26.

19   Council of Trent, Session XIII, *Decree on the Holy Eucharist*, c. 5.

20   Council of Trent, Session XXII, *Doctrine on the Holy Sacrifice of the Mass*, c. 2.

21   See St. Augustine, *Tractatus in Ioannem*, VI, n. 7.

22   See Rev. 21:2; Col. 3:1; Heb. 8:2.

23   See Phil. 3:20; Col. 3:4.

24   See John 17:3; Luke 24:27; Acts 2:38.

25   See Matt. 28:20.

26   Postcommunion for both Masses of Easter Sunday.

27   Collect of the Mass for Tuesday of Easter Week.

28   See 2 Cor. 6:1.

29   See Matt. 6:6.

30   See 1 Thess. 5:17.

31   See 2 Cor. 4:10–11.

32   Secret for Monday of Pentecost Week.

33   St. Cyprian, *On the Unity of the Catholic Church*, 7; see *Letter* 66, n. 8, 3.

34   See Council of Trent, Session XXII, *Doctrine on the Holy Sacrifice of the Mass*, c. 8.

35   See St. Ignatius of Antioch, *To the Smyrnians*, 8; *To the Magnesians*, 7; *To the Philadelphians*, 4.

CHAPTER II

36   See St. Augustine, *Tractatus in Ioannem*, VI, n. 13.

37   Roman Breviary, feast of Corpus Christi, Second Vespers, antiphon to the Magnificat.

38   See St. Cyril of Alexandria, *Commentary on the Gospel of John*, book XI, chap. XI–XII: Migne, Patrologia Graeca, 74, 557–564.

39   See 1 Tim. 2:1–2.

40   Session XXI, July 16, 1562. *Doctrine on Communion under Both Species*, chap. 1–3: Condlium Tridentinum. *Diariorum, Actorum, Epistolarum,* Tractatuum nova collectio ed. Soc. Goerresiana, tome VIII (Freiburg in Br., 1919), 698–699.

CHAPTER III

41   Council of Trent, Session XXIV, November 11, 1563, *On Reform*, chap. I. See Roman Ritual, title VIII, chap. II, n. 6.

CHAPTER VI

42   See Eph. 5:19; Col. 3:16.

GAUDIUM ET SPES

*Pastoral Constitution on
the Church in the Modern World*

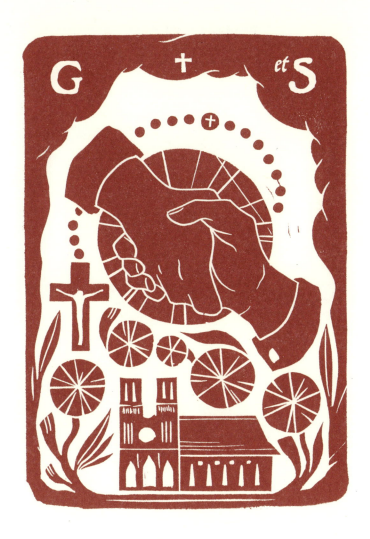

PROMULGATED *by* HIS HOLINESS
POPE PAUL VI
on DECEMBER 7, 1965

The Priority of Christ

Introduction to *Gaudium et Spes* by Bishop Robert Barron

Gaudium et Spes is perhaps the most controversial of the Vatican II documents. It is by far the longest—in fact, the longest document in the history of the Church's ecumenical councils—and in the eyes of many of its interpreters, the most important. Indeed, theologians as prominent as Henri de Lubac, Yves Congar, and Karol Wojtyła had a role in its writing. On the other hand, its rhetorical style is famously verbose, giving rise to a whole series of criticisms, beginning with Joseph Ratzinger's vigorous critique written in the immediate wake of the document's publication, continuing with Karl Rahner's criticism, and culminating in very recent years with Tracey Rowland's even more trenchant criticism. More than any other of the Vatican II documents, it seems to give voice to the optimistic "spirit of the council," making it for its advocates the most eloquent and for its detractors the most problematic.

However, it is important to underscore that *Gaudium et Spes* is characterized by the council fathers as a "pastoral constitution," as opposed to *Sacrosanctum Concilium*, which is a constitution, and *Lumen Gentium* and *Dei Verbum*, both *dogmatic* constitutions. What this means precisely is a bit vague, though perhaps the simplest reading is that, as a pastoral constitution, *Gaudium et Spes*—while having dogmatic elements and principles—has more to do with some of the shifting facts of this present time and is hence open to greater debate.

Despite its controversial legacy and pastoral designation, *Gaudium et Spes* offers a beautiful vision of the Church going out to meet a modern world hungry for God. The opening words of this document are perhaps the most famous of any conciliar statement: "The joys and the hopes, the griefs and the anxieties of the men of this age, especially those who are poor or in any way afflicted, these are the joys and hopes, the griefs and anxieties of the followers of Christ." Despite the lyrical and balanced quality of this line, immediately we see one of the central interpretive issues: Who positions whom? Are the Church and the world simply coequal dialogue partners? Or does the Church have clear primacy? Is the world in any meaningful sense "outside" of Christ? Outside of the one who determines it in every detail? In a word, is "the world" setting the agenda for the Church, or vice versa?

Thus, it is critical to remember at the outset that Vatican II was *not* about modernizing the Church. Some modernization was called for— yes, indeed—but modern culture, like every culture, is evangelically ambiguous. There are positive aspects, to be sure, but we also see great violence, great moral drift, and "the dictatorship of relativism" as Benedict XVI termed it. Rather, the purpose of Vatican II was to Christify the world. There is a tight connection between the Church and the world, for the Church exists for the sake of the world. This is because the Church is the new Israel, and Israel was intended to be the magnet that would draw all nations to the worship of the true God. That's why the joys and hopes and griefs and anxieties of the world are the joys and hopes and griefs and anxieties of the Church: not because the world is setting the agenda for the Church, but because the Church has this transformative mission within the world. We don't come hat in hand to this deeply ambiguous modern culture seeking to accommodate ourselves; rather, we proclaim Christ in and to that culture.

That is the proper dialogical relationship between the Church and the modern world—and that, ultimately, is the right way to read *Gaudium et Spes*.

GAUDIUM ET SPES

Pastoral Constitution
on the Church in the Modern World

PREFACE

1. The joys and the hopes, the griefs and the anxieties of the men of this age, especially those who are poor or in any way afflicted, these are the joys and hopes, the griefs and anxieties of the followers of Christ. Indeed, nothing genuinely human fails to raise an echo in their hearts. For theirs is a community composed of men. United in Christ, they are led by the Holy Spirit in their journey to the Kingdom of their Father and they have welcomed the news of salvation which is meant for every man. That is why this community realizes that it is truly linked with mankind and its history by the deepest of bonds.

2. Hence this Second Vatican Council, having probed more profoundly into the mystery of the Church, now addresses itself without hesitation, not only to the sons of the Church and to all who invoke the name of Christ, but to the whole of humanity. For the council yearns to explain to everyone how it conceives of the presence and activity of the Church in the world of today.[1]

Therefore, the council focuses its attention on the world of men, the whole human family along with the sum of those realities in the midst of which it lives; that world which is the theater of man's history, and the heir of his energies, his tragedies, and his triumphs; that world which the Christian sees as created and sustained by its Maker's love, fallen indeed into the bondage of sin, yet emancipated now by Christ, Who was

The Day of Christian Hope

Gaudium et Spes 1

**Pope
St. John Paul II**

Dies Domini 38

Sunday is not only the day of faith, but is also *the day of Christian hope*. To share in "the Lord's Supper" is to anticipate the eschatological feast of the "marriage of the Lamb" (Rev. 19:9). Celebrating this memorial of Christ, risen and ascended into heaven, the Christian community waits "in joyful hope for the coming of our Savior, Jesus Christ." Renewed and nourished by this intense weekly rhythm, Christian hope becomes the leaven and the light of human hope. This is why the Prayer of the Faithful responds not only to the needs of the particular Christian community but also to those of all humanity; and the Church, coming together for the Eucharistic celebration, shows to the world that she makes her own "the joys and the hopes, the griefs and the anxieties of the men of this age, especially those who are poor or in any way afflicted." With the offering of the Sunday Eucharist, the Church crowns the witness which her children strive to offer every day of the week by proclaiming the Gospel and practicing charity in the world of work and in all the many tasks of life; thus she shows forth more plainly her identity as "a sacrament or as a sign and instrument both of a very closely knit union with God and of the unity of the whole human race" (LG 1).

crucified and rose again to break the stranglehold of personified evil, so that the world might be fashioned anew according to God's design and reach its fulfillment.

3. Though mankind is stricken with wonder at its own discoveries and its power, it often raises anxious questions about the current trend of the world, about the place and role of man in the universe, about the meaning of its individual and collective strivings, and about the ultimate destiny of reality and of humanity. Hence, giving witness and voice to the faith of the whole people of God gathered together by Christ, this council can provide

no more eloquent proof of its solidarity with, as well as its respect and love for the entire human family with which it is bound up, than by engaging with it in conversation about these various problems. The council brings to mankind light kindled from the Gospel, and puts at its disposal those saving resources which the Church herself, under the guidance of the Holy Spirit, receives from her Founder. For the human person deserves to be preserved; human society deserves to be renewed. Hence the focal point of our total presentation will be man himself, whole and entire, body and soul, heart and conscience, mind and will.

Therefore, this sacred synod, proclaiming the noble destiny of man and championing the Godlike seed which has been sown in him, offers to mankind the honest assistance of the Church in fostering that brotherhood of all men which corresponds to this destiny of theirs. Inspired by no earthly ambition, the Church seeks but a solitary goal: to carry forward the work of Christ under the lead of the befriending Spirit. And Christ entered this world to give witness to the truth, to rescue and not to sit in judgment, to serve and not to be served.[2]

INTRODUCTORY STATEMENT
The Situation of Men in the Modern World

4. To carry out such a task, the Church has always had the duty of scrutinizing the signs of the times and of interpreting them in the light of the Gospel. Thus, in language intelligible to each generation, she can respond to the perennial questions which men ask about this present life and the life to come, and about the relationship of the one to the other. We must therefore recognize and understand the world in which we live, its explanations, its longings, and its often dramatic characteristics. Some of the main features of the modern world can be sketched as follows.

Today, the human race is involved in a new stage of history. Profound and rapid changes are spreading by degrees around the whole world. Triggered by the intelligence and creative energies of man, these changes recoil upon him, upon his decisions and desires, both individual and collective, and upon his manner of thinking and acting with respect to things and to people. Hence we can already speak of a true cultural and social transformation, one which has repercussions on man's religious life as well.

As happens in any crisis of growth, this transformation has brought serious difficulties in its wake. Thus while man extends his power in every direction, he does not always succeed in subjecting it to his own welfare. Striving to probe more profoundly into the deeper recesses of his own mind, he frequently appears more unsure of himself. Gradually and more precisely he lays bare the laws of society, only to be paralyzed by uncertainty about the direction to give it.

Never has the human race enjoyed such an abundance of wealth, resources, and economic power, and yet a huge proportion of the world's citizens are still tormented by hunger and poverty, while countless numbers suffer from total illiteracy. Never before has man had so keen an understanding of freedom, yet at the same time new forms of social and psychological slavery make their appearance. Although the world of today has a very vivid awareness of its unity and of how one man depends on another in needful solidarity, it is most grievously torn into opposing camps by conflicting forces. For political, social, economic, racial, and ideological disputes still continue bitterly, and with them the peril of a war which would reduce everything to ashes. True, there is a growing exchange of ideas, but the very words by which key concepts are expressed take on quite different meanings in diverse ideological systems. Finally, man painstakingly searches for a better world, without a corresponding spiritual advancement.

Influenced by such a variety of complexities, many of our contemporaries are kept from accurately identifying permanent values and adjusting them properly to fresh discoveries. As a result, buffeted between hope and anxiety and pressing one another with questions about the present course of events, they are burdened down with uneasiness. This same course of events leads men to look for answers; indeed, it forces them to do so.

The Signs of the Times

Gaudium et Spes 4 | Bishop Barron

In *Gaudium et Spes* 4, we read, "The Church has always had the duty of scrutinizing the signs of the times and of interpreting them in the light of the Gospel." When I was coming of age, "the signs of the times" were almost always seen as positive, and the teaching of the council was presented as a call for the Church to adjust itself to the present situation. But the thousands killed by gun violence in our city streets, the millions of unborn children murdered since the passage of *Roe v. Wade*, the moral drift in our culture, the rise of the "nones," and aggressive forms of atheism—these, too, are signs of our times. Our job is not to accommodate ourselves to the times, but rather to scrutinize the signs of the times—both good and bad—and interpret them "in the light of the Gospel." They are data to be read; the reader is the Christian, and the interpretive lens is revelation.

Later in the document we read: "Under the light of Christ, the image of the unseen God, the firstborn of every creature, the council wishes to speak to all men in order to shed light on the mystery of man" (GS 10). It is in light of Christ, the image of the invisible God, that the council proposes to elucidate the mystery of mankind—not the other way around.

The dialogue with the culture has been, since the council, perhaps the principal preoccupation of the Church. But far too often, the conversation has been one-sided, the Church straining to make itself understandable to the culture, and the culture making precious little effort to reciprocate. Perhaps the very hostility of the culture today is compelling the Church to revisit the treasure house of its own tradition: the Bible, the saints, art and architecture, metaphysics, etc. And perhaps it is serving as a summons to an army of smart and spiritually alert catechists, evangelists, and witnesses willing to give their lives to the great task before them.

---

5. Today's spiritual agitation and the changing conditions of life are part of a broader and deeper revolution. As a result of the latter, intellectual formation is ever increasingly based on the mathematical and natural sciences and on those dealing with man himself, while in the practical order the technology which stems from these sciences takes on mounting importance.

This scientific spirit has a new kind of impact on the cultural sphere and on modes of thought. Technology is now transforming the face of the earth, and is already trying to master outer space. To a certain extent, the human intellect is also broadening its dominion over time: over the past by means of historical knowledge; over the future, by the art of projecting and by planning.

Advances in biology, psychology, and the social sciences not only bring men hope of improved self-knowledge; in conjunction with technical methods, they are helping men exert direct influence on the life of social groups.

At the same time, the human race is giving steadily-increasing thought to forecasting and regulating its own population growth. History itself speeds along on so rapid a course that an individual person can scarcely keep abreast of it. The destiny of the human community has become all of a piece, where once the various groups of men had a kind of private history of their own.

Thus, the human race has passed from a rather static concept of reality to a more dynamic, evolutionary one. In consequence there has arisen a new series of problems, a series as numerous as can be, calling for efforts of analysis and synthesis.

6. By this very circumstance, the traditional local communities such as families, clans, tribes, villages, various groups and associations stemming from social contacts, experience more thorough changes every day.

The industrial type of society is gradually being spread, leading some nations to economic affluence, and radically transforming ideas and social conditions established for centuries.

Likewise, the cult and pursuit of city living has grown, either because of a multiplication of cities and their inhabitants, or by a transplantation of city life to rural settings.

New and more efficient media of social communication are contributing to the knowledge of events; by setting off chain reactions they are giving the swiftest and widest possible circulation to styles of thought and feeling.

It is also noteworthy how many men are being induced to migrate on various counts, and are thereby changing their manner of life. Thus a man's ties with his fellows are constantly being multiplied, and at the same time "socialization" brings further ties, without however always promoting appropriate personal development and truly personal relationships.

This kind of evolution can be seen more clearly in those nations which already enjoy the conveniences of economic and technological progress, though it is also astir among peoples still striving for such progress and eager to secure for themselves the advantages of an industrialized and urbanized society. These peoples, especially those among them who are attached to older traditions, are simultaneously undergoing a movement toward more mature and personal exercise of liberty.

7. A change in attitudes and in human structures frequently calls accepted values into question, especially among young people, who have grown impatient on more than one occasion, and indeed become rebels in their distress. Aware of their own influence in the life of society, they want a part in it sooner. This frequently causes parents and educators to experience greater difficulties day by day in discharging their tasks. The institutions, laws, and modes of thinking and feeling as handed down from previous generations do not always seem to be well adapted to the contemporary state of affairs; hence arises an upheaval in the manner and even the norms of behavior.

Finally, these new conditions have their impact on religion. On the one hand a more critical ability to distinguish religion from a magical view of the world and from the superstitions which still circulate purifies it and exacts day by day a more personal and explicit adherence to faith. As a result many persons are achieving a more vivid sense of God. On the other hand, growing numbers of people are abandoning religion in practice. Unlike former days, the denial of God or of religion, or the abandonment of them, are no longer unusual and individual occurrences. For today it is not rare for such things to be presented as requirements of scientific progress or of a certain new humanism. In numerous places these views are voiced not only in the teachings of philosophers, but on every side they influence literature, the arts, the interpretation of the humanities and of history, and civil laws themselves. As a consequence, many people are shaken.

8. This development coming so rapidly and often in a disorderly fashion, combined with keener awareness itself of the inequalities in the world beget or intensify contradictions and imbalances.

Within the individual person there develops rather frequently an imbalance between an intellect which is modern in practical matters and a theoretical system of thought which can neither master the sum total of its ideas, nor arrange them adequately into a synthesis. Likewise an imbalance arises between a concern for practicality and efficiency, and the demands of moral conscience; also very often between the conditions of collective existence and the requisites of personal thought, and even of contemplation. At length there develops an imbalance between specialized human activity and a comprehensive view of reality.

As for the family, discord results from population, economic and social pressures, or from difficulties which arise between succeeding generations, or from new social relationships between men and women.

Differences crop up too between races and between various kinds of social orders; between wealthy nations and those which are less influential or are needy; finally, between international institutions born of the popular desire for peace, and the ambition to propagate one's own ideology, as well as collective greeds existing in nations or other groups.

What results is mutual distrust, enmities, conflicts, and hardships. Of such is man at once the cause and the victim.

9. Meanwhile the conviction grows not only that humanity can and should increasingly consolidate its control over creation, but even more, that it devolves on humanity to establish a political, social, and economic order which will growingly serve man and help individuals as well as groups to affirm and develop the dignity proper to them.

As a result many persons are quite aggressively demanding those benefits of which with vivid awareness they judge themselves to be deprived either through injustice or unequal distribution. Nations on the road to progress, like those recently made independent, desire to participate in the goods of modern civilization, not only in the political field but also economically, and to play their part freely on the world scene. Still they continually fall behind while very often their economic and other dependence on wealthier nations advances more rapidly.

People hounded by hunger call upon those better off. Where they have not yet won it, women claim for themselves an equity with men before the law and in fact. Laborers and farmers seek not only to provide for the necessities of life, but to develop the gifts of their personality by their labors and indeed to take part in regulating economic, social, political, and cultural life. Now, for the first time in human history all people are convinced that the benefits of culture ought to be and actually can be extended to everyone.

Still, beneath all these demands lies a deeper and more widespread longing: persons and societies thirst for a full and free life worthy of man; one in which they can subject to their own welfare all that the modern world can offer them so abundantly. In addition, nations try harder every day to bring about a kind of universal community.

Since all these things are so, the modern world shows itself at once powerful and weak, capable of the noblest deeds or the foulest; before it lies the path to freedom or to slavery, to progress or retreat, to brotherhood or hatred. Moreover, man is becoming aware that it is his responsibility to guide aright the forces which he has unleashed and which can enslave him or minister to him. That is why he is putting questions to himself.

10. The truth is that the imbalances under which the modern world labors are linked with that more basic imbalance which is rooted in the heart of man. For in man himself many elements wrestle with one another. Thus, on the one hand, as a creature he experiences his limitations in a multitude of ways; on the other he feels himself to be boundless in his desires and summoned to a higher life. Pulled by manifold attractions he is constantly forced to choose among them and renounce some. Indeed, as a weak and sinful being, he often does what he would not, and fails to do what he would.[1] Hence he suffers from internal divisions, and from these flow so many and such great discords in society. No doubt many whose lives are infected with a practical materialism are blinded against any sharp insight into this kind of dramatic situation; or else, weighed down by unhappiness they are prevented from giving the matter any thought. Thinking they have found serenity in an interpretation of reality everywhere proposed these days, many look forward to a genuine and total emancipation of humanity wrought solely by human effort; they are convinced that the future rule of man over the earth will satisfy every desire of his heart. Nor are there lacking men who despair of any meaning to life and praise the boldness of those who think that human existence is devoid of any inherent significance and strive to confer a total meaning on it by their own ingenuity alone.

Nevertheless, in the face of the modern development of the world, the number constantly swells of the people who raise the most basic questions or recognize them with a new sharpness: what is man? What is this sense of sorrow, of evil, of death, which continues to exist despite so much progress? What purpose have these victories purchased at so high a cost? What can man offer to society, what can he expect from it? What follows this earthly life?

The Church firmly believes that Christ, who died and was raised up for all,[2] can through His Spirit offer man the light and the strength to measure up to his supreme destiny. Nor has any other name under heaven been given to man by which it is fitting for him to be saved.[3] She likewise holds that in her most benign Lord and Master can be found the key, the focal point, and the goal of man, as well as of all human history. The Church also maintains that beneath all changes there are many realities which do not change and which have their ultimate foundation in Christ, Who is the same yesterday and today, yes and forever.[4] Hence under the light of Christ, the image of the unseen God, the firstborn of every creature,[5] the council wishes to speak to all men in order to shed light on the mystery of man and to cooperate in finding the solution to the outstanding problems of our time.

The Situation of Modern Man
Gaudium et Spes 10

**Pope
St. John Paul II**

———

*Redemptor
Hominis* 14

It was . . . man in all the truth of his life, in his conscience, in his continual inclination to sin and at the same time in his continual aspiration to truth, the good, the beautiful, justice, and love that the Second Vatican Council had before its eyes when, in outlining his situation in the modern world, it always passed from the external elements of this situation to the truth within humanity: "In man himself many elements wrestle with one another. Thus, on the one hand, as a creature he experiences his limitations in a multitude of ways; on the other he feels himself to be boundless in his desires and summoned to a higher life. Pulled by manifold attractions he is constantly forced to choose among them and renounce some. Indeed, as a weak and sinful being, he often does what he would not, and fails to do what he would. Hence he suffers from internal divisions, and from these flow so many and such great discords in society."

This man is the way for the Church—a way that, in a sense, is the basis of all the other ways that the Church must walk—because man—every man without any exception whatever—has been redeemed by Christ, and because with man—with each man without any exception whatever—Christ is in a way united, even when man is unaware of it: "Christ, who died and was raised up for all, can through His Spirit offer man"—each man and every man—"the light and the strength to measure up to his supreme destiny."

Since this man is the way for the Church, the way for her daily life and experience, for her mission and toil, the Church of today must be aware in an always new manner of man's "situation." That means that she must be aware of his possibilities, which keep returning to their proper bearings and thus revealing themselves. She must likewise be aware of the threats to man and of all that seems to oppose the endeavor to make human life "more human" (GS 38) and make every element of this life correspond to man's true dignity—in a word, she must be aware of all that is opposed to that process.

PART I

The Church and Man's Calling

11. The People of God believes that it is led by the Lord's Spirit, Who fills the earth. Motivated by this faith, it labors to decipher authentic signs of God's presence and purpose in the happenings, needs, and desires in which this People has a part along with other men of our age. For faith throws a new light on everything, manifests God's design for man's total vocation, and thus directs the mind to solutions which are fully human.

This council, first of all, wishes to assess in this light those values which are most highly prized today and to relate them to their divine source. Insofar as they stem from endowments conferred by God on man, these values are exceedingly good. Yet they are often wrenched from their rightful function by the taint in man's heart, and hence stand in need of purification.

What does the Church think of man? What needs to be recommended for the upbuilding of contemporary society? What is the ultimate significance of human activity throughout the world? People are waiting for an answer to these questions. From the answers it will be increasingly clear that the People of God and the human race in whose midst it lives render service to each other. Thus the mission of the Church will show its religious, and by that very fact, its supremely human character.

CHAPTER I
The Dignity of the Human Person

12. According to the almost unanimous opinion of believers and unbelievers alike, all things on earth should be related to man as their center and crown.

But what is man? About himself he has expressed, and continues to express, many divergent and even contradictory opinions. In these he often exalts himself as the absolute measure of all things or debases himself to the point of despair. The result is doubt and anxiety. The Church certainly understands these problems. Endowed with light from God, she can offer solutions to them, so that man's true situation can be portrayed and his defects explained, while at the same time his dignity and destiny are justly acknowledged.

For Sacred Scripture teaches that man was created "to the image of God," is capable of knowing and loving his Creator, and was appointed by Him as master of all earthly creatures[1] that he might subdue them and use them to God's glory.[2] "What is man that you should care for him? You have made him little less than the angels, and crowned him with glory and honor. You have given him rule over the works of your hands, putting all things under his feet" (Ps. 8:5–7).

But God did not create man as a solitary, for from the beginning "male and female he created them" (Gen. 1:27). Their companionship produces the primary form of interpersonal communion. For by his innermost nature man is a social being, and unless he relates himself to others he can neither live nor develop his potential.

Therefore, as we read elsewhere in Holy Scripture God saw "all that he had made, and it was very good" (Gen. 1:31).

13. Although he was made by God in a state of holiness, from the very onset of his history man abused his liberty, at the urging of the Evil One. Man set himself against God and sought to attain his goal apart from God. Although they knew God, they did not glorify Him as God, but their senseless minds were darkened and they served the creature rather

than the Creator.[3] What divine revelation makes known to us agrees with experience. Examining his heart, man finds that he has inclinations toward evil too, and is engulfed by manifold ills which cannot come from his good Creator. Often refusing to acknowledge God as his beginning, man has disrupted also his proper relationship to his own ultimate goal as well as his whole relationship toward himself and others and all created things.

Therefore man is split within himself. As a result, all of human life, whether individual or collective, shows itself to be a dramatic struggle between good and evil, between light and darkness. Indeed, man finds that by himself he is incapable of battling the assaults of evil successfully, so that everyone feels as though he is bound by chains. But the Lord Himself came to free and strengthen man, renewing him inwardly and casting out that "prince of this world" (John 12:31) who held him in the bondage of sin.[4] For sin has diminished man, blocking his path to fulfillment.

The call to grandeur and the depths of misery, both of which are a part of human experience, find their ultimate and simultaneous explanation in the light of this revelation.[5]

The Greatness and Misery

Gaudium et Spes 12–13 | Bishop Barron

The first section of the main body of *Gaudium et Spes* has to do with human dignity, and the document is a rather typically modern document in the measure that it places a special stress on humanity. It does so, however, in a biblical way, drawing our attention to the idea of humanity offered in Genesis—as being made in the image and likeness of God. Our dignity comes, not from the state or the culture or our achievements, but from God as a gift of grace.

Now, for those who say *Gaudium et Spes* is too one-sidedly optimistic, remember this line: "From the very onset of his history man abused his liberty, at the urging of the Evil One." The council fathers knew that this *imago Dei*, though real, is severely compromised by sin, which comes from the Evil One. Hence (and here revelation and experience coincide), we find ourselves divided, with both a fundamental orientation toward God and a leaning toward evil, so that all of human life is "a dramatic struggle between good and evil, between light and darkness." As Ratzinger pointed out and as the concluding line of this section suggests, the philosopher Blaise Pascal was influential here, especially his teaching on the *grandeur et misère* (greatness and misery) of man.

Man Set Himself Against God

Gaudium et Spes 13

**Pope
St. John Paul II**

*Dominum et
Vivificantem 36*

According to the witness concerning the beginning which we find in the Scriptures and in Tradition, after the first (and also more complete) description in the Book of Genesis, sin in its original form is understood as "disobedience," and this means simply and directly transgression of a prohibition laid down by God (see Gen. 2:16). But in the light of the whole context it is also obvious that the ultimate roots of this disobedience are to be sought in the whole real situation of man. Having been called into existence, the human being—man and woman—is a creature. The "image of God," consisting in rationality and freedom, expresses the greatness and dignity of the human subject, who is a person. But this personal subject is also always a creature: in his existence and essence he depends on the Creator. According to the Book of Genesis, "the tree of the knowledge of good and evil" was to express and constantly remind man of the "limit" impassable for a created being. God's prohibition is to be understood in this sense: the Creator forbids man and woman to eat of the fruit of the tree of the knowledge of good and evil. The words of the enticement, that is to say the temptation, as formulated in the sacred text, are an inducement to transgress this prohibition—that is to say, to go beyond that "limit": "When you eat of it your eyes will be opened, and you will be like God ["like gods"], knowing good and evil" (Gen. 3:5).

"Disobedience" means precisely going beyond that limit, which remains impassable to the will and the freedom of man as a created being. For God the Creator is the one definitive source of the moral order in the world created by him. Man cannot decide by himself what is good and what is evil—cannot "know good and evil, like God." In the created world God indeed remains the first and sovereign source for deciding about good and evil, through the intimate truth of being, which is the reflection of the Word, the eternal Son, consubstantial with the Father. To man, created to the image of God, the Holy Spirit gives the gift of conscience, so that in this conscience the image may faithfully reflect its model, which is both Wisdom and eternal Law, the source of the moral order in man and in the world. "Disobedience," as the original dimension of sin, means the rejection of this source, through man's claim to become an independent and exclusive source for deciding about good and evil. The Spirit who "searches the depths of God," and who at the same time is for man the light of conscience and the source of the moral order, knows in all its fullness this dimension of the sin inscribed in the mystery of man's beginning. And the Spirit does not cease "convincing the world of it" in connection with the Cross of Christ on Golgotha.

14. Though made of body and soul, man is one. Through his bodily composition he gathers to himself the elements of the material world; thus they reach their crown through him, and through him raise their voice in free praise of the Creator.[6] For this reason man is not allowed to despise his bodily life, rather he is obliged to regard his body as good and honorable since God has created it and will raise it up on the last day. Nevertheless, wounded by sin, man experiences rebellious stirrings in his body. But the very dignity of man postulates that man glorify God in his body and forbid it to serve the evil inclinations of his heart.

Now, man is not wrong when he regards himself as superior to bodily concerns, and as more than a speck of nature or a nameless constituent of the city of man. For by his interior qualities he outstrips the whole sum of mere things. He plunges into the depths of reality whenever he enters into his own heart; God, Who probes the heart,[7] awaits him there; there he discerns his proper destiny beneath the eyes of God. Thus, when he recognizes in himself a spiritual and immortal soul, he is not being mocked by a fantasy born only of physical or social influences, but is rather laying hold of the proper truth of the matter.

15. Man judges rightly that by his intellect he surpasses the material universe, for he shares in the light of the divine mind. By relentlessly employing his talents through the ages he has indeed made progress in the practical sciences and in technology and the liberal arts. In our times he has won superlative victories, especially in his probing of the material world and in subjecting it to himself. Still he has always searched for more penetrating truths, and finds them. For his intelligence is not confined to observable data alone, but can with genuine certitude attain to reality itself as knowable, though in consequence of sin that certitude is partly obscured and weakened.

The intellectual nature of the human person is perfected by wisdom and needs to be, for wisdom gently attracts the mind of man to a quest and a love for what is true and good. Steeped in wisdom, man passes through visible realities to those which are unseen.

Our era needs such wisdom more than bygone ages if the discoveries made by man are to be further humanized. For the future of the world stands in peril unless wiser men are forthcoming. It should also be pointed out that many nations, poorer in economic goods, are quite rich in wisdom and can offer noteworthy advantages to others.

It is, finally, through the gift of the Holy Spirit that man comes by faith to the contemplation and appreciation of the divine plan.[8]

Reason and Faith
Gaudium et Spes 15

Pope Benedict XVI
———
Spe Salvi 23

Reason is God's great gift to man, and the victory of reason over unreason is also a goal of the Christian life. But when does reason truly triumph? When it is detached from God? When it has become blind to God? Is the reason behind action and capacity for action the whole of reason? If progress, in order to be progress, needs moral growth on the part of humanity, then the reason behind action and capacity for action is likewise urgently in need of integration through reason's openness to the saving forces of faith, to the differentiation between good and evil. Only thus does reason become truly human.

It becomes human only if it is capable of directing the will along the right path, and it is capable of this only if it looks beyond itself. Otherwise, man's situation, in view of the imbalance between his material capacity and the lack of judgment in his heart, becomes a threat for him and for creation. Thus where freedom is concerned, we must remember that human freedom always requires a convergence of various freedoms. Yet this convergence cannot succeed unless it is determined by a common intrinsic criterion of measurement, which is the foundation and goal of our freedom. Let us put it very simply: man needs God, otherwise he remains without hope. . . . There is no doubt, therefore, that a "Kingdom of God" accomplished without God—a kingdom therefore of man alone—inevitably ends up as the "perverse end" of all things as described by Kant: we have seen it, and we see it over and over again. Yet neither is there any doubt that God truly enters into human affairs only when, rather than being present merely in our thinking, he himself comes towards us and speaks to us. Reason therefore needs faith if it is to be completely itself: reason and faith need one another in order to fulfill their true nature and their mission.

16. In the depths of his conscience, man detects a law which he does not impose upon himself, but which holds him to obedience. Always summoning him to love good and avoid evil, the voice of conscience when necessary speaks to his heart: do this, shun that. For man has in his heart a law written by God; to obey it is the very dignity of man; according to it he will be judged.[9] Conscience is the most secret core and sanctuary of a man. There he is alone with God, Whose voice echoes in his depths.[10] In a wonderful manner conscience reveals that law which is fulfilled by love of God and neighbor.[11] In fidelity to conscience, Christians are joined with the rest of men in the search for truth, and for the genuine solution to the numerous problems which arise in the life of individuals from social relationships. Hence the more right conscience holds sway, the more persons and groups turn aside from blind choice and strive to be guided by the objective norms of morality. Conscience frequently errs from invincible ignorance without losing its dignity. The same cannot be said for a man who cares but little for truth and goodness, or for a conscience which by degrees grows practically sightless as a result of habitual sin.

17. Only in freedom can man direct himself toward goodness. Our contemporaries make much of this freedom and pursue it eagerly; and rightly to be sure. Often however they foster it perversely as a license for doing whatever pleases them, even if it is evil. For its part, authentic freedom is an exceptional sign of the divine image within man. For God has willed that man remain "under the control of his own decisions,"[12] so that he can seek his Creator spontaneously, and come freely to utter and blissful perfection through loyalty to Him. Hence man's dignity demands that he act according to a knowing and free choice that is personally motivated and prompted from within, not under blind internal impulse nor by mere external pressure. Man achieves such dignity when, emancipating himself from all captivity to passion, he pursues his goal in a spontaneous choice of what is good, and procures for himself through effective and skillful action, apt helps to that end. Since man's freedom has been damaged by sin, only by the aid of God's grace can he bring such a relationship with God into full flower. Before the judgment seat of God each man must render an account of his own life, whether he has done good or evil.[13]

Three Signs of Human Dignity

Gaudium et Spes 15–17 | Bishop Barron

Gaudium et Spes 15–17 outlines three special signs of the dignity of the human person: intellect, conscience, and freedom. Influenced undoubtedly by Karl Rahner's theological anthropology, the council teaches that the first sign is the intellectual power that orients the human being to the whole of reality and finally to that invisible intelligibility that transcends the visible world. The mind is hungry for truth, and to a degree, finds it in philosophy, the sciences, and all the great academic disciplines. But no matter how much we know, our minds are never satisfied; in fact, the more we know, the more the mind is awakened. Bernard Lonergan, the great Catholic philosopher, said that the mind finally wants to know "everything about everything." Ultimately, it wants the beatific vision; it wants to know the essence of God.

Secondly, *Gaudium et Spes* says, the dignity of man is displayed "in the depths of his conscience." The reference here is to that strangely compelling interior voice that tells us right from wrong, that urges us—with an uncompromising, unconditioned authority—to do what we must do and avoid what we must avoid. Like the mind, the conscience does not want just particular goods; what the conscience finally wants is the good itself—the unlimited, unconditioned good. "Conscience is the most secret core and sanctuary of a man. There he is alone with God, Whose voice echoes in his depths." Here we see the influence of John Henry Newman, who said that the conscience is the "aboriginal Vicar of Christ" in the soul.

Finally, in number seventeen, we find the assertion that "only in freedom can man direct himself toward goodness." How typically modern this sounds; and yet the council fathers are quick to distinguish true freedom from license: "Authentic freedom is an exceptional sign of the divine image within man." In the modern sense, freedom means primarily liberty of self-expression, of choice. I am free in the measure that I can say "yes" or "no," that I can decide for myself what path to pursue. But in the Bible, freedom is the disciplining of desire so as to make the achievement of the good first possible and then effortless. It is not a freedom in opposition to the good and to value, but precisely in surrender to it. Freedom doesn't stand opposed to God, but rather finds itself precisely in relation to God, the supreme good.

---

18. It is in the face of death that the riddle a human existence grows most acute. Not only is man tormented by pain and by the advancing deterioration of his body, but even more so by a dread of perpetual extinction. He rightly follows the intuition of his heart when he abhors and repudiates the utter ruin and total disappearance of his own person. He rebels against death because he bears in himself an eternal seed which cannot be reduced to sheer matter. All the endeavors of technology, though useful in the extreme, cannot calm his anxiety; for prolongation of biological life is unable to satisfy that desire for higher life which is inescapably lodged in his breast.

Although the mystery of death utterly beggars the imagination, the Church has been taught by divine revelation and firmly teaches that man has been created by God for a blissful purpose beyond the reach of earthly misery. In addition, that bodily death from which man would have been immune had he not sinned[14] will be vanquished, according to the Christian faith, when man who was ruined by his own doing is restored to wholeness by an almighty and merciful Savior. For God has called man and still calls him so that with his entire being he might be joined to Him in an endless sharing of a divine life beyond all corruption. Christ won this victory when He rose to life, for by His death He freed man from death. Hence to every thoughtful man a solidly established faith provides the answer to his anxiety about what the future holds for him. At the same time faith gives him the power to be united in Christ with his loved ones who have already been snatched away by death; faith arouses the hope that they have found true life with God.[15]

19. The root reason for human dignity lies in man's call to communion with God. From the very circumstance of his origin man is already invited to converse with God. For man would not exist were he not created by God's love and constantly preserved by it; and he cannot live fully according to truth unless he freely acknowledges that love and devotes himself to his Creator. Still, many of our contemporaries have never recognized this intimate and vital link with God, or have explicitly rejected it. Thus atheism must be accounted among the most serious problems of this age, and is deserving of closer examination.

The word atheism is applied to phenomena which are quite distinct from one another. For while God is expressly denied by some, others believe that man can assert absolutely nothing about Him. Still others use such a method to scrutinize the question of God as to make it seem devoid of meaning. Many, unduly transgressing the limits of the positive sciences, contend that everything can be explained by this kind of scientific reasoning alone, or by contrast, they altogether disallow that there is any absolute truth. Some laud man so extravagantly that their faith in God lapses into a kind of anemia, though they seem more inclined to affirm man than to deny God. Again some form for themselves such a fallacious idea of God that when they repudiate this figment they are by no means rejecting the God of the Gospel. Some never get to the point of raising questions about God, since they seem to experience no religious stirrings nor do they see why they should trouble themselves about religion. Moreover, atheism results not rarely from a violent protest against the evil in this world, or from the absolute character with which certain human values are unduly invested, and which thereby already accords them the stature of God. Modern civilization itself often complicates the approach to God not for any essential reason but because it is so heavily engrossed in earthly affairs.

Undeniably, those who willfully shut out God from their hearts and try to dodge religious questions are not following the dictates of their consciences, and hence are not free of blame; yet believers themselves frequently bear some responsibility for this situation. For, taken as a whole, atheism is not a spontaneous development but stems from a variety of causes, including a critical reaction against religious beliefs, and in some places against the Christian religion in particular. Hence believers can have more than a little to do with the birth of atheism. To the extent that they neglect their own training in the faith, or teach erroneous doctrine, or are deficient in their religious, moral, or social life, they must be said to conceal rather than reveal the authentic face of God and religion.

20. Modern atheism often takes on a systematic expression which, in addition to other causes, stretches the desires for human independence to such a point that it poses difficulties against any kind of dependence on God. Those who profess atheism of this sort maintain that it gives man freedom to be an end unto himself, the sole artisan and creator of his own history. They claim that this freedom cannot be reconciled with the affirmation of a Lord Who is author and purpose of all things, or at least that this freedom makes such an affirmation altogether superfluous. Favoring this doctrine can be the sense of power which modern technical progress generates in man.

Not to be overlooked among the forms of modern atheism is that which anticipates the liberation of man especially through his economic and social emancipation. This form argues that by its nature religion thwarts this liberation by arousing man's hope for a deceptive future life, thereby diverting him from the constructing of the earthly city. Consequently when the proponents of this doctrine gain governmental power they vigorously fight against religion, and promote atheism by using, especially in the education of youth, those means of pressure which public power has at its disposal.

21. In her loyal devotion to God and men, the Church has already repudiated[16] and cannot cease repudiating, sorrowfully but as firmly as possible, those poisonous doctrines and actions which contradict reason and the common experience of humanity, and dethrone man from his native excellence.

Still, she strives to detect in the atheistic mind the hidden causes for the denial of God; conscious of how weighty are the questions which atheism raises, and motivated by love for all men, she believes these questions ought to be examined seriously and more profoundly.

The Church holds that the recognition of God is in no way hostile to man's dignity, since this dignity is rooted and perfected in God. For man was made an intelligent and free member of society by God Who created him, but even more important, he is called as a son to commune with God and share in His happiness. She further teaches that a hope related to the end of time does not diminish the importance of intervening duties but rather undergirds the fulfillment of them with fresh incentives. By contrast, when a divine instruction and the hope of life eternal are wanting, man's dignity is most grievously lacerated, as current events often attest; riddles of life and death, of guilt and of grief go unsolved with the frequent result that men succumb to despair.

Meanwhile every man remains to himself an unsolved puzzle, however obscurely he may perceive it. For on certain occasions no one can entirely escape the kind of self-questioning mentioned earlier, especially when life's major events take place. To this questioning only God fully and most certainly provides an answer as He summons man to higher knowledge and humbler probing.

The remedy which must be applied to atheism, however, is to be sought in a proper presentation of the Church's teaching as well as in the integral life of the Church and her members. For it is the function of the Church, led by the Holy Spirit Who renews and purifies her ceaselessly,[17] to make God the Father and His Incarnate Son present and in a sense visible. This result is achieved chiefly by the witness of a living and mature faith, namely, one trained to see difficulties clearly and to master them. Many martyrs have given luminous witness to this faith and continue to do so. This faith needs to prove its fruitfulness by penetrating the believer's entire life, including its worldly dimensions, and by activating him toward justice and love, especially regarding the needy. What does the most reveal God's presence, however, is the brotherly charity of the faithful who are united in spirit as they work together for the faith of the Gospel[18] and who prove themselves a sign of unity.

While rejecting atheism, root and branch, the Church sincerely professes that all men, believers and unbelievers alike, ought to work for the rightful betterment of this world in which all alike live; such an ideal cannot be realized, however, apart from sincere and prudent dialogue. Hence the Church protests against the distinction which some state

Atheist Humanism

Gaudium et Spes 19–21 | Bishop Barron

Gaudium et Spes explores a number of reasons why atheism has reasserted itself in modern times, but they put particular emphasis on the "humanist" objection to belief in God. With its roots in the speculation of Ludwig Feuerbach, this argument holds that the affirmation of God results in the denigration of humanity. Feuerbach himself opined that "the no to God is the yes to man." Karl Marx, an ardent disciple of Feuerbach, characterized religion as the "opium of the people." And Sigmund Freud, moving down the same avenue of thought, argued that religious faith is an infantile fantasy, a dream from which an enlightened humanity should wake.

Now, what is the answer to this trenchant objection? The council fathers do not offer a fully developed rebuttal, but *Gaudium et Spes* 21 gives a classically Catholic response: that God must not be construed in a competitive manner with our dignity and happiness. "The Church holds that the recognition of God is in no way hostile to man's dignity, since this dignity is rooted and perfected in God. For man was made an intelligent and free member of society by God Who created him, but even more important, he is called as a son to commune with God and share in His happiness."

Atheism is born of the suspicion that God represents a threat to full human flourishing. This notion, in turn, comes from a fundamental misconception of God as a supreme being alongside of other beings. A supreme being would indeed compete with other conditioned things in the measure that they would all need to occupy together the same metaphysical space. But the God in whom Christians believe is the God of the burning bush: on fire, but not consumed. The closer the true God comes to a creature, the more radiant and beautiful that creature becomes. Thus, the God presented by classical Catholic philosophy is not one being, however supreme, among many, but rather is the sheer act of to-be itself, *ipsum esse subsistens*, in Aquinas' pithy formulation. This distinction is pivotal, for it implies that God and creatures are not caught in a desperate zero-sum game, whereby the more God is glorified the more creatures are denigrated, and vice versa. Rather, as St. Irenaeus has it, "The glory of God is a human being fully alive."

authorities make between believers and unbelievers, with prejudice to the fundamental rights of the human person. The Church calls for the active liberty of believers to build up in this world God's temple too. She courteously invites atheists to examine the Gospel of Christ with an open mind.

Above all the Church knows that her message is in harmony with the most secret desires of the human heart when she champions the dignity of the human vocation, restoring hope to those who have already despaired of anything higher than their present lot. Far from diminishing man, her message brings to his development light, life, and freedom. Apart from this message nothing will avail to fill up the heart of man: "Thou hast made us for Thyself," O Lord, "and our hearts are restless till they rest in Thee."[19]

22. The truth is that only in the mystery of the incarnate Word does the mystery of man take on light. For Adam, the first man, was a figure of Him Who was to come,[20] namely Christ the Lord. Christ, the final Adam, by the revelation of the mystery of the Father and His love, fully reveals man to man himself and makes his supreme calling clear. It is not surprising, then, that in Him all the aforementioned truths find their root and attain their crown.

He Who is "the image of the invisible God" (Col. 1:15),[21] is Himself the perfect man. To the sons of Adam He restores the divine likeness which had been disfigured from the first sin onward. Since human nature as He assumed it was not annulled,[22] by that very fact it has been raised up to a divine dignity in our respect too. For by His incarnation the Son of God has united Himself in some fashion with every man. He worked with human hands, He thought with a human mind, acted by human choice,[23] and loved with a human heart. Born of the Virgin Mary, He has truly been made one of us, like us in all things except sin.[24]

As an innocent lamb He merited for us life by the free shedding of His own blood. In Him God reconciled us[25] to Himself and among ourselves; from bondage to the devil and sin He delivered us, so that each one of us can say with the Apostle: The Son of God "loved me and gave Himself up for me" (Gal. 2:20). By suffering for us He not only provided us with an example for our imitation,[26] He blazed a trail, and if we follow it, life and death are made holy and take on a new meaning.

The Christian man, conformed to the likeness of that Son Who is the firstborn of many brothers,[27] received "the first-fruits of the Spirit"

(Rom. 8:23) by which he becomes capable of discharging the new law of love.[28] Through this Spirit, who is "the pledge of our inheritance" (Eph. 1:14), the whole man is renewed from within, even to the achievement of "the redemption of the body" (Rom. 8:23): "If the Spirit of him who raised Jesus from the death dwells in you, then he who raised Jesus Christ from the dead will also bring to life your mortal bodies because of his Spirit who dwells in you" (Rom. 8:11).[29] Pressing upon the Christian to be sure, are the need and the duty to battle against evil through manifold tribulations and even to suffer death. But, linked with the paschal mystery and patterned on the dying Christ, he will hasten forward to resurrection in the strength which comes from hope.[30]

All this holds true not only for Christians, but for all men of good will in whose hearts grace works in an unseen way.[31] For, since Christ died for all men,[32] and since the ultimate vocation of man is in fact one, and divine, we ought to believe that the Holy Spirit in a manner known only to God offers to every man the possibility of being associated with this paschal mystery.

Such is the mystery of man, and it is a great one, as seen by believers in the light of Christian revelation. Through Christ and in Christ, the riddles of sorrow and death grow meaningful. Apart from His Gospel, they overwhelm us. Christ has risen, destroying death by His death; He has lavished life upon us[33] so that, as sons in the Son, we can cry out in the Spirit: Abba, Father.[34]

The Light of Christ

Gaudium et Spes 22 | Bishop Barron

One of the most important sections of *Gaudium et Spes* is number 22. Karol Wojtyła particularly loved and used this passage in his magisterium over and over again. Here are the key lines: "The truth is that only in the mystery of the incarnate Word does the mystery of man take on light. . . . Christ, the final Adam, by the revelation of the mystery of the Father and His love, fully reveals man to man himself and makes his supreme calling clear."

If Karol Wojtyła is right, this incarnational vision is the interpretive grid for this entire document. Often, *Gaudium et Spes* appears to present the modern world in a one-sidedly positive way—despite the fact that, by 1965, it had produced two World Wars, several attempts at genocide, the rape of the environment, a potentially disastrous cold war, and the dropping of two atomic bombs. But in contending that the mystery of humanity is properly understood only in light of the mystery of the Word made flesh, this paragraph offers the necessary corrective. In Christ, we see the world aright and properly assess both its darkness and its light.

The adoption of this theme also has extremely important methodological implications, for it reverses the momentum of so much liberal theological speculation, which has tended to read (and hence misread) Christ in light of man instead of vice versa. As the God-human, Jesus is the key to understanding both divinity and humanity. The humanity of Jesus is the luminous icon of his divinity, but it is also the great lens by which we read the signs of the times. Christ is not an addendum to a generally humanist project, not window dressing to a program of secular progress; rather, Jesus is the interpretive key to humanity, that through which

human beings properly understand themselves.

Finally, it points to the great humanism implied in this "supreme calling." As the "image of the invisible God" (Col. 1:15), Christ is the restoration of the lost *imago* in Adam, the renewal of the likeness unto God. In becoming incarnate in Christ, the Son of God, in a certain sense, united himself to the whole human race. "He worked with human hands, He thought with a human mind, acted by human choice, and loved with a human heart." But as the council fathers point out, Christ not only provided humanity with "an example for our imitation"; he also "blazed a trail" by which we are "conformed to the likeness of that Son" and "renewed from within, even to the achievement of 'the redemption of the body' (Rom. 8:23)." God became man, as St. Athanasius put it, so that man might become God. There is simply no greater humanism on offer; there never has been, and there never will be.

CHAPTER II
The Community of Mankind

23. One of the salient features of the modern world is the growing interdependence of men one on the other, a development promoted chiefly

by modern technical advances. Nevertheless brotherly dialogue among men does not reach its perfection on the level of technical progress, but on the deeper level of interpersonal relationships. These demand a mutual respect for the full spiritual dignity of the person. Christian revelation contributes greatly to the promotion of this communion between persons, and at the same time leads us to a deeper understanding of the laws of social life which the Creator has written into man's moral and spiritual nature.

Since rather recent documents of the Church's teaching authority have dealt at considerable length with Christian doctrine about human society,[1] this council is merely going to call to mind some of the more basic truths, treating their foundations under the light of revelation. Then it will dwell more at length on certain of their implications having special significance for our day.

24. God, Who has fatherly concern for everyone, has willed that all men should constitute one family and treat one another in a spirit of brotherhood. For having been created in the image of God, Who "from one man has created the whole human race and made them live all over the face of the earth" (Acts 17:26), all men are called to one and the same goal, namely God Himself.

For this reason, love for God and neighbor is the first and greatest commandment. Sacred Scripture, however, teaches us that the love of God cannot be separated from love of neighbor: "If there is any other commandment, it is summed up in this saying: Thou shalt love thy neighbor as thyself. . . . Love therefore is the fulfillment of the Law" (Rom. 13:9–10; see 1 John 4:20). To men growing daily more dependent on one another, and to a world becoming more unified every day, this truth proves to be of paramount importance.

Indeed, the Lord Jesus, when He prayed to the Father, "that all may be one . . . as we are one" (John 17:21–22) opened up vistas closed to human reason, for He implied a certain likeness between the union of the divine Persons, and the unity of God's sons in truth and charity. This likeness reveals that man, who is the only creature on earth which God willed for itself, cannot fully find himself except through a sincere gift of himself.[2]

Salvation Is a Communal Reality

Gaudium et Spes 24 | Bishop Barron

One of the most important shapers of *Gaudium et Spes* was the French Jesuit Henri de Lubac. In the 1940s, de Lubac wrote a text entitled *Catholicism* in which he argued for the social dimension of every doctrine within Catholic dogmatics. The influence of this perspective is especially evident in this second chapter of the constitution.

The council fathers argue that salvation is a communal rather than individual reality: "God, Who has fatherly concern for everyone, has willed that all men should constitute one family and treat one another in a spirit of brotherhood." This means that the advancement of the human being and the cultivation of human society go hand in hand. Politically speaking, this means that we must stress the common good, understood as the conditions that make possible the full flourishing of each individual.

The Gift of Self

Gaudium et Spes 24

Pope St. John Paul II

—

Mulieris Dignitatem 7

In the chapter on "The Community of Mankind" in the Pastoral Constitution *Gaudium et Spes*, we read: "The Lord Jesus, when He prayed to the Father, 'that all may be one . . . as we are one' (John 17:21–22) opened up vistas closed to human reason, for He implied a certain likeness between the union of the divine Persons, and the unity of God's sons in truth and charity. This likeness reveals that man, who is the only creature on earth which God willed for itself, cannot fully find himself except through a sincere gift of himself."

With these words, the Council text presents a summary of the whole truth about man and woman—a truth which is already outlined in the first chapters of the Book of Genesis, and which is the structural basis of biblical and Christian anthropology. *Man*—whether man or woman—

is *the only being among the creatures* of the visible world *that God the Creator has "willed for itself"*; that creature is thus a person. Being a person means striving towards self-realization (the Council text speaks of self-discovery), which can only be achieved "through a sincere gift of himself." The model for this interpretation of the person is God himself as Trinity, as a communion of Persons. To say that man is created in the image and likeness of God means that man is called to exist "for" others, to become a gift.

This applies to every human being, whether woman or man, who live it out in accordance with the special qualities proper to each.

25. Man's social nature makes it evident that the progress of the human person and the advance of society itself hinge on one another. For the beginning, the subject, and the goal of all social institutions is and must be the human person which for its part and by its very nature stands completely in need of social life.[3] Since this social life is not something added on to man, through his dealings with others, through reciprocal duties, and through fraternal dialogue he develops all his gifts and is able to rise to his destiny.

Among those social ties which man needs for his development some, like the family and political community, relate with greater immediacy to his innermost nature; others originate rather from his free decision. In our era, for various reasons, reciprocal ties and mutual dependencies increase day by day and give rise to a variety of associations and organizations, both public and private. This development, which is called socialization, while certainly not without its dangers, brings with it many advantages with respect to consolidating and increasing the qualities of the human person, and safeguarding his rights.[4]

But if by this social life the human person is greatly aided in responding to his destiny, even in its religious dimensions, it cannot be denied that men are often diverted from doing good and spurred toward and by the social circumstances in which they live and are immersed from their birth. To be sure the disturbances which so frequently occur in the social order result in part from the natural tensions of economic, political, and social forms. But at a deeper level they flow from man's pride and selfishness, which contaminate even the social sphere. When the structure of affairs is flawed by the consequences of sin, man, already born with a bent toward evil, finds there new inducements to sin, which cannot be overcome without strenuous efforts and the assistance of grace.

26. Every day human interdependence grows more tightly drawn and spreads by degrees over the whole world. As a result the common good, that is, the sum of those conditions of social life which allow social groups and their individual members relatively thorough and ready access to their own fulfillment, today takes on an increasingly universal complexion and consequently involves rights and duties with respect to the whole human race. Every social group must take account of the needs and legitimate aspirations of other groups, and even of the general welfare of the entire human family.[5]

At the same time, however, there is a growing awareness of the exalted dignity proper to the human person, since he stands above all things, and his rights and duties are universal and inviolable. Therefore, there must be made available to all men everything necessary for leading a life truly human, such as food, clothing, and shelter; the right to choose a state of life freely and to found a family, the right to education, to employment, to a good reputation, to respect, to appropriate information, to activity in accord with the upright norm of one's own conscience, to protection of privacy and rightful freedom even in matters religious.

Hence, the social order and its development must invariably work to the benefit of the human person if the disposition of affairs is to be subordinate to the personal realm and not contrariwise, as the Lord indicated when He said that the Sabbath was made for man, and not man for the Sabbath.[6]

This social order requires constant improvement. It must be founded on truth, built on justice, and animated by love; in freedom it should grow every day toward a more humane balance.[7] An improvement in attitudes and abundant changes in society will have to take place if these objectives are to be gained.

God's Spirit, Who with a marvelous providence directs the unfolding of time and renews the face of the earth, is not absent from this development. The ferment of the Gospel too has aroused and continues to arouse in man's heart the irresistible requirements of his dignity.

27. Coming down to practical and particularly urgent consequences, this council lays stress on reverence for man; everyone must consider his every neighbor without exception as another self, taking into account first of all His life and the means necessary to living it with dignity,[8] so as not to imitate the rich man who had no concern for the poor man Lazarus.[9]

In our times a special obligation binds us to make ourselves the neighbor of every person without exception and of actively helping him when he comes across our path, whether he be an old person abandoned by all, a foreign laborer unjustly looked down upon, a refugee, a child born of an unlawful union and wrongly suffering for a sin he did not commit, or a hungry person who disturbs our conscience by recalling the voice of the Lord, "As long as you did it for one of these the least of my brethren, you did it for me" (Matt. 25:40).

Furthermore, whatever is opposed to life itself, such as any type of murder, genocide, abortion, euthanasia, or willful self-destruction, whatever violates the integrity of the human person, such as mutilation, torments inflicted on body or mind, attempts to coerce the will itself; whatever insults human dignity, such as subhuman living conditions, arbitrary imprisonment, deportation, slavery, prostitution, the selling of women and children; as well as disgraceful working conditions, where men are treated as mere tools for profit, rather than as free and responsible persons; all these things and others of their like are infamies indeed. They poison human society, but they do more harm to those who practice them than those who suffer from the injury. Moreover, they are supreme dishonor to the Creator.

The Defense of the Unborn

Gaudium et Spes 27

Pope Francis

—

Evangelii Gaudium
213–214

Among the vulnerable for whom the Church wishes to care with particular love and concern are unborn children, the most defenseless and innocent among us. Nowadays efforts are made to deny them their human dignity and to do with them whatever one pleases, taking their lives and passing laws preventing anyone from standing in the way of this. Frequently, as a way of ridiculing the Church's effort to defend their lives, attempts are made to present her position as ideological, obscurantist, and conservative. Yet this defense of unborn life is closely linked to the defense of each and every other human right. It involves the conviction that a human being is always sacred and inviolable, in any situation and at every stage of development. Human beings are ends in themselves and never a means of resolving other problems. Once this conviction disappears, so do solid and lasting foundations for the defense of human rights, which would always be subject to the passing whims of the powers that be. Reason alone is sufficient to recognize the inviolable value of each single human life, but if we also look at the issue from the standpoint of faith, "every violation of the personal dignity of the human being cries out in vengeance to God and is an offence against the creator of the individual."

Precisely because this involves the internal consistency of our message about the value of the human person, the Church cannot be expected to change her position on this question. I want to be completely honest in this regard. This is not something subject to alleged reforms or "modernizations." It is not "progressive" to try to resolve problems by eliminating a human life. On the other hand, it is also true that we have done little to adequately accompany women in very difficult situations, where abortion appears as a quick solution to their profound anguish, especially when the life developing within them is the result of rape or a situation of extreme poverty. Who can remain unmoved before such painful situations?

28. Respect and love ought to be extended also to those who think or act differently than we do in social, political, and even religious matters. In fact, the more deeply we come to understand their ways of thinking through such courtesy and love, the more easily will we be able to enter into dialogue with them.

This love and good will, to be sure, must in no way render us indifferent to truth and goodness. Indeed love itself impels the disciples of Christ to speak the saving truth to all men. But it is necessary to distinguish between error, which always merits repudiation, and the person in error, who never loses the dignity of being a person even when he is flawed by false or inadequate religious notions.[10] God alone is the judge and searcher of hearts; for that reason He forbids us to make judgments about the internal guilt of anyone.[11]

The teaching of Christ even requires that we forgive injuries,[12] and extends the law of love to include every enemy, according to the command of the New Law: "You have heard that it was said: Thou shalt love thy neighbor and hate thy enemy. But I say to you: love your enemies, do good to those who hate you, and pray for those who persecute and calumniate you" (Matt. 5:43–44).

29. Since all men possess a rational soul and are created in God's likeness, since they have the same nature and origin, have been redeemed by Christ, and enjoy the same divine calling and destiny, the basic equality of all must receive increasingly greater recognition.

True, all men are not alike from the point of view of varying physical power and the diversity of intellectual and moral resources. Nevertheless, with respect to the fundamental rights of the person, every type of discrimination, whether social or cultural, whether based on sex, race, color, social condition, language, or religion, is to be overcome and eradicated as contrary to God's intent. For in truth it must still be regretted that fundamental personal rights are still not being universally honored. Such is the case of a woman who is denied the right to choose a husband freely, to embrace a state of life, or to acquire an education or cultural benefits equal to those recognized for men.

Therefore, although rightful differences exist between men, the equal dignity of persons demands that a more humane and just condition of life be brought about. For excessive economic and social differences between the members of the one human family or population groups cause scandal, and militate against social justice, equity, the dignity of the human person, as well as social and international peace.

Human institutions, both private and public, must labor to minister to the dignity and purpose of man. At the same time let them put up a stubborn fight against any kind of slavery, whether social or political, and safeguard the basic rights of man under every political system. Indeed human institutions themselves must be accommodated by degrees to the highest of all realities, spiritual ones, even though meanwhile, a long enough time will be required before they arrive at the desired goal.

Rights Are Rooted in God

Gaudium et Spes 29 | Bishop Barron

Great stress is placed in this chapter, and in this number in particular, on rights. But we must insist upon a contrast between a Hobbesian and a Catholic understanding of the term. For Thomas Hobbes, as well as for his disciple John Locke, we have a right to those things that we are incapable of not desiring—for instance, life and liberty. But for *Gaudium et Spes*, rights are rooted not so much in unavoidable desires but in the dignity that comes to us through creation and redemption: "Since all men possess a rational soul and are created in God's likeness, since they have the same nature and origin, have been redeemed by Christ, and enjoy the same divine calling and destiny, the basic equality of all must receive increasingly greater recognition."

30. Profound and rapid changes make it more necessary that no one ignoring the trend of events or drugged by laziness, content himself with a merely individualistic morality. It grows increasingly true that the obligations of justice and love are fulfilled only if each person, contributing to the common good, according to his own abilities and the needs of others, also promotes and assists the public and private institutions dedicated to bettering the conditions of human life. Yet there are those who, while possessing grand and rather noble sentiments, nevertheless in reality live always as if they cared nothing for the needs of society. Many in various places even make light of social laws and precepts, and do not hesitate to resort to various frauds and deceptions in avoiding just taxes or other debts due to society. Others think little of certain norms of social life, for example those designed for the protection of health, or laws establishing speed limits; they do not even avert to the fact that by such indifference they imperil their own life and that of others.

Let everyone consider it his sacred obligation to esteem and observe social necessities as belonging to the primary duties of modern man. For the more unified the world becomes, the more plainly do the offices of men extend beyond particular groups and spread by degrees to the whole world. But this development cannot occur unless individual men and their associations cultivate in themselves the moral and social virtues, and promote them in society; thus, with the needed help of divine grace men who are truly new and artisans of a new humanity can be forthcoming.

31. In order for individual men to discharge with greater exactness the obligations of their conscience toward themselves and the various groups to which they belong, they must be carefully educated to a higher degree of culture through the use of the immense resources available today to the human race. Above all the education of youth from every social background has to be undertaken, so that there can be produced not only men and women of refined talents, but those great-souled persons who are so desperately required by our times.

Now a man can scarcely arrive at the needed sense of responsibility, unless his living conditions allow him to become conscious of his dignity, and to rise to his destiny by spending himself for God and for others. But human freedom is often crippled when a man encounters extreme poverty just as it withers when he indulges in too many of life's comforts and imprisons himself in a kind of splendid isolation. Freedom acquires new strength, by contrast, when a man consents to the unavoidable requirements of social life, takes on the manifold demands of human partnership, and commits himself to the service of the human community.

Hence, the will to play one's role in common endeavors should be everywhere encouraged. Praise is due to those national procedures which allow the largest possible number of citizens to participate in public affairs with genuine freedom. Account must be taken, to be sure, of the actual conditions of each people and the decisiveness required by public authority. If every citizen is to feel inclined to take part in the activities of the various groups which make up the social body, these must offer advantages which will attract members and dispose them to serve others. We can justly consider that the future of humanity lies in the hands of those who are strong enough to provide coming generations with reasons for living and hoping.

32. As God did not create man for life in isolation, but for the formation of social unity, so also "God . . . does not make men holy and save them merely as individuals, without bond or link between one another. Rather has it pleased Him to bring men together as one people, a people which acknowledges Him in truth and serves Him in holiness."[13] So from the

beginning of salvation history He has chosen men not just as individuals but as members of a certain community. Revealing His mind to them, God called these chosen ones "His people" (Exod. 3:7–12), and even made a covenant with them on Sinai.[14]

This communitarian character is developed and consummated in the work of Jesus Christ. For the very Word made flesh willed to share in the human fellowship. He was present at the wedding of Cana, visited the house of Zacchaeus, ate with publicans and sinners. He revealed the love of the Father and the sublime vocation of man in terms of the most common of social realities and by making use of the speech and the imagery of plain everyday life. Willingly obeying the laws of his country He sanctified those human ties, especially family ones, which are the source of social structures. He chose to lead the life proper to an artisan of His time and place.

In His preaching He clearly taught the sons of God to treat one another as brothers. In His prayers He pleaded that all His disciples might be "one." Indeed as the redeemer of all, He offered Himself for all even to point of death. "Greater love than this no one has, that one lay down his life for his friends" (John 15:13). He commanded His Apostles to preach to all peoples the Gospel's message that the human race was to become the Family of God, in which the fullness of the Law would be love.

As the firstborn of many brethren and by the giving of His Spirit, He founded after His death and resurrection a new brotherly community composed of all those who receive Him in faith and in love. This He did through His Body, which is the Church. There everyone, as members one of the other, would render mutual service according to the different gifts bestowed on each.

This solidarity must be constantly increased until that day on which it will be brought to perfection. Then, saved by grace, men will offer flawless glory to God as a family beloved of God and of Christ their Brother.

CHAPTER III
Man's Activity Throughout the World

33. Through his labors and his native endowments man has ceaselessly striven to better his life. Today, however, especially with the help of science and technology, he has extended his mastery over nearly the whole of nature and continues to do so. Thanks to increased opportunities for many

kinds of social contact among nations, the human family is gradually recognizing that it comprises a single world community and is making itself so. Hence many benefits once looked for, especially from heavenly powers, man has now enterprisingly procured for himself.

In the face of these immense efforts which already preoccupy the whole human race, men agitate numerous questions among themselves. What is the meaning and value of this feverish activity? How should all these things be used? To the achievement of what goal are the strivings of individuals and societies heading? The Church guards the heritage of God's word and draws from it moral and religious principles without always having at hand the solution to particular problems. As such she desires to add the light of revealed truth to mankind's store of experience, so that the path which humanity has taken in recent times will not be a dark one.

34. Throughout the course of the centuries, men have labored to better the circumstances of their lives through a monumental amount of individual and collective effort. To believers, this point is settled: considered in itself, this human activity accords with God's will. For man, created to God's image, received a mandate to subject to himself the earth and all it contains, and to govern the world with justice and holiness;[1] a mandate to relate himself and the totality of things to Him Who was to be acknowledged as the Lord and Creator of all. Thus, by the subjection of all things to man, the name of God would be wonderful in all the earth.[2]

This mandate concerns the whole of everyday activity as well. For while providing the substance of life for themselves and their families, men and women are performing their activities in a way which appropriately benefits society. They can justly consider that by their labor they are unfolding the Creator's work, consulting the advantages of their brother men, and are contributing by their personal industry to the realization in history of the divine plan.[3]

Thus, far from thinking that works produced by man's own talent and energy are in opposition to God's power, and that the rational creature exists as a kind of rival to the Creator, Christians are convinced that the triumphs of the human race are a sign of God's grace and the flowering of His own mysterious design. For the greater man's power becomes, the farther his individual and community responsibility extends. Hence it is clear that men are not deterred by the Christian message from building up the world, or impelled to neglect the welfare of their fellows, but that they are rather more stringently bound to do these very things.[4]

35. Human activity, to be sure, takes its significance from its relationship to man. Just as it proceeds from man, so it is ordered toward man. For when a man works he not only alters things and society, he develops himself as well. He learns much, he cultivates his resources, he goes outside of himself and beyond himself. Rightly understood this kind of growth is of greater value than any external riches which can be garnered. A man is more precious for what he is than for what he has.[5] Similarly, all that men do to obtain greater justice, wider brotherhood, a more humane disposition of social relationships has greater worth than technical advances. For these advances can supply the material for human progress, but of themselves alone they can never actually bring it about.

Hence, the norm of human activity is this: that in accord with the divine plan and will, it harmonize with the genuine good of the human race, and that it allow men as individuals and as members of society to pursue their total vocation and fulfill it.

36. Now many of our contemporaries seem to fear that a closer bond between human activity and religion will work against the independence of men, of societies, or of the sciences.

If by the autonomy of earthly affairs we mean that created things and societies themselves enjoy their own laws and values which must be gradually deciphered, put to use, and regulated by men, then it is entirely right to demand that autonomy. Such is not merely required by modern man, but harmonizes also with the will of the Creator. For by the very circumstance of their having been created, all things are endowed with their own stability, truth, goodness, proper laws, and order. Man must respect these as he isolates them by the appropriate methods of the individual sciences or arts. Therefore if methodical investigation within every branch of learning is carried out in a genuinely scientific manner and in accord with moral norms, it never truly conflicts with faith, for earthly matters and the concerns of faith derive from the same God.[6] Indeed whoever labors to penetrate the secrets of reality with a humble and steady mind, even though he is unaware of the fact, is nevertheless being led by the hand of God, who holds all things in existence, and gives them their identity. Consequently, we cannot but deplore certain habits of mind, which are sometimes found too among Christians, which do not sufficiently attend to the rightful independence of science and which, from the arguments and controversies they spark, lead many minds to conclude that faith and science are mutually opposed.[7]

But if the expression, the independence of temporal affairs, is taken to mean that created things do not depend on God, and that man can use them without any reference to their Creator, anyone who acknowledges God will see how false such a meaning is. For without the Creator the creature would disappear. For their part, however, all believers of whatever religion always hear His revealing voice in the discourse of creatures. When God is forgotten, however, the creature itself grows unintelligible.

The Dialogue Between Science and Faith
Gaudium et Spes 36

Pope Francis
———
Evangelii Gaudium
242

Whereas positivism and scientism "refuse to admit the validity of forms of knowledge other than those of the positive sciences," the Church proposes another path, which calls for a synthesis between the responsible use of methods proper to the empirical sciences and other areas of knowledge such as philosophy, theology, as well as faith itself, which elevates us to the mystery transcending nature and human intelligence. Faith is not fearful of reason; on the contrary, it seeks and trusts reason, since "the light of reason and the light of faith both come from God" and cannot contradict each other. Evangelization is attentive to scientific advances and wishes to shed on them the light of faith and the natural law so that they will remain respectful of the centrality and supreme value of the human person at every stage of life. All of society can be enriched thanks to this dialogue, which opens up new horizons for thought and expands the possibilities of reason.

When God Is Forgotten

Gaudium et Spes 36

**Pope
St. John Paul II**

---

*Evangelium Vitae
22*

When the sense of God is lost, the sense of man is also threatened and poisoned, as the Second Vatican Council concisely states: "Without the Creator the creature would disappear. . . . When God is forgotten . . . the creature itself grows unintelligible." Man is no longer able to see himself as "mysteriously different" from other earthly creatures; he regards himself merely as one more living being, as an organism which, at most, has reached a very high stage of perfection. Enclosed in the narrow horizon of his physical nature, he is somehow reduced to being "a thing," and no longer grasps the "transcendent" character of his "existence as man." He no longer considers life as a splendid gift of God, something "sacred" entrusted to his responsibility and thus also to his loving care and "veneration." Life itself becomes a mere "thing," which man claims as his exclusive property, completely subject to his control and manipulation.

Thus, in relation to life at birth or at death, man is no longer capable of posing the question of the truest meaning of his own existence, nor can he assimilate with genuine freedom these crucial moments of his own history. He is concerned only with "doing," and, using all kinds of technology, he busies himself with programming, controlling, and dominating birth and death. Birth and death, instead of being primary experiences demanding to be "lived," become things to be merely "possessed" or "rejected."

Moreover, once all reference to God has been removed, it is not surprising that the meaning of everything else becomes profoundly distorted. Nature itself, from being "mater" (mother), is now reduced to being "matter," and is subjected to every kind of manipulation. This is the direction in which a certain technical and scientific way of thinking, prevalent in present-day culture, appears to be leading when it rejects the very idea that there is a truth of creation which must be acknowledged, or a plan of God for life which must be respected. Something similar happens when concern about the consequences of such a "freedom without law" leads some people to the opposite position of a "law without freedom," as for example in ideologies which consider it unlawful to interfere in any way with nature, practically "divinizing" it. Again, this is a misunderstanding of nature's dependence on the plan of the Creator. Thus it is clear that the loss of contact with God's wise design is the deepest root of modern man's confusion, both when this loss leads to a freedom without rules and when it leaves man in "fear" of his freedom.

By living "as if God did not exist," man not only loses sight of the mystery of God, but also of the mystery of the world and the mystery of his own being.

37. Sacred Scripture teaches the human family what the experience of the ages confirms: that while human progress is a great advantage to man, it brings with it a strong temptation. For when the order of values is jumbled and bad is mixed with the good, individuals and groups pay heed solely to their own interests, and not to those of others. Thus it happens that the world ceases to be a place of true brotherhood. In our own day, the magnified power of humanity threatens to destroy the race itself.

For a monumental struggle against the powers of darkness pervades the whole history of man. The battle was joined from the very origins of the world and will continue until the last day, as the Lord has attested.[8] Caught in this conflict, man is obliged to wrestle constantly if he is to cling to what is good, nor can he achieve his own integrity without great efforts and the help of God's grace.

That is why Christ's Church, trusting in the design of the Creator, acknowledges that human progress can serve man's true happiness, yet she cannot help echoing the Apostle's warning: "Be not conformed to this world" (Rom. 12:2). Here by the world is meant that spirit of vanity and malice which transforms into an instrument of sin those human energies intended for the service of God and man.

Hence if anyone wants to know how this unhappy situation can be overcome, Christians will tell him that all human activity, constantly imperiled by man's pride and deranged self-love, must be purified and perfected by the power of Christ's cross and resurrection. For redeemed by Christ and made a new creature in the Holy Spirit, man is able to love the things themselves created by God, and ought to do so. He can receive them from God and respect and reverence them as flowing constantly from the hand of God. Grateful to his Benefactor for these creatures, using and enjoying them in detachment and liberty of spirit, man is led forward into a true possession of them, as having nothing, yet possessing all things.[9] "All are yours, and you are Christ's, and Christ is God's" (1 Cor. 3:22–23).

The Threat of Destruction
Gaudium et Spes 37

Pope St. John Paul II

Centesimus Annus 37–38

In his desire to have and to enjoy rather than to be and to grow, man consumes the resources of the earth and his own life in an excessive and disordered way. At the root of the senseless destruction of the natural environment lies an anthropological error, which unfortunately is widespread in our day. Man, who discovers his capacity to transform and in a certain sense create the world through his own work, forgets that this is always based on God's prior and original gift of the things that are. Man thinks that he can make arbitrary use of the earth, subjecting it without restraint to his will, as though it did not have its own requisites and a prior God-given purpose, which man can indeed develop but must not betray. Instead of carrying out his role as a co-operator with God in the work of creation, man sets himself up in place of God and thus ends up provoking a rebellion on the part of nature, which is more tyrannized than governed by him.

In all this, one notes first the poverty or narrowness of man's outlook, motivated as he is by a desire to possess things rather than to relate them to the truth, and lacking that disinterested, unselfish, and aesthetic attitude that is born of wonder in the presence of being and of the beauty which enables one to see in visible things the message of the invisible God who created them. In this regard, humanity today must be conscious of its duties and obligations towards future generations.

In addition to the irrational destruction of the natural environment, we must also mention the more serious destruction of the human environment, something which is by no means receiving the attention it deserves. Although people are rightly worried—though much less than they should be—about preserving the natural habitats of the various animal species threatened with extinction, because they realize that each of these species makes its particular contribution to the balance of nature in general, too little effort is made to safeguard the moral conditions for an authentic "human ecology." Not only has God given the earth to man, who must use it with respect for the original good purpose for which it was given to him, but man too is God's gift to man. He must therefore respect the natural and moral structure with which he has been endowed. In this context, mention should be made of the serious problems of modern urbanization, of the need for urban planning which is concerned with how people are to live, and of the attention which should be given to a "social ecology" of work.

38. For God's Word, through Whom all things were made, was Himself made flesh and dwelt on the earth of men.[10] Thus He entered the world's history as a perfect man, taking that history up into Himself and summarizing it.[11] He Himself revealed to us that "God is love" (1 John 4:8) and at the same time taught us that the new command of love was the basic law of human perfection and hence of the world's transformation.

To those, therefore, who believe in divine love, He gives assurance that the way of love lies open to men and that the effort to establish a universal brotherhood is not a hopeless one. He cautions them at the same time that this charity is not something to be reserved for important matters, but must be pursued chiefly in the ordinary circumstances of life. Undergoing death itself for all of us sinners,[12] He taught us by example that we too must shoulder that cross which the world and the flesh inflict upon those who search after peace and justice. Appointed Lord by His resurrection and given plenary power in heaven and on earth,[13] Christ is now at work in the hearts of men through the energy of His Holy Spirit, arousing not only a desire for the age to come, but by that very fact animating, purifying, and strengthening those noble longings too by which the human family makes its life more human and strives to render the whole earth submissive to this goal.

Now, the gifts of the Spirit are diverse: while He calls some to give clear witness to the desire for a heavenly home and to keep that desire green among the human family, He summons others to dedicate themselves to the earthly service of men and to make ready the material of the celestial realm by this ministry of theirs. Yet He frees all of them so that by putting aside love of self and bringing all earthly resources into the service of human life they can devote themselves to that future when humanity itself will become an offering accepted by God.[14]

The Lord left behind a pledge of this hope and strength for life's journey in that sacrament of faith where natural elements refined by man are gloriously changed into His Body and Blood, providing a meal of brotherly solidarity and a foretaste of the heavenly banquet.

39. We do not know the time for the consummation of the earth and of humanity,[15] nor do we know how all things will be transformed. As deformed by sin, the shape of this world will pass away;[16] but we are taught that God is preparing a new dwelling place and a new earth where justice will abide,[17] and whose blessedness will answer and surpass all the longings for peace which spring up in the human heart.[18] Then, with death overcome, the sons of God will be raised up in Christ, and what was sown in weakness and corruption will be invested with incorruptibility.[19] Enduring with charity and its fruits,[20] all that creation[21] which God made on man's account will be unchained from the bondage of vanity.

Therefore, while we are warned that it profits a man nothing if he gain the whole world and lose himself,[22] the expectation of a new earth must not weaken but rather stimulate our concern for cultivating this one. For here grows the body of a new human family, a body which even now is able to give some kind of foreshadowing of the new age.

Hence, while earthly progress must be carefully distinguished from the growth of Christ's kingdom, to the extent that the former can contribute to the better ordering of human society, it is of vital concern to the Kingdom of God.[23]

For after we have obeyed the Lord, and in His Spirit nurtured on earth the values of human dignity, brotherhood, and freedom, and indeed all the good fruits of our nature and enterprise, we will find them again, but freed of stain, burnished and transfigured, when Christ hands over to the Father a kingdom eternal and universal: "a kingdom of truth and life, of holiness and grace, of justice, love, and peace."[24] On this earth that Kingdom is already present in mystery. When the Lord returns it will be brought into full flower.

Nothing Will Have Been in Vain

Gaudium et Spes 39

**Pope
St. John Paul II**

*Sollicitudo Rei
Socialis*
48

The Church well knows that no temporal achievement is to be identified with the Kingdom of God, but that all such achievements simply reflect and in a sense anticipate the glory of the Kingdom, the Kingdom which we await at the end of history, when the Lord will come again. But that expectation can never be an excuse for lack of concern for people in their concrete personal situations and in their social, national, and international life, since the former is conditioned by the latter, especially today.

However imperfect and temporary are all the things that can and ought to be done through the combined efforts of everyone and through divine grace, at a given moment of history, in order to make people's lives "more human," nothing will be lost or will have been in vain. This is the teaching of the Second Vatican Council, in an enlightening passage of the Pastoral Constitution *Gaudium et Spes*: "After we have obeyed the Lord, and in His Spirit nurtured on earth the values of human dignity, brotherhood, and freedom, and indeed all the good fruits of our nature and enterprise, we will find them again, but freed of stain, burnished and transfigured, when Christ hands over to the Father a kingdom eternal and universal. . . . On this earth that Kingdom is already present in mystery."

The Kingdom of God becomes present above all in the celebration of the sacrament of the Eucharist, which is the Lord's Sacrifice. In that celebration the fruits of the earth and the work of human hands—the bread and wine—are transformed mysteriously, but really and substantially, through the power of the Holy Spirit and the words of the minister, into the Body and Blood of the Lord Jesus Christ, the Son of God and Son of Mary, through whom the Kingdom of the Father has been made present in our midst.

The goods of this world and the work of our hands—the bread and wine—serve for the coming of the definitive Kingdom, since the Lord, through his Spirit, takes them up into himself in order to offer himself to the Father and to offer us with himself in the renewal of his one Sacrifice, which anticipates God's Kingdom and proclaims its final coming.

Thus the Lord unites us with himself through the Eucharist—Sacrament and Sacrifice—and he unites us with himself and with one another by a bond stronger than any natural union; and thus united, he sends us into the whole world to bear witness, through faith and works, to God's love, preparing the coming of his Kingdom and anticipating it, though in the obscurity of the present time.

All of us who take part in the Eucharist are called to discover, through this sacrament, the profound meaning of our actions in the world in favor of development and peace; and to receive from it the strength to commit ourselves ever more generously, following the example of Christ, who in this sacrament lays down his life for his friends (see John 15:13). Our personal commitment, like Christ's and in union with his, will not be in vain but certainly fruitful.

CHAPTER IV
The Role of the Church in the Modern World

40. Everything we have said about the dignity of the human person, and about the human community and the profound meaning of human activity, lays the foundation for the relationship between the Church and

the world, and provides the basis for dialogue between them.[1] In this chapter, presupposing everything which has already been said by this council concerning the mystery of the Church, we must now consider this same Church inasmuch as she exists in the world, living and acting with it.

Coming forth from the eternal Father's love,[2] founded in time by Christ the Redeemer and made one in the Holy Spirit,[3] the Church has a saving and an eschatological purpose which can be fully attained only in the future world. But she is already present in this world, and is composed of men, that is, of members of the earthly city who have a call to form the family of God's children during the present history of the human race, and to keep increasing it until the Lord returns. United on behalf of heavenly values and enriched by them, this family has been "constituted and organized in the world as a society"[4] by Christ, and is equipped "with those means which befit it as a visible and social union."[5] Thus the Church, at once "the visible assembly and the spiritual community,"[6] goes forward together with humanity and experiences the same earthly lot which the world does. She serves as a leaven and as a kind of soul for human society[7] as it is to be renewed in Christ and transformed into God's family.

That the earthly and the heavenly city penetrate each other is a fact accessible to faith alone; it remains a mystery of human history, which sin will keep in great disarray until the splendor of God's sons is fully revealed. Pursuing the saving purpose which is proper to her, the Church does not only communicate divine life to men but in some way casts the reflected light of that life over the entire earth, most of all by its healing and elevating impact on the dignity of the person, by the way in which it strengthens the seams of human society and imbues the everyday activity of men with a deeper meaning and importance. Thus through her individual matters and her whole community, the Church believes she can contribute greatly toward making the family of man and its history more human.

In addition, the Catholic Church gladly holds in high esteem the things which other Christian Churches and ecclesial communities have done or are doing cooperatively by way of achieving the same goal. At the same time, she is convinced that she can be abundantly and variously helped by the world in the matter of preparing the ground for the Gospel. This help she gains from the talents and industry of individuals and from human society as a whole. The council now sets forth certain general principles for the proper fostering of this mutual exchange and assistance in concerns which are in some way common to the world and the Church.

41. Modern man is on the road to a more thorough development of his own personality, and to a growing discovery and vindication of his own rights. Since it has been entrusted to the Church to reveal the mystery of God, Who is the ultimate goal of man, she opens up to man at the same time the meaning of his own existence, that is, the innermost truth about himself. The Church truly knows that only God, Whom she serves, meets the deepest longings of the human heart, which is never fully satisfied by what this world has to offer.

She also knows that man is constantly worked upon by God's spirit, and hence can never be altogether indifferent to the problems of religion. The experience of past ages proves this, as do numerous indications in our own times. For man will always yearn to know, at least in an obscure way, what is the meaning of his life, of his activity, of his death. The very presence of the Church recalls these problems to his mind. But only God, Who created man to His own image and ransomed him from sin, provides the most adequate answer to the questions, and this He does through what He has revealed in Christ His Son, Who became man. Whoever follows after Christ, the perfect man, becomes himself more of a man.

Thanks to this belief, the Church can anchor the dignity of human nature against all tides of opinion, for example those which undervalue the human body or idolize it. By no human law can the personal dignity and liberty of man be so aptly safeguarded as by the Gospel of Christ which has been entrusted to the Church. For this Gospel announces and proclaims the freedom of the sons of God, and repudiates all the bondage which ultimately results from sin;[8] it has a sacred reverence for the dignity of conscience and its freedom of choice, constantly advises that all human talents be employed in God's service and men's, and, finally, commends all to the charity of all (see Matt. 22:39).[9]

This agrees with the basic law of the Christian dispensation. For though the same God is Savior and Creator, Lord of human history as well as of salvation history, in the divine arrangement itself, the rightful autonomy of the creature, and particularly of man is not withdrawn, but is rather re-established in its own dignity and strengthened in it.

The Church, therefore, by virtue of the Gospel committed to her, proclaims the rights of man; she acknowledges and greatly esteems the dynamic movements of today by which these rights are everywhere fostered. Yet these movements must be penetrated by the spirit of the Gospel and protected against any kind of false autonomy. For we are tempted to think that our personal rights are fully ensured only when we are exempt from every requirement of divine law. But this way lies not the maintenance of the dignity of the human person, but its annihilation.

42. The union of the human family is greatly fortified and fulfilled by the unity, founded on Christ,[10] of the family of God's sons.

Christ, to be sure, gave His Church no proper mission in the political, economic, or social order. The purpose which He set before her is a religious one.[11] But out of this religious mission itself come a function, a light, and an energy which can serve to structure and consolidate the human community according to the divine law. As a matter of fact, when circumstances of time and place produce the need, she can and indeed should initiate activities on behalf of all men, especially those designed for the needy, such as the works of mercy and similar undertakings.

The Church recognizes that worthy elements are found in today's social movements, especially an evolution toward unity, a process of wholesome socialization and of association in civic and economic realms. The promotion of unity belongs to the innermost nature of the Church, for she is "in Christ like a sacrament or as a sign and instrument both of a very closely knit union with God and of the unity of the whole human race."[12] Thus she shows the world that an authentic union, social and external, results from a union of minds and hearts, namely from that faith and charity by which her own unity is unbreakably rooted in the Holy Spirit. For the force which the Church can inject into the modern society of man consists in that faith and charity put into vital practice, not in any external dominion exercised by merely human means.

Moreover, since in virtue of her mission and nature she is bound to no particular form of human culture, nor to any political, economic, or social system, the Church by her very universality can be a very close bond between diverse human communities and nations, provided these trust her and truly acknowledge her right to true freedom in fulfilling her mission. For this reason, the Church admonishes her own sons, but also humanity as a whole, to overcome all strife between nations and races in this family spirit of God's children, and in the same way, to give internal strength to human associations which are just.

With great respect, therefore, this council regards all the true, good, and just elements inherent in the very wide variety of institutions which the human race has established for itself and constantly continues to establish.

The council affirms, moreover, that the Church is willing to assist and promote all these institutions to the extent that such a service depends on her and can be associated with her mission. She has no fiercer desire than that in pursuit of the welfare of all she may be able to develop herself freely under any kind of government which grants recognition to the basic rights of person and family, to the demands of the common good, and to the free exercise of her own mission.

43. This council exhorts Christians, as citizens of two cities, to strive to discharge their earthly duties conscientiously and in response to the Gospel spirit. They are mistaken who, knowing that we have here no abiding city but seek one which is to come,[13] think that they may therefore shirk their earthly responsibilities. For they are forgetting that by the faith itself they are more obliged than ever to measure up to these duties, each according to his proper vocation.[14] Nor, on the contrary, are they any less wide of the mark who think that religion consists in acts of worship alone and in the discharge of certain moral obligations, and who imagine they can plunge themselves into earthly affairs in such a way as to imply that these are altogether divorced from the religious life. This split between the faith which many profess and their daily lives deserves to be counted among the more serious errors of our age. Long since, the Prophets of the Old Testament fought vehemently against this scandal[15] and even more so did Jesus Christ Himself in the New Testament threaten it with grave punishments.[16] Therefore, let there be no false opposition between professional and social activities on the one part, and religious life on the other. The Christian who neglects his temporal duties, neglects his duties toward his neighbor and even God, and jeopardizes his eternal salvation. Christians should rather rejoice that, following the example of Christ Who worked as an artisan, they are free to give proper exercise to all their earthly activities and to their humane, domestic, professional, social, and technical enterprises by gathering them into one vital synthesis with religious values, under whose supreme direction all things are harmonized unto God's glory.

Secular duties and activities belong properly although not exclusively to laymen. Therefore acting as citizens in the world, whether individually or socially, they will keep the laws proper to each discipline, and labor to equip themselves with a genuine expertise in their various fields. They will gladly work with men seeking the same goals. Acknowledging the demands of faith and endowed with its force, they will unhesitatingly devise new enterprises, where they are appropriate, and put them into action. Laymen should also know that it is generally the function of their well-formed Christian conscience to see that the divine law is inscribed in the life of the earthly city; from priests they may look for spiritual light and nourishment. Let the layman not imagine that his pastors are always such experts, that to every problem which arises, however complicated, they can readily give him a concrete solution, or even that such is their mission. Rather, enlightened by Christian wisdom and giving close attention to the teaching authority of the Church,[17] let the layman take on his own distinctive role.

Often enough the Christian view of things will itself suggest some specific solution in certain circumstances. Yet it happens rather frequently, and legitimately so, that with equal sincerity some of the faithful will disagree with others on a given matter. Even against the intentions of their proponents, however, solutions proposed on one side or another may be easily confused by many people with the Gospel message. Hence it is necessary for people to remember that no one is allowed in the aforementioned situations to appropriate the Church's authority for his opinion. They should always try to enlighten one another through honest discussion, preserving mutual charity and caring above all for the common good.

Since they have an active role to play in the whole life of the Church, laymen are not only bound to penetrate the world with a Christian spirit, but are also called to be witnesses to Christ in all things in the midst of human society.

Bishops, to whom is assigned the task of ruling the Church of God, should, together with their priests, so preach the news of Christ that all the earthly activities of the faithful will be bathed in the light of the Gospel. All pastors should remember too that by their daily conduct and concern[18] they are revealing the face of the Church to the world, and men will judge the power and truth of the Christian message thereby. By their lives and speech, in union with Religious and their faithful, may they demonstrate that even now the Church by her presence alone and by all the gifts which she contains, is an unspent fountain of those virtues which the modern world needs the most.

By unremitting study they should fit themselves to do their part in establishing dialogue with the world and with men of all shades of opinion.

Above all let them take to heart the words which this council has spoken: "Because the human race today is joining more and more into a civic, economic, and social unity, it is that much the more necessary that priests, by combined effort and aid, under the leadership of the bishops and the Supreme Pontiff, wipe out every kind of separateness, so that the whole human race may be brought into the unity of the family of God."[19]

Although by the power of the Holy Spirit the Church will remain the faithful spouse of her Lord and will never cease to be the sign of salvation on earth, still she is very well aware that among her members,[20] both clerical and lay, some have been unfaithful to the Spirit of God during the course of many centuries; in the present age, too, it does not escape the Church how great a distance lies between the message she offers and the human failings of those to whom the Gospel is entrusted. Whatever be the judgment of history on these defects, we ought to be conscious of them, and struggle against them energetically, lest they inflict harm on the spread of the Gospel. The Church also realizes that in working out her relationship with the world she always has great need of the ripening which comes with the experience of the centuries. Led by the Holy Spirit, Mother Church unceasingly exhorts her sons "to purification and renewal so that the sign of Christ may shine more brightly over the face of the earth."[21]

44. Just as it is in the world's interest to acknowledge the Church as an historical reality, and to recognize her good influence, so the Church herself knows how richly she has profited by the history and development of humanity.

The experience of past ages, the progress of the sciences, and the treasures hidden in the various forms of human culture, by all of which the nature of man himself is more clearly revealed and new roads to truth are opened, these profit the Church, too. For, from the beginning of her history she has learned to express the message of Christ with the help of the ideas and terminology of various philosophers, and has tried to clarify it with their wisdom, too. Her purpose has been to adapt the Gospel to the grasp of all as well as to the needs of the learned, insofar as such was appropriate. Indeed this accommodated preaching of the revealed word ought to remain the law of all evangelization. For thus the ability to express Christ's message in its own way is developed in each nation, and at the same time there is fostered a living exchange between the Church and the diverse cultures of people.[22] To promote such exchange, especially in our days, the Church requires the special help of those who live in the world, are versed in different institutions and specialties, and grasp their innermost significance in the eyes of both believers and unbelievers. With the help of the Holy Spirit, it is the task of the entire People of God, especially pastors and theologians, to hear, distinguish, and interpret the many voices of our age, and to judge them in the light of the divine word, so that revealed truth can always be more deeply penetrated, better understood, and set forth to greater advantage.

Since the Church has a visible and social structure as a sign of her unity in Christ, she can and ought to be enriched by the development of human social life, not that there is any lack in the constitution given her by Christ, but that she can understand it more penetratingly, express it better, and adjust it more successfully to our times. Moreover, she gratefully understands that in her community life no less than in her individual sons, she receives a variety of helps from men of every rank and condition, for whoever promotes the human community at the family level, culturally, in its economic, social, and political dimensions, both nationally and internationally, such a one, according to God's design, is contributing greatly to the Church as well, to the extent that she depends on things outside herself. Indeed, the Church admits that she has greatly profited and still profits from the antagonism of those who oppose or who persecute her.[23]

45. While helping the world and receiving many benefits from it, the Church has a single intention: that God's kingdom may come, and that the salvation of the whole human race may come to pass. For every benefit which the People of God during its earthly pilgrimage can offer to the human family stems from the fact that the Church is "the universal sacrament of salvation,"[24] simultaneously manifesting and exercising the mystery of God's love.

For God's Word, by whom all things were made, was Himself made flesh so that as perfect man He might save all men and sum up all things in Himself. The Lord is the goal of human history, the focal point of the longings of history and of civilization, the center of the human race, the joy of every heart, and the answer to all its yearnings.[25] He it is Whom the Father raised from the dead, lifted on high, and stationed at His right hand, making Him judge of the living and the dead. Enlivened and united in His Spirit, we journey toward the consummation of human history, one which fully accords with the counsel of God's love: "To reestablish all things in Christ, both those in the heavens and those on the earth" (Eph. 1:10).

The Lord Himself speaks: "Behold I come quickly! And my reward is with me, to render to each one according to his works. I am the Alpha and the Omega, the first and the last, the beginning and the end" (Rev. 22:12–13).

The Nature of God's Kingdom

Gaudium et Spes 45

Pope St. John Paul II

———

Redemptoris Missio 15–17

The kingdom aims at transforming human relationships; it grows gradually as people slowly learn to love, forgive, and serve one another. Jesus sums up the whole Law, focusing it on the commandment of love (see Matt. 22:34–40; Luke 10:25–28). Before leaving his disciples, he gives them a "new commandment": "Love one another; even as I have loved you" (John 13:34; see 15:12). Jesus' love for the world finds its highest expression in the gift of his life for mankind (see John 15:13), which manifests the love which the Father has for the world (see John 3:16). The kingdom's nature, therefore, is one of communion among all human beings— with one another and with God.

The kingdom is the concern of everyone: individuals, society, and the world. Working for the kingdom means acknowledging and promoting God's activity, which is present in human history and transforms it. Building the kingdom means working for liberation from evil in all its forms. In a word, the kingdom of God is the manifestation and the realization of God's plan of salvation in all its fullness.

By raising Jesus from the dead, God has conquered death, and in Jesus he has definitely inaugurated his kingdom.

During his earthly life, Jesus was the Prophet of the kingdom; after his passion, resurrection, and ascension into heaven he shares in God's power and in his dominion over the world (see Matt. 28:18; Acts 2:36; Eph. 1:18–21). The resurrection gives a universal scope to Christ's message, his actions and whole mission. The disciples recognize that the kingdom is already present in the person of Jesus and is slowly being established within man and the world through a mysterious connection with him.

Indeed, after the resurrection, the disciples preach the kingdom by proclaiming Jesus crucified and risen from the dead. In Samaria, Philip "preached good news about the kingdom of God and the name of Jesus Christ" (Acts 8:12). In Rome, we find Paul "preaching the kingdom of God and teaching about the Lord Jesus Christ" (Acts 28:31). The first Christians also proclaim "the kingdom of Christ and of God" (Eph. 5:5; see Rev. 11:15; 12:10), or "the kingdom of our Lord and Savior Jesus Christ" (2 Pet. 1:11). The preaching of the early Church was centered on the proclamation of Jesus Christ, with whom the kingdom was identified. Now, as then, there is a need to unite the proclamation of the kingdom of God (the content of Jesus' own "kerygma") and the proclamation of the Christ-event (the "kerygma" of the apostles). The two proclamations are complementary; each throws light on the other.

Nowadays the kingdom is much spoken of, but not always in a way consonant with the thinking of the Church. In fact, there are ideas about salvation and mission which can be called "anthropocentric" in the reductive sense of the word, inasmuch as they are focused on man's earthly needs. In this view, the kingdom tends to become something completely human and secularized; what counts are programs and struggles for a liberation which is socio-economic, political, and even cultural, but within a horizon that is closed to the transcendent. Without denying that on this level too there are values to be promoted, such a notion nevertheless remains within the confines of a kingdom of man, deprived of its authentic and profound dimensions. Such a view easily translates into one more ideology of purely earthly progress. The kingdom of God, however, "is not of this world . . . is not from the world" (John 18:36).

PART II
Some Problems of Special Urgency

46. This council has set forth the dignity of the human person, and the work which men have been destined to undertake throughout the world both as individuals and as members of society. There are a number of particularly urgent needs characterizing the present age, needs which go to the roots of the human race. To a consideration of these in the light of the Gospel and of human experience, the council would now direct the attention of all.

Of the many subjects arousing universal concern today, it may be helpful to concentrate on these: marriage and the family, human progress, life in its economic, social, and political dimensions, the bonds between the family of nations, and peace. On each of these may there shine the radiant ideals proclaimed by Christ. By these ideals may Christians be led, and all mankind enlightened, as they search for answers to questions of such complexity.

CHAPTER I
Fostering the Nobility of Marriage and the Family

47. The well-being of the individual person and of human and Christian society is intimately linked with the healthy condition of that community produced by marriage and family. Hence Christians and all men who hold this community in high esteem sincerely rejoice in the various ways by which men today find help in fostering this community of love and perfecting its life, and by which parents are assisted in their lofty calling. Those who rejoice in such aids look for additional benefits from them and labor to bring them about.

Yet the excellence of this institution is not everywhere reflected with equal brilliance, since polygamy, the plague of divorce, so-called free love, and other disfigurements have an obscuring effect. In addition, married love is too often profaned by excessive self-love, the worship of pleasure, and illicit practices against human generation. Moreover, serious disturbances are caused in families by modern economic conditions, by influences at once social and psychological, and by the demands of civil society. Finally, in certain parts of the world problems resulting from population growth are generating concern.

All these situations have produced anxiety of consciences. Yet, the power and strength of the institution of marriage and family can also be seen in the fact that time and again, despite the difficulties produced, the profound changes in modern society reveal the true character of this institution in one way or another.

Therefore, by presenting certain key points of Church doctrine in a clearer light, this sacred synod wishes to offer guidance and support to those Christians and other men who are trying to preserve the holiness and to foster the natural dignity of the married state and its superlative value.

48. The intimate partnership of married life and love has been established by the Creator and qualified by His laws, and is rooted in the conjugal covenant of irrevocable personal consent. Hence by that human act whereby spouses mutually bestow and accept each other a relationship arises which by divine will and in the eyes of society too is a lasting one. For the good of the spouses and their offspring as well as of society, the existence of the sacred bond no longer depends on human decisions alone. For, God Himself is the author of matrimony, endowed as it is with various benefits and purposes.[1] All of these have a very decisive bearing on the continuation of the human race, on the personal development and eternal destiny of the individual members of a family, and on the dignity, stability, peace, and prosperity of the family itself and of human society as a whole. By their very nature, the institution of matrimony itself and conjugal love are ordained for the procreation and education of children, and find in them their ultimate crown. Thus a man and a woman, who by their compact of conjugal love "are no longer two, but one flesh" (Matt. 19:6ff), render mutual help and service to each other through an intimate union of their persons and of their actions. Through this union they experience the meaning of their oneness and attain to it with growing perfection day by day. As a mutual gift of two persons, this intimate union and the good of the children impose total fidelity on the spouses and argue for an unbreakable oneness between them.[2]

Christ the Lord abundantly blessed this many-faceted love, welling up as it does from the fountain of divine love and structured as it is on the model of His union with His Church. For as God of old made Himself present[3] to His people through a covenant of love and fidelity, so now the Savior of men and the Spouse[4] of the Church comes into the lives of married Christians through the sacrament of matrimony. He abides with them thereafter so that just as He loved the Church and handed Himself over on her behalf,[5] the spouses may love each other with perpetual fidelity through mutual self-bestowal.

Authentic married love is caught up into divine love and is governed and enriched by Christ's redeeming power and the saving activity of the Church, so that this love may lead the spouses to God with powerful effect and may aid and strengthen them in the sublime office of being a father or a mother.[6] For this reason Christian spouses have a special sacrament by which they are fortified and receive a kind of consecration in the duties and dignity of their state.[7] By virtue of this sacrament, as spouses fulfill their conjugal and family obligation, they are penetrated with the spirit of Christ, which suffuses their whole lives with faith, hope, and charity. Thus they increasingly advance the perfection of their own personalities, as well as their mutual sanctification, and hence contribute jointly to the glory of God.

As a result, with their parents leading the way by example and family prayer, children and indeed everyone gathered around the family hearth will find a readier path to human maturity, salvation, and holiness. Graced with the dignity and office of fatherhood and motherhood, parents will energetically carry out a duty which devolves primarily on them, namely education and especially religious education.

As living members of the family, children contribute in their own way to making their parents holy. For they will respond to the kindness of their parents with sentiments of gratitude, with love and trust. They will stand by them as children should when hardships overtake their parents and old age brings its loneliness. Widowhood, accepted bravely as a continuation of the marriage vocation, should be esteemed by all.[8] Families too will share their spiritual riches generously with other families. Thus the Christian family, which springs from marriage as a reflection of the loving covenant uniting Christ with the Church,[9] and as a participation in that covenant, will manifest to all men Christ's living presence in the world, and the genuine nature of the Church. This the family will do by the mutual love of the spouses, by their generous fruitfulness, their solidarity and faithfulness, and by the loving way in which all members of the family assist one another.

Partners Open to Fruitfulness

Gaudium et Spes 48

Pope Francis

———

Amoris Laetitia
80

Marriage is firstly an "intimate partnership of . . . life and love" which is a good for the spouses themselves, while sexuality is "ordered to the conjugal love of man and woman." It follows that "spouses to whom God has not granted children can have a conjugal life full of meaning, in both human and Christian terms." Nonetheless, the conjugal union is ordered to procreation "by [its] very nature." The child who is born "does not come from outside as something added on to the mutual love of the spouses, but springs from the very heart of that mutual giving, as its fruit and fulfilment." He or she does not appear at the end of a process, but is present from the beginning of love as an essential feature, one that cannot be denied without disfiguring that love itself. From the outset, love refuses every impulse to close in on itself; it is open to a fruitfulness that draws it beyond itself. Hence no genital act of husband and wife can refuse this meaning, even when for various reasons it may not always in fact beget a new life.

49. The biblical Word of God several times urges the betrothed and the married to nourish and develop their wedlock by pure conjugal love and undivided affection.[10] Many men of our own age also highly regard true love between husband and wife as it manifests itself in a variety of ways depending on the worthy customs of various peoples and times.

This love is an eminently human one since it is directed from one person to another through an affection of the will; it involves the good of the whole person, and therefore can enrich the expressions of body and mind with a unique dignity, ennobling these expressions as special ingredients and signs of the friendship distinctive of marriage. This love God has judged worthy of special gifts, healing, perfecting, and exalting gifts of grace and of charity. Such love, merging the human with the divine,

Your Marriage Is Not About You

Gaudium et Spes **48** | Bishop Barron

In the second major section of *Gaudium et Spes* we find a discussion of a theme that became central to Pope John Paul II's magisterium: marriage and family.

The council teaches that "authentic married love is caught up into divine love," in such a way that the family functions as an image and symbol of the divine love at work in the world: "Thus the Christian family, which springs from marriage as a reflection of the loving covenant uniting Christ with the Church, and as a participation in that covenant, will manifest to all men Christ's living presence in the world, and the genuine nature of the Church." God is appreciated as the author of marriage, and hence marriage, at its best, represents a fulfillment of God's purposes. More to it, marriage is, according to the Pauline image, a symbol of Christ's love for his Church. The love of husband and wife must therefore pass beyond eros to true self-giving love.

When I was doing full-time parish work, young couples would often come to me for marriage preparation. I would invariably ask them, "Why do you want to get married in church?" Most couples would say something along the lines of "Well, because we love each other." And I would say, "I'm delighted that you love each other, but that's no reason to get married in church." Usually, they looked stunned. I explained that a couple should come to church to be married before God and his people only when they are convinced that their marriage is not, finally, about them; that it is, in fact, about God and about serving God's purposes. A man and a woman should get married in a church only when they believe that they have been brought together by the divine love to be a radiant sign of that love to the world.

---

leads the spouses to a free and mutual gift of themselves, a gift providing itself by gentle affection and by deed; such love pervades the whole of their lives:[11] indeed by its busy generosity it grows better and grows greater. Therefore it far excels mere erotic inclination, which, selfishly pursued, soon enough fades wretchedly away.

This love is uniquely expressed and perfected through the appropriate enterprise of matrimony. The actions within marriage by which the couple are united intimately and chastely are noble and worthy ones. Expressed in a manner which is truly human, these actions promote that mutual self-giving by which spouses enrich each other with a joyful and a ready will. Sealed by mutual faithfulness and hallowed above all by Christ's sacrament, this love remains steadfastly true in body and in mind, in bright days or dark. It will never be profaned by adultery or divorce. Firmly established by the Lord, the unity of marriage will radiate from the equal personal dignity of wife and husband, a dignity acknowledged by mutual and total love. The constant fulfillment of the duties of this Christian vocation demands notable virtue. For this reason, strengthened by grace for holiness of life, the couple will painstakingly cultivate and pray for steadiness of love, large heartedness, and the spirit of sacrifice.

Authentic conjugal love will be more highly prized, and wholesome public opinion created about it if Christian couples give outstanding witness to faithfulness and harmony in their love, and to their concern for educating their children, and also, if they do their part in bringing about the needed cultural, psychological, and social renewal on behalf of marriage and the family. Especially in the heart of their own families, young people should be aptly and seasonably instructed in the dignity, duty, and work of married love. Trained thus in the cultivation of chastity, they will be able at a suitable age to enter a marriage of their own after an honorable courtship.

50. Marriage and conjugal love are by their nature ordained toward the begetting and educating of children. Children are really the supreme gift of marriage and contribute very substantially to the welfare of their parents. The God Himself Who said, "it is not good for man to be alone" (Gen. 2:18) and "Who made man from the beginning male and female" (Matt. 19:4), wishing to share with man a certain special participation in His own creative work, blessed male and female, saying: "Increase and multiply" (Gen. 1:28). Hence, while not making the other purposes of matrimony of less account, the true practice of conjugal love, and the whole meaning of the family life which results from it, have this aim: that the couple be ready with stout hearts to cooperate with the love of the Creator and the Savior, Who through them will enlarge and enrich His own family day by day.

Parents should regard as their proper mission the task of transmitting human life and educating those to whom it has been transmitted. They should realize that they are thereby cooperators with the love of God the

Creator, and are, so to speak, the interpreters of that love. Thus they will fulfill their task with human and Christian responsibility, and, with docile reverence toward God, will make decisions by common counsel and effort. Let them thoughtfully take into account both their own welfare and that of their children, those already born and those which the future may bring. For this accounting they need to reckon with both the material and the spiritual conditions of the times as well as of their state in life. Finally, they should consult the interests of the family group, of temporal society, and of the Church herself. The parents themselves and no one else should ultimately make this judgment in the sight of God. But in their manner of acting, spouses should be aware that they cannot proceed arbitrarily, but must always be governed according to a conscience dutifully conformed to the divine law itself, and should be submissive toward the Church's teaching office, which authentically interprets that law in the light of the Gospel. That divine law reveals and protects the integral meaning of conjugal love, and impels it toward a truly human fulfillment. Thus, trusting in divine Providence and refining the spirit of sacrifice,[12] married Christians glorify the Creator and strive toward fulfillment in Christ when with a generous human and Christian sense of responsibility they carry out the duty to procreate. Among the couples who fulfill their God-given task in this way, those merit special mention who with a gallant heart and with wise and common deliberation, undertake to bring up suitably even a relatively large family.[13]

Marriage to be sure is not instituted solely for procreation; rather, its very nature as an unbreakable compact between persons, and the welfare of the children, both demand that the mutual love of the spouses be embodied in a rightly ordered manner, that it grow and ripen. Therefore, marriage persists as a whole manner and communion of life, and maintains its value and indissolubility, even when despite the often intense desire of the couple, offspring are lacking.

The Features of Married Life
Gaudium et Spes 47–50

Pope St. Paul VI
—
Humanae Vitae 9

[Married] love is above all fully human, a compound of sense and spirit. It is not, then, merely a question of natural instinct or emotional drive. It is also, and above all, an act of the free will, whose trust is such that it is meant not only to survive the joys and sorrows of daily life, but also to grow, so that husband and wife become in a way one heart and one soul, and together attain their human fulfillment.

It is a love which is total—that very special form of personal friendship in which husband and wife generously share everything, allowing no unreasonable exceptions and not thinking solely of their own convenience. Whoever really loves his partner loves not only for what he receives, but loves that partner for the partner's own sake, content to be able to enrich the other with the gift of himself.

Married love is also faithful and exclusive of all other, and this until death. This is how husband and wife understood it on the day on which, fully aware of what they were doing, they freely vowed themselves to one another in marriage. Though this fidelity of husband and wife sometimes presents difficulties, no one has the right to assert that it is impossible; it is, on the contrary, always honorable and meritorious. The example of countless married couples proves not only that fidelity is in accord with the nature of marriage, but also that it is the source of profound and enduring happiness.

Finally, this love is fecund. It is not confined wholly to the loving interchange of husband and wife; it also contrives to go beyond this to bring new life into being. "Marriage and conjugal love are by their nature ordained toward the begetting and educating of children. Children are really the supreme gift of marriage and contribute very substantially to the welfare of their parents."

A Fecund Union and Mutual Love

Gaudium et Spes 50 | Bishop Barron

The council insists that married love is directed toward the procreation of children, who "are really the supreme gift of marriage," and urges Catholic couples to "fulfill their task with human and Christian responsibility." And it insists that "those merit special mention who with a gallant heart and with wise and common deliberation, undertake to bring up suitably even a relatively large family."

Some years ago, *TIME Magazine's* cover story "The Childfree Life" generated a good deal of controversy and commentary. The photo that graced the cover of the edition pretty much summed up the argument: a young, fit couple lounge languidly on a beach and gaze up at the camera with blissful smiles—and no child anywhere in sight. What the editors wanted us to accept is that this scenario is not just increasingly a fact in our country, but that it is morally acceptable as well, a lifestyle choice that people may legitimately make.

There is no question that childlessness is on the rise in the United States. Our birthrate is the lowest in recorded history, surpassing even the decline in reproduction that followed the economic crash of the 1930s. We have not yet reached the drastic levels found in Europe (in Italy, for example, one in four women never give birth), but childlessness has risen in our country across all ethnic and racial groups, even those that have traditionally put a particular premium on large families.

And this represents a sea change in cultural orientation. Up until very recent times, the decision whether or not to have children would never have been simply "up to the individual." Rather, a person's choice would have been situated in the context of a whole series of values that properly condition and shape the will: family, neighborhood, society, culture, the human race, nature, and ultimately, God and his desire that life flourish: "And you, be fruitful and multiply, abound on the earth and multiply in it" (Gen. 9:7). *Gaudium et Spes* very clearly calls Catholic couples to be signs of the divine love in the world— and one of those signs is fecundity.

But then the council fathers add that procreation is not the only end of marriage: "Marriage to be sure is not instituted solely for procreation; rather, its very nature as an unbreakable compact between persons, and the welfare of the children, both demand that the mutual love of the spouses be embodied in a rightly ordered manner, that it grow and ripen." We may be used to this idea now, but at the time *Gaudium et Spes* was written, this was a revolutionary statement. Married life must be open to new life, yes—but this is not all that marriage is. One of its principles and purposes is also the mutual love of husband and wife.

51. This council realizes that certain modern conditions often keep couples from arranging their married lives harmoniously, and that they find themselves in circumstances where at least temporarily the size of their families should not be increased. As a result, the faithful exercise of love and the full intimacy of their lives is hard to maintain. But where the intimacy of married life is broken off, its faithfulness can sometimes be imperiled and its quality of fruitfulness ruined, for then the upbringing of the children and the courage to accept new ones are both endangered.

To these problems there are those who presume to offer dishonorable solutions indeed; they do not recoil even from the taking of life. But the Church issues the reminder that a true contradiction cannot exist between the divine laws pertaining to the transmission of life and those pertaining to authentic conjugal love.

For God, the Lord of life, has conferred on men the surpassing ministry of safeguarding life in a manner which is worthy of man. Therefore from the moment of its conception life must be guarded with the greatest care, while abortion and infanticide are unspeakable crimes. The sexual characteristics of man and the human faculty of reproduction wonderfully exceed the dispositions of lower forms of life. Hence the acts themselves which are proper to conjugal love and which are exercised in accord with genuine human dignity must be honored with great reverence. Hence when there is question of harmonizing conjugal love with the responsible transmission of life, the moral aspect of any procedure does not depend solely on sincere intentions or on an evaluation of motives, but must be determined by objective standards. These, based on the nature of the human person and his acts, preserve the full sense of mutual self-giving and human procreation in the context of true love. Such a goal cannot be achieved unless the virtue of conjugal chastity is sincerely practiced. Relying on these principles, sons of the Church may not undertake methods of birth control which are found blameworthy by the teaching authority of the Church in its unfolding of the divine law.[14]

All should be persuaded that human life and the task of transmitting it are not realities bound up with this world alone. Hence they cannot be measured or perceived only in terms of it, but always have a bearing on the eternal destiny of men.

**Pope
St. Paul VI**

*Humanae Vitae
11, 14*

Excluding the Exclusion of Life

Gaudium et Spes 51

The sexual activity, in which husband and wife are intimately and chastely united with one another, through which human life is transmitted, is, as the recent Council recalled, "noble and worthy" (GS 49). It does not, moreover, cease to be legitimate even when, for reasons independent of their will, it is foreseen to be infertile. For its natural adaptation to the expression and strengthening of the union of husband and wife is not thereby suppressed. The fact is, as experience shows, that new life is not the result of each and every act of sexual intercourse. God has wisely ordered laws of nature and the incidence of fertility in such a way that successive births are already naturally spaced through the inherent operation of these laws. The Church, nevertheless, in urging men to the observance of the precepts of the natural law, which it interprets by its constant doctrine, teaches that each and every marital act must of necessity retain its intrinsic relationship to the procreation of human life. . . .

Therefore We base Our words on the first principles of a human and Christian doctrine of marriage when We are obliged once more to declare that the direct interruption of the generative process already begun and, above all, all direct abortion, even for therapeutic reasons, are to be absolutely excluded as lawful means of regulating the number of children. Equally to be condemned, as the magisterium of the Church has affirmed on many occasions, is direct sterilization, whether of the man or of the woman, whether permanent or temporary.

Similarly excluded is any action which either before, at the moment of, or after sexual intercourse, is specifically intended to prevent procreation—whether as an end or as a means. . . .

It is a serious error to think that a whole married life of otherwise normal relations can justify sexual intercourse which is deliberately contraceptive and so intrinsically wrong.

52. The family is a kind of school of deeper humanity. But if it is to achieve the full flowering of its life and mission, it needs the kindly communion of minds and the joint deliberation of spouses, as well as the painstaking cooperation of parents in the education of their children. The active presence of the father is highly beneficial to their formation. The children, especially the younger among them, need the care of their mother at home. This domestic role of hers must be safely preserved, though the legitimate social progress of women should not be underrated on that account.

Children should be so educated that as adults they can follow their vocation, including a religious one, with a mature sense of responsibility and can choose their state of life; if they marry, they can thereby establish their family in favorable moral, social, and economic conditions. Parents or guardians should by prudent advice provide guidance to their young with respect to founding a family, and the young ought to listen gladly. At the same time no pressure, direct or indirect, should be put on the young to make them enter marriage or choose a specific partner.

Thus the family, in which the various generations come together and help one another grow wiser and harmonize personal rights with the other requirements of social life, is the foundation of society. All those, therefore, who exercise influence over communities and social groups should work efficiently for the welfare of marriage and the family. Public authority should regard it as a sacred duty to recognize, protect, and promote their authentic nature, to shield public morality, and to favor the prosperity of home life. The right of parents to beget and educate their children in the bosom of the family must be safeguarded. Children too who unhappily lack the blessing of a family should be protected by prudent legislation and various undertakings and assisted by the help they need.

Christians, redeeming the present time[15] and distinguishing eternal realities from their changing expressions, should actively promote the values of marriage and the family, both by the examples of their own lives and by cooperation with other men of good will. Thus when difficulties arise, Christians will provide, on behalf of family life, those necessities and helps which are suitably modern. To this end, the Christian instincts of the faithful, the upright moral consciences of men, and the wisdom and experience of persons versed in the sacred sciences will have much to contribute.

Those too who are skilled in other sciences, notably the medical, biological, social, and psychological, can considerably advance the welfare of marriage and the family along with peace of conscience if by pooling their efforts they labor to explain more thoroughly the various conditions favoring a proper regulation of births.

It devolves on priests duly trained about family matters to nurture the vocation of spouses by a variety of pastoral means, by preaching God's word, by liturgical worship, and by other spiritual aids to conjugal and family life; to sustain them sympathetically and patiently in difficulties, and to make them courageous through love, so that families which are truly illustrious can be formed.

Various organizations, especially family associations, should try by their programs of instruction and action to strengthen young people and spouses themselves, particularly those recently wed, and to train them for family, social, and apostolic life.

Finally, let the spouses themselves, made to the image of the living God and enjoying the authentic dignity of persons, be joined to one another[16] in equal affection, harmony of mind, and the work of mutual sanctification. Thus, following Christ who is the principle of life,[17] by the sacrifices and joys of their vocation and through their faithful love, married people can become witnesses of the mystery of love which the Lord revealed to the world by His dying and His rising up to life again.[18]

CHAPTER II
The Proper Development of Culture

53. Man comes to a true and full humanity only through culture, that is through the cultivation of the goods and values of nature. Wherever human life is involved, therefore, nature and culture are quite intimately connected one with the other.

The word "culture" in its general sense indicates everything whereby man develops and perfects his many bodily and spiritual qualities; he strives by his knowledge and his labor, to bring the world itself under his control. He renders social life more human both in the family and the civic community, through improvement of customs and institutions. Throughout the course of time he expresses, communicates, and conserves in his works, great spiritual experiences and desires, that they might be of advantage to the progress of many, even of the whole human family.

Thence it follows that human culture has necessarily a historical and social aspect and the word "culture" also often assumes a sociological and ethnological sense. According to this sense we speak of a plurality of cultures. Different styles of life and multiple scales of values arise from the diverse manner of using things, of laboring, of expressing oneself, of practicing religion, of forming customs, of establishing laws and juridic institutions, of cultivating the sciences, the arts, and beauty. Thus the customs handed down to it form the patrimony proper to each human community. It is also in this way that there is formed the definite, historical milieu which enfolds the man of every nation and age and from which he draws the values which permit him to promote civilization.

SECTION 1
The Circumstances of Culture in the World Today

54. The circumstances of the life of modern man have been so profoundly changed in their social and cultural aspects, that we can speak of a new age of human history.[1] New ways are open, therefore, for the perfection and the further extension of culture. These ways have been prepared by the enormous growth of natural, human, and social sciences, by technical progress, and advances in developing and organizing means whereby men can communicate with one another. Hence the culture of today possesses particular characteristics: sciences which are called exact greatly develop critical judgment; the more recent psychological studies more profoundly explain human activity; historical studies make it much easier to see things in their mutable and evolutionary aspects, customs and usages are becoming more and more uniform; industrialization, urbanization, and other causes which promote community living create a mass-culture from which are born new ways of thinking, acting, and making use of leisure. The increase of commerce between the various nations and human groups opens more widely to all the treasures of different civilizations and thus little by little, there develops a more universal form of human culture, which better promotes and expresses the unity of the human race to the degree that it preserves the particular aspects of the different civilizations.

55. From day to day, in every group or nation, there is an increase in the number of men and women who are conscious that they themselves are the authors and the artisans of the culture of their community. Throughout the whole world there is a mounting increase in the sense of autonomy as well as of responsibility. This is of paramount importance for the spiritual and moral maturity of the human race. This becomes more clear if we consider the unification of the world and the duty which is imposed upon us, that we build a better world based upon truth and justice. Thus we are witnesses of the birth of a new humanism, one in which man is defined first of all by this responsibility to his brothers and to history.

56. In these conditions, it is no cause of wonder that man, who senses his responsibility for the progress of culture, nourishes a high hope but also looks with anxiety upon many contradictory things which he must resolve:

What is to be done to prevent the increased exchanges between cultures, which should lead to a true and fruitful dialogue between groups and nations, from disturbing the life of communities, from destroying the wisdom received from ancestors, or from placing in danger the character proper to each people?

How is the dynamism and expansion of a new culture to be fostered without losing a living fidelity to the heritage of tradition? This question is of particular urgency when a culture which arises from the enormous progress of science and technology must be harmonized with a culture nourished by classical studies according to various traditions.

How can we quickly and progressively harmonize the proliferation of particular branches of study with the necessity of forming a synthesis of them, and of preserving among men the faculties of contemplation and observation which lead to wisdom?

What can be done to make all men partakers of cultural values in the world, when the human culture of those who are more competent is constantly becoming more refined and more complex?

Finally how is the autonomy which culture claims for itself to be recognized as legitimate without generating a notion of humanism which is merely terrestrial, and even contrary to religion itself?

In the midst of these conflicting requirements, human culture must evolve today in such a way that it can both develop the whole human person and aid man in those duties to whose fulfillment all are called, especially Christians fraternally united in one human family.

SECTION 2
Some Principles for the Proper Development of Culture

57. Christians, on pilgrimage toward the heavenly city, should seek and think of these things which are above.[2] This duty in no way decreases, rather it increases, the importance of their obligation to work with all men in the building of a more human world. Indeed, the mystery of the Christian faith furnishes them with an excellent stimulant and aid to fulfill this duty more courageously and especially to uncover the full meaning of this activity, one which gives to human culture its eminent place in the integral vocation of man.

When man develops the earth by the work of his hands or with the aid of technology, in order that it might bear fruit and become a dwelling worthy of the whole human family and when he consciously takes part in the life of social groups, he carries out the design of God manifested at the beginning of time, that he should subdue the earth, perfect creation, and develop himself. At the same time he obeys the commandment of Christ that he place himself at the service of his brethren.[3]

Furthermore, when man gives himself to the various disciplines of philosophy, history, and of mathematical and natural science, and when he cultivates the arts, he can do very much to elevate the human family to a more sublime understanding of truth, goodness, and beauty, and to the formation of considered opinions which have universal value. Thus mankind may be more clearly enlightened by that marvelous Wisdom which was with God from all eternity, composing all things with him, rejoicing in the earth, delighting in the sons of men.[4]

In this way, the human spirit, being less subjected to material things, can be more easily drawn to the worship and contemplation of the Creator. Moreover, by the impulse of grace, he is disposed to acknowledge the Word of God, Who before He became flesh in order to save all and to sum up all in Himself was already "in the world" as "the true light which enlightens every man" (John 1:9–10).[5]

Indeed today's progress in science and technology can foster a certain exclusive emphasis on observable data, and an agnosticism about everything else. For the methods of investigation which these sciences use can be wrongly considered as the supreme rule of seeking the whole truth. By virtue of their methods these sciences cannot penetrate to the intimate notion of things. Indeed the danger is present that man, confiding too much in the discoveries of today, may think that he is sufficient unto himself and no longer seek the higher things.

Those unfortunate results, however, do not necessarily follow from the culture of today, nor should they lead us into the temptation of not acknowledging its positive values. Among these values are included:

Culture and Transcendence

Gaudium et Spes 57 | Bishop Barron

What, according to *Gaudium es Spes*, are the principles that ought to govern the development of culture? First, a healthy culture is predicated upon the faith—that is to say, upon an orientation toward transcendent goods: "Christians, on pilgrimage toward the heavenly city, should seek and think of these things which are above. This duty in no way decreases, rather it increases, the importance of their obligation to work with all men in the building of a more human world. Indeed, the mystery of the Christian faith furnishes them with an excellent stimulant and aid to fulfill this duty more courageously and especially to uncover the full meaning of this activity, one which gives to human culture its eminent place in the integral vocation of man."

Those who cultivate the culture in the best way are those who do not look to this world for their ultimate fulfillment. Why? Because every culture is animated by the three great transcendental drives of the human spirit—toward truth, goodness, and beauty. Think of newspapers, universities, education, books—all of which are reflective of the human desire for truth. Think of our legal structures, the judicial system—all trying to establish the good, to seek justice and righteousness. Think of everything from painting and sculpture to dance and theater and even (to some degree) television and the internet—all are attempts to achieve the beautiful.

But these longings do not order us simply to particular expressions of the true, the good, or the beautiful; rather, they direct us to truth, goodness, and beauty in their unconditioned forms. When the transcendent aspiration is denied, these drives are frustrated and tend to turn in on themselves. Hence, the longing for truth is reduced to a narrow scientism, the aspiration for the good devolves into moral relativism, and the drive for the beautiful becomes a preoccupation with surface prettiness.

scientific study and fidelity toward truth in scientific inquiries, the necessity of working together with others in technical groups, a sense of international solidarity, a clearer awareness of the responsibility of experts to aid and even to protect men, the desire to make the conditions of life more favorable for all, especially for those who are poor in culture or who are deprived of the opportunity to exercise responsibility. All of these provide some preparation for the acceptance of the message of the Gospel, a preparation which can be animated by divine charity through Him Who has come to save the world.

58. There are many ties between the message of salvation and human culture. For God, revealing Himself to His people to the extent of a full manifestation of Himself in His Incarnate Son, has spoken according to the culture proper to each epoch.

Likewise the Church, living in various circumstances in the course of time, has used the discoveries of different cultures so that in her preaching she might spread and explain the message of Christ to all nations, that she might examine it and more deeply understand it, that she might give it better expression in liturgical celebration and in the varied life of the community of the faithful.

But at the same time, the Church, sent to all peoples of every time and place, is not bound exclusively and indissolubly to any race or nation, any particular way of life or any customary way of life recent or ancient. Faithful to her own tradition and at the same time conscious of her universal mission, she can enter into communion with the various civilizations, to their enrichment and the enrichment of the Church herself.

The Gospel of Christ constantly renews the life and culture of fallen man; it combats and removes the errors and evils resulting from the permanent allurement of sin. It never ceases to purify and elevate the morality of peoples. By riches coming from above, it makes fruitful, as it were from within, the spiritual qualities and traditions of every people of every age. It strengthens, perfects, and restores[6] them in Christ. Thus the Church, in the very fulfillment of her own function,[7] stimulates and advances human and civic culture; by her action, also by her liturgy, she leads them toward interior liberty.

59. For the above reasons, the Church recalls to the mind of all that culture is to be subordinated to the integral perfection of the human person, to the

good of the community and of the whole society. Therefore it is necessary to develop the human faculties in such a way that there results a growth of the faculty of admiration, of intuition, of contemplation, of making personal judgment, of developing a religious, moral, and social sense.

Culture, because it flows immediately from the spiritual and social character of man, has constant need of a just liberty in order to develop; it needs also the legitimate possibility of exercising its autonomy according to its own principles. It therefore rightly demands respect and enjoys a certain inviolability within the limits of the common good, as long, of course, as it preserves the rights of the individual and the community, whether particular or universal.

This Sacred Synod, therefore, recalling the teaching of the first Vatican Council, declares that there are "two orders of knowledge" which are distinct, namely faith and reason; and that the Church does not forbid that "the human arts and disciplines use their own principles and their proper method, each in its own domain"; therefore "acknowledging this just liberty," this Sacred Synod affirms the legitimate autonomy of human culture and especially of the sciences.[8]

All this supposes that, within the limits of morality and the common utility, man can freely search for the truth, express his opinion, and publish it; that he can practice any art he chooses; that finally, he can avail himself of true information concerning events of a public nature.[9]

As for public authority, it is not its function to determine the character of the civilization, but rather to establish the conditions and to use the means which are capable of fostering the life of culture among all, even within the minorities of a nation.[10] It is necessary to do everything possible to prevent culture from being turned away from its proper end and made to serve as an instrument of political or economic power.

Faith Does Not Compete with Reason

Gaudium et Spes 59 | Bishop Barron

As John Henry Newman taught in his *Idea of a University*, faith stands at the center of a healthy culture. But as *Gaudium et Spes* affirms, "The Church does not forbid that 'the human arts and disciplines use their own principles and their proper method, each in its own domain.'" Just as God is not competitive with his creation, so faith is not competitive with reason, nor the principles of theology competitive with the principles of the human sciences.

The Wings of Faith and Reason
Gaudium et Spes 59

**Pope
St. John Paul II**

Fides et Ratio
Blessing

Faith and reason are like two wings on which the human spirit rises to the contemplation of truth; and God has placed in the human heart a desire to know the truth—in a word, to know himself—so that, by knowing and loving God, men and women may also come to the fullness of truth about themselves (see Exod. 33:18; Ps. 27:8–9; 63:2–3; John 14:8; 1 John 3:2).

SECTION 3
Some More Urgent Duties of Christians in Regard to Culture

60. It is now possible to free most of humanity from the misery of ignorance. Therefore the duty most consonant with our times, especially for Christians, is that of working diligently for fundamental decisions to be taken in economic and political affairs, both on the national and international level which will everywhere recognize and satisfy the right of all to a human and social culture in conformity with the dignity of the human person without any discrimination of race, sex, nation, religion, or social condition. Therefore it is necessary to provide all with a sufficient quantity of cultural benefits, especially of those which constitute the so-called fundamental culture lest very many be prevented from cooperating in the promotion of the common good in a truly human manner because of illiteracy and a lack of responsible activity.

We must strive to provide for those men who are gifted the possibility of pursuing higher studies; and in such a way that, as far as possible, they may occupy in society those duties, offices, and services which are in harmony with their natural aptitude and the competence they have acquired.[11] Thus each man and the social groups of every people will be able to attain the full development of their culture in conformity with their qualities and traditions.

Everything must be done to make everyone conscious of the right to culture and the duty he has of developing himself culturally and of helping others. Sometimes there exist conditions of life and of work which impede the cultural striving of men and destroy in them the eagerness for culture. This is especially true of farmers and workers. It is necessary to provide for them those working conditions which will not impede their human culture but rather favor it. Women now work in almost all spheres. It is fitting that they are able to assume their proper role in accordance with their own nature. It will belong to all to acknowledge and favor the proper and necessary participation of women in the cultural life.

61. Today it is more difficult to form a synthesis of the various disciplines of knowledge and the arts than it was formerly. For while the mass and the diversity of cultural factors are increasing, there is a decrease in each man's faculty of perceiving and unifying these things, so that the image of "universal man" is being lost sight of more and more. Nevertheless it remains each man's duty to retain an understanding of the whole human person in which the values of intellect, will, conscience, and fraternity are preeminent. These values are all rooted in God the Creator and have been wonderfully restored and elevated in Christ.

The Feminine Genius

Gaudium et Spes 60

Pope Francis
———
Evangelii Gaudium 103

The Church acknowledges the indispensable contribution which women make to society through the sensitivity, intuition, and other distinctive skill sets which they, more than men, tend to possess. I think, for example, of the special concern which women show to others, which finds a particular, even if not exclusive, expression in motherhood. I readily acknowledge that many women share pastoral responsibilities with priests, helping to guide people, families, and groups and offering new contributions to theological reflection. But we need to create still broader opportunities for a more incisive female presence in the Church. Because "the feminine genius is needed in all expressions in the life of society, the presence of women must also be guaranteed in the workplace" and in the various other settings where important decisions are made, both in the Church and in social structures.

A Mother's Presence

Gaudium et Spes 60

Pope Francis
—
Amoris Laetitia
173

Nowadays we acknowledge as legitimate and indeed desirable that women wish to study, work, develop their skills, and have personal goals. At the same time, we cannot ignore the need that children have for a mother's presence, especially in the first months of life. Indeed, "the woman stands before the man as a mother, the subject of the new human life that is conceived and develops in her, and from her is born into the world." The weakening of this maternal presence with its feminine qualities poses a grave risk to our world. I certainly value feminism, but one that does not demand uniformity or negate motherhood. For the grandeur of women includes all the rights derived from their inalienable human dignity but also from their feminine genius, which is essential to society. Their specifically feminine abilities—motherhood in particular—also grant duties, because womanhood also entails a specific mission in this world, a mission that society needs to protect and preserve for the good of all.

The family is, as it were, the primary mother and nurse of this education. There, the children, in an atmosphere of love, more easily learn the correct order of things, while proper forms of human culture impress themselves in an almost unconscious manner upon the mind of the developing adolescent.

Opportunities for the same education are to be found also in the societies of today, due especially to the increased circulation of books and to the new means of cultural and social communication which can foster a universal culture. With the more or less generalized reduction of working hours, the leisure time of most men has increased. May this leisure be used properly to relax, to fortify the health of soul and body through spontaneous study and activity, through tourism which refines man's character and enriches him with understanding of others, through sports activity which helps to preserve equilibrium of spirit even in the community, and to establish fraternal relations among men of all conditions, nations, and races. Let Christians cooperate so that the cultural manifestations and collective activity characteristic of our time may be imbued with a human and a Christian spirit.

All these leisure activities however are not able to bring man to a full cultural development unless there is at the same time a profound inquiry into the meaning of culture and science for the human person.

62. Although the Church has contributed much to the development of culture, experience shows that, for circumstantial reasons, it is sometimes difficult to harmonize culture with Christian teaching. These difficulties do not necessarily harm the life of faith, rather they can stimulate the mind to a deeper and more accurate understanding of the faith. The recent studies and findings of science, history, and philosophy raise new questions which affect life and which demand new theological investigations. Furthermore, theologians, within the requirements and methods proper to theology, are invited to seek continually for more suitable ways of communicating doctrine to the men of their times; for the deposit of Faith or the truths are one thing and the manner in which they are enunciated, in the same meaning and understanding, is another.[12] In pastoral care, sufficient use must be made not only of theological principles, but also of the findings of the secular sciences, especially of psychology and sociology, so that the faithful may be brought to a more adequate and mature life of faith.

Literature and the arts are also, in their own way, of great importance to the life of the Church. They strive to make known the proper nature of man, his problems, and his experiences in trying to know and perfect both himself and the world. They have much to do with revealing man's place in history and in the world; with illustrating the miseries and joys, the needs and strengths of man and with foreshadowing a better life for him. Thus they are able to elevate human life, expressed in multifold forms according to various times and regions.

Efforts must be made so that those who foster these arts feel that the Church recognizes their activity and so that, enjoying orderly liberty, they may initiate more friendly relations with the Christian community. The Church acknowledges also new forms of art which are adapted to our age and are in keeping with the characteristics of various nations and regions. They may be brought into the sanctuary since they raise the mind to God, once the manner of expression is adapted and they are conformed to liturgical requirements.[13]

Thus the knowledge of God is better manifested and the preaching of the Gospel becomes clearer to human intelligence and shows itself to be relevant to man's actual conditions of life.

May the faithful, therefore, live in very close union with the other men of their time and may they strive to understand perfectly their way of thinking and judging, as expressed in their culture. Let them blend new sciences and theories and the understanding of the most recent discoveries with Christian morality and the teaching of Christian doctrine, so that their religious culture and morality may keep pace with scientific knowledge and with the constantly progressing technology. Thus they will be able to interpret and evaluate all things in a truly Christian spirit.

Let those who teach theology in seminaries and universities strive to collaborate with men versed in the other sciences through a sharing of their resources and points of view. Theological inquiry should pursue a profound understanding of revealed truth; at the same time it should not neglect close contact with its own time that it may be able to help these men skilled in various disciplines to attain to a better understanding of the faith. This common effort will greatly aid the formation of priests, who will be able to present to our contemporaries the doctrine of the Church concerning God, man, and the world, in a manner more adapted to them so that they may receive it more willingly.[14] Furthermore, it is to be hoped that many of the laity will receive a sufficient formation in the sacred sciences and that some will dedicate themselves professionally to these studies, developing and deepening them by their own labors. In order that they may fulfill their function, let it be recognized that all the faithful, whether clerics or laity, possess a lawful freedom of inquiry, freedom of thought, and of expressing their mind with humility and fortitude in those matters on which they enjoy competence.[15]

CHAPTER III
Economic and Social Life

63. In the economic and social realms, too, the dignity and complete vocation of the human person and the welfare of society as a whole are to be respected and promoted. For man is the source, the center, and the purpose of all economic and social life.

Like other areas of social life, the economy of today is marked by man's increasing domination over nature, by closer and more intense relationships between citizens, groups, and countries and their mutual dependence, and by the increased intervention of the state. At the same time progress in the methods of production and in the exchange of goods and services has made the economy an instrument capable of better meeting the intensified needs of the human family.

Reasons for anxiety, however, are not lacking. Many people, especially in economically advanced areas, seem, as it were, to be ruled by economics, so that almost their entire personal and social life is permeated with a certain economic way of thinking. Such is true both of nations that favor a collective economy and of others. At the very time when the development of economic life could mitigate social inequalities (provided that it be guided and coordinated in a reasonable and human way), it is often made to embitter them; or, in some places, it even results in a decline of the social status of the underprivileged and in contempt for the poor. While an immense number of people still lack the absolute necessities of life, some, even in less advanced areas, live in luxury or squander wealth. Extravagance and wretchedness exist side by side. While a few enjoy very great power of choice, the majority are deprived of almost all possibility of acting on their own initiative and responsibility, and often subsist in living and working conditions unworthy of the human person.

A similar lack of economic and social balance is to be noticed between agriculture, industry, and the services, and also between different parts of one and the same country. The contrast between the economically more advanced countries and other countries is becoming more serious day by day, and the very peace of the world can be jeopardized thereby.

Our contemporaries are coming to feel these inequalities with an ever sharper awareness, since they are thoroughly convinced that the ampler technical and economic possibilities which the world of today enjoys can and should correct this unhappy state of affairs. Hence, many reforms in the socioeconomic realm and a change of mentality and attitude are required of all. For this reason the Church down through the centuries and in the light of the Gospel has worked out the principles of justice and equity demanded by right reason both for individual and social life and for international life, and she has proclaimed them especially in recent times. This sacred council intends to strengthen these principles according to the circumstances of this age and to set forth certain guidelines, especially with regard to the requirements of economic development.[1]

SECTION 1
Economic Development

64. Today more than ever before attention is rightly given to the increase of the production of agricultural and industrial goods and of the rendering of services, for the purpose of making provision for the growth of population and of satisfying the increasing desires of the human race. Therefore, technical progress, an inventive spirit, an eagerness to create and to expand enterprises, the application of methods of production, and the strenuous efforts of all who engage in production—in a word, all the elements making for such development—must be promoted. The fundamental finality of this production is not the mere increase of products nor profit or control but rather the service of man, and indeed of the whole man with regard for the full range of his material needs and the demands of his intellectual, moral, spiritual, and religious life; this applies to every man whatsoever and to every group of men, of every race and of every part of the world. Consequently, economic activity is to be carried on according to its own methods and laws within the limits of the moral order,[2] so that God's plan for mankind may be realized.[3]

65. Economic development must remain under man's determination and must not be left to the judgment of a few men or groups possessing too much economic power or of the political community alone or of certain more powerful nations. It is necessary, on the contrary, that at every level the largest possible number of people and, when it is a question of international relations, all nations have an active share in directing that development. There is need as well of the coordination and fitting and harmonious combination of the spontaneous efforts of individuals and of free groups with the undertakings of public authorities.

Growth is not to be left solely to a kind of mechanical course of the economic activity of individuals, nor to the authority of government. For this reason, doctrines which obstruct the necessary reforms under the guise of a false liberty, and those which subordinate the basic rights of individual persons and groups to the collective organization of production must be shown to be erroneous.[4]

Citizens, on the other hand, should remember that it is their right and duty, which is also to be recognized by the civil authority, to contribute to the true progress of their own community according to their ability.

Especially in underdeveloped areas, where all resources must urgently be employed, those who hold back their unproductive resources or who deprive their community of the material or spiritual aid that it needs— saving the personal right of migration—gravely endanger the common good.

The Wide Diffusion of Power

Gaudium et Spes 65 | Bishop Barron

The council fathers observe that participation in the economic life ought to be open to the widest possible swath of the population and not restricted to a small elite coterie: "Economic development must remain under man's determination and must not be left to the judgment of a few men or groups possessing too much economic power or of the political community alone or of certain more powerful nations."

This is a very good summary of a key aspect of Catholic social teaching. From *Rerum Novarum* in the late nineteenth century all the way through to Benedict XVI in the early twenty-first century, the Church has insisted that power, both economic and political, should be widely diffused throughout the society and not concentrated in a few hands. If someone is extraordinarily wealthy, what is he called to do? He ought to invest that money creatively for the benefit of the wider community. In this manner, the two great principles of solidarity and subsidiarity would be simultaneously honored.

66. To satisfy the demands of justice and equity, strenuous efforts must be made, without disregarding the rights of persons or the natural qualities of each country, to remove as quickly as possible the immense economic inequalities, which now exist and in many cases are growing and which are connected with individual and social discrimination. Likewise, in many areas, in view of the special difficulties of agriculture relative to the raising and selling of produce, country people must be helped both to increase and to market what they produce, and to introduce the necessary development and renewal and also obtain a fair income. Otherwise, as too often happens, they will remain in the condition of lower-class citizens. Let farmers themselves, especially young ones, apply themselves to perfecting their professional skill, for without it, there can be no agricultural advance.[5]

Justice and equity likewise require that the mobility, which is necessary in a developing economy, be regulated in such a way as to keep the life of individuals and their families from becoming insecure and precarious. When workers come from another country or district and contribute to the economic advancement of a nation or region by their labor, all discrimination as regards wages and working conditions must be carefully avoided. All the people, moreover, above all the public authorities, must treat them not as mere tools of production but as persons, and must help them to bring their families to live with them and to provide themselves with a decent dwelling; they must also see to it that these workers are incorporated into the social life of the country or region that receives them. Employment opportunities, however, should be created in their own areas as far as possible.

In economic affairs which today are subject to change, as in the new forms of industrial society in which automation, for example, is advancing, care must be taken that sufficient and suitable work and the possibility of the appropriate technical and professional formation are furnished. The livelihood and the human dignity especially of those who are in very difficult conditions because of illness or old age must be guaranteed.

SECTION 2
Certain Principles Governing Socio-Economic Life as a Whole

67. Human labor which is expended in the production and exchange of goods or in the performance of economic services is superior to the other elements of economic life, for the latter have only the nature of tools.

This labor, whether it is engaged in independently or hired by someone else, comes immediately from the person, who as it were stamps the things of nature with his seal and subdues them to his will. By his labor a man ordinarily supports himself and his family, is joined to his fellow men and serves them, and can exercise genuine charity and be a partner in the work of bringing divine creation to perfection. Indeed, we hold that through labor offered to God man is associated with the redemptive work of Jesus Christ, Who conferred an eminent dignity on labor when at Nazareth He worked with His own hands. From this there follows for every man the duty of working faithfully and also the right to work. It is the duty of society, moreover, according to the circumstances prevailing in it, and in keeping with its role, to help the citizens to find sufficient employment.

Finally, remuneration for labor is to be such that man may be furnished the means to cultivate worthily his own material, social, cultural, and spiritual life and that of his dependents, in view of the function and productiveness of each one, the conditions of the factory or workshop, and the common good.[6]

Since economic activity for the most part implies the associated work of human beings, any way of organizing and directing it which may be detrimental to any working men and women would be wrong and inhuman. It happens too often, however, even in our days, that workers are reduced to the level of being slaves to their own work. This is by no means justified by the so-called economic laws. The entire process of productive work, therefore, must be adapted to the needs of the person and to his way of life, above all to his domestic life, especially in respect to mothers of families, always with due regard for sex and age. The opportunity, moreover, should be granted to workers to unfold their own abilities and personality through the performance of their work. Applying their time and strength to their employment with a due sense of responsibility, they should also all enjoy sufficient rest and leisure to cultivate their familial, cultural, social, and religious life. They should also have the opportunity freely to develop the energies and potentialities which perhaps they cannot bring to much fruition in their professional work.

The Superiority of Labor

Gaudium et Spes 67 | Bishop Barron

Gaudium et Spes 67 affirms the priority of labor over capital. In a teaching that John Paul would echo in *Laborem Exercens*, the council fathers say,

"Human labor which is expended in the production and exchange of goods or in the performance of economic services is superior to the other elements of economic life, for the latter have only the nature of tools."

---

68. In economic enterprises it is persons who are joined together, that is, free and independent human beings created to the image of God. Therefore, with attention to the functions of each—owners or employers, management or labor—and without doing harm to the necessary unity of management, the active sharing of all in the administration and profits of these enterprises in ways to be properly determined is to be promoted.[7] Since more often, however, decisions concerning economic and social

**Pope
St. Paul VI**

*Populorum
Progressio
27–28*

The Concept of Work
Gaudium et Spes 67

The concept of work can turn into an exaggerated mystique. Yet, for all that, it is something willed and approved by God. Fashioned in the image of his Creator, "man must cooperate with Him in completing the work of creation and engraving on the earth the spiritual imprint which he himself has received." God gave man intelligence, sensitivity, and the power of thought—tools with which to finish and perfect the work He began. Every worker is, to some extent, a creator—be he artist, craftsman, executive, laborer, or farmer.

Bent over a material that resists his efforts, the worker leaves his imprint on it, at the same time developing his own powers of persistence, inventiveness, and concentration. Further, when work is done in common—when hope, hardship, ambition, and joy are shared—it brings together and firmly unites the wills, minds, and hearts of men. In its accomplishment, men find themselves to be brothers.

Work, too, has a double edge. Since it promises money, pleasure, and power, it stirs up selfishness in some and incites others to revolt. On the other hand, it also fosters a professional outlook, a sense of duty, and love of neighbor. Even though it is now being organized more scientifically and efficiently, it still can threaten man's dignity and enslave him; for work is human only if it results from man's use of intellect and free will.

Our predecessor John XXIII stressed the urgent need of restoring dignity to the worker and making him a real partner in the common task: "Every effort must be made to ensure that the enterprise is indeed a true human community, concerned about the needs, the activities, and the standing of each of its members."

Considered from a Christian point of view, work has an even loftier connotation. It is directed to the establishment of a supernatural order here on earth, a task that will not be completed until we all unite to form that perfect manhood of which St. Paul speaks, "the mature measure of the fullness of Christ" (Eph. 4:13).

conditions, on which the future lot of the workers and of their children depends, are made not within the business itself but by institutions on a higher level, the workers themselves should have a share also in determining these conditions—in person or through freely elected delegates.

Among the basic rights of the human person is to be numbered the right of freely founding unions for working people. These should be able truly to represent them and to contribute to the organizing of economic life in the right way. Included is the right of freely taking part in the activity of these unions without risk of reprisal. Through this orderly participation joined to progressive economic and social formation, all will grow day by day in the awareness of their own function and responsibility, and thus they will be brought to feel that they are comrades in the whole task of economic development and in the attainment of the universal common good according to their capacities and aptitudes.

When, however, socio-economic disputes arise, efforts must be made to come to a peaceful settlement. Although recourse must always be had first to a sincere dialogue between the parties, a strike, nevertheless, can remain even in present-day circumstances a necessary, though ultimate, aid for the defense of the workers' own rights and the fulfillment of their just desires. As soon as possible, however, ways should be sought to resume negotiation and the discussion of reconciliation.

69. God intended the earth with everything contained in it for the use of all human beings and peoples. Thus, under the leadership of justice and in the company of charity, created goods should be in abundance for all in like manner.[8] Whatever the forms of property may be, as adapted to the legitimate institutions of peoples, according to diverse and changeable

circumstances, attention must always be paid to this universal destination of earthly goods. In using them, therefore, man should regard the external things that he legitimately possesses not only as his own but also as common in the sense that they should be able to benefit not only him but also others.[9] On the other hand, the right of having a share of earthly goods sufficient for oneself and one's family belongs to everyone. The Fathers and Doctors of the Church held this opinion, teaching that men are obliged to come to the relief of the poor and to do so not merely out of their superfluous goods.[10] If one is in extreme necessity, he has the right to procure for himself what he needs out of the riches of others.[11] Since there are so many people prostrate with hunger in the world, this sacred council urges all, both individuals and governments, to remember the aphorism of the Fathers, "Feed the man dying of hunger, because if you have not fed him, you have killed him,"[12] and really to share and employ their earthly goods, according to the ability of each, especially by supporting individuals or peoples with the aid by which they may be able to help and develop themselves.

In economically less advanced societies the common destination of earthly goods is partly satisfied by means of the customs and traditions proper to the community, by which the absolutely necessary things are furnished to each member. An effort must be made, however, to avoid regarding certain customs as altogether unchangeable, if they no longer answer the new needs of this age. On the other hand, imprudent action should not be taken against respectable customs which, provided they are suitably adapted to present-day circumstances, do not cease to be very useful. Similarly, in highly developed nations a body of social institutions dealing with protection and security can, for its own part, bring to reality the common destination of earthly goods. Family and social services, especially those that provide for culture and education, should be further promoted. When all these things are being organized, vigilance is necessary to prevent the citizens from being led into a certain inactivity vis-à-vis society or from rejecting the burden of taking up office or from refusing to serve.

**Pope
St. Paul VI**

—

*Populorum
Progressio
22*

Created Goods Are for All

Gaudium et Spes 69

In the very first pages of Scripture we read these words: "Fill the earth and subdue it" (Gen. 1:28). This teaches us that the whole of creation is for man, that he has been charged to give it meaning by his intelligent activity, to complete and perfect it by his own efforts and to his own advantage.

Now if the earth truly was created to provide man with the necessities of life and the tools for his own progress, it follows that every man has the right to glean what he needs from the earth. The recent Council reiterated this truth: "God intended the earth with everything contained in it for the use of all human beings and peoples. Thus, under the leadership of justice and in the company of charity, created goods should be in abundance for all in like manner."

All other rights, whatever they may be, including the rights of property and free trade, are to be subordinated to this principle. They should in no way hinder it; in fact, they should actively facilitate its implementation. Redirecting these rights back to their original purpose must be regarded as an important and urgent social duty.

Pope Francis

—

*Evangelii Gaudium
187–190*

Growing in Solidarity

Gaudium et Spes 69

The old question always returns: "How does God's love abide in anyone who has the world's goods, and sees a brother or sister in need and yet refuses help?" (1 John 3:17). Let us recall also how bluntly the apostle James speaks of the cry of the oppressed: "The wages of the laborers who mowed your fields, which you kept back by fraud, cry out, and the cries of the harvesters have reached the ears of the Lord of hosts" (James 5:4).

The Church has realized that the need to heed this plea is itself born of the liberating action of grace within each of us, and thus it is not a question of a mission reserved only to a few: "The Church, guided by the Gospel of mercy and by love for mankind, hears the cry for justice and intends to respond to it with all her might." In this context we can understand Jesus' command to his disciples: "You yourselves give them something to eat!" (Mark 6:37): it means working to eliminate the structural causes of poverty and to promote the integral development of the poor, as well as small daily acts of solidarity in meeting the real needs which we encounter. The word "solidarity" is a little worn and at times poorly understood, but it refers to something more than a few sporadic acts of generosity. It presumes the creation of a new mindset which thinks in terms of community and the priority of the life of all over the appropriation of goods by a few.

Solidarity is a spontaneous reaction by those who recognize that the social function of property and the universal destination of goods are realities which come before private property. The private ownership of goods is justified by the need to protect and increase them, so that they can better serve the common good; for this reason, solidarity must be lived as the decision to restore to the poor what belongs to them. These convictions and habits of solidarity, when they are put into practice, open the way to other structural transformations and make them possible. Changing structures without generating new convictions and attitudes will only ensure that those same structures will become, sooner or later, corrupt, oppressive, and ineffectual.

Sometimes it is a matter of hearing the cry of entire peoples, the poorest peoples of the earth, since "peace is founded not only on respect for human rights, but also on respect for the rights of peoples." Sadly, even human rights can be used as a justification for an inordinate defense of individual rights or the rights of the richer peoples. With due respect for the autonomy and culture of every nation, we must never forget that the planet belongs to all mankind and is meant for all mankind; the mere fact that some people are born in places with fewer resources or less development does not justify the fact that they are living with less dignity. It must be reiterated that "the more fortunate should renounce some of their rights so as to place their goods more generously at the service of others." To speak properly of our own rights, we need to broaden our perspective and to hear the plea of other peoples and other regions than those of our own country. We need to grow in a solidarity which "would allow all peoples to become the artisans of their destiny," since "every person is called to self-fulfillment."

70. Investments, for their part, must be directed toward procuring employment and sufficient income for the people both now and in the future. Whoever makes decisions concerning these investments and the planning of the economy—whether they be individuals or groups of public authorities—are bound to keep these objectives in mind and to recognize their serious obligation of watching, on the one hand, that provision be made for the necessities required for a decent life both of individuals and of the whole community and, on the other, of looking out for the future and of establishing a right balance between the needs of present-day consumption, both individual and collective, and the demands of investing for the generation to come. They should also always bear in mind the urgent needs of underdeveloped countries or regions. In monetary matters they should beware of hurting the welfare of their own country or of other countries. Care should also be taken lest the economically weak countries unjustly suffer any loss from a change in the value of money.

71. Since property and other forms of private ownership of external goods contribute to the expression of the personality, and since, moreover, they furnish one an occasion to exercise his function in society and in the economy, it is very important that the access of both individuals and communities to some ownership of external goods be fostered.

Private property or some ownership of external goods confers on everyone a sphere wholly necessary for the autonomy of the person and the family, and it should be regarded as an extension of human freedom. Lastly, since it adds incentives for carrying on one's function and charge, it constitutes one of the conditions for civil liberties.[13]

The forms of such ownership or property are varied today and are becoming increasingly diversified. They all remain, however, a cause of security not to be underestimated, in spite of social funds, rights, and services provided by society. This is true not only of material property but also of immaterial things such as professional capacities.

The right of private ownership, however, is not opposed to the right inherent in various forms of public property. Goods can be transferred to the public domain only by the competent authority, according to the demands and within the limits of the common good, and with fair compensation. Furthermore, it is the right of public authority to prevent anyone from abusing his private property to the detriment of the common good.[14]

By its very nature private property has a social quality which is based on the law of the common destination of earthly goods.[15] If this social quality is overlooked, property often becomes an occasion of passionate desires for wealth and serious disturbances, so that a pretext is given to the attackers for calling the right itself into question.

In many underdeveloped regions there are large or even extensive rural estates which are only slightly cultivated or lie completely idle for the sake of profit, while the majority of the people either are without land or have only very small fields, and, on the other hand, it is evidently urgent to increase the productivity of the fields. Not infrequently those who are hired to work for the landowners or who till a portion of the land as tenants receive a wage or income unworthy of a human being, lack decent housing, and are exploited by middlemen. Deprived of all security, they live under such personal servitude that almost every opportunity of acting on their own initiative and responsibility is denied to them and all advancement in human culture and all sharing in social and political life is forbidden to them. According to the different cases, therefore, reforms are necessary: that income may grow, working conditions should be improved, security in employment increased, and an incentive to working on one's own initiative given. Indeed, insufficiently cultivated estates should be distributed to those who can make these lands fruitful; in this case, the necessary things and means, especially educational aids and the right facilities for cooperative organization, must be supplied. Whenever, nevertheless, the common good requires expropriation, compensation must be reckoned in equity after all the circumstances have been weighed.

The Universal Destination of Goods

Gaudium et Spes 71 | Bishop Barron

In *Rerum Novarum*, Pope Leo XIII, the founder of the modern Catholic social tradition, strenuously defended private property and, using a number of arguments, repudiated socialist economic arrangements. *Gaudium et Spes* does not repudiate these views; however, in line with the totality of Catholic social teaching, it reiterates the Thomistic distinction between the ownership and the use of private property: "By its very nature private property has a social quality which is based on the law of the common destination of earthly goods."

St. Thomas Aquinas made the relevant distinction in question 66 of the *secunda secundae* of the *Summa theologiae*. For a variety of reasons, Thomas argues, people have the right to "procure and dispense" the goods of the world and hence to hold them as "property." But in regard to the use of what they legitimately own, they must always keep the general welfare first in mind: "On

this respect man ought to possess external things, not as his own, but as common, so that, to wit, he is ready to communicate them to others in their need."

Now, in regard to this distinction, Thomas himself was the inheritor of an older tradition, stretching back to the Church Fathers. St. John Chrysostom said, "Not to enable the poor to share in our goods is to steal from them and deprive them of life. The goods we possess are not ours, but theirs." And St. Gregory the Great in the same vein declared, "When we provide the needy with their basic needs, we are giving them what belongs to them, not to us." The simplest way to grasp the distinction between ownership and use is to imagine the scenario of a starving man coming to the door of your house late at night and asking for sustenance. Though you are in your own home, which you legitimately own, and behind a door that you have understandably locked against intruders, you would nevertheless be morally obligated to give away some of your property to the beggar in such desperate need.

72. Christians who take an active part in present-day socio-economic development and fight for justice and charity should be convinced that they can make a great contribution to the prosperity of mankind and to the peace of the world. In these activities let them, either as individuals or as members of groups, give a shining example. Having acquired the absolutely necessary skill and experience, they should observe the right order in their earthly activities in faithfulness to Christ and His Gospel. Thus their whole life, both individual and social, will be permeated with the spirit of the beatitudes, notably with a spirit of poverty.

Whoever in obedience to Christ seeks first the Kingdom of God, takes therefrom a stronger and purer love for helping all his brethren and for perfecting the work of justice under the inspiration of charity.[16]

CHAPTER IV
The Life of the Political Community

73. In our day, profound changes are apparent also in the structure and institutions of peoples. These result from their cultural, economic, and social evolution. Such changes have a great influence on the life of the political community, especially regarding the rights and duties of all in the exercise of civil freedom and in the attainment of the common good, and in organizing the relations of citizens among themselves and with respect to public authority.

The present keener sense of human dignity has given rise in many parts of the world to attempts to bring about a politico-juridical order which will give better protection to the rights of the person in public life. These include the right freely to meet and form associations, the right to express one's own opinion and to profess one's religion both publicly and privately. The protection of the rights of a person is indeed a necessary condition so that citizens, individually or collectively, can take an active part in the life and government of the state.

Along with cultural, economic, and social development, there is a growing desire among many people to play a greater part in organizing the life of the political community. In the conscience of many arises an increasing concern that the rights of minorities be recognized, without any neglect for their duties toward the political community. In addition, there is a steadily growing respect for men of other opinions or other religions. At the same time, there is wider cooperation to guarantee the actual exercise of personal rights to all citizens, and not only to a few privileged individuals.

However, those political systems, prevailing in some parts of the world are to be reproved which hamper civic or religious freedom, victimize large numbers through avarice and political crimes, and divert the exercise of authority from the service of the common good to the interests of one or another faction or of the rulers themselves.

There is no better way to establish political life on a truly human basis than by fostering an inward sense of justice and kindliness, and of service to the common good, and by strengthening basic convictions as to the true nature of the political community and the aim, right exercise, and sphere of action of public authority.

74. Men, families, and the various groups which make up the civil community are aware that they cannot achieve a truly human life by their own unaided efforts. They see the need for a wider community, within which each one makes his specific contribution every day toward an ever broader realization of the common good.[1] For this purpose they set up a political community according to various forms. The political community exists, consequently, for the sake of the common good, in which it finds its full justification and significance, and the source of its inherent legitimacy. Indeed, the common good embraces the sum of those conditions of the social life whereby men, families, and associations more adequately and readily may attain their own perfection.[2]

Yet the people who come together in the political community are many and diverse, and they have every right to prefer divergent solutions. If the political community is not to be torn apart while everyone follows his own opinion, there must be an authority to direct the energies of all citizens toward the common good, not in a mechanical or despotic fashion, but by acting above all as a moral force which appeals to each one's freedom and sense of responsibility.

It is clear, therefore, that the political community and public authority are founded on human nature and hence belong to the order designed by God, even though the choice of a political regime and the appointment of rulers are left to the free will of citizens.[3]

It follows also that political authority, both in the community as such and in the representative bodies of the state, must always be exercised within the limits of the moral order and directed toward the common good—with a dynamic concept of that good—according to the juridical order legitimately established or due to be established. When authority is so exercised, citizens are bound in conscience to obey.[4] Accordingly, the responsibility, dignity, and importance of leaders are indeed clear.

But where citizens are oppressed by a public authority overstepping its competence, they should not protest against those things which are objectively required for the common good; but it is legitimate for them to defend their own rights and the rights of their fellow citizens against the abuse of this authority, while keeping within those limits drawn by the natural law and the Gospels.

According to the character of different peoples and their historic development, the political community can, however, adopt a variety of concrete solutions in its structures and the organization of public authority. For the benefit of the whole human family, these solutions must always contribute to the formation of a type of man who will be cultivated, peace-loving, and well-disposed towards all his fellow men.

75. It is in full conformity with human nature that there should be juridico-political structures providing all citizens in an ever better fashion and without any discrimination the practical possibility of freely and actively taking part in the establishment of the juridical foundations of the political community and in the direction of public affairs, in fixing the terms of reference of the various public bodies, and in the election of political leaders.[5] All citizens, therefore, should be mindful of the right and also the duty to use their free vote to further the common good. The Church praises and esteems the work of those who for the good of men devote themselves to the service of the state and take on the burdens of this office.

If the citizens' responsible cooperation is to produce the good results which may be expected in the normal course of political life, there must be a statute of positive law providing for a suitable division of the functions and bodies of authority and an efficient and independent system for the protection of rights. The rights of all persons, families, and groups, and their practical application, must be recognized, respected, and furthered, together with the duties binding on all citizens.[6] Among the latter, it will be well to recall the duty of rendering the political community such material and personal service as are required by the common good. Rulers must be careful not to hamper the development of family, social, or cultural groups, nor that of intermediate bodies or organizations, and not to deprive them of opportunities for legitimate and constructive activity; they should willingly seek rather to promote the orderly pursuit of such activity. Citizens, for their part, either individually or collectively, must be careful not to attribute excessive power to public authority, not to make exaggerated and untimely demands upon it in their own interests, lessening in this way the responsible role of persons, families, and social groups.

The complex circumstances of our day make it necessary for public authority to intervene more often in social, economic, and cultural matters in order to bring about favorable conditions which will give more effective help to citizens and groups in their free pursuit of man's total well-being. The relations, however, between socialization and the autonomy and development of the person can be understood in different ways according to various regions and the evolution of peoples. But when the exercise of rights is restricted temporarily for the common good, freedom should be restored immediately upon change of circumstances. Moreover, it is inhuman for public authority to fall back on dictatorial systems or totalitarian methods which violate the rights of the person or social groups.[7]

Citizens must cultivate a generous and loyal spirit of patriotism, but without being narrow-minded. This means that they will always direct their attention to the good of the whole human family, united by the different ties which bind together races, people, and nations.

All Christians must be aware of their own specific vocation within the political community. It is for them to give an example by their sense of responsibility and their service of the common good. In this way they are to demonstrate concretely how authority can be compatible with freedom, personal initiative with the solidarity of the whole social organism, and the advantages of unity with fruitful diversity. They must recognize the legitimacy of different opinions with regard to temporal solutions, and respect citizens, who, even as a group, defend their points of view by honest methods. Political parties, for their part, must promote those things which in their judgment are required for the common good; it is never allowable to give their interests priority over the common good.

Great care must be taken about civic and political formation, which is of the utmost necessity today for the population as a whole, and especially for youth, so that all citizens can play their part in the life of the political community. Those who are suited or can become suited should prepare themselves for the difficult, but at the same time, the very noble art of politics,[8] and should seek to practice this art without regard for their own interests or for material advantages. With integrity and wisdom, they must take action against any form of injustice and tyranny, against arbitrary domination by an individual or a political party, and any intolerance. They should dedicate themselves to the service of all with sincerity and fairness, indeed, with the charity and fortitude demanded by political life.

76. It is very important, especially where a pluralistic society prevails, that there be a correct notion of the relationship between the political community and the Church, and a clear distinction between the tasks which Christians undertake, individually or as a group, on their own responsibility as citizens guided by the dictates of a Christian conscience, and the activities which, in union with their pastors, they carry out in the name of the Church.

The Church, by reason of her role and competence, is not identified in any way with the political community nor bound to any political system. She is at once a sign and a safeguard of the transcendent character of the human person.

The Church and the political community in their own fields are autonomous and independent from each other. Yet both, under different titles, are devoted to the personal and social vocation of the same men. The more that both foster sounder cooperation between themselves with due consideration for the circumstances of time and place, the more effectively will their service be exercised for the good of all. For man's horizons are not limited only to the temporal order; while living in the context of human history, he preserves intact his eternal vocation. The Church, for her part, founded on the love of the Redeemer, contributes toward the reign of justice and charity within the borders of a nation and between nations. By preaching the truths of the Gospel, and bringing to bear on all fields of human endeavor the light of her doctrine and of a Christian witness, she respects and fosters the political freedom and responsibility of citizens.

The Apostles, their successors, and those who cooperate with them, are sent to announce to mankind Christ, the Savior. Their apostolate is based on the power of God, Who very often shows forth the strength of the Gospel on the weakness of its witnesses. All those dedicated to the ministry of God's Word must use the ways and means proper to the Gospel which in a great many respects differ from the means proper to the earthly city.

There are, indeed, close links between earthly things and those elements of man's condition which transcend the world. The Church herself makes use of temporal things insofar as her own mission requires it. She, for her part, does not place her trust in the privileges offered by civil authority. She will even give up the exercise of certain rights which have been legitimately acquired, if it becomes clear that their use will cast doubt on the sincerity of her witness or that new ways of life demand new methods. It is only right, however, that at all times and in all places, the Church should have true freedom to preach the faith, to teach her social doctrine, to exercise her role freely among men, and also to pass moral judgment in those matters which regard public order when the fundamental rights of a person or the salvation of souls require it. In this, she should make use of all the means—but only those—which accord with the Gospel and which correspond to the general good according to the diversity of times and circumstances.

While faithfully adhering to the Gospel and fulfilling her mission to the world, the Church, whose duty it is to foster and elevate[9] all that is found to be true, good, and beautiful in the human community, strengthens peace among men for the glory of God.[10]

The Church's Role in Society
Gaudium et Spes 76

**Pope
Benedict XVI**
———
*Deus Caritas Est
29*

The formation of just structures is not directly the duty of the Church, but belongs to the world of politics, the sphere of the autonomous use of reason. The Church has an indirect duty here, in that she is called to contribute to the purification of reason and to the reawakening of those moral forces without which just structures are neither established nor prove effective in the long run.

CHAPTER V
The Fostering of Peace and the Promotion of a Community of Nations

77. In our generation when men continue to be afflicted by acute hardships and anxieties arising from the ravages of war or the threat of it, the whole

human family faces an hour of supreme crisis in its advance toward maturity. Moving gradually together and everywhere more conscious already of its unity, this family cannot accomplish its task of constructing for all men everywhere a world more genuinely human unless each person devotes himself to the cause of peace with renewed vigor. Thus it happens that the Gospel message, which is in harmony with the loftier strivings and aspirations of the human race, takes on a new luster in our day as it declares that the artisans of peace are blessed "because they will be called the sons of God" (Matt. 5:9).

Consequently, as it points out the authentic and noble meaning of peace and condemns the frightfulness of war, the Council wishes passionately to summon Christians to cooperate, under the help of Christ the author of peace, with all men in securing among themselves a peace based on justice and love and in setting up the instruments of peace.

78. Peace is not merely the absence of war; nor can it be reduced solely to the maintenance of a balance of power between enemies; nor is it brought about by dictatorship. Instead, it is rightly and appropriately called an enterprise of justice. Peace results from that order structured into human society by its divine Founder, and actualized by men as they thirst after ever greater justice. The common good of humanity finds its ultimate meaning in the eternal law. But since the concrete demands of this common good are constantly changing as time goes on, peace is never attained once and for all, but must be built up ceaselessly. Moreover, since the human will is unsteady and wounded by sin, the achievement of peace requires a constant mastering of passions and the vigilance of lawful authority.

But this is not enough. This peace on earth cannot be obtained unless personal well-being is safeguarded and men freely and trustingly share with one another the riches of their inner spirits and their talents. A firm determination to respect other men and peoples and their dignity, as well as the studied practice of brotherhood are absolutely necessary for the establishment of peace. Hence peace is likewise the fruit of love, which goes beyond what justice can provide.

That earthly peace which arises from love of neighbor symbolizes and results from the peace of Christ which radiates from God the Father. For by the cross the incarnate Son, the prince of peace reconciled all men with God. By thus restoring all men to the unity of one people and one body, He slew hatred in His own flesh; and, after being lifted on high by His resurrection, He poured forth the spirit of love into the hearts of men.

For this reason, all Christians are urgently summoned to do in love what the truth requires, and to join with all true peacemakers in pleading for peace and bringing it about.

Motivated by this same spirit, we cannot fail to praise those who renounce the use of violence in the vindication of their rights and who resort to methods of defense which are otherwise available to weaker parties too, provided this can be done without injury to the rights and duties of others or of the community itself.

Insofar as men are sinful, the threat of war hangs over them, and hang over them it will until the return of Christ. But insofar as men vanquish sin by a union of love, they will vanquish violence as well and make these words come true: "They shall turn their swords into plough-shares, and their spears into sickles. Nation shall not lift up sword against nation, neither shall they learn war any more" (Isa. 2:4).

SECTION 1
The Avoidance of War

79. Even though recent wars have wrought physical and moral havoc on our world, the devastation of battle still goes on day by day in some part of the world. Indeed, now that every kind of weapon produced by modern science is used in war, the fierce character of warfare threatens to lead the combatants to a savagery far surpassing that of the past. Furthermore, the complexity of the modern world and the intricacy of international relations allow guerrilla warfare to be drawn out by new methods of deceit and subversion. In many cases the use of terrorism is regarded as a new way to wage war.

Contemplating this melancholy state of humanity, the council wishes, above all things else, to recall the permanent binding force of universal natural law and its all-embracing principles. Man's conscience itself gives ever more emphatic voice to these principles. Therefore, actions which deliberately conflict with these same principles, as well as orders commanding such actions are criminal, and blind obedience cannot excuse those who yield to them. The most infamous among these are actions designed for the methodical extermination of an entire people, nation, or ethnic minority. Such actions must be vehemently condemned as horrendous crimes. The courage of those who fearlessly and openly resist those who issue such commands merits supreme commendation.

On the subject of war, quite a large number of nations have subscribed to international agreements aimed at making military activity and its consequences less inhuman. Their stipulations deal with such matters as the treatment of wounded soldiers and prisoners. Agreements of this sort must be honored. Indeed they should be improved upon so that the frightfulness of war can be better and more workably held in check. All men, especially government officials and experts in these matters, are bound to do everything they can to effect these improvements. Moreover, it seems right that laws make humane provisions for the case of those who for reasons of conscience refuse to bear arms, provided however, that they agree to serve the human community in some other way.

Certainly, war has not been rooted out of human affairs. As long as the danger of war remains and there is no competent and sufficiently powerful authority at the international level, governments cannot be denied the right to legitimate defense once every means of peaceful settlement has been exhausted. State authorities and others who share public responsibility have the duty to conduct such grave matters soberly and to protect the welfare of the people entrusted to their care. But it is one thing to undertake military action for the just defense of the people, and something else again to seek the subjugation of other nations. Nor, by the same token, does the mere fact that war has unhappily begun mean that all is fair between the warring parties.

Those too who devote themselves to the military service of their country should regard themselves as the agents of security and freedom of peoples. As long as they fulfill this role properly, they are making a genuine contribution to the establishment of peace.

80. The horror and perversity of war is immensely magnified by the addition of scientific weapons. For acts of war involving these weapons can inflict massive and indiscriminate destruction, thus going far beyond the bounds of legitimate defense. Indeed, if the kind of instruments which can now be found in the armories of the great nations were to be employed to their fullest, an almost total and altogether reciprocal slaughter of each side by the other would follow, not to mention the widespread devastation that would take place in the world and the deadly aftereffects that would be spawned by the use of weapons of this kind.

All these considerations compel us to undertake an evaluation of war with an entirely new attitude.[1] The men of our time must realize that they will have to give a somber reckoning of their deeds of war, for the course of the future will depend greatly on the decisions they make today.

With these truths in mind, this most holy synod makes its own the condemnations of total war already pronounced by recent popes,[2] and issues the following declaration.

Any act of war aimed indiscriminately at the destruction of entire cities or extensive areas along with their population is a crime against God and man himself. It merits unequivocal and unhesitating condemnation.

The unique hazard of modern warfare consists in this: it provides those who possess modern scientific weapons with a kind of occasion for perpetrating just such abominations; moreover, through a certain inexorable chain of events, it can catapult men into the most atrocious decisions. That such may never truly happen in the future, the bishops of the whole world gathered together, beg all men, especially government officials and military leaders, to give unremitting thought to their gigantic responsibility before God and the entire human race.

81. To be sure, scientific weapons are not amassed solely for use in war. Since the defensive strength of any nation is considered to be dependent upon its capacity for immediate retaliation, this accumulation of arms, which increases each year, likewise serves, in a way heretofore unknown, as deterrent to possible enemy attack. Many regard this procedure as the most effective way by which peace of a sort can be maintained between nations at the present time.

Whatever be the facts about this method of deterrence, men should be convinced that the arms race in which an already considerable number of countries are engaged is not a safe way to preserve a steady peace, nor is the so-called balance resulting from this race a sure and authentic peace. Rather than being eliminated thereby, the causes of war are in danger of being gradually aggravated. While extravagant sums are being spent for the furnishing of ever new weapons, an adequate remedy cannot be provided for the multiple miseries afflicting the whole modern world. Disagreements between nations are not really and radically healed; on the contrary, they spread the infection to other parts of the earth. New approaches based on reformed attitudes must be taken to remove this trap and to emancipate the world from its crushing anxiety through the restoration of genuine peace.

Therefore, we say it again: the arms race is an utterly treacherous trap for humanity, and one which ensnares the poor to an intolerable degree. It is much to be feared that if this race persists, it will eventually spawn all the lethal ruin whose path it is now making ready. Warned by the calamities which the human race has made possible, let us make use of the interlude granted us from above and for which we are thankful to become more conscious of our own responsibility and to find means for resolving our disputes in a manner more worthy of man. Divine Providence urgently demands of us that we free ourselves from the age-old slavery of war. If we refuse to make this effort, we do not know where we will be led by the evil road we have set upon.

It is our clear duty, therefore, to strain every muscle in working for the time when all war can be completely outlawed by international consent. This goal undoubtedly requires the establishment of some universal public authority acknowledged as such by all and endowed with the power to safeguard on the behalf of all, security, regard for justice, and respect for rights. But before this hoped for authority can be set up, the highest existing international centers must devote themselves vigorously to the pursuit of better means for obtaining common security. Since peace must be born of mutual trust between nations and not be imposed on them through a fear of the available weapons, everyone must labor to put an end at last to the arms race, and to make a true beginning of disarmament, not unilaterally indeed, but proceeding at an equal pace according to agreement, and backed up by true and workable safeguards.[3]

Just War

Gaudium et Spes 79–81 | Bishop Barron

The council fathers stand with the Catholic tradition in asserting the right to legitimate national self-defense "once every means of peaceful settlement has been exhausted." But they remind us, following John XXIII, that the weapons of modern war have compelled us to adjust our understanding of the just war criteria:

"Any act of war aimed indiscriminately at the destruction of entire cities or extensive areas along with their population is a crime against God and man himself. It merits unequivocal and unhesitating condemnation."

Further, they strongly condemn the arms race, "an utterly treacherous trap for humanity, and one which ensnares the poor to an intolerable degree." The council fathers even go so far as to issue a passionate call for an end to all war: "Divine Providence urgently demands of us that we free ourselves from the age-old slavery of war. . . . It is our clear duty, therefore, to strain every muscle in working for the time when all war can be completely outlawed by international consent."

In connection with this, they call for a truly international authority "with the power to safeguard on the behalf of all, security, regard for justice, and respect for rights."

According to the Catholic social teaching tradition, going to war can be undertaken morally only when definite criteria are met. These are 1) declaration by a competent authority,

2) the presence of a just cause, 3) some proportion between the good to be achieved and the negativity of the war, 4) right intention on the part of those engaged in the conflict, 5) the war being undertaken only after all other attempts to resolve the conflict have been exhausted, and 6) a reasonable hope of success.

The Church does not stake out a pacifist position. It holds that sometimes, in our finite and conflictual world, violence has to be used in defense of certain basic goods. However, it clearly insists that the criteria provided by the just war theory—as *Gaudium et Spes* reminds us in this passage—should be strictly rather than loosely applied.

---

82. In the meantime, efforts which have already been made and are still underway to eliminate the danger of war are not to be underrated. On the contrary, support should be given to the good will of the very many leaders who work hard to do away with war, which they abominate. These men, although burdened by the extremely weighty preoccupations of their high office, are nonetheless moved by the very grave peacemaking task to which they are bound, even if they cannot ignore the complexity of matters as they stand. We should fervently ask God to give these men the strength to go forward perseveringly and to follow through courageously on this work of building peace with vigor. It is a work of supreme love for mankind. Today it certainly demands that they extend their thoughts and their spirit beyond the confines of their own nation, that they put aside national selfishness and ambition to dominate other nations, and that they nourish a profound reverence for the whole of humanity, which is already making its way so laboriously toward greater unity.

The problems of peace and of disarmament have already been the subject of extensive, strenuous, and constant examination. Together with international meetings dealing with these problems, such studies should be regarded as the first steps toward solving these serious questions, and should be promoted with even greater urgency by way of yielding concrete results in the future.

Nevertheless, men should take heed not to entrust themselves only to the efforts of some, while not caring about their own attitudes. For government officials who must at one and the same time guarantee the good of their own people and promote the universal good are very greatly dependent on public opinion and feeling. It does them no good to work for peace as long as feelings of hostility, contempt, and distrust, as well as racial hatred and unbending ideologies, continue to divide men and place them in opposing camps. Consequently there is above all a pressing need for a renewed education of attitudes and for new inspiration in public opinion. Those who are dedicated to the work of education, particularly of the young, or who mold public opinion, should consider it their most weighty task to instruct all in fresh sentiments of peace. Indeed, we all need a change of heart as we regard the entire world and those tasks which we can perform in unison for the betterment of our race.

But we should not let false hope deceive us. For unless enmities and hatred are put away and firm, honest agreements concerning world peace are reached in the future, humanity, which already is in the middle of a grave crisis, even though it is endowed with remarkable knowledge, will perhaps be brought to that dismal hour in which it will experience no peace other than the dreadful peace of death. But, while we say this, the Church of Christ, present in the midst of the anxiety of this age, does not cease to hope most firmly. She intends to propose to our age over and over again, in season and out of season, this apostolic message: "Behold, now is the acceptable time for a change of heart; behold! now is the day of salvation."[4]

SECTION 2
Setting Up An International Community

83. In order to build up peace above all the causes of discord among men, especially injustice, which foment wars must be rooted out. Not a few of these causes come from excessive economic inequalities and from putting

off the steps needed to remedy them. Other causes of discord, however, have their source in the desire to dominate and in a contempt for persons. And, if we look for deeper causes, we find them in human envy, distrust, pride, and other egotistical passions. Man cannot bear so many ruptures in the harmony of things. Consequently, the world is constantly beset by strife and violence between men, even when no war is being waged. Besides, since these same evils are present in the relations between various nations as well, in order to overcome or forestall them and to keep violence once unleashed within limits it is absolutely necessary for countries to cooperate more advantageously and more closely together and to organize together international bodies and to work tirelessly for the creation of organizations which will foster peace.

84. In view of the increasingly close ties of mutual dependence today between all the inhabitants and peoples of the earth, the apt pursuit and efficacious attainment of the universal common good now require of the community of nations that it organize itself in a manner suited to its present responsibilities, especially toward the many parts of the world which are still suffering from unbearable want.

To reach this goal, organizations of the international community, for their part, must make provision for men's different needs, both in the fields of social life—such as food supplies, health, education, labor, and also in certain special circumstances which can crop up here and there, e.g., the need to promote the general improvement of developing countries, or to alleviate the distressing conditions in which refugees dispersed throughout the world find themselves, or also to assist migrants and their families.

Already existing international and regional organizations are certainly well-deserving of the human race. These are the first efforts at laying the foundations on an international level for a community of all men to work for the solution to the serious problems of our times, to encourage progress everywhere, and to obviate wars of whatever kind. In all of these activities the Church takes joy in the spirit of true brotherhood flourishing between Christians and non-Christians as it strives to make ever more strenuous efforts to relieve abundant misery.

85. The present solidarity of mankind also calls for a revival of greater international cooperation in the economic field. Although nearly all peoples have become autonomous, they are far from being free of every

form of undue dependence, and far from escaping all danger of serious internal difficulties.

The development of a nation depends on human and financial aids. The citizens of each country must be prepared by education and professional training to discharge the various tasks of economic and social life. But this in turn requires the aid of foreign specialists who, when they give aid, will not act as overlords, but as helpers and fellow-workers. Developing nations will not be able to procure material assistance unless radical changes are made in the established procedures of modern world commerce. Other aid should be provided as well by advanced nations in the form of gifts, loans, or financial investments. Such help should be accorded with generosity and without greed on the one side, and received with complete honesty on the other side.

If an authentic economic order is to be established on a world-wide basis, an end will have to be put to profiteering, to national ambitions, to the appetite for political supremacy, to militaristic calculations, and to machinations for the sake of spreading and imposing ideologies.

The Reform of International Organizations
Gaudium et Spes 84–85

Pope Benedict XVI

Caritas in Veritate 67

There is urgent need of a true world political authority, as my predecessor Blessed John XXIII indicated some years ago. Such an authority would need to be regulated by law, to observe consistently the principles of subsidiarity and solidarity, to seek to establish the common good, and *to make a commitment to securing authentic integral human development inspired by the values of charity in truth.* Furthermore, such an authority would need to be universally recognized and to be vested with the effective power to ensure security for all, regard for justice, and respect for rights (see GS 81). Obviously it would have to have the authority to ensure compliance with its decisions from all parties, and also with the coordinated measures adopted in various international forums. Without this, despite the great progress accomplished in various sectors, international law would risk being conditioned by the balance of power among the strongest nations. The integral development of peoples and international cooperation require the establishment of a greater degree of international ordering, marked by subsidiarity, for the management of globalization. They also require the construction of a social order that at last conforms to the moral order, to the interconnection between moral and social spheres, and to the link between politics and the economic and civil spheres, as envisaged by the Charter of the United Nations.

86. The following norms seem useful for such cooperation:

a) Developing nations should take great pains to seek as the object for progress to express and secure the total human fulfillment of their citizens. They should bear in mind that progress arises and grows above all out of the labor and genius of the nations themselves because it has to be based, not only on foreign aid, but especially on the full utilization of their own resources, and on the development of their own culture and traditions. Those who exert the greatest influence on others should be outstanding in this respect.

b) On the other hand, it is a very important duty of the advanced nations to help the developing nations in discharging their above-mentioned responsibilities. They should therefore gladly carry out on their own home front those spiritual and material readjustments that are required for the realization of this universal cooperation.

Consequently, in business dealings with weaker and poorer nations, they should be careful to respect their profit, for these countries need the income they receive on the sale of their homemade products to support themselves.

c) It is the role of the international community to coordinate and promote development, but in such a way that the resources earmarked for this purpose will be allocated as effectively as possible, and with complete equity. It is likewise this community's duty, with due regard for the principle of subsidiarity, so to regulate economic relations throughout the world that these will be carried out in accordance with the norms of justice.

Suitable organizations should be set up to foster and regulate international business affairs, particularly with the underdeveloped countries, and to compensate for losses resulting from an excessive inequality of power among the various nations. This type of organization, in unison with technical, cultural, and financial aid, should provide the help which developing nations need so that they can advantageously pursue their own economic advancement.

d) In many cases there is an urgent need to revamp economic and social structures. But one must guard against proposals of technical solutions that are untimely. This is particularly true of those solutions providing man with material conveniences, but nevertheless contrary to man's spiritual nature and advancement. For "not by bread alone does man live, but by every word which proceeds from the mouth of God" (Matt. 4:4). Every sector of the family of man carries within itself and in its best traditions some portion of the spiritual treasure entrusted by God to humanity, even though many may not be aware of the source from which it comes.

87. International cooperation is needed today especially for those peoples who, besides facing so many other difficulties, likewise undergo pressures due to a rapid increase in population. There is an urgent need to explore, with the full and intense cooperation of all, and especially of the wealthier nations, ways whereby the human necessities of food and a suitable education can be furnished and shared with the entire human community. But some peoples could greatly improve upon the conditions of their life if they would change over from antiquated methods of farming to the new technical methods, applying them with needed prudence according to their own circumstances. Their life would likewise be improved by the establishment of a better social order and by a fairer system for the distribution of land ownership.

Governments undoubtedly have rights and duties, within the limits of their proper competency, regarding the population problem in their respective countries, for instance, in the line of social and family life legislation, or regarding the migration of country-dwellers to the cities, or with respect to information concerning the condition and needs of the country. Since men today are giving thought to this problem and are so greatly disturbed over it, it is desirable in addition that Catholic specialists, especially in the universities, skillfully pursue and develop studies and projects on all these matters.

But there are many today who maintain that the increase in world population, or at least the population increase in some countries, must be radically curbed by every means possible and by any kind of intervention on the part of public authority. In view of this contention, the council urges everyone to guard against solutions, whether publicly or privately supported, or at times even imposed, which are contrary to the moral law. For in keeping with man's inalienable right to marry and generate children, a decision concerning the number of children they will have depends on the right judgment of the parents and it cannot in any way be left to the judgment of public authority. But since the judgment of the parents presupposes a rightly formed conscience, it is of the utmost importance that the way be open for everyone to develop a correct and genuinely human responsibility which respects the divine law and takes into consideration the circumstances of the situation and the time. But sometimes this requires an improvement in educational and social conditions, and, above all, formation in religion or at least a complete moral training. Men should discreetly be informed, furthermore, of scientific advances in exploring methods whereby spouses can be helped in regulating the number of their children and whose safeness has been well proven and whose harmony with the moral order has been ascertained.

88. Christians should cooperate willingly and wholeheartedly in establishing an international order that includes a genuine respect for all freedoms and amicable brotherhood between all. This is all the more pressing since the greater part of the world is still suffering from so much poverty that it is as if Christ Himself were crying out in these poor to beg the charity of the disciples. Do not let men, then, be scandalized because some countries with a majority of citizens who are counted as Christians have an abundance of wealth, whereas others are deprived of the necessities of life and are tormented with hunger, disease, and every kind of misery. The spirit of poverty and charity are the glory and witness of the Church of Christ.

Those Christians are to be praised and supported, therefore, who volunteer their services to help other men and nations. Indeed, it is the duty of the whole People of God, following the word and example of the bishops, to alleviate as far as they are able the sufferings of the modern age. They should do this too, as was the ancient custom in the Church, out of the substance of their goods, and not only out of what is superfluous.

The procedure of collecting and distributing aids, without being inflexible and completely uniform, should nevertheless be carried on in an orderly fashion in dioceses, nations, and throughout the entire world. Wherever it seems convenient, this activity of Catholics should be carried on in unison with other Christian brothers. For the spirit of charity does not forbid, but on the contrary commands that charitable activity be carried out in a careful and orderly manner. Therefore, it is essential for those who intend to dedicate themselves to the services of the developing nations to be properly trained in appropriate institutes.

89. Since, in virtue of her mission received from God, the Church preaches the Gospel to all men and dispenses the treasures of grace, she contributes to the ensuring of peace everywhere on earth and to the placing of the fraternal exchange between men on solid ground by imparting knowledge of the divine and natural law. Therefore, to encourage and stimulate cooperation among men, the Church must be clearly present in the midst of the community of nations both through her official channels and through the full and sincere collaboration of all Christians—a collaboration motivated solely by the desire to be of service to all.

This will come about more effectively if the faithful themselves, conscious of their responsibility as men and as Christians will exert their influence in their own milieu to arouse a ready willingness to cooperate with the international community. Special care must be given, in both religious and civil education, to the formation of youth in this regard.

New Forms of the Areopagus
Gaudium et Spes 89

Pope St. John Paul II

———

Redemptoris Missio
37

The first Areopagus of the modern age is the world of communications, which is unifying humanity and turning it into what is known as a "global village." The means of social communication have become so important as to be for many the chief means of information and education, of guidance and inspiration in their behavior as individuals, families, and within society at large. In particular, the younger generation is growing up in a world conditioned by the mass media. To some degree perhaps this Areopagus has been neglected. Generally, preference has been given to other means of preaching the Gospel and of Christian education, while the mass media are left to the initiative of individuals or small groups and enter into pastoral planning only in a secondary way. Involvement in the mass media, however, is not meant merely to strengthen the preaching of the Gospel. There is a deeper reality involved here: since the very evangelization of modern culture depends to a great extent on the influence of the media, it is not enough to use the media simply to spread the Christian message and the Church's authentic teaching. It is also necessary to integrate that message into the "new culture" created by modern communications. This is a complex issue, since the "new culture" originates not just from whatever content is eventually expressed, but from the very fact that there exist new ways of communicating, with new languages, new techniques, and a new psychology. Pope Paul VI said that "the split between the Gospel and culture is undoubtedly the tragedy of our time," and the field of communications fully confirms this judgment.

There are many other forms of the "Areopagus" in the modern world toward which the Church's missionary activity ought to be directed; for example, commitment to peace, development, and the liberation of peoples; the rights of individuals and peoples, especially those of minorities; the advancement of women and children; safeguarding the created world. These too are areas which need to be illuminated with the light of the Gospel.

We must also mention the immense "Areopagus" of culture, scientific research, and international relations which promote dialogue and open up new possibilities. We would do well to be attentive to these modern areas of activity and to be involved in them. People sense that they are, as it were, traveling together across life's sea, and that they are called to ever greater unity and solidarity. Solutions to pressing problems must be studied, discussed, and worked out with the involvement of all. That is why international organizations and meetings are proving increasingly important in many sectors of human life, from culture to politics, from the economy to research. Christians who live and work in this international sphere must always remember their duty to bear witness to the Gospel.

90. An outstanding form of international activity on the part of Christians is found in the joint efforts which, both as individuals and in groups, they contribute to institutes already established or to be established for the encouragement of cooperation among nations. There are also various Catholic associations on an international level which can contribute in many ways to the building up of a peaceful and fraternal community of nations. These should be strengthened by augmenting in them the number of well qualified collaborators, by increasing needed resources, and by advantageously fortifying the coordination of their energies. For today both effective action and the need for dialogue demand joint projects. Moreover, such associations contribute much to the development of a universal outlook—something certainly appropriate for Catholics. They also help to form an awareness of genuine universal solidarity and responsibility.

Finally, it is very much to be desired that Catholics, in order to fulfill their role properly in the international community, will seek to cooperate actively and in a positive manner both with their separated brothers who together with them profess the Gospel of charity and with all men thirsting for true peace.

The council, considering the immensity of the hardships which still afflict the greater part of mankind today, regards it as most opportune that an organism of the universal Church be set up in order that both the justice and love of Christ toward the poor might be developed everywhere. The role of such an organism would be to stimulate the Catholic community to promote progress in needy regions and international social justice.

CONCLUSION

91. Drawn from the treasures of Church teaching, the proposals of this sacred synod look to the assistance of every man of our time, whether he believes in God, or does not explicitly recognize Him. If adopted, they will

promote among men a sharper insight into their full destiny, and thereby lead them to fashion the world more to man's surpassing dignity, to search for a brotherhood which is universal and more deeply rooted, and to meet the urgencies of our age with a gallant and unified effort born of love.

Undeniably this conciliar program is but a general one in several of its parts; and deliberately so, given the immense variety of situations and forms of human culture in the world. Indeed while it presents teaching already accepted in the Church, the program will have to be followed up and amplified since it sometimes deals with matters in a constant state of development. Still, we have relied on the word of God and the spirit of the Gospel. Hence we entertain the hope that many of our proposals will prove to be of substantial benefit to everyone, especially after they have been adapted to individual nations and mentalities by the faithful, under the guidance of their pastors.

92. By virtue of her mission to shed on the whole world the radiance of the Gospel message, and to unify under one Spirit all men of whatever nation, race, or culture, the Church stands forth as a sign of that brotherhood which allows honest dialogue and gives it vigor.

Such a mission requires in the first place that we foster within the Church herself mutual esteem, reverence, and harmony, through the full recognition of lawful diversity. Thus all those who compose the one People of God, both pastors and the general faithful, can engage in dialogue with ever abounding fruitfulness. For the bonds which unite the faithful are mightier than anything dividing them. Hence, let there be unity in what is necessary; freedom in what is unsettled, and charity in any case.

Our hearts embrace also those brothers and communities not yet living with us in full communion; to them we are linked nonetheless by our profession of the Father and the Son and the Holy Spirit, and by the bond of charity. We do not forget that the unity of Christians is today awaited and desired by many, too, who do not believe in Christ; for the farther it advances toward truth and love under the powerful impulse of the Holy Spirit, the more this unity will be a harbinger of unity and peace for the world at large. Therefore, by common effort and in ways which are today increasingly appropriate for seeking this splendid goal effectively, let us take pains to pattern ourselves after the Gospel more exactly every day, and thus work as brothers in rendering service to the human family. For, in Christ Jesus this family is called to the family of the sons of God.

We think cordially too of all who acknowledge God, and who preserve in their traditions precious elements of religion and humanity. We want frank conversation to compel us all to receive the impulses of the Spirit faithfully and to act on them energetically.

For our part, the desire for such dialogue, which can lead to truth through love alone, excludes no one, though an appropriate measure of prudence must undoubtedly be exercised. We include those who cultivate outstanding qualities of the human spirit, but do not yet acknowledge the Source of these qualities. We include those who oppress the Church and harass her in manifold ways. Since God the Father is the origin and purpose of all men, we are all called to be brothers. Therefore, if we have been summoned to the same destiny, human and divine, we can and we should work together without violence and deceit in order to build up the world in genuine peace.

The Meaning of Dialogue

Gaudium et Spes 92

**Pope
St. John Paul II**

———

Ut Unum Sint 28

If prayer is the "soul" of ecumenical renewal and of the yearning for unity, it is the basis and support for *everything the Council defines as "dialogue."* This definition is certainly not unrelated to today's *personalist way of thinking*. The capacity for "dialogue" is rooted in the nature of the person and his dignity. As seen by philosophy, this approach is linked to the Christian truth concerning man as expressed by the Council: man is in fact "the only creature on earth which God willed for itself"; thus he cannot "fully find himself except through a sincere gift of himself" (GS 24). Dialogue is an indispensable step along the path *towards human self-realization*, the self-realization both of *each individual* and of *every human community*. Although the concept of "dialogue" might appear to give priority to the cognitive dimension (*dia-logos*), all dialogue implies a global, existential dimension. It involves the human subject in his or her entirety; dialogue between communities involves in a particular way the subjectivity of each.

This truth about dialogue, so profoundly expressed by Pope Paul VI in his Encyclical *Ecclesiam Suam*, was also taken up by the Council in its teaching and ecumenical activity. Dialogue is not simply an exchange of ideas. In some way it is always a "sharing of gifts" (LG 13).

93. Mindful of the Lord's saying: "by this will all men know that you are my disciples, if you have love for one another" (John 13:35), Christians cannot yearn for anything more ardently than to serve the men of the modern world with mounting generosity and success. Therefore, by holding faithfully to the Gospel and benefiting from its resources, by joining with every man who loves and practices justice, Christians have shouldered a gigantic task for fulfillment in this world, a task concerning which they must give a reckoning to Him who will judge every man on the last of days.

Not everyone who cries, "Lord, Lord," will enter into the kingdom of heaven, but those who do the Father's will by taking a strong grip on the work at hand. Now, the Father wills that in all men we recognize Christ our brother and love Him effectively, in word and in deed. By thus giving witness to the truth, we will share with others the mystery of the heavenly Father's love. As a consequence, men throughout the world will be aroused to a lively hope—the gift of the Holy Spirit—that some day at last they will be caught up in peace and utter happiness in that fatherland radiant with the glory of the Lord.

"Now to Him who is able to accomplish all things in a measure far beyond what we ask or conceive, in keeping with the power that is at work in us—to Him be glory in the Church and in Christ Jesus, down through all the ages of time without end. Amen" (Eph. 3:20–21).

NOTES

PREFACE

1   The Pastoral Constitution "De Ecclesia in Mundo Huius Temporis" is made up of two parts; yet it constitutes an organic unity. By way of explanation: the constitution is called "pastoral" because, while resting on doctrinal principles, it seeks to express the relation of the Church to the world and modern mankind. The result is that, on the one hand, a pastoral emphasis is not overlooked in the first part, and, on the other hand, a doctrinal emphasis is not overlooked in the second part. In the first part, the Church develops her teaching on man, on the world which is the enveloping context of man's existence, and on man's relations to his fellow men. In part two, the Church gives closer consideration to various aspects of modern life and human society; special consideration is given to those questions and problems which, in this general area, seem to have a greater urgency in our day. As a result in part two the subject matter which is viewed in the light of doctrinal principles is made up of diverse elements. Some elements have a permanent value; others, only a transitory one. Consequently, the constitution must be interpreted according to the general norms of theological interpretation. Interpreters must bear in mind—especially in part two— the changeable circumstances which the subject matter, by its very nature, involves.

2   See John 18:37; Matt. 20:28; Mark 10:45.

INTRODUCTION

1   See Rom. 7:14 ff.

2   See 2 Cor. 5:15.

3   See Acts 4:12.

4   See Heb. 13:8.

5   See Col. 1:15.

PART I

CHAPTER I

1   See Gen. 1:26, Wis. 2:23.

2   See Sir. 17:3–10.

3   See Rom. 1:21–25.

4   See John 8:34.

5   See Dan. 3:57–90.

6   See 1 Cor. 6:13–20.

7   See 1 Kings 16:7; Jer. 17:10.

8   See Sir. 17:7–8.

9   See Rom. 2:15–16.

10   See Pius XII, *Radio address on the correct formation of a Christian conscience in the young*, March 23, 1952: AAS (1952), p. 271.

11   See Matt. 22:37–40; Gal. 5:14.

12   See Sir. 15:14.

13   See 2 Cor. 5:10.

14   See Wis. 1:13; 2:23–24; Rom. 5:21; 6:23; James 1:15.

15   See 1 Cor. 15:56–57.

16   See Pius XI, encyclical letter *Divini Redemptoris*, March 19, 1937: AAS 29 (1937), pp. 65–106; Pius XII, encyclical letter *Ad Apostolorum Principis*, June 29, 1958: AAS 50 (1958) pp. 601–614; John XXIII, encyclical letter *Mater et Magistra* May 15, 1961: AAS 53 (1961), pp. 451–453; Paul VI, *Ecclesiam Suam*, Aug. 6, 1964: AAS 56 (1964), pp. 651–653.

17   See *Dogmatic Constitution on the Church*, Chapter I, n. 8.

18   See Phil. 1:27.

19   St. Augustine, *Confessions* 1, 1: PL 32, 661.

20   See Rom. 5:14. See Tertullian, *De carnis resurrectione* 6: "The shape that the slime of the earth was given was intended with a view to Christ, the future man.": P. 2, 282; CSEL 47, p. 33, l. 12–13.

21   See 2 Cor. 4:4.

22   See *Second Council of Constantinople*, canon 7: "The divine Word was not changed into a human nature, nor was a human nature absorbed by the Word." Denzinger 219 (428); see also Third Council of Constantinople: "For just as His most holy and immaculate human nature, though deified, was not destroyed (theotheisa ouk anerethe), but rather remained in its proper state and mode of being": Denzinger 291 (556); see Council of Chalcedon: "to be acknowledged in two natures, without confusion, change, division, or separation." Denzinger 148 (302).

23   See *Third Council of Constantinople*: "and so His human will, though deified, is not destroyed": Denzinger 291 (556).

24   See Heb. 4:15.

25   See 2 Cor. 5:18–19; Col. 1:20–22.

26   See 1 Pet. 2:21; Matt. 16:24; Luke 14:27.

27   See Rom. 8:29; Col. 3:10–14.

28   See Rom. 8:1–11.

29   See 2 Cor. 4:14.

30   See Phil. 3:19; Rom. 8:17.

31   See *Dogmatic Constitution on the Church*, Chapter 2, n. 16.

32   See Rom. 8:32.

33   See *The Byzantine Easter Liturgy*.

34   See Rom. 8:15 and Gal. 4:6; see also John 1:22 and John 3:1–2.

CHAPTER II

1   See John XXIII, encyclical letter *Mater et Magistra*, May 15, 1961: AAS 53 (1961), pp. 401–464, and encyclical letter *Pacem in Terris*, April 11, 1963: AAS 55 (1963), pp. 257–304; Paul VI, encyclical letter *Ecclesiam Suam*, Aug. 6, 1964: AAS 54 (1864) pp. 609–659.

2   See Luke 17:33.

3   See St. Thomas, 1 *Ethica Lect.* 1.

4   See John XXIII, encyclical letter *Mater et Magistra*: AAS 53 (1961), p. 418. See also Pius XI, encyclical letter *Quadragesimo Anno*: AAS 23 (1931), p. 222 ff.

5   See John XXIII, encyclical letter *Mater et Magistra*: AAS 53 (1961).

6   See Mark 2:27.

7   See John XXIII, encyclical letter *Pacem in Terris*: AAS 55 (1963), p. 266.

8   See James 2:15–16.

9   See Luke 16:18–31.

10   See John XXIII, encyclical letter *Pacem in Terris*: AAS 55 (1963), p. 299 and 300.

11   See Luke 6:37–38; Matt. 7:1–2; Rom. 2:1–11; 14:10, 14:10–12.

12   See Matt. 5:43–47.

13   See *Dogmatic Constitution on the Church*, Chapter II, n. 9.

14   See Exod. 24:1–8.

CHAPTER III

1   See Gen. 1:26–27; 9:3; Wis. 9:3.

2   See Ps. 8:7 and 10.

3   See John XXIII, encyclical letter *Pacem in Terris*: AAS 55 (1963), p. 297.

4   See Message to all mankind sent by the Fathers at the beginning of the Second Vatican Council, Oct. 20, 1962: AAS 54 (1962), p. 823.

5   See Paul VI, Address to the diplomatic corps, Jan 7, 1965: AAS 57 (1965), p. 232.

6   See First Vatican Council, *Dogmatic Constitution on the Catholic Faith*, Chapter III: Denz. 1785–1786 (3004–3005).

7   See Msgr. Pio Paschini, *Vita e opere di Galileo Galilei*, 2 volumes, Vatican Press (1964).

8   See Matt. 24:13; 13:24–30 and 36–43.

9   See 2 Cor. 6:10.

10   See John 1:3 and 14.

11   See Eph. 1:10.

12   See John 3:16; Rom. 5:8.

13   See Acts 2:36; Matt. 28:18.

14   See Rom. 15:16.

15   See Acts 1:7.

16   See 1 Cor. 7:31; St. Irenaeus, *Adversus haereses,* V, 36, PG, VIII, 1221.

17   See 2 Cor. 5:2; 2 Pet. 3:13.

18   See 1 Cor. 2:9; Rev. 21:4–5.

19   See 1 Cor. 15:42 and 53.

20   See 1 Cor. 13:8; 3:14.

21   See Rom. 8:19–21.

22   See Luke 9:25.

23   See Pius XI, encyclical letter *Quadragesimo Anno*: AAS 23 (1931), p. 207.

24   Preface of the Feast of Christ the King.

CHAPTER IV

1   See Paul VI, encyclical letter *Ecclesiam Suam*, III: AAS 56 (1964), pp. 637–659.

2   See Titus 3:4: "love of mankind."

3   See Eph. 1:3; 5:6; 13–14, 23.

4   *Dogmatic Constitution on the Church*, Chapter I, n. 8.

5   Ibid., Chapter II, no. 9.

6   Ibid., Chapter I, n. 8.

7   See ibid., Chapter IV, n. 38, with note 9*.

8   See Rom. 8:14–17.

9   See Matt. 22:39.

10   *Dogmatic Constitution on the Church,* Chapter II, n. 9.

11   See Pius XII, Address to the International Union of Institutes of Archeology, History and History of Art, March 9, 1956: AAS 48 (1965), p. 212: "Its divine Founder, Jesus Christ, has not given it any mandate or fixed any end of the cultural order. The goal which Christ assigns to it is strictly religious. . . . The Church must lead men to God, in order that they may be given over to him without reserve. . . . The Church can never lose sight of the strictly religious, supernatural goal. The meaning of all its activities, down to the last canon of its Code, can only cooperate directly or indirectly in this goal."

12   *Dogmatic Constitution on the Church,* Chapter I, n. 1.

13   See Heb. 13:14.

14   See 2 Thess. 3:6–13; Eph. 4:28.

15   See Isa. 58:1–12.

16   See Matt. 23:3–23; Mark 7:10–13.

17   See John XXIII, encyclical letter *Mater et Magistra,* IV: AAS 53 (1961), pp. 456–457; see I: AAS loc. cit., pp. 407, 410–411.

18   See *Dogmatic Constitution on the Church,* Chapter III, n. 28.

19   Ibid., n. 28.

20   See St. Ambrose, *De virginitate,* Chapter VIII, n. 48: ML 16, 278.

21   See *Dogmatic Constitution on the Church,* Chapter II, n. 15.

22   See *Dogmatic Constitution on the Church,* Chapter II, n. 13.

23   See Justin, *Dialogus cum Tryphone,* Chapter 110; MG 6, 729 (ed. Otto), 1897, pp. 391–393: ". . . but the greater the number of persecutions which are inflicted upon us, so much the greater the number of other men who become devout believers through the name of Jesus." See Tertullian, *Apologeticus,* Chapter L, 13: "Every time you mow us down like grass, we increase in number: the blood of Christians is a seed!" See *Dogmatic Constitution on the Church,* Chapter II, n. 9.

24   See *Dogmatic Constitution on the Church,* Chapter VII, n. 48.

25   See Paul VI, address given on Feb. 3, 1965.

PART II

CHAPTER I

1   See St. Augustine, *De Bene coniugali* PL 40, 375–376 and 394, St. Thomas, *Summa Theologica,* Suppl. Quaest. 49, art. 3 ad 1, *Decretum pro Armenis*: Denz.-Schoen. 1327; Pius XI, encyclical letter *Casti Connubii*: AAS 22 (1930), pp. 547–548; Denz.-Schoen. 3703–3714.

2   See Pius XI, encyclical letter *Casti Connubii*: AAS 22 (1930), pp. 546–547; Denz.-Schoen. 3706.

3   See Hosea 2; Jer. 3:6–13; Ezek. 16 and 23; Isa. 54.

4   See Matt. 9:15; Mark 2:19–20; Luke 5:34–35; John 3:29; see also 2 Cor. 11:2; Eph. 5:27; Rev. 19:7–8; 21:2 and 9.

5   See Eph. 5:25.

6   See *Dogmatic Constitution on the Church,* Chapter II, n. 11, para. 2; Chapter IV, n. 35, para. 3; Chapter V, n. 41, para. 5.

7   Pius XI, encyclical letter *Casti Connubii*: AAS 22 (1930), p. 583.

8   See 1 Tim. 5:3.

9   See Eph. 5:32.

10   See Gen. 2:22–24, Prov. 5:15–20; 31:10–31; Tob. 8:4–8; Cant. 1:2–3; 1:16; 4:16–5:1; 7:8–11; 1 Cor. 7:3–6; Eph. 5:25–33.

11   See Pius XI, encyclical letter *Casti Connubii*: AAS 22 (1930), p. 547 and 548; Denz.-
     Schoen. 3707.

12   See 1 Cor. 7:5.

13   See Pius XII, Address *Tra le visite*, Jan. 20, 1958: AAS 50 (1958), p. 91.

14   See Pius XI, encyclical letter *Casti Connubii*: AAS 22 (1930): Denz.-Schoen. 3716–
     3718, Pius XII, *Allocutio Conventui Unionis Italicae inter Obstetrices*, Oct. 29, 1951:
     AAS 43 (1951), pp. 835–854, Paul VI, *Address to a group of cardinals*, June 23 1964:
     AAS 56 (1964), pp. 581–589. Certain questions which need further and more careful
     investigation have been handed over, at the command of the Supreme Pontiff, to a
     commission for the study of population, family, and births, in order that, after it
     fulfills its function, the Supreme Pontiff may pass judgment. With the doctrine of
     the magisterium in this state, this holy synod does not intend to propose immediately
     concrete solutions.

15   See Eph. 5:16; Col. 4:5.

16   See *Sacramentarium Gregorianum*: PL 78, 262.

17   See Rom. 5:15 and 18; 6:5–11; Gal. 2:20.

18   See Eph. 5:25–27.

CHAPTER II

1   See Introductory statement of this constitution, n. 4 ff.

2   See Col. 3:2.

3   See Gen. 1:28.

4   See Prov. 8:30–31.

5   See St. Irenaeus, *Adversus haereses*, III, 11, 8 (ed. Sagnard p. 200; see ibid., 16, 6: pp.
     290–292; 21, 10–22: pp. 370–372; 22 3: p. 378; etc.).

6   See Eph. 1:10.

7   See the words of Pius XI to Father M. D. Roland-Gosselin: "It is necessary never to
     lose sight of the fact that the objective of the Church is to evangelize, not to civilize. If
     it civilizes, it is for the sake of evangelization." (Semaines sociales de France, Versailles,
     1936, pp. 461–462).

8   First Vatican Council, *Constitution on the Catholic Faith*: Denzinger 1795, 1799 (3015,
     3019). See Pius XI, encyclical letter *Quadragesimo Anno*: AAS 23 (1931), p. 190.

9   See John XXIII, encyclical letter *Pacem in Terris*: AAS 55 (1963), p. 260.

10   See John XXIII, encyclical letter *Pacem in Terris*: AAS 55 (1963), p. 283; Pius XII,
     Radio address, Dec. 24, 1941: AAS 34 (1942), pp. 16–17.

11   John XXIII, encyclical letter *Pacem in Terris:* AAS 55 (1963), p. 260.

12   See John XXIII, prayer delivered on Oct. 11, 1962, at the beginning of the council:
     AAS 54 (1962), p. 792.

13   See *Constitution on the Sacred Liturgy*, n. 123: AAS 56 (1964), p. 131; Paul VI,
     Discourse to the artists of Rome: AAS 56 (1964), pp. 439–442.

14   See Second Vatican Council, *Decree on Priestly Training* and *Declaration on Christian
     Education*.

15   See *Dogmatic Constitution on the Church*, Chapter IV, n. 37.

CHAPTER III

1   See Pius XII, Address on March 23, 1952: AAS 44 (1953), p. 273; John XXIII,
     Allocution to the Catholic Association of Italian Workers, May 1, 1959: AAS 51
     (1959), p. 358.

2   See Pius XI, encyclical letter *Quadragesimo Anno*: AAS 23 (1931), p. 190 ff; Pius XII, Address of March 23, 1952: AAS 44 (1952), p. 276 ff; John XXIII, encyclical letter *Mater et Magistra*: AAS 53 (19ff), p. 450; Vatican Council II, *Decree on the Media of Social Communication*, Chapter I, n. 6 AAS 56 (1964), p. 147.

3   See Matt. 16:26, Luke 16:1–31, Col. 3:17.

4   See Leo XIII, encyclical letter *Libertas*, in Acta Leonis XIII, t. VIII, p. 220 ff; Pius XI, encyclical letter *Quadragesimo Anno*: AAS 23 (1931), p. 191 ff; Pius XI, encyclical letter *Divini Redemptoris*: AAS 39 (1937), p. 65 ff; Pius XII, Nuntius natalicius 1941: AAS 34 (1942), p. 10 ff: John XXIII, encyclical letter *Mater et Magistra*: AAS 53 (1961), pp. 401–464.

5   In reference to agricultural problems see especially John XXIII, encyclical letter *Mater et Magistra*: AAS 53 (1961).

6   See Leo XIII, encyclical letter *Rerum Novarum*: AAS 23 (1890–91), p. 649, p. 662; Pius XI, encyclical letter *Quadragesimo Anno*: AAS 23 (1931), pp. 200–201; Pius XI, encyclical letter *Divini Redemptoris*: AAS 29 (1937), p. 92; Pius XII, Radio address on Christmas Eve 1942: AAS 35 (1943) p. 20; Pius XII, Allocution of June 13, 1943: AAS 35 (1943), p. 172; Pius XII, Radio address to the workers of Spain, March 11, 1951: AAS 43 (1951), p. 215; John XXIII, encyclical letter *Mater et Magistra*: AAS 53 (1961), p. 419.

7   See John XXIII, encyclical letter *Mater et Magistra*: AAS 53 (1961), pp. 408, 424, 427; however, the word "curatione" has been taken from the Latin text of the encyclical letter *Quadragesimo Anno*: AAS 23 (1931) p. 199. Under the aspect of the evolution of the question see also: Pius XII, Allocution of June 3, 1950: AAS 42 (1950) pp. 485–488; Paul VI, Allocution of June 8, 1964: AAS 56 (1964), pp. 573–579.

8   See Pius XII, encyclical *Sertum Laetitiae*: AAS 31 (1939), p. 642, John XXIII, Consistorial allocution: AAS 52 (1960), pp. 5–11; John XXIII, encyclical letter *Mater et Magistra*: AAS 53 (1961), p. 411.

9   See St. Thomas, *Summa Theologica*: II–II, q. 32, a. 5 ad 2; Ibid. q. 66, a. 2: see explanation in Leo XIII, encyclical letter *Rerum Novarum*: AAS 23 (1890–91) p. 651; see also Pius XII Allocution of June 1, 1941: AAS 33 (1941), p. 199; Pius XII, Birthday radio address 1954: AAS 47 (1955), p. 27.

10   See St. Basil, *Hom. in illud Lucae "Destruam horrea mea,"* n. 2 (PG 31, 263); Lactantius, *Divinarum institutionum*, lib. V. on justice (PL 6, 565 B); St. Augustine, *In Ioann*. Ev. tr. 50, n. 6 (PL 35, 1760); St. Augustine, *Enarratio* in Ps. CXLVII, 12 (PL 37, 192); St. Gregory the Great, *Homiliae* in Ev., hom. 20 (PL 76, 1165); St. Gregory the Great, *Regulae Pastoralis liber*, pars III c. 21 (PL 77 87); St. Bonaventure, *In III Sent*. d. 33, dub. 1 (ed Quaracchi, III, 728); St. Bonaventure, *In IV Sent*. d. 15, p. II, a. a q. 1 (ed. cit. IV, 371 b); q. de superfluo (ms. Assisi Bibl. Comun. 186, ff. 112a–113a); St. Albert the Great, *In III Sent*., d. 33, a.3, sol. 1 (ed. Borgnet XXVIII, 611); Id. *In IV Sent*. d. 15, a. 1 (ed. cit. XXIX, 494–497). As for the determination of what is superfluous in our day and age, see John XXIII, Radio-television message of Sept. 11, 1962: AAS 54 (1962) p. 682: "The obligation of every man, the urgent obligation of the Christian man, is to reckon what is superfluous by the measure of the needs of others, and to see to it that the administration and the distribution of created goods serve the common good."

11   In that case, the old principle holds true: "In extreme necessity all goods are common, that is, all goods are to be shared." On the other hand, for the order, extension, and manner by which the principle is applied in the proposed text, besides the modern

authors: see St. Thomas, *Summa Theologica* II–II, q. 66, a. 7. Obviously, for the correct application of the principle, all the conditions that are morally required must be met.

12   See Gratiam, *Decretum*, C. 21, dist. LXXXVI (ed. Friedberg I, 302). This axiom is also found already in PL 54, 591 A (see in Antonianum 27 (1952) 349–366) i.

13   See Leo XIII, encyclical letter *Rerum Novarum*: AAS 23 (1890–91) pp. 643–646, Pius XI, encyclical letter *Quadragesimo Anno*: AAS 23 (1931) p. 191; Pius XII, Radio message of June 1, 1941: AAS 33 (1941), p. 199; Pius XII, Radio message on Christmas Eve 1942: AAS 35 (1943), p. 17; Pius XII, Radio message of Sept. 1, 1944: AAS 36 (1944) p. 253; John XXIII, encyclical letter *Mater et Magistra*: AAS 53 (1961) pp. 428–429.

14   See Pius XI, encyclical letter *Quadragesimo Anno*: AAS 23 (1931) p. 214; John XXIII, encyclical letter *Mater et Magistra*: AAS 53 (1961), p. 429.

15   See Pius XII, Radio message of Pentecost 1941: AAS 44 (1941) p. 199, John XXIII, encyclical letter *Mater et Magistra*: AAS 53 (1961) p. 430.

16   For the right use of goods according to the doctrine of the New Testament, see Luke 3:11, 10:30 ff; 11:41; 1 Pet. 5:3, Mark 8:36; 12:39–41; James 5:1–6; 1 Tim. 6:8; Eph. 4:28; 1 Cor. 8:13; 1 John 3:17 ff.

CHAPTER IV

1   See John XXIII, encyclical letter *Mater et Magistra*: AAS 53 (1961), p. 417.

2   See John XXIII, ibid.

3   See Rom. 13:1–5.

4   See Rom. 13:5.

5   See Pius XII, Radio message, Dec. 24, 1942: AAS 35 (1943) pp. 9–24; Dec. 24, 1944: AAS 37 (1945), pp. 11–17; John XXIII encyclical letter *Pacem in Terris*: AAS 55 (1963), pp. 263, 271, 277, and 278.

6   See Pius XII, Radio message of June 7, 1941: AAS 33 (1941) p. 200: John XXIII, encyclical letter *Pacem in Terris*: l.c., p. 273 and 274.

7   See John XXIII, encyclical letter *Mater et Magistra*: AAS 53 (1961), p. 416.

8   Pius XI, Allocution "Ai dirigenti della Federazione Universitaria Cattolica." Discorsi di Pio XI (ed. Bertetto), Turin, vol. 1 (1960), p. 743.

9   See *Dogmatic Constitution on the Church*, Chapter II, n. 13.

10   See Luke 2:14.

CHAPTER V

1   See John XXIII, encyclical letter *Pacem in Terris*, April 11, 1963: AAS 55 (1963), p. 291; "Therefore in this age of ours which prides itself on its atomic power, it is irrational to believe that war is still an apt means of vindicating violated rights."

2   See Pius XII, Allocution of Sept. 30, 1954: AAS 46 (1954) p. 589; Radio message of Dec. 24, 1954: AAS 47 (1955), pp. 15 ff, John XXIII, encyclical letter *Pacem in Terris*: AAS 55 (1963), pp. 286–291; Paul VI, Allocution to the United Nations, Oct. 4, 1965.

3   See John XXIII, encyclical letter *Pacem in Terris*, where reduction of arms is mentioned: AAS 55 (1963), p. 287.

4   See 2 Cor. 2:6.

Closing Address to the Council

Pope St. Paul VI

Today we are concluding the Second Vatican Council. We bring it to a close at the fullness of its efficiency: the presence of so many of you here clearly demonstrates it; the well-ordered pattern of this assembly bears testimony to it; the normal conclusion of the work done by the council confirms it; the harmony of sentiments and decisions proclaims it. And if quite a few questions raised during the course of the council itself still await appropriate answers, this shows that its labors are now coming to a close not out of weariness, but in a state of vitality which this universal synod has awakened. In the post-conciliar period this vitality will apply, God willing, its generous and well-regulated energies to the study of such questions.

This council bequeaths to history an image of the Catholic Church symbolized by this hall, filled, as it is, with shepherds of souls professing the same faith, breathing the same charity, associated in the same communion of prayer, discipline, and activity and—what is marvelous— all desiring one thing: namely, to offer themselves like Christ, our Master and Lord, for the life of the Church and for the salvation of the world. This council hands over to posterity not only the image of the Church but also the patrimony of her doctrine and of her commandments, the "deposit" received from Christ and meditated upon through centuries, lived and expressed now and clarified in so many of its parts, settled and arranged in its integrity. The deposit, that is, which lives on by the divine power of truth and of grace which constitutes it, and is, therefore, able to vivify anyone who receives it and nourishes with it his own human existence.

What then was the council? What has it accomplished? The answer to these questions would be the logical theme of our present meditation. But it would require too much of our attention and time: this final and stupendous hour would not perhaps give us enough tranquility of mind to make such a synthesis. We should like to devote this precious moment to one single thought which bends down our spirits in humility and at the same time raises them up to the summit of our aspirations. And that thought is this: what is the religious value of this council? We refer to it as religious because of its direct relationship with the living God, that relationship which is the raison d'être of the Church, of all that she believes, hopes, and loves; of all that she is and does.

Could we speak of having given glory to God, of having sought knowledge and love of Him, of having made progress in our effort of contemplating Him, in our eagerness for honoring Him, and in the art of proclaiming Him to men who look up to us as to pastors and masters of the life of God? In all sincerity we think the answer is yes. Also because from this basic purpose there developed the guiding principle which was to give direction to the future council. Still fresh in our memory are the words uttered in this basilica by our venerated predecessor, John XXIII, whom we may in truth call the originator of this great synod. In his opening address to the council he had this to say: "The major interest of the Ecumenical Council is this: that the sacred heritage of Christian truth be safeguarded and expounded with greater efficacy. . . . Christ our Lord said: 'Seek first the kingdom of God and His justice,' and this word 'first' indicates what the primary direction of all our thoughts and energies must be."

His great purpose has now been achieved. To appreciate it properly it is necessary to remember the time in which it was realized: a time which everyone admits is orientated toward the conquest of the kingdom of earth rather than of that of heaven; a time in which forgetfulness of God has become habitual, and seems, quite wrongly, to be prompted by the progress of science; a time in which the fundamental act of the human person, more conscious now of himself and of his liberty, tends to pronounce in favor of his own absolute autonomy, in emancipation from every transcendent law; a time in which secularism seems the legitimate consequence of modern thought and the highest wisdom in the temporal ordering of society; a time, moreover, in which the soul of man has plumbed the depths of irrationality and desolation; a time, finally, which is characterized by upheavals and a hitherto unknown decline even in the great world religions.

It was at such a time as this that our council was held to the honor of God, in the name of Christ, and under the impulse of the Spirit: who "searcheth all things," "making us understand God's gifts to us" (cf. 1 Cor. 2:10–12), and who is now quickening the Church, giving her a vision at once profound and all-embracing of the life of the world. The theocentric and theological concept of man and the universe, almost in defiance of the charge of anachronism and irrelevance, has been given a new prominence by the council, through claims which the world will at first judge to be foolish, but which, we hope, it will later come to recognize as being truly human, wise, and salutary: namely, God is—and more, He is real, He lives, a personal, provident God, infinitely good; and not only good in Himself, but also immeasurably good to us. He will be recognized as Our Creator, our truth, our happiness; so much so that the effort to look on Him, and to center our heart in Him which we call contemplation, is the highest, the most perfect act of the spirit, the act which even today can and must be at the apex of all human activity.

Men will realize that the council devoted its attention not so much to divine truths, but rather, and principally, to the Church—her nature and composition, her ecumenical vocation, her apostolic and missionary activity. This secular religious society, which is the Church, has endeavored to carry out an act of reflection about herself, to know herself better, to define herself better and, in consequence, to set aright what she feels and what she commands. So much is true. But this introspection has not been an end in itself, has not been simply an exercise of human understanding or of a merely worldly culture. The Church has gathered herself together in deep spiritual awareness, not to produce a learned analysis of religious psychology, or an account of her own experiences, not even to devote herself to reaffirming her rights and explaining her laws. Rather, it was to find in herself, active and alive, the Holy Spirit, the word of Christ; and to probe more deeply still the mystery, the plan, and the presence of God above and within herself; to revitalize in herself that faith which is the secret of her confidence and of her wisdom, and that love which impels her to sing without ceasing the praises of God. "Cantare amantis est" (Song is the expression of a lover), says St. Augustine (Serm. 336; P. L. 38, 1472).

The council documents—especially the ones on divine revelation, the liturgy, the Church, priests, Religious, and the laity—leave wide open to view this primary and focal religious intention, and show how clear and fresh and rich is the spiritual stream which contact with the living God causes to well up in the heart of the Church, and flow out from it over the dry wastes of our world.

But we cannot pass over one important consideration in our analysis of the religious meaning of the council: it has been deeply committed to the study of the modern world. Never before perhaps, so much as on this occasion, has the Church felt the need to know, to draw near to, to understand, to penetrate, serve, and evangelize the society in which she lives; and to get to grips with it, almost to run after it, in its rapid and continuous change. This attitude, a response to the distances and divisions we have witnessed over recent centuries, in the last century and in our own especially, between the Church and secular society—this attitude has been strongly and unceasingly at work in the council; so much so that some have been inclined to suspect that an easy-going and excessive responsiveness to the outside world, to passing events, cultural fashions, temporary needs, an alien way of thinking . . . may have swayed persons and acts of the ecumenical synod, at the expense of the fidelity which is due to tradition, and this to the detriment of the religious orientation of the council itself. We do not believe that this shortcoming should be imputed to it, to its real and deep intentions, to its authentic manifestations.

We prefer to point out how charity has been the principal religious feature of this council. Now, no one can reprove as want of religion or infidelity to the Gospel such a basic orientation, when we recall that it is Christ Himself who taught us that love for our brothers is the distinctive mark of His disciples (cf. John 13:35); when we listen to the words of the apostle: "If he is to offer service pure and unblemished in the sight of God, who is our Father, he must take care of orphans and widows in their need, and keep himself untainted by the world" (James 1:27); and again: "He has seen his brother, and has no love for him; what love can he have for the God he has never seen?" (1 John 4:20).

Yes, the Church of the council has been concerned, not just with herself and with her relationship of union with God, but with man—man as he really is today: living man, man all wrapped up in himself, man who makes himself not only the center of his every interest but dares to claim that he is the principle and explanation of all reality. Every perceptible element in man, every one of the countless guises in which he appears, has, in a sense, been displayed in full view of the council Fathers, who, in their turn, are mere men, and yet all of them are pastors and brothers whose position accordingly fills them with solicitude and love. Among these guises we may cite man as the tragic actor of his own plays; man as the superman of yesterday and today, ever frail, unreal, selfish, and savage; man unhappy with himself as he laughs and cries; man the versatile actor ready to perform any part; man the narrow devotee of nothing but scientific reality; man as he is, a creature who thinks and loves and toils and is always waiting for something, the "growing son" (Gen. 49:22); man sacred because of the innocence of his childhood, because of the mystery of his poverty, because of the dedication of his suffering; man as an individual and man in society; man who lives in the glories of the past and dreams of those of the future; man the sinner and man the saint, and so on.

Secular humanism, revealing itself in its horrible anti-clerical reality has, in a certain sense, defied the council. The religion of the God who became man has met the religion (for such it is) of man who makes himself God. And what happened? Was there a clash, a battle, a condemnation? There could have been, but there was none. The old story of the Samaritan has been the model of the spirituality of the council. A feeling of boundless sympathy has permeated the whole of it. The attention of our council has been absorbed by the discovery of human needs (and these needs grow in proportion to the greatness which the son of the earth claims for himself). But we call upon those who term themselves modern humanists, and who have renounced the transcendent value of the highest realities, to give the council credit at least for one quality and to recognize our own new type of humanism: we, too, in fact, we more than any others, honor mankind.

And what aspect of humanity has this august senate studied? What goal under divine inspiration did it set for itself? It also dwelt upon humanity's ever twofold facet, namely, man's wretchedness and his greatness, his profound weakness—which is undeniable and cannot be cured by himself—and the good that survives in him which is ever marked by a hidden beauty and an invincible serenity. But one must realize that this council, which exposed itself to human judgment, insisted very much more upon this pleasant side of man, rather than on his unpleasant one. Its attitude was very much and deliberately optimistic. A wave of affection and admiration flowed from the council over the modern world of humanity. Errors were condemned, indeed, because charity demanded this no less than did truth, but for the persons themselves there was only warning, respect, and love. Instead of depressing diagnoses, encouraging remedies; instead of direful prognostics, messages of trust issued from the council to the present-day world. The modern world's values were not only respected but honored, its efforts approved, its aspirations purified and blessed.

You see, for example, how the countless different languages of peoples existing today were admitted for the liturgical expression of men's communication with God and God's communication with men: to man as such was recognized his fundamental claim to enjoy full possession of his rights and to his transcendental destiny. His supreme aspirations to life, to personal dignity, to his just liberty, to culture, to the renewal of the social order, to justice and peace were purified and promoted; and to all men was addressed the pastoral and missionary invitation to the light of the Gospel.

We can now speak only too briefly on the very many and vast questions, relative to human welfare, with which the council dealt. It did not attempt to resolve all the urgent problems of modern life; some of these have been reserved for a further study which the Church intends to make of them, many of them were presented in very restricted and general terms, and for that reason are open to further investigation and various applications.

But one thing must be noted here, namely, that the teaching authority of the Church, even though not wishing to issue extraordinary dogmatic pronouncements, has made thoroughly known its authoritative teaching on a number of questions which today weigh upon man's conscience and activity, descending, so to speak, into a dialogue with him, but ever preserving its own authority and force; it has spoken with the accommodating friendly voice of pastoral charity; its desire has been to be heard and understood by everyone; it has not merely concentrated on intellectual understanding but has also sought to express itself in simple, up-to-date, conversational style, derived from actual experience and a cordial approach which make it more vital, attractive, and persuasive; it has spoken to modern man as he is.

Another point we must stress is this: all this rich teaching is channeled in one direction, the service of mankind, of every condition, in every weakness and need. The Church has, so to say, declared herself the servant of humanity, at the very time when her teaching role and her pastoral government have, by reason of the council's solemnity, assumed greater splendor and vigor: the idea of service has been central.

It might be said that all this and everything else we might say about the human values of the council have diverted the attention of the Church in council to the trend of modern culture, centered on humanity. We would say not diverted but rather directed. Any careful observer of the council's prevailing interest for human and temporal values cannot deny that it is from the pastoral character that the council has virtually made its program, and must recognize that the same interest is never divorced from the most genuine religious interest, whether by reason of charity, its sole inspiration (where charity is, God is!), or the council's constant, explicit attempts to link human and temporal values with those that are specifically spiritual, religious, and everlasting; its concern is with man and with earth, but it rises to the kingdom of God.

The modern mind, accustomed to assess everything in terms of usefulness, will readily admit that the council's value is great if only because everything has been referred to human usefulness. Hence no one should ever say that a religion like the Catholic religion is without use, seeing that when it has its greatest self-awareness and effectiveness, as it has in council, it declares itself entirely on the side of man and in his service. In this way the Catholic religion and human life reaffirm their alliance with one another, the fact that they converge on one single human reality: the Catholic religion is for mankind. In a certain sense it is the life of mankind. It is so by the extremely precise and sublime interpretation that our religion gives of humanity (surely man by himself is a mystery to himself) and gives this interpretation in virtue of its knowledge of God: a knowledge of God is a prerequisite for a knowledge of man as he really is, in all his fullness; for proof of this let it suffice for now to recall the ardent expression of St. Catherine of Siena, "In your nature, Eternal God, I shall know my own." The Catholic religion is man's life because it determines life's nature and destiny; it gives life its real meaning, it establishes the supreme law of life and infuses it with that mysterious activity which we may say divinizes it.

Consequently, if we remember, venerable brothers and all of you, our children, gathered here, how in everyone we can and must recognize the countenance of Christ (see Matt. 25:40), the Son of Man, especially when tears and sorrows make it plain to see, and if we can and must recognize in Christ's countenance the countenance of our heavenly Father, "He who sees me," Our Lord said, "sees also the Father" (John 14:9), our humanism becomes Christianity, our Christianity becomes centered on God; in such sort that we may say, to put it differently: a knowledge of man is a prerequisite for a knowledge of God.

Would not this council, then, which has concentrated principally on man, be destined to propose again to the world of today the ladder leading to freedom and consolation? Would it not be, in short, a simple, new, and solemn teaching to love man in order to love God? To love man, we say, not as a means but as the first step toward the final and transcendent goal which is the basis and cause of every love. And so this council can be summed up in its ultimate religious meaning, which is none other than a pressing and friendly invitation to mankind of today to rediscover in fraternal love the God "to turn away from whom is to fall, to turn to whom is to rise again, to remain in whom is to be secure . . . to return to whom is to be born again, in whom to dwell is to live" (St. Augustine, Solil. I, 1, 3; PL 32, 870).

This is our hope at the conclusion of this Second Vatican Ecumenical Council and at the beginning of the human and religious renewal which the council proposed to study and promote; this is our hope for you, brothers and Fathers of the council; this is our hope for the whole of mankind which here we have learned to love more and to serve better.

To this end we again invoke the intercession of St. John the Baptist and of St. Joseph, who are the patrons of the ecumenical council; of the holy Apostles Peter and Paul, the foundations and columns of the Holy Church; and with them of St. Ambrose, the bishop whose feast we celebrate today, as it were uniting in him the Church of the East and of the West. We also earnestly implore the protection of the most Blessed Mary, the Mother of Christ and therefore called by us also Mother of the Church. With one voice and with one heart we give thanks and glory to the living and true God, to the one and sovereign God, to the Father, to the Son, and to the Holy Spirit. Amen.

—December 7, 1965
Delivered During the Last General Meeting of the Council

Afterword

Matthew Levering

All Catholics should agree that Vatican II was an authoritative ecumenical council. As befits a council of the Church, its value rests primarily upon its proclamation of Jesus Christ as the incarnate Lord and Savior of the world. Thus, *Dei Verbum* emphasizes that Jesus Christ is not receding into the past but remains a person we can encounter and know today. In a brief compass, it engages in a balanced manner with historical research, both with regard to the historical composition of Scripture and to the historical unfolding of doctrine. It strongly affirms that the Church has truthfully handed on divine revelation as found preeminently in the words and deeds of Christ.

Lumen Gentium portrays the Church as sharing in Christ's priestly, prophetic, and royal offices. Christ is the Head of the Church, and Christ's baptized people, his Mystical Body, follow him in the Spirit on the new Exodus that he has inaugurated to the Jerusalem above. The Church is a seed and a sign of the consummated kingdom, the new creation. The Blessed Virgin Mary has already attained to this triumph, having been supremely configured to Christ's cross and Resurrection.

Sacrosanctum Concilium invites believers to find in the Eucharistic liturgy the apex of the Christian faith. Sharing in Christ's one sacrificial offering for the salvation of the world, we commune in his risen Body and

347

Blood and are drawn into his life as adopted sons and daughters in the Son. We must actively participate, interiorly and also through external acts, in the Eucharistic liturgy that builds up Christ's Church in love.

Last among the council's four constitutions, *Gaudium et Spes* addresses issues that have arisen in the modern world, such as the emergence of a global community, the danger of nuclear war, and environmental problems. It affirms that only in Jesus Christ is the human being made intelligible. Only in Christ can the desires and hopes of modern humankind be realized. Christ is the center of all history.[1]

What was the modern world to which the council spoke? For one thing, the bishops gathered less than two decades after the unspeakable horror of the Nazi Holocaust. It was clear that the Church's longstanding total rejection of the spiritual worth of ongoing Judaism had been a terrible mistake. Thus, Vatican II's Declaration on the Relation of the Church to Non-Christians Religions, *Nostra Aetate*, stands as a powerful step forward.

The modern world of the early 1960s was also one in which non-Catholics had relatively recently received the right to participate fully in politics and in other aspects of society in majority-Catholic countries. In the course of the century prior to the council, the popes had warned against religious indifferentism, and they had also warned against deformations of society that would be caused by the Church no longer having a guiding influence. Pope Pius IX's *Syllabus of Errors*, for instance, condemns propositions such as the following: "The Church does not have the power of defining dogmatically that the religion of the Catholic Church is the only true religion," and "The Church is to be separated from the State, and the State from the Church."[2] His 1864 encyclical *Quantum Cura* condemns the view that "the Church has no right of restraining by temporal punishments those who violate her laws."[3] These teachings are not at odds with *Dignitatis Humanae*, Vatican II's Declaration on Religious Liberty, although a valuable doctrinal development does take place in this document. *Dignitatis Humanae* teaches that "a wrong is done when government imposes upon its people, by force or fear or other means, the profession or repudiation of any religion, or when it hinders men from joining or leaving a religious community."[4] At the same time, *Dignitatis Humanae* affirms both that the doctrine of religious freedom "leaves untouched traditional Catholic doctrine on the moral duty of men and societies toward the true religion and toward the one Church of Christ" and that the "one true religion subsists in the Catholic and Apostolic Church."[5]

Vatican II also teaches that the Church appreciates the elements of truth within non-Catholic forms of Christianity. Although the council repeatedly affirms that the one Church established by Christ is the Catholic Church, the council parts ways with early twentieth-century papal rejection of ecumenism, so long as it does not entail a false understanding of unity. After hundreds of years of animosity and suspicion toward Orthodox and Protestant Christians, *Unitatis Redintegratio*, the council's Decree on Ecumenism, emphasizes that "men of both sides were to blame" for the divisions. In addition, *Unitatis Redintegratio* laudably remarks that "the children who are born into these Communities [Orthodox and Protestant] and who grow up believing in Christ cannot be accused of the sin involved in the separation, and the Catholic Church embraces them as brothers, with respect and affection."[6]

Prior to the council, almost nothing from the Old Testament, excepting the Psalms, was read as part of the Eucharistic liturgy. Matters such as this are addressed in *Sacrosanctum Concilium*. When, after Vatican I, the pope began to appoint all the bishops directly and to govern the Church more fully through the Curia, the bishops lost some of the ecclesiastical place belonging to them as members of the apostolic college. This situation is addressed by *Lumen Gentium* and also by *Christus Dominus*, the council's Decree concerning the Pastoral Office of Bishops in the Church.

Looking at the council as a whole, its roots can be found partly in a controversy over religious liberalism that arose within Catholicism in the late nineteenth century and that had roiled Protestantism a century earlier. Religious liberalism—which should be distinguished from political liberalism—arose in Protestant Germany in the late eighteenth century. It was a response to two problems. First, Enlightenment philosophers argued that we cannot really know the divine but instead can only know our own experience of the divine. Second, historical research had produced doubts about the literal truth of the Old Testament and the Gospels.

For the liberal Catholicism that came into focus in the first few years of the twentieth century, the main question was the status of Catholic dogma: for instance, what the Church means by teaching that Christ is the incarnate Son of God. According to religious liberalism, dogma is a concrete way of speaking about religious experience. Dogma has its use, but we should not cling to it. It can become outdated, in which case the Christian community will need to find new ways of expressing the community's liberative experience of "Christ." Religious liberalism holds that dogma is of value so long as it resonates with and expresses the community's religious experience; but as epochs change, dogma will need to change to reflect the evolving religious experience of humankind. On this view, the dogma of the divinity of Christ is true insofar as it expresses the religious experience of believers that the mystery of the divine can be uniquely encountered in Christ. The dogma is a claim not so much about the real Jesus of Nazareth as it is a claim about the religious experience of believers. Therefore, the truth it expresses will evolve and will require new culturally contextualized language in different epochs.

Liberal Catholicism—also known in its original form as "modernism"—was condemned by Pope Pius X in his 1907 encyclical *Pascendi Dominici Gregis*. Pius X bemoans the fact that liberal Catholics not only "make consciousness and revelation synonymous," but also hold that since religious experiences change, it follows that "the formulae too, which we call dogmas, must be subject to these vicissitudes, and are, therefore, liable to change."[7] In fact, the roots of religious liberalism in Enlightenment philosophy had already drawn a papal response. In 1879, Pope Leo XIII published his encyclical *Aeterni Patris*, "On the Restoration of Christian Philosophy in Catholic Schools in the Spirit of the Angelic Doctor, St. Thomas Aquinas," with the goal of strengthening the teaching of scholastic and Thomistic thought to correct the dead ends of Enlightenment philosophy.

By the 1930s, two preeminent modes of Catholic intellectual critique of religious liberalism had emerged. The first, scholastic or "neo-scholastic" theology, focused largely upon addressing the philosophical roots of religious liberalism. The second, *nouvelle théologie* or *ressourcement* theology, focused more upon addressing the historical-critical roots of religious liberalism. Of course, many historians of the time held to the presuppositions of Enlightenment philosophy, and so the two modes often engaged the same figures, though with different emphases. Scholastic theologians also addressed historical matters, but not with the depth or erudition that one finds in the best representatives of *ressourcement* theology. In general, one finds in scholastic theologians a deeper philosophical erudition.

Why is this important for understanding Vatican II? It is important because, by the end of World War II, the two modes of Catholic response to religious liberalism were locked in mortal combat with each other. Both sides identified weaknesses in the other to which the other was impervious. Both sides predicted a dire and lifeless future for Catholicism if the other side were not soundly defeated; and both sides linked the other, in different ways, with rationalism. Even today, adherents of either side generally can find little good in the leading preconciliar exponents of the other side.

In the 1950s, the Vatican clamped down on *ressourcement* theology, and many prominent theologians were removed from their teaching positions and prohibited from publishing on certain topics. In the 1960s, the ecclesiastical tide turned, and scholastic theologians found themselves widely vilified and marginalized in the theological academy and in the Church. Indeed, by the end of the council, scholastic theology was pretty much dead.[8]

Convened from 1962–1965, the Second Vatican Council was dominated by *ressourcement* theologians, even if the council's documents reflect both scholastic and *ressourcement* perspectives. On the key issues—the universal truth of dogma, the veracity of the Gospels, the infallibility of solemn papal and conciliar teaching, the standing of the Catholic Church as the one Church founded by Christ, the universal redemptive work of Christ, and the power of the sacraments—the council taught firmly against religious liberalism.

Yet already during the council, Henri de Lubac, at that time the preeminent *ressourcement* theologian, sounded the alarm. He remarked that a group motivated in certain ways by religious liberalism was on the ascendant. As soon became evident, the scholastic and *ressourcement* theologians had exhausted themselves in their decades-long battle, and the younger theologians (and some older ones too, revealing their true colors) were flocking to the banner of religious liberalism. After the council, liberal Catholicism exploded onto the scene like a rocket.

In the first two decades after the council, liberal Catholic theologians of various stripes dominated the teaching of Catholic theology in universities worldwide and in most seminaries as well. They published a raft of books with titles such as *Do We Need the Church?*; *The Church in Anguish: Has the Vatican Betrayed Vatican II?*; *Infallible?: An Unresolved Enquiry*; *Toward Vatican III: The Work That Needs to Be Done*; *Vatican II: The Unfinished Agenda: A Look to the Future*; and so on. Often the focus was on sexual matters: if the Church could only change its consistent teaching on contraceptive intercourse, or on homosexual acts, or on marital indissolubility, then the liberation that Jesus had intended to bring would soon arrive. Another major focus was the ordination of women and tearing down hierarchical structures in favor of democratic leadership and open communion. Frequently, the focus was on dogmatic points such as whether the "Incarnation" as classically conceived allows for Jesus' full humanity, or whether other religions are God's chosen paths for the salvation of non-Christians. Various books challenged classical dogmatic teachings regarding such things as the Real Presence of Christ in the Eucharist, or the unchanging transcendence of God, or whether Mary's body decomposed in Palestine, or whether any of the Apostles saw the risen Jesus with their bodily eyes, or original sin, or the virgin birth. The power of the pope was bemoaned, and the postconciliar popes were depicted as failing to live up to the promise of the council. During this period, the "spirit of the council" was often invoked against its "letter," since the "letter" was seen as too traditional whereas the "spirit" was seen as preparing the way for sweeping changes, correcting and changing many solemn teachings of Vatican II's own dogmatic constitutions.

I can attest that when I arrived at Boston College as a doctoral student in the mid-nineties, Joseph Ratzinger was seen as an arch-reactionary. Typical was the claim by Hermann Häring in his 1986 essay "Joseph Ratzinger's 'Nightmare Theology.'" Häring opines, "A tragic aspect of [Ratzinger's] development is that he has not been inspired by the breadth of vision of an Yves Congar but rather by the antimodern predisposition of a Hans Urs von Balthasar," with the result that Ratzinger's "own call upon Catholic identity can no longer be qualified as catholic."[9]

Ressourcement theologians such as de Lubac, Hans Urs von Balthasar, and Jean Daniélou, all of whom were well over sixty after the council ended, sharply criticized this liberal reception of the council. In representative fashion, Louis Bouyer shifted from an ecstatic response to *Sacrosanctum Concilium* in his 1964 *The Liturgy Revived: A Doctrinal Commentary of the Conciliar Constitution on the Liturgy*, to near despair by the end of the decade. Bouyer's change was partly a reaction to a hasty decision after the council, without basis in *Sacrosanctum Concilium*, to part ways with the Catholic tradition and with the practice of the Eastern Orthodox churches by having the priest face the people during the Eucharistic prayer, the high point of the self-offering of the whole congregation—both priest and people—in union with Christ's sacrifice to the Father through the Spirit. Bouyer also recognized that the new Eucharistic prayers had been composed too quickly—including one that he himself wrote—and that the new music and architecture would need reform.

By the 2000s, publications such as Robert Barron's *Thomas Aquinas:*

Spiritual Master had begun to bring together the scholastic (or Thomistic) and *ressourcement* modes. Thomistic theology began to revive. At the same time, scholarly study of the major *ressourcement* theologians began to enter into most of the leading universities. The seminaries had been invigorated by the publication of the *Catechism of the Catholic Church* and other developments in the early 1990s. Pope John Paul II led enormously popular World Youth Days, and the Church in various places, such as China, began to flourish or to recover.

Yet many Catholics still preferred a doctrinally and morally fluid Catholicism, attuned preeminently to the changing norms and interests of the contemporary world. In recent years, there has been no letup in the flood of academically mainstream books that reject the "letter" of the council in various ways, as for example *A Council That Will Never End:* Lumen Gentium *and the Church Today*; *Why the Catholic Church Needs Vatican III*; *True Reform: Liturgy and Ecclesiology in* Sacrosanctum Concilium; *Steps Toward Vatican III: Catholics Pathfinding a Global Spirituality with Islam and Buddhism*; and so on. At the same time, there are disturbing indications that some Catholic laity, from the opposite perspective and (mistakenly) in the name of fidelity to divine revelation, are likewise rejecting the "letter" of Vatican II.

In sum, the reception of Vatican II—that is, of the actual documents—has run into unexpected difficulties over the years, while also being graced and blessed at important junctures, such as the 1985 Synod that approved the plan for the *Catechism* and that laid down a framework for properly interpreting the council.[10] To provide historical perspective, I have highlighted one tragedy that undermined the council's reception—namely, the preconciliar battle between the scholastic and the *ressourcement* theologians that damaged both sides and produced wounds that are still unhealed. This healing needs to happen as soon as possible, since the problem of religious liberalism is as pressing as ever. Elsewhere, I have encouraged a "*ressourcement* Thomism" in which the two sides make a good faith effort to find good things to say about the other side.[11] Above all, given the tendency of the Church's pendulum to swing rapidly, Catholics need to hold firm to what gives balance and weight to the Church: its enduringly true dogmatic and sacramental sharing in Jesus Christ.

At present, then, proper appreciation for Vatican II requires sifting the permanent things from the passing things. Without yielding to the centrifugal pressures of our time, Catholics should seek Jesus

Christ together. Catholics know, with *Dei Verbum*, that "the four Gospels . . . faithfully hand on what Jesus Christ, while living among men, really did and taught for their eternal salvation" (DV 19). We know that, "in His gracious goodness, God has seen to it that what He had revealed for the salvation of all nations would abide perpetually in its full integrity and be handed on to all generations" (DV 7). We know, in words from *Dei Verbum* that should awaken our hearts, that God's will was that men, "through Christ, the Word made flesh . . . might in the Holy Spirit have access to the Father, and come to share in the divine nature" (DV 2).

We know that, as *Lumen Gentium* says, God "planned to assemble in the holy Church all those who would believe in Christ" (LG 2), and "all men are called to this union with Christ, who is the light of the world, from whom we go forth, through whom we live, and toward whom our whole life strains" (LG 3). We know that "by her preaching she brings forth to a new and immortal life the sons who are born to her in baptism, conceived of the Holy Spirit and born of God. She herself is a virgin, who keeps the faith given to her by her Spouse whole and entire " (LG 64). We know, as *Lumen Gentium* underscores, that "when either the Roman Pontiff or the Body of Bishops together with him defines a judgment, they pronounce it in accordance with Revelation itself. . . . The Revelation . . . under the guiding light of the Spirit of truth is religiously preserved and faithfully expounded in the Church" (LG 25).

Catholics know, as *Sacrosanctum Concilium* says, that "it is of the essence of the Church that she be both human and divine, visible and yet invisibly equipped, eager to act and yet intent on contemplation, present in this world and yet not at home in it; and she is all these things in such wise that in her the human is directed and subordinated to the divine . . . and this present world to that city yet to come, which we seek" (SC 2). We know that it is the liturgy "'through which the work of our redemption is accomplished,' most of all in the divine sacrifice of the Eucharist'" (SC 2).

We know, in the famous lines of *Gaudium et Spes*, that "only in the mystery of the incarnate Word does the mystery of man take on light. For Adam, the first man, was a figure of Him Who was to come, namely Christ the Lord. Christ, the final Adam, by the very revelation of the mystery of the Father and His love, fully reveals man to man himself and makes his supreme calling clear" (GS 22). We know that, as *Gaudium et Spes* says, "The Father wills that in all men we recognize Christ our brother and love Him effectively, in word and in deed. By thus giving witness to the truth, we will share with others the mystery of the heavenly Father's love" (GS 93).

The more that these central truths are obscured and denied, the more we as Catholics are called to penetrate interiorly into these teachings of Vatican II. Let us bear witness to these truths with patient endurance, as Christians called by the Lord to be sanctified through real faith, hope, and love, willing to suffer rather than to depart in word or deed from Christ who makes himself present in the Church.

In 1999, Pope John Paul II dedicated Europe to the care of three great saints: St. Catherine of Siena, St. Bridget of Sweden, and St. Edith Stein.[12] These three women lived in times when the Church and the world were collapsing. At the heart of the world, at the heart of the Church, Christ shone through these great saints. Their witness to the world resounded with the power of the truths that we have heard from the documents of the Second Vatican Council. May we, prepared by the council, go forth on mission in the Church and the world.

NOTES

1   For further discussion, see my *An Introduction to Vatican II as an Ongoing Theological Event* (Washington, DC: The Catholic University of America Press, 2017).

2   Heinrich Denzinger, *Compendium of Creeds, Definitions, and Declarations on Matters of Faith and Morals*, revised and enlarged and edited by Peter Hünermann with Helmut Hoping, 43rd ed., English edition edited by Robert Fastiggi and Anne Englund Nash (San Francisco: Ignatius Press, 2012), nos. 2921, 2955.

3   Pope Pius IX, *Quanta Cura*, 5, encyclical letter, Papal Encyclicals Online, https://www.papalencyclicals.net/Pius09/p9quanta.htm.

4   *Dignitatis Humanae*, 6, Vatican website, December 7, 1965, http://www.vatican.va/archive/hist_councils/ii_vatican_council/documents/vat-ii_decl_19651207_dignitatis-humanae_en.html.

5   *Dignitatis Humanae*, 1. For discussion, see Nicholas J. Healy, Jr., "*Dignitatis Humanae*," in *The Reception of Vatican II*, ed. Matthew L. Lamb and Matthew Levering (Oxford: Oxford University Press, 2017), 367–392.

6   *Unitatis Redintegratio*, 3, Vatican website, November 21, 1964, https://www.vatican.va/archive/hist_councils/ii_vatican_council/documents/vat-ii_decree_19641121_unitatis-redintegratio_en.html.

7   Pope Pius X, *Pascendi Dominici Gregis*, 8, 13, encyclical letter, Vatican website, September 8, 1907, http://www.vatican.va/content/pius-x/en/encyclicals/documents/hf_p-x_enc_19070908_pascendi-dominici-gregis.html.

8   Although Archbishop Lefebvre's schismatic movement (rejecting parts of Vatican II as heretical) identified itself with scholastic theology, this movement had no major scholastic theologians as participants.

9   Hermann Häring, "Joseph Ratzinger's 'Nightmare Theology,'" in *The Church in Anguish: Has the Vatican Betrayed Vatican II?*, ed. Hans Küng and Leonard Swidler (New York: Harper & Row, 1987), 87.

10 Archbishop Elias Zoghby's response to the projected *Catechism* is typical of countless others at the time: "In effect, to publish at the present time a Universal Catechism, a form of common and solemn profession of faith, which would benefit from the quasi-infallible approval of the pope, would mean freezing the decrees of the Council, which are now only in a projected form, into a quasi-definitive formulation, which would make them the final term of a reform which has so far hardly been sketched out" (Zoghby, "The Universal Catechism Proposed by the Extraordinary Synod of Bishops, Considered from a Cultural and Pastoral Viewpoint," trans. Lawrence H. Ginn, in *Synod 1985—An Evaluation*, ed. Giuseppe Alberigo and James Provost, English ed. Marcus Lefébure [Edinburgh: T & T Clark, 1986], 87).

11 See my *The Achievement of Hans Urs von Balthasar* (Washington, DC: The Catholic University of America Press, 2019).

12 Pope John Paul II, "Apostolic Letter Issued Motu Proprio Proclaiming Saint Bridget of Sweden, Saint Catherine of Siena, and Saint Teresa Benedicta of the Cross Co-patronesses of Europe," Vatican website, October 1, 1999, http://www.vatican.va/content/john-paul-ii/en/motu_proprio/documents/hf_jp-ii_motu-proprio_01101999_co-patronesses-europe.html.

KEY TERMS AND FIGURES

Key Terms

DV - *Dei Verbum*
LG - *Lumen Gentium*
SC - *Sacrosanctum Concilium*
GS - *Gaudium et Spes*

ACTIVE PARTICIPATION

(SC 14–21, 27, 30, 41, 50, 79, 113, 114, 121, 124)

A mystical sharing in the Mass by the faithful, both through interior attention and exterior action, that is "the primary and indispensable source from which the faithful are to derive the true Christian spirit" (SC 14).

CANON

(DV 8, 11, 20)

From the Greek *kanon* (straight rod or ruler that is a standard of excellence), typically the list of books in Scripture authoritatively recognized by the Church as inspired; however, it can also refer to a recognized rule or standard in the Church's life (e.g., SC 128) or a member of a religious order (e.g., SC 95).

CATECHUMENATE

(LG 14; SC 64, 66)

The process of initiation for the unbaptized desiring to enter the Catholic Church ("catechumens"), which is focused on revelation and the Church's history, beliefs, and practices, and commonly referred to as the Rite of Christian Initiation of Adults (RCIA).

CHURCH FATHERS (ALSO FATHERS OF THE CHURCH, HOLY FATHERS, FATHERS)

(DV 8, 23; LG 2, 6, 7, 21, 43, 56, 67; SC 50, 92, 112; GS 69)

Christian theologians (many of them saints, and some Doctors of the Church) between the first and seventh centuries, whose writings—together with Sacred Scripture—helped to shape the early Church's life and thought.

COMMON PRIESTHOOD (OR PRIESTHOOD OF ALL BELIEVERS)

(LG 10, 31; SC 14, 48)

The participation in the priesthood of Jesus Christ shared by all the faithful, including the laity, by virtue of their Baptism, especially by joining their own lives to the offering of the Eucharist by ministerial priests.

COUNCIL FATHERS

(LG 69, Appendix; SC 122)

The bishops from around the world, under the headship of the pope, who participated in the four sessions of the Second Vatican Council (2,448 at session one, 2,488 at session two, 2,468 at session three, and 2,625 at session four).

DOGMATIC

(DV title; LG title, 69; SC 16, 55)

Relating to those divinely revealed truths, solemnly defined as such by the Church, in which the faithful are obliged to believe.

ECONOMY OF SALVATION (OR ECONOMY, PLAN)

(DV 2, 4, 14–15; LG 36, 55)

From the Greek *oeconomia* (house management), God's saving plan and design for humanity shown in creation, the story of Israel, and most fully, in the redemptive work of Christ.

ECCLESIAL COMMUNITIES (OR ECCLESIASTICAL COMMUNITIES)

(LG 15, GS 40)

Christian communities of faith that do not fully partake in the constitutive elements of the Church—namely, apostolic succession, the priesthood, and the Eucharist.

ESCHATOLOGICAL

(LG chapter VII, GS 40)

From the Greek *eschaton* (the last things), relating to the Church's teaching on death, judgment, heaven, and hell.

HIERARCHY

(LG chapter III)

From the Greek *heirarkhes* (rule of priests or holy order), the levels of holy orders—bishops, priests, and deacons—who have been tasked with "the nurturing and constant growth of the People of God" (LG 18).

INFALLIBILITY

(LG 18, 25)

The charism (or gift) given to the Church by which (under certain conditions) doctrines pertaining to faith or morals are preserved from error.

INSPIRATION

(DV 9, 11, 18, 20; LG 43)

From the Latin for "in the spirit," the divine influence upon the human authors of Sacred Scripture, such that God, acting "in them and through them" (DV 11), truly becomes the author of these books and makes them his Word.

LAITY

(LG chapter IV; SC 28, 55, 100; GS 43, 62)

From the Greek *laos* (people), all the baptized members of the Church who, though not a part of its ecclesiastical hierarchy or a religious order, partake in the life of the Spirit and are called to holiness and the sanctification of the world.

LITURGY

(DV 21, 23, 24, 25; LG 6, 11, 21, 23, 26, 29, 42, 45, 50, 51, 67, Appendix; SC; GS 52, 58)

The official worship of God offered by the Church, participating in Christ's total self-gift to the Father and culminating in the "fount and apex of the whole Christian life" (LG 11): the Eucharistic sacrifice of the Mass.

MAGISTERIUM (OR TEACHING OFFICE)

(DV 10; LG 25, 67)

The authoritative teaching body of the Church, which is the whole college of bishops united with the pope.

MINISTERIAL PRIESTHOOD (OR HIERARCHICAL PRIESTHOOD)

(LG 10, 20–21, 28, 41; SC 7, 16–19, 22, 33, 35, 41, 48, 55, 57, 68, 77, 84, 86–87, 90, 99–100, 127; GS 43, 52, 62)

> Those members of the Church set apart and ordained to act in the person of Christ and in the name of the whole Church, administering the sacraments, primarily the Eucharist, to build up the common priesthood of the baptized.

MODERN

(SC 4, 88, 107; GS)

> From the Latin *modo* (just now, recent times), the era of history stretching from the eighteenth century to the present day, which is marked by distinct social and political perspectives and scientific and technological breakthroughs.

MYSTICAL BODY OF CHRIST

(LG 8, 23, 26, 50, 54; SC 7, 99)

> Another term for the Church, emphasizing that her members have been incorporated (made into one body) with Christ, their Head, through Baptism and the Holy Spirit.

PASCHAL MYSTERY

(SC 5–6, 61, 104, 106; GS 22)

> From the Greek *pascha* (of or pertaining to Passover or Easter), the redemption effected by Christ through his Passion, Death, Resurrection, and Ascension, in which Christians participate through the sacraments and the whole of their lives.

PASTORAL

(DV 24; LG 23, 27, 28, 41, 45, 51, Appendix; SC 14–15, 23, 33, 43–44, 49, 63, 86; GS title, 52, 62)

> Relating to the spiritual accompaniment and care of the people of God by the Church's shepherds.

PEOPLE OF GOD

(DV 23, LG chapter II, 18, 22–23, 28–33, 40–41, 44–45, 50, 66, 68–69; GS 3, 11, 44–45, 88, 92)

> Another term for the Church, emphasizing not a democratic character

but its role as the new Israel, the continuation of the family constituted by God.

PILGRIM CHURCH
(DV 6, LG 48, 50)

The Church as it exists in this passing world, emphasizing its journeying quality and eschatological longing for the new heavens and new earth.

SECULAR
(LG 31, 35–36; SC 18, 57; GS 43, 62)

Concerned with the things of the world.

SENSUS FIDEI
(LG 12, 35)

Translated as "understanding of the faith" or "discernment in matters of faith," that supernatural and theological faith among the members of the Church that, as such, cannot err.

UNIVERSAL CALL TO HOLINESS
(LG chapter V)

The divine summons to all Christians, "of whatever rank or status" (LG 40), to strive to be saints and to transform the world by their witness of sanctity.

Key Figures

HANS URS VON BALTHASAR
(1905–1988)

A Swiss priest, theologian, and author of eighty-five books, the most well-known of which is his fifteen-volume trilogy on beauty (*The Glory of the Lord*), goodness (*Theo-Drama*), and truth (*Theo-Logic*). Balthasar was associated with the *nouvelle théologie* (new theology) and a cofounder, with Henri de Lubac and Joseph Ratzinger, of the *Communio* journal. Balthasar did not himself participate in the Second Vatican Council, but his theological writings influenced many there in the years during and after, including Pope St. John Paul II[1] and Pope Benedict XVI.[2]

YVES CONGAR
(1904–1995)

A French Dominican friar and theologian known for his writings on ecclesiology, ecumenism, and the Holy Spirit. He served as a *peritus* or theological expert at Vatican II, serving on the preparatory commission and contributing to eight documents, including the four constitutions. As Bishop Barron has observed, "By most accounts, he proved the most influential theologian at that epic gathering."[3]

JEAN DANIÉLOU
(1905–1974)

A French Jesuit priest, theologian, and historian who was part of the *ressourcement* (return to the sources) movement in theology and drew on the writings of the Church Fathers. Daniélou was a *peritus* at the Second Vatican Council and was named a cardinal by Pope Paul VI in 1969.

HENRI DE LUBAC
(1896–1991)

A French Jesuit priest and theologian considered one of the most influential Catholic thinkers of the twentieth century. De Lubac was appointed to the preparatory commission for Vatican II and served as a *peritus* during the council. His thought had a tremendous influence on the council, particularly on the constitutions *Lumen Gentium* and *Gaudium et Spes*. Pope John Paul II, who reverenced de Lubac and worked with him on *Gaudium et Spes*,[4] made him a cardinal in 1983.

ROMANO GUARDINI

(1885–1968)

An Italian-born German priest and academic whose book *The Spirit of the Liturgy* influenced the Liturgical Movement. Leaders of this movement—following the promptings of Pope Pius X—called for a renewal in the Mass, including greater incorporation of patristic sources and increased participation of the laity. Guardini was an important forerunner to the reforms of *Sacrosanctum Concilium*, and has influenced both Pope Benedict XVI and Pope Francis.

REYNOLD HILLENBRAND

(1904–1979)

An American priest, seminary rector, and leader of the Liturgical Movement and Catholic Action Movement. As Bishop Barron observes in his commentary on *Lumen Gentium* 31–36, the views of Hillenbrand and his colleagues on the liturgy—including an emphasis on the active participation of the laity and the relevance of the liturgy for the political and economic realms—were later adopted at Vatican II.

ST. JOHN HENRY NEWMAN

(1801–1890)

A nineteenth-century English convert, theologian, and saint. Although St. John Henry Newman died over seventy years before Vatican II was convoked, his theological work greatly influenced many of the key thinkers of the council. His influence is especially apparent in the emphasis on conscience (LG 16, GS 15–17) and the idea of development in the Church's teaching (DV 8).

JOSEPH RATZINGER (POPE BENEDICT XVI)

(1927–)

The pope of the Catholic Church from April 19, 2005, to February 28, 2013. Ratzinger was present at the council as a *peritus* to Cardinal Joseph Frings, Archbishop of Cologne. He influenced the development of *Dei Verbum*, and he also worked (together with Yves Congar) on the final draft of the document *Ad Gentes*, the Decree on the Mission Activity of the Church.

POPE ST. JOHN XXIII

(1881–1963)

The pope of the Catholic Church from October 28, 1958, to June 3, 1963. Pope John XXIII opened the council on October 11, 1962, and died the following year after the council's first session. He was canonized a saint on April 27, 2014.

KAROL WOJTYŁA (POPE ST. JOHN PAUL II)

(1920–2005)

The pope of the Catholic Church from October 16, 1978, to April 2, 2005. Wojtyła was present at the council as Auxiliary Bishop and later Archbishop of Kraków, making important contributions to *Gaudium et Spes* as well as *Dignitatis Humanae*, the Declaration on Religious Freedom. As Bishop Barron observes, *Gaudium et Spes* 22, in particular, became an important passage for Wojtyła throughout his pontificate. He was canonized a saint on April 27, 2014.

POPE ST. PAUL VI

(1897–1978)

The pope of the Catholic Church from June 21, 1963, to August 6, 1978. Pope Paul VI promulgated the sixteen documents of the Second Vatican Council, and closed the council on December 8, 1965. He was canonized a saint on October 14, 2018.

KARL RAHNER

(1904–1984)

A German Jesuit priest, theologian, and author. Prior to the council, Rahner was associated with the *nouvelle théologie*. But as Bishop Barron notes in his introduction, Ratzinger (with whom Rahner worked closely at the council), de Lubac, and Balthasar eventaully split from Rahner and other founders of the *Concilium* journal, who came to represent a more liberal reading of the council. Rahner was a *peritus* at Vatican II, and influenced passages in *Dei Verbum, Lumen Gentium,* and *Gaudium et Spes.*

NOTES

1   "All who knew the priest, von Balthasar, are shocked, and grieve over the loss of a great son of the Church, an outstanding man of theology and of the arts, who deserves a special place of honor in contemporary ecclesiastical and cultural life." From a telegram sent by Pope John Paul II to Cardinal Ratzinger after the death of Balthasar. Quoted in "Introduction to the Life and Work of Hans Urs von Balthasar," Ignatius Insight, http://www.ignatiusinsight.com/authors/vonbalthasar.asp.

2   "With great pleasure I join you in spirit in the celebration of the centenary of the birth of Hans Urs von Balthasar, the distinguished Swiss theologian whom I knew and had the joy of meeting regularly. I consider that his theological reflection keeps its deep actuality intact to this day and still stirs many to penetrate ever further into the depths of the mystery of faith, holding the hand of this most authoritative guide. . . . I hope that you will all continue with interest and enthusiasm to study von Balthasar's work and will find ways to apply it effectively." Pope Benedict XVI, "Message of His Holiness Benedict XVI for the Centenary of the Birth of Fr Hans Urs von Balthasar," Vatican website, October 6, 2005, http://www.vatican.va/content/benedict-xvi/en/messages/pont-messages/2005/documents/hf_ben-xvi_mes_20051006_von-balthasar.html.

3   Bishop Robert Barron, "Yves Congar and the Meaning of Vatican II," Word on Fire, June 29, 2012, https://www.wordonfire.org/resources/article/yves-congar-and-the-meaning-of-vatican-ii/445.

4   Bishop Robert Barron, "Cardinal Etchegaray, Henri de Lubac, and Vatican II," Word on Fire, September 17, 2019, https://www.wordonfire.org/resources/article/cardinal-etchegaray-henri-de-lubac-and-john-paul-ii/25260.

FREQUENTLY ASKED QUESTIONS

1. What is Vatican II?

Vatican II, or the Second Vatican Council, was the twenty-first (and most recent) ecumenical council of the Catholic Church. Ecumenical councils, which go back to the Council of Nicaea in 325, are gatherings of bishops from around the world, under the leadership of the pope, to authoritatively discuss and define Church doctrine and discipline.

An ecumenical council is an extremely rare occurrence, a "solemn" exercise of episcopal power.[1] It is the highest ranked and most important of seven types of general councils possible in the life of the Catholic Church.

Vatican II was opened under Pope St. John XXIII on October 11, 1962, and closed under Pope St. Paul VI on December 8, 1965. The council culminated in sixteen documents[2] promulgated by Pope St. Paul VI, including four central "constitutions":

> *Dei Verbum* (Dogmatic Constitution on Divine Revelation)
> *Lumen Gentium* (Dogmatic Constitution on the Church)
> *Sacrosanctum Concilium* (Constitution on the Sacred Liturgy)
> *Gaudium et Spes* (Pastoral Constitution on the Church in the Modern World)

These documents—not a nebulous "spirit of Vatican II" that misrepresents or misapplies them, or a narrow "traditionalism" that reacts by rejecting them—are the soul of Vatican II.

2. Did Vatican II define any new dogmas or condemn any heresies?

No. Unlike many other ecumenical councils, Vatican II did not in an extraordinary way define any new dogmas of the Church or condemn any heresies.

But it is not unique in this respect. In fact, three ecumenical councils—the First Lateran Council (1123), the Second Lateran Council (1139), and the Third Lateran Council (1179)—were disciplinary councils. Not only did these ecumenical councils not define any new dogmas; they did not address matters of doctrine at all.

3. Was Vatican II merely a "pastoral" council?

No. While the Council did not define any new dogmas (see question 2), and while its *aims* were largely pastoral, Vatican II also reaffirmed dogmas of the faith and developed key doctrines. In other words, the council's substance—as the names of its four constitutions make clear (see question 1)—are not merely dealing with pastoral matters.

4. Are Vatican II's teachings infallible and binding, or fallible and optional?

This is a false dilemma. First, as stated in question 3, Vatican II does affirm infallible dogmas of the faith. These affirmations require the assent of faith on the part of Catholics.

But even when it is not affirming infallible dogma, the Second Vatican Council presents the teachings of the supreme ordinary Magisterium through an ecumenical council of the Church. This means that these teachings are assisted by the Holy Spirit,[3] are promulgated by the pope in communion with the "authentic teachers of the apostolic faith endowed with the authority of Christ,"[4] and require "religious assent which, though distinct from the assent of faith, is nonetheless an extension of it."[5] In short, the teachings are guarded from doctrinal error and are binding on all Catholics; they are not optional.

5. Did Pope Paul VI say that Vatican II was ordinary, pastoral, and fallible?

On January 12, 1966, Pope St. Paul VI said in an audience: "Given the Council's pastoral character, it avoided pronouncing, in an extraordinary manner, dogmas endowed with the note of infallibility." This quote has often been used to suggest the council's teachings and decrees are not binding on Catholics.

However, as Dr. Jeff Mirus has explained,[6] all this is really saying is what is described in the previous three questions: that Vatican II, while largely pastoral in nature, did not in an extraordinary way (i.e., invoking infallibility) define any new dogmas. Pope Paul VI was not saying that Vatican II is *merely* pastoral, subject to doctrinal error, or not binding.

On the contrary, in the very next sentence he adds, "But [the Council] has invested its teachings with the authority of the supreme ordinary magisterium, which ordinary magisterium is so obviously authentic that it must be accepted with docility and sincerity by all the faithful, according to the mind of the Council as expressed in the nature and aims of the individual documents."

6. Are Catholics free to ignore, disparage, or reject Vatican II?

No. In light of questions 1–5, this is not a valid option for Catholics. To ignore, disparage, or reject Vatican II is to call into question the living teaching authority of the Church itself, which was given by Christ[7] and is accomplished in the Holy Spirit.[8] It is to place oneself in a dangerous spiritual attitude with respect to "the fullness of the means of salvation"[9]—the one, holy, catholic, and apostolic Church—by setting oneself above its Magisterium as judge.

Pope St. Pius X warned against this attitude in 1909:

> Do not allow yourselves to be deceived by the cunning statements of those who persistently claim to wish to be with the Church, to love the Church, to fight so that people do not leave Her . . . but judge them by their works. If they despise the shepherds of the Church and even the Pope, if they attempt all means of evading their authority in order to elude their directives and judgments . . . then about which Church do these men mean to speak? Certainly not about that established on the foundations of the apostles and prophets, with Christ Jesus himself as the cornerstone.[10]

7. Could parts of Vatican II's doctrine be removed or reversed in the future?

No. It has been suggested that this could happen to Vatican II in light of two apparent errors in past councils that were later corrected: one attributed to the Council of Constance, and one to the Council of Florence.

But as distinguished historian Cardinal Walter Brandmüller pointed out,[11] neither of these cases is analogous to reversing doctrine from Vatican II. In the case of Constance, the decrees in question were issued earlier by a schismatic assembly that had no authority. Only later on did the gathering become a true ecumenical council; therefore, none of its earlier decisions were authoritative or binding. In the case of Florence, the reversal did not have to do with doctrine at all—only a disciplinary matter.

The doctrine articulated by Vatican II is, under the guidance of the Holy Spirit, part of the Catholic Church's official magisterial teaching. It may be deepened or clarified in the future, but it cannot be removed or reversed.

8. Is Vatican II in continuity with tradition, or a rupture?

These terms originate in an address given by Pope Benedict XVI in 2005.[12] In that speech, he contrasts two "hermeneutics," or ways of interpreting, Vatican II. On the one hand is "the hermeneutic of discontinuity or rupture," the idea that Vatican II is a split or break with Catholic tradition. On the other hand is "the hermeneutic of reform" or continuity, the idea that Vatican II is consistent with Catholic tradition.

Both those on the extreme "left" and the extreme "right" have interpreted Vatican II as a rupture—a good rupture and a bad rupture, respectively.

But Pope Benedict XVI championed the hermeneutic of continuity, saying, "The Church, both before and after the Council, was and is the same Church, one, holy, catholic, and apostolic, journeying on through time." Vatican II was not a break or rupture; it must be interpreted in continuity with the tradition that came before.

This position has also been defended more recently by Cardinal Robert Sarah. In his book *The Day Is Now Far Spent,* he argues:

> The hermeneutic of reform in continuity that Benedict XVI taught so clearly is an indispensable condition of unity. Those who make sensational announcements of change and rupture are false prophets. They do not seek the good of the flock. They are mercenaries who have been smuggled into the sheepfold. Our unity will be forged around the truth of Catholic doctrine. There are no other means.[13]

9. Did thinkers behind Vatican II deliberately use ambiguity to change Church teaching?

Theologian Edward Schillebeeckx has been quoted as saying, "We have used ambiguous phrases during the Council and we know how we will interpret them afterwards." The suggestion is that conspirators planted certain phrases within the Vatican II documents that appeared vague and innocent on the surface, but would later be exploited by those wishing to overturn traditional Church teaching.

However, this quotation is not found in Schillebeeckx's own writings but in a book titled *Open Letter to Confused Catholics,* written years after the council by Archbishop Marcel Lefebvre. Lefebvre was an ardent critic of Vatican II who founded the once schismatic and still canonically irregular SSPX society. In the book, Archbishop Lefebvre shares the quote apparently from memory, without any source or citation, and adds, "Fr. Schillebeeckx admitted it. . . . Those people knew what they were doing." The source casts serious doubt on the truth of this quotation, which is not corroborated anywhere else, and thus offers no support for the idea that those who influenced Vatican II deliberately used ("weaponized") ambiguity to distort Church teaching. There is simply no evidence of such a conspiracy.

(It's also worth noting that Fr. Schillebeeckx was not a bishop and thus had no vote about the language used in the final Vatican II texts.)

Absent any reliable evidence to the contrary, Ven. Fulton Sheen's assessment in his autobiography seems far more trustworthy and reasonable:

> Those who read the Documents of Vatican Council II have no idea how much care and preparation went into every word they contained. . . . I can testify to how we would discuss various Latin words for a day in order to arrive at a precise meaning. Then, after a chapter was prepared, printed, and given to the Council Fathers, the debates on each subject went on for months until finally there were hammered out documents that were acceptable to all except a very few who voted against them.

Finally, it's worth adding that sometimes, including in the Councils of Trent and Nicaea, theologians are not in full agreement, and so somewhat ambiguous statements must be used in the final documents. For example, at Nicaea the term *homoousios* is applied to the Son but not to the Spirit—and this was done to placate a minority of disagreeing bishops. That ambiguity could later be exploited unfaithfully, but it could equally be developed faithfully under the guidance of the Holy Spirit by later councils—which is indeed what happened.

As another example, the Council of Trent did not resolve various theological disputes about the Eucharist between Jesuits, Dominicans, and others. The language used is ambiguous enough to allow for diverse theological opinions.

The key point is this: all councils employ some theological language that is inevitably ambiguous in certain ways. It may be that there are theologians present at a council—contributors to a conciliar text—that hope to employ the ambiguous language in a wrong way later. But the Church has a guardrail against this—namely, the Holy Spirit, who guides the Church in interpreting its councils and handing on the faith. The *Catechism of the Catholic Church* is an example of the Church rightly interpreting the council's words, and there are many other examples as well.

10. Did Vatican II forbid Latin, Gregorian Chant, pipe organs, and *ad orientem* worship in the Mass?

No. *Sacrosanctum Concilium*, the Constitution on the Sacred Liturgy, did not forbid any of these things.

On the contrary, it preserved Latin as the official language of the Latin rite, and had this to say of the use of Latin in the Mass: "Steps should be taken so that the faithful may also be able to say or to sing together in Latin those parts of the Ordinary of the Mass which pertain to them" (SC 54).

Regarding Gregorian Chant, it said: "The Church acknowledges Gregorian chant as specially suited to the Roman liturgy: therefore, other things being equal, it should be given pride of place in liturgical services" (SC 116).

Regarding pipe organs, it said: "In the Latin Church the pipe organ is to be held in high esteem, for it is the traditional musical instrument which adds a wonderful splendor to the Church's ceremonies and powerfully lifts up man's mind to God and to higher things" (SC 120).

It said nothing about liturgical orientation—that is, whether the priest celebrates the Mass *ad orientem* (facing the altar) or *versus populum* (facing the people). In fact, many churches have incorporated *ad orientem* worship into the Ordinary Form of the Mass.

11. Does supporting the Traditional Latin Mass mean you have to reject Vatican II—or vice versa?

No. The same Magisterium that gave us the ecumenical council of Vatican II has also allowed for continued celebration of the Latin Mass under certain conditions. To be a Catholic who reveres the Church's tradition, which is a living tradition, is to accept both the Extraordinary Form and the Ordinary Form of the Mass as valid.

12. Did Vatican II cause the erosion we are seeing the Church—clerical corruption, the rise of the "nones," the drop in vocations, the lack of belief in the Real Presence?

No. It is important to note, first of all, that Catholicism is a global Church, and this erosion is a largely Western phenomenon. As the World Christian Database confirms, Catholic Church membership has *significantly increased* since Vatican II, with the most dramatic growth in Africa and Latin America (Central America, the Caribbean, and South America).[14] (In fact, the only place where the Church has not been growing since Vatican II is in Europe.) It is projected that, by 2050, the largest percentage of Catholics will be in these two regions of the world:

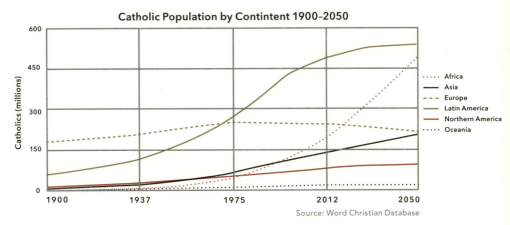

Catholic Population by Contintent 1900-2050

Source: Word Christian Database

Why has this moral and spiritual erosion occurred in our Western context?

There are two points to keep in mind, both of which were pointed out by Ven. Fulton Sheen: first, that the spirit of the age is what has eroded the faith of so many Catholics; and second, that turbulence is to be expected in the wake of any council.

In 1970, William F. Buckley asked Sheen if the drop-off in churchgoing and overall erosion of faith was caused by the *zeitgeist* (the spirit of the times), or by the ecumenism of the Second Vatican Council. Sheen responded, "No, I should not say that ecumenism was the cause of the erosion. Certainly, the *zeitgeist* is partly the cause—and very much the cause."[15] (The statistics showing an erosion in faith across Christian denominations, and indeed across other religions, is evidence that Sheen was right.) It is also important to reiterate (see question 1) that Vatican II is distinct from "the spirit of Vatican II." The latter was sometimes invoked to distort the Council according to the *zeitgeist*—often with disastrous results.

Later, Buckley challenges Sheen: If Vatican II was a missionary council, why is this erosion still happening around us? Sheen responds, with great humility and wisdom: "It's going to take a long time for the yeast to work through the dough."[16] In fact, Sheen pointed out in his autobiography, *Treasure in Clay*, that a period of turbulence is to be expected in the wake of any ecumenical council. He writes:

> The tensions which developed after the Council are not surprising to those who know the whole history of the Church. It is a historical fact that whenever there is an outpouring of the Holy Spirit as in a General Council of the Church, there is always an extra show of force by the anti-Spirit or the demonic. Even at the beginning, immediately after Pentecost and the descent of the Spirit upon the Apostles, there began a persecution and the murder of Stephen. If a General Council did not provoke the spirit of turbulence, one might almost doubt the operation of the Third Person of the Trinity over the Assembly.[17]

We are all living through this time of great turbulence. But our hope is in the Holy Spirit, working through Sacred Scripture, Sacred Tradition, and the Magisterium, to renew the Church and use it to proclaim Christ to the modern world—but on God's time, and in God's way, rather than our own.

NOTES

1   *Catechism of the Catholic Church*, no. 884 (New York: Image Books, 1995), 255.

2   "Documents of the Second Vatican Council," Vatican website, http://www.vatican.va/archive/hist_councils/ii_vatican_council/index.htm.

3   *Catechism*, no. 688, 198.

4   *Catechism*, no. 888, 256.

5   *Catechism*, no. 892, 257.

6   Dr. Jeff Mirus, "Pope Paul VI on Vatican II," Catholic Culture, November 4, 2011, https://www.catholicculture.org/commentary/pope-paul-vi-on-vatican-ii/.

7   *Catechism*, no. 874, 252.

8   *Catechism*, no. 78, 30.

9   *Catechism*, no. 824, 237.

10 Quoted in "Which Pope said this?", Where Peter Is, July 18, 2020, https://wherepeteris.com/which-pope-said-this-100.

11 Sandro Magister, "The 'Fake News' of Viganò and Company. Unmasked by a Cardinal," L'Espresso, July 13, 2020, http://magister.blogautore.espresso.repubblica.it/2020/07/13/the-"fake-news"-of-vigano-and-company-unmasked-by-a-cardinal/.

12 Pope Benedict XVI, "Address of His Holiness Benedict XVI to the Roman Curia Offering Them His Christmas Greetings," Vatican website, December 22, 2005, http://www.vatican.va/content/benedict-xvi/en/speeches/2005/december/documents/hf_ben_xvi_spe_20051222_roman-curia.html.

13 Robert Cardinal Sarah with Nicolas Diat, *The Day Is Now Far Spent* (San Francisco: Ignatius Press, 2019), 17.

14 Data source: Todd M. Johnson and Gina A. Zurlo, eds., World Christian Database (Leiden/Boston: Brill, accessed December 2020). Used by permission.

15 Firing Line with William F. Buckley, Jr., "Firing Line with William F. Buckley Jr.: Skepticism and Disorder," YouTube video, July 4, 2019, 24:57, https://youtu.be/-ZwcU4EfJYM.

16 "Skepticism and Disorder," YouTube video, 36:48.

17 Fulton J. Sheen, *Treasure in Clay: The Autobiography of Fulton J. Sheen* (San Francisco: Ignatius Press, [1980] 1993), 292–293.